Telling Images

fecisti : et expectabo nomen tuum quoniam b
spectu sanctorum tuorum. In finem intell
videat si est intelligens aut requirens deum
declinaverunt simul inutiles facti sunt : no

V.A. KOLVE

Telling Images

CHAUCER AND THE IMAGERY OF NARRATIVE II

STANFORD UNIVERSITY PRESS
STANFORD, CALIFORNIA

Stanford University Press
Stanford, California

Printed in the United States of America on acid-free, archival-quality paper

Library of Congress Cataloging-in-Publication Data

Kolve, V. A.
Telling images : Chaucer and the imagery of narrative II / V.A. Kolve.
p. cm.
Sequel to: Chaucer and the imagery of narrative.
Includes bibliographical references and index.
ISBN 978-0-8047-5583-2 (cloth : alk. paper)
1. Chaucer, Geoffrey, d. 1400. Canterbury tales. 2. Chaucer, Geoffrey, d. 1400--Symbolism. 3. Christian pilgrims and pilgrimages in literature. 4. Narration (Rhetoric)--History--To 1500. 5. Art and literature--England--History--To 1500. 6. Art, Medieval--Themes, motives. 7. Rhetoric, Medieval. I. Title. PR1875.A44K644 2009
821'.1--dc22

2008050524

Typeset by Bruce Lundquist in 11/12 Bembo

THIS BOOK TOO IS FOR LARRY LUCHTEL

Contents

Illustrations

Preface

LITERATURE, it has been said, is not so much about things as about ways of seeing things. Yet *seeing*, as a figure of speech, itself allows for several meanings, sometimes little more than framing a moral at the end, or (better) having a perspective on the whole, or (better still) exploring a way of thinking about it. In these chapters, as in *Chaucer and the Imagery of Narrative: The First Five Canterbury Tales*,[1] the book to which this is a sequel, I have used it in another sense as well, having to do with the way we "see" things in our minds as we read or listen to a story.

Though the making of mental images is likely to elude exact description forever, it is a cognitive function all of us share and most of us acknowledge. The degree to which we think "visually" no doubt varies—some are more inclined that way than others—but this much seems clear: the mental images we make, even of things never seen, draw upon (are indeed constructed from) images already stored in the memory—the visual residue of things and events previously experienced in the material world, including the representation of such things in the visual arts. In the Middle Ages, church walls were painted and their windows lit with sacred stories, noble halls were hung with heroic or allegorical tapestries, and almost every deluxe book was furnished with a program of illustrations. Poets and preachers too took pains to make their verbal discourse "pictorially" vivid, using their rhetorical skills to make it accessible to the eye of the mind. Relatively little of this visual tradition was decorative merely: it sought instead to give memorable form to the major themes and master narratives that shaped the medieval understanding of the world.

This book too attempts to show how some knowledge of this imagery can guide and enrich our experience of Chaucer's narrative art. But it means to confirm as well an empirical observation central to my earlier volume: namely, that in Chaucer's mature practice one or two such images characteristically emerge as dominant in the course of a tale, or in the case of his longer poems, in each of their constituent parts. Because they emerge *from* the story rather than being imposed upon it—that is, as the setting of an action or the essential configuration of an important event—they carry symbolic meaning almost effortlessly, without needing to emphasize their function. Naturalized by their place in the plot and masked by a screen of realistic detail, they gracefully usher into the poem the cultural paradigms its fiction will test, interrogate, or affirm, often to surprising end. The narrative coherence of Chaucer's poetry rarely depends upon the affiliations of such an image being recognized; the poem or tale will make self-contained sense even if the symbolic function of that image remains obscure. But for anyone, then or now, interested in thinking about the narrative in its full historical dimension—in responding to it thoughtfully as it plays out, and in reflecting on "what is remembered" when it is over—these images and their affiliations link Chaucer's fictions to culturally validated truth in a distinctively medieval way. Charles Owen, Jr., in a brief but suggestive essay written long ago, called them "governing images"—getting their function right, although he made no reference to the visual arts.[2]

In this book, as in its predecessor, I have tried to remedy that omission and carry the insight further. In introductory chapters to *Chaucer and the Imagery of Narrative: The First Five Canterbury Tales*, I surveyed the historicist grounds for doing so, stressing the essential role the Middle Ages assigned to mental imagery in such distinctively human activities as *remembering* what we have experienced, *imagining* things we have not experienced, and thinking deeply (*meditating*) upon both. Material images, of course, served as "books for the unlearned"—the vast majority of the population being unable to read. But they were not addressed to the illiterate only, and they had an important afterlife in the memory, the chambers of the mind.

For all these reasons, I think of Chaucer's first audiences as bringing to his art not only a widely shared habit of visual imagining, responsive to both oral and written texts, but also a storehouse of images popular, courtly, and religious in nature—traditional images *known from poems and tales and sermons as well as from the visual arts*—ready to deepen and enrich their response to narrative. What use, I here ask again, did Chaucer make of this iconographic "literacy," this culturally shared habit of mind? On what terms does his poetry engage with this visual language, and with what ends in view?

The chapters that follow, here collected and augmented for the first time, were written over a period of more than twenty-five years, with the earliest-written of them—on *The Legend of Good Women* and the iconography of St. Cecilia—exceeding the scope of my first volume (limited to the first five *Canterbury Tales*) and predating it a little in publication. Apart from the two linked chapters on *The Merchant's Tale*, new in this volume, they are all "occasional" pieces first published in collections of conference papers, or as Festschrift essays in honor of distinguished colleagues, or as major addresses (the honorary "Chaucer Lecture" and the Presidential Address) to international conferences of the New Chaucer Society. But they are not, I trust, "occasional" in the sense of being slight, or casual, or focused on matters of only passing interest.

It has not been my practice to publish things twice, and I do not lightly break that custom here. *The Play Called Corpus Christi* was entirely new to print, and the first volume of *Chaucer and the Imagery of Narrative* nearly so.[3] But this is how I always intended a second volume on Chaucer and the visual culture of his time to come into being—one essay at a time, as occasions presented themselves—until there was a book as substantial as the first. Because still other occasions (invited essays and named lecture series on subjects unrelated to Chaucer) also came along, the volumes in which these chapters first appeared are now mostly out of print, and some of them, in the nature of scholarly publishing, never had a wide distribution. In the belief that these readings may still have value, and with gratitude to Stanford University Press for its continuing interest, I bring them together here, continuing a project first announced in an essay called "Chaucer and the Visual Arts" in 1975.[4] Since I am now well into my seventh decade, with two other books long underway, but still to finish, this volume must serve as that project's conclusion. Though the essays on *Troilus* that open and close it end in reflections on the "otherness" of Chaucer's art and religion sweeping enough to be placed in a chapter called "Conclusions," I have chosen to end this book as Chaucer did his *Canterbury Tales*, allowing each fiction (and my critical response to it) its own integrity. In the opening pages of the final chapter, "God-Denying Fools"—an argument conceived, in imitation of Chaucer, as a modernist's "Retraction"—I privilege my personal situation for the first time, confessing to a dilemma I have never wholly resolved: how to teach and write "from within" Christian systems of thought without appearing to acquiesce in beliefs I do not share.

Because this book continues something already substantially begun, I choose to offer this preface in lieu of a full-scale introduction—partly because that introduction has already been written in the two lengthy chapters that open the previous volume: "Audience and Image: Some Medieval Hypotheses," and "Chaucerian Aesthetic: The Image in the Poem." Those pages and their many pictures still serve my purpose well enough, in that they tread reasonably lightly, assume no prior knowledge, and have Chaucer's poetic practice ultimately in mind. But I have other reasons as well. Since the publication of my book in 1984, two studies by Mary J. Carruthers, *The Book of Memory: A Study of Memory in Medieval Culture* (1990) and *The Craft of Thought: Meditation, Rhetoric, and the Making of Images, 400–1200* (1998), have profoundly increased our understanding of the role played by images in the medieval conception of memory and its powers—including its *creative* potential, which goes well beyond "recollection" narrowly conceived. Any interested reader will find in these books a wealth of new evidence and ideas strengthening the medieval case for visual/verbal "equivalency" that I made in my earlier introductory chapters.[5] And anyone interested in how these theoretical issues might be reformulated today will read with interest an important essay by Michael Riffaterre, "The Mind's Eye: Memory and Textuality" (1991), in which he argues that "the principal mechanism of the *written* text is memory"—emphasis mine—and that "reading the text is not a matter of decoding contiguous signs in linear sequence, but of matching those signs against simultaneous memories stacked in paradigms." In our minds as we read, he argues, there is present not only "a vast terra incognita of other texts but also, and perhaps above all, a terra incognita of mythologemes, ideologemes, descriptive systems and sememic structures" that feeds into the text before us; it is, he suggests, "the stuff, the precast, prefabricated stuff of literature." Beneath that daunting pile-up of technical language there lies some simple good sense, leading Riffaterre to a conclusion he deems "inescapable," however paradoxical, and which I find entirely sympathetic with my own: "The text's unwritten component is vastly more developed than the written. . . . Memory is the essence of textuality."[6]

Because many readers will consult the present volume one chapter at a time, independent of the whole, I've let stand (as first written) the brief introduction to method that opens each. The redundancy is not great, and anyone already familiar with the general cast of my work is invited to pass over those opening paragraphs lightly—except, please, in one special case. The opening pages of "Looking at the Sun" introduce more fully than has been relevant before the kind of imagery advocated by the medieval "arts of memory"—imagery intentionally bizarre and unnatural—as a guide to Chaucer's use of dream images in *Troilus and Criseyde*. Those startling, fantastical dreams, one invented for each lover, serve not only as gateways to the center of a great poem, yielding a deeper understanding of character and theme, but also (coincidentally) as a gateway to the argument of this book, because they diverge so greatly from Chaucer's more usual practice, the art of the embedded image, outlined above and explored in the chapters that follow.

To bring together essays written over so many years is an activity that invites retrospection, tempting one, at best, to an account—at worst, to a defense—of how "one's light was spent" and how they came to be. Since I feel neither especially defensive nor boastful, I shall mention only a matter or two that comes as a surprise even to me.

I am struck, in looking back, by how much my undergraduate interest in the stage, both medieval and modern, led to this way of reading and thinking about Chaucer. After two years at Oxford (1955–57), reading the Honours B.A. in English—in those days a degree heavily in favor of literature written before 1400—I found myself choosing a field of specialization quite different from the one that had brought me there. It was not to be modern poetry (most particularly the poetry of William Butler Yeats), as I imagined when I was competing for a Rhodes Scholarship from the University of Wisconsin, but instead the world of *Beowulf* and the Old English elegies,

Piers Plowman, *Sir Gawain and the Green Knight*, the *Revelations* of Julian of Norwich, the plays of the Wakefield Master, the medieval lyric both secular and religious, and the Arthurian romances of Sir Thomas Malory—a distant world unknown before, to which my Oxford studies eventually gave me access. Chaucer, oddly enough, played almost no part in that decision. His works were assigned to me in my first term at Oxford, before I had any skill in the language (this predated student editions glossed in the margins), and before I had got my critical feet on the ground. And so, in that first term, fearful of exposing my new-world ineptitude, I didn't so much read "Chaucer" as read widely in what had been published on his work (pre-1955), trusting it to tell me what I might find valuable there were I able to read him on my own. It didn't come close. In the course of the next two years, however, as my linguistic competence grew, the medieval texts mentioned above became a major source of interest, feeding and being reinforced by my growing interest in medieval art. What finally tipped the scale was a visit to the York Festival in the summer of 1957, shortly after doing "Schools" (twenty-seven hours of comprehensive written exams), to see the York plays performed in the ruins of St. Mary's Abbey, along with another staged on a pageant wagon pulled through the city streets. A Yorkshire girl named Judy Dench, still in drama school in London, played the Virgin Mary that year. Moved by the plays' scope and ambition, and by the strength and simplicity of their means, I chose the surviving cycles of medieval England, including that of York, as the subject of my Oxford doctoral research. It became my first book, *The Play Called Corpus Christi* (1966).

I read the texts of those four vast plays intensively, enabled, no doubt, by my American training in historically based "close reading." (Thank you, Ruth Wallerstein and Madeleine Doran.) But I read them as well against a great number of works in the vernacular from the same period—works that retold, versified, commented upon, or preached from those same biblical stories—asking myself over and over what made the drama versions distinctive. The best answers I could frame always seemed to have something to do with declared mode (medieval drama as "play" and "game") and with stage image (medieval drama as a "visual" art). Though I published no pictures in that first book, in the course of its writing I looked at (and learned from) medieval art in European churches and cathedrals, read books about it (they were far fewer then), and gained privileged access to the thing itself in illuminated manuscripts, having recognized early on that the visual arts were part of the drama's essential context. Together these two interests helped me imagine the way a play might be enacted on a stage: how it might be set; how its players might interact with the audience; and how it might leave a residual "image" in the minds of those who wished to recall what they had seen, in order to think about it some more.

My interest in theatrical mode and stage image had been coincidentally nourished by an undergraduate first year spent "doing theater" in Oxford, initially in two productions for the Experimental Theatre Club, and then in a late-night cabaret for the Oxford Theatre Group, "on the fringe" at the Edinburgh Festival in 1956. Because we played there in a small hall with a minimal set, on a thrust stage with the audience on three sides, I learned things about drama in performance I could never have guessed from the proscenium stage and its illusory "fourth-wall"—at the time an almost universal theatrical convention in the West. But I had been readied for it by one singular exception—the first London production of Samuel Beckett's *Waiting for Godot* (1955), a shattering experience that prepared me, better than anything else, to attempt a new kind of book about medieval drama and (later) about Chaucer and the visual arts. It instructed me in the *power* of stage images (even in a setting most bare, and in a play where almost nothing happens), and in the way that dialogue and action (even inaction) can define such an image, call it into question, erase it even (to the point where only traces remain visible), and yet acknowledge the witness it bears to something important in our cultural past (possibly in our human nature) that will not go away, however abject and even embarrassing its continuing half-life. I wrote about the play in just such terms in an essay called "Religious Language in *Waiting for Godot*,"[7] published a year after *The Play Called Corpus Christi*. That essay seems to me in retrospect a bridge to others I would write about medieval drama,[8] and more to the present point, to the work I was beginning to do on Chaucer.

My first experience of Brecht on stage was almost as important—an Oxford student production in 1956 of *The Good Woman of Sezuan*, as it was then called, the first production (if memory serves) ever mounted in England. It was directed by Dennis Potter, now dead, an awkward and angry undergraduate who went on to become a celebrated television playwright (*Pennies from Heaven*; *The Singing Detective*). Brecht's polemical call for an "epic" theater free of theatrical illusion further encouraged me to approach with respect, and as a given, the modalities of the medieval stage and the sweep of its ambition. For students of my generation, Beckett and Brecht represented "the shock of the new" in ways that went well beyond the history of drama.

When Chaucer next came my way, as a young professor at Stanford, this immersion in medieval drama and the stage images it "set before the eyes"—in the moment of performance, in the memory, and in even a reader's imagination—was a major part of what I brought, almost unaware, to his poetry. In my second year, 1963, I was assigned on very short notice the required (and therefore highly enrolled) lecture course on Chaucer; it was there that my first real engagement with his work began. Quite apart from two other new courses running in tandem, one of them a graduate seminar (we taught three-three-three in those days), this one on its own would have been a challenging experience: three hour-and-a-quarter lectures a week, on an author I'd never really studied, delivered to some 140 students (master-degree candidates and undergraduates together) in a vast auditorium at eight o'clock in the morning. Because I had never addressed an audience so large, I wrote out my lectures in full—and did so, for an eight-week term, every night far into the small hours of the morning. I found it all exhilarating rather than exhausting. Though I had little advance notion of what I was going to find in those texts, I felt unexpectedly able to engage with them on their own terms. Though mysterious still, they no longer seemed foreign—and at least some of the time I found myself saying things that seemed unlike anything I'd encountered in the Chaucer criticism I'd read before.

In that sense, my studies in medieval drama and its background were serving me well. But Chaucer's texts themselves, week by week, were teaching me that I needed to know much more. And so, by the time *The Play Called Corpus Christi* appeared between hard covers, I had set out upon a broadly based, highly "empirical" study of medieval art, eager to discover what the contents of the medieval visual imaginary might be. Over the next decade I read books on art history, visited medieval churches and cathedrals, and (most important of all) examined countless illuminated manuscripts in many of the great libraries of Europe and America, making notes toward other potential projects, while giving priority to the new questions and new ideas (born of lecture) that I had about Chaucer. It was a privileged introduction to the visual culture of medieval Europe. Everything I've published since, and intend to publish in the future, has been rooted in that ground.

My interest in thinking about text and image together thus predates, and owes relatively little, to the example of D. W. Robertson, Jr., whose monumental *A Preface to Chaucer: Studies in Medieval Perspectives* (1962) was the first to significantly employ pictures and argue for iconographic meaning in Chaucer's poems.[9] But the power and challenge of that book (and of Robbie's gruff personal charisma) was nevertheless a decisive force in the shaping of my career—as it was for many medievalists of my generation. His larger claims for the allegorical nature of all medieval literature, so bracing (even frightening) when they were new, are, I think, no longer widely entertained. But for at least a decade they set the terms of a debate that brought everything into clearer focus, on both sides of the bench. More important, I think, was the way Robertson redefined our sense of what it might be useful to know, even necessary to know, to write responsibly about medieval literature—not only the Bible, the writings of the Fathers, and medieval iconography, as he did at the beginning of his career, but social and economic history, as he did toward its end. In Robertson's wake, genial literary appreciation would no longer suffice; belles lettres would not see one through. Though his work is no longer at the center of current controversies, and probably never will be again, recent conference symposia assessing his influence point to a renewed respect for the power and consequence of his intervention.[10]

I first met him in 1958 over lunch in an Oxford pub, to discuss the possibility of doing graduate work at Princeton. He was working in the Bodleian on what would become his monumental *Preface to Chaucer*, and I was beginning my research into the medieval drama. It was an odd and uneasy meeting, punctuated by ex cathedra pronouncements and terse obiter dicta, some of which left me puzzled indeed. He had not yet become a name for a school of thought. Short and stocky, nattily dressed in a black suit, a dark maroon shirt, and a black tie—a costume unthinkable in England of the 1950s—he looked (I thought) like George Raft or some gangster from the *Movietone News*. Years later, I would encounter him in Princeton dressed in summer whites and a fine straw hat, looking for all the world like the owner of a Southern plantation. Though he was kind and encouraged my interest in working with him at Princeton, a research fellowship at St. Edmund Hall (unforeseen at that moment) allowed me to stay on in Oxford and finish my D.Phil. there. In retrospect, it was an outcome all to the good. Robertson did not brook disagreement lightly, certainly not face to face, and not often (I would guess) even from those he most fostered. But I always valued the friendly, if guarded, acquaintance we maintained over the years. He said to me once, in his brusque sort of way, "You're the one I worry about," leaving me unclear whether he worried about my failure to read medieval literature in a fully correct, Robertsonian way, or that, by challenging some of his imperatives, I might lead others from the true path. (However unlikely, the second interpretation is the one I choose to prefer.) I recently came upon the letter he wrote me after *Chaucer and the Imagery of Narrative* was published, a letter characteristically "Robbie" in tone. After praising the book as "magnificently printed and most attractively illustrated," "sure to find many enthusiastic readers," he continues: "There are, of course, many matters about which we disagree," and then takes me to task for a couple, before ending with this remark: "However, this is a very impressive book, and any objections I might have to it would undoubtedly be met with observations like, 'There *he* goes again!'" I consider it an honor to have been allowed even that much room.

Robertson could be fearsome in argument, and did not always play fair, not even in casual academic discussion. But he was a very great scholar, and his work energized the work of many others. *A Preface to Chaucer* was a shot across the bow of medieval studies, a call to arms whether for and against, that raised the ante and changed the face of Chaucer criticism for years to come. In my case, it gave me a book to admire, a new level of scholarship to try to emulate, and a set of conclusions that seemed worth calling into question, in search of an account more inclusive and possibly more true. However he might fail, a beginning scholar couldn't wish for more.

The chapters that follow amount to a portrait of "Chaucer among the commonplaces," a poet among the topics and themes fundamental to the medieval worldview.[11] Though most of these topoi (as they are called) can be traced back to literary texts inherited from the classical, biblical and earlier medieval past, they have a long history in the visual arts as well, being at once familiar—"common" to many "places"—yet also varied and endlessly transformable. Chaucer typically uncovered them within an inherited narrative—he did not invent his own stories—most often in some sort of binary relationship: the vainglory of the tomb alongside the horror of the grave; man "in the middle" between heaven and hell, Christ and Satan; youth against age; woman "on top," dominating man; true art versus magic and false illusion; the place of chastity in a world that must be peopled; "courtly" love and religious idolatry. The *finding* of such images (called, in Latin, their "invention") is essential to Chaucer's narrative art—part of the process of its telling—even as their likeness to certain other images current in the culture identifies them as "telling" in a larger sense, bearing symbolic significance not limited to a specific fiction. In literature of this kind, the "commonplace" emerges both strengthened and refreshed, its claims to authority demonstrated anew.

Symbolic traditions in the visual arts, like the great topics of literature, are never simple and rarely univocal. Both emerge from histories of use, respond to changing interests and needs, and do not readily reduce to dictionary equivalences—though handbooks of iconography sometimes pretend they do. I have chosen instead to survey a range of their meanings *in use*, though even brief surveys risk overshadowing for a time the Chaucerian texts that provide their occasion. I accept that risk, first of all, because I do not mean these readings to be coercive: in the face of all this rich material, other responses are not only possible, they should be positively invited. But I do so too because the visual culture of Chaucer's time, taken at the large, is my other ongoing subject in these books, a culture not only fascinating in its own right but too little and too seldom represented in critical thought about his poetry. Like the first volume of *Chaucer and the Imagery of Narrative*, this book is a "twofer"—a two-for-one that surveys, chapter by chapter, a range of images such as those the poet and his audience might have summoned to mind, before suggesting how Chaucer may have used that tradition within a specific poem.

Chaucer was not a "painterly" poet, nor do I present him in those terms. Character and action, dialogue and ethical reflection interested him more. He can, of course, be counted on for visual detail sufficient to set a scene, supply some local color, enrich a characterization, or flesh out an action. But he never aims at pictorialism for its own sake.[12] Indeed, the absence of virtuoso description in his verse means that even those settings and events he describes with greatest care emerge as "iconographic" rather than "painterly," sharing with the visual arts a symbolic language based upon a limited number of essential elements rather than on an abundance of secondary or merely circumstantial detail. In these chapters, as in those of my first volume, I have sought to recover that language in (1) pictures of a kind he and his first audiences *could* have known, and would certainly have understood;

and (2) in literary texts he and his first audiences almost certainly knew, confirming the public accessibility of these traditions, and on occasion (usefully for us) stipulating their symbolic meaning.

I trace the history and dispersion of these images beyond Chaucer's death (1400) by at least a decade or two, and often by fifty years or more, because—this bears repeating—I think of these traditions as being in their own right a major subject in these books, and because they have rather seldom been written about in this way, not even by art historians. But I have other, more urgent reasons as well. What survives to us from the late fourteenth century, often almost by chance, is not so complete, so transparent, and so assuredly representative that we can afford to exclude everything made later, in hope of a putatively exact "historical" reading of texts from that period. The iconographic traditions that are my subject did not lose currency or meaning in the year 1400, nor did Chaucer's fifteenth-century audiences think it necessary to exclude the art and literature of their own time in order to read him free of anachronism—an ideal they would neither have understood nor embraced. I have of course sought to avoid substantial anachronism; these are essays in historical criticism. But if a tradition flourished well before the end of the fourteenth century—most of those I deal with go back much further—I have assumed that variants on it available to his early fifteenth-century audiences are of legitimate interest to us too. Too many things have been lost from the earlier century to pretend otherwise, while many things produced within the decades that followed—stylistic matters apart—preserve earlier symbolic traditions largely unchanged.

A colloquium, "The Afterlife of Origins," at the New Chaucer Society Conference held in Glasgow in 2004 and published in 2006, posed a related question—how should we define "source study" in a postmodern age? The answers there returned are of considerable interest here.[13] Several of the participants, having contributed chapters to the new two-volume *Sources and Analogues of the Canterbury Tales*, speak of the way traditional definitions of a "source" proved an impediment to their work. Kenneth Bleeth, for example, in "*The Physician's Tale* and Remembered Texts," argues from his experience that the origins of that tale cannot be traced just to actual books Chaucer might have had at hand but must also include "remembered texts, semantic fields, and pictorial images—the cultural topics stored in the mental retrieval systems of both author and audience, and ready to be activated by what the poet's readers and hearers discover in the primary text." Peter G. Beidler, also a contributor, in "New Terminology for Sources and Analogues; or, Let's Forget the Lost French Source for *The Miller's Tale*," proposes a new and more flexible way of categorizing such materials, sorting them out into "hard source," "soft source," "hard analogue," "soft analogue," and "lost source"—significantly reopening the meaning of "invention" (how and where a poet finds his material). Another contributor, Amy W. Goodwin, in "Chaucer's *Clerk's Tale*: Sources, Influences, and Allusions," points to "two different kinds of sources—a source text and, let us say, a source of invention"—suggesting the second may yield as much or more than the first "with respect to the insights they provide into Chaucer's poetic process or other issues." Nancy Mason Bradbury, in "Proverb Tradition as a Soft Source for the *Canterbury Tales*," suggests that "what best distinguishes a soft source is not that its influence on Chaucer's work is general or distant, but rather that it need not be a single written text. A soft source might be a pictorial image, cultural practice, oral tradition, set of conventions, or real event," as long as it "leaves a distinct verbal imprint on the work in question to indicate its special relevance." Carolyn P. Collette, coeditor of the chapter on *The Canon's Yeoman's Tale* in the new collection, after confirming the absence of a direct written source for the tale's alchemical lore, makes the reasonable claim that "for an artist like Chaucer, living in the city of London, the city and its inhabitants, his reading, his colleagues and their shared culture all become part of the sources of his art." She ends by acknowledging, in witty resignation, "There is no way to trace or document this fact. And so we say the tale has no sources." Earlier in her essay, she defended "our current interest in what a previous generation may have termed *analogues*, the verbal echoes, structural parallels, similarities of theme and phrase that occur within a range of time that does not necessarily predate the composition of Chaucer's work," allowing "a more open conception of connections and affinities than a previous generation of Chaucerians felt comfortable with or needed." Revisionary papers by Dolores Warwick Frese on the politics of translation and Betsy McCormick on ideas of "cultural capital" and the *habitus* strikingly formulated by Pierre Bourdieu add to this list. In a formal "Response," Ruth Evans calls attention to the fact all these papers conceive of "authorship, influences, and the literary in more complex ways" than does traditional source study, bound by rules of demonstrable textual indebtedness and (too often) kept rigorously separate from literary intepretation.[14]

It comes down to this: though we cannot become "fourteenth-century readers" even if we try—a goal theoretically naïve and only hypothetically attractive—enough survives from the fourteenth century and before, as well as from the decades that follow, to allow an informed reader to plausibly attempt a "late-medieval," "fourteenth- or early fifteenth-century reading" of a poem. That construct will inevitably be of our own time as well and speculative to a degree—no matter how diligently we attempt to recover the artistic life of something no longer entirely legible, not even to historical criticism. But if that is as close as we can get, it is also (I suggest) close enough to be valuable, allowing us to revisit imaginatively a time when changes in style did not occur often or quickly and when iconographic traditions evolved more slowly still. Because literary criticism puts no lives at risk and is unlikely to cure our mortal condition—it is not rocket science, nor brain surgery, nor an investigation of the mysteries of the atom—even historicist critics may legitimately claim a space not unreasonably anxious and constricted in which to exercise our pleasurable craft. There is no way we can exclude from our experience of Chaucer everything we know about the literature and art that came immediately after him—nor should we want to. Even for the historically minded, conversations with the distant past take place in present time.

The introduction to my first volume concluded with this sentence: "I make no claim that Chaucer looked upon any of these pictures, only that he would have understood them, and that he could have counted on some substantial part of his audience to share with him that skill." That is the part of his audience I have done my best to join.[15]

When I first set out, long ago, to *discover* rather than impose a theory of how Chaucer's poetic art related to the visual arts of his time, I began with a simple question: "What comes first to mind?" when I seek to recall the essence of a given tale. That highly pragmatic, not very theoretical, question still has, it seems to me, two considerable advantages: (1) it invites a variety of answers, making room not only for my own but for other people's experience of the tales; and (2) unlike a good deal of modern theory, the answers it returns are neither predetermined by the theory nor contained within the question itself. It leads one outward, to centers of thought and reflection ("telling images") embedded in particular narratives. At the same time—I think this too should count in its favor—the answers elicted by such a question are unlikely to surprise anyone who has actually read and thought about these tales. Though these images become more "telling" when their iconographic affiliations are recognized, they are plainly and openly present in each narrative, simply as images "told."

Grandly schematic images mattered to Chaucer too, especially at the beginning of his career: images that could generate the form and detail of a work, deriving it from a central idea. *The Hous of Fame* offers an example, as does the allegorical Goddess Nature, the bird parliament, and the parklike setting of *The Parlement of Foules*.[16] The narrative images that furnish me my subject, in contrast, forward his fictions in advance of, and independent of, their symbolic meaning. Because they emerge from a complex narrative, they seldom yield simple moral lessons. But neither do they emerge from a "realistic" representation entirely divorced from idea. By their means Chaucer was able to build his house of fiction within the neighborhood of truth—or at least, granted the always contested nature of that neighborhood, "truth" as it used to be conceived.

I take the ideals of Chaucer's poetry seriously because they are essential to his art and refreshing to the modern spirit, however disenchanted the world in which we live and read him. For similar reasons, I speak of his or the poem's "intention," not because I imagine such an intention is wholly recoverable or strictly verifiable, but because as a phrase it happily coincides with my own wish, however limited its success, to understand him in his own terms. As Lee Patterson has recently remarked, it is difficult to imagine any serious human communication aiming at anything less. Even the most skeptical among us want us to understand their explanation of why the attempt to understand is doomed.

In paying these images such sustained attention, I hope to have added something distinctive to Chaucer criticism, and to have suggested to his modern readers, if only in part, the subtlety and interest of the visual culture of his age.

Acknowledgments

A COLLECTION of essays written over more than a quarter of a century rests on so many debts, personal and professional, that one despairs of remembering them all, much less of expressing suitable thanks, however briefly, here. I can only hope that none went unacknowledged at the time, and that those who aided me then will take pleasure in the ongoing life of these essays they helped me prepare. I feel more secure in giving institutional thanks, first of all to the University of Virginia and its Center for Advanced Study, which appointed me as a fellow twice in seventeen years, reducing my teaching load each time and underwriting the costs of my pictorial research. The University of California, Los Angeles, whose UCLA Foundation Chair I was privileged to hold for fifteen years, provided research funds that enabled a good deal of the writing and research represented in this second volume. I am indebted as well to the UCLA Center for Medieval and Renaissance Studies for creating a community in which students of early history and literature find collegial friendship, a wide range of expertise, and enlightened support for our work.

If I cannot hope to remember all those who first helped bring these essays into public print, let me thank in their stead (there will be significant overlap here) a select group of students it has been my good fortune to teach at Oxford, Stanford, the University of Virginia, and UCLA over the course of more than forty years. Even this, I am aware, carries a risk of omission. I have kept no orderly record, and any number of persons with good claim not to be forgotten will no doubt come to mind the moment this book is in print. But since this, my third and final book on Chaucer, feels a bit like a valedictory occasion, let me thank at least some of those who enriched my life and work in their student days, and whose books (many of which began as dissertations I directed or codirected) have contributed something public and substantial to our understanding of medieval English literature. The earliest group includes Gabriel Josopovici, Terry Jones, Richard Firth Green, and Stephen Knight, from tutorials in Oxford when they were undergraduates and we all were young. There followed Robert Yeager and Jorie (Marjorie Curry) Woods, from undergraduate studies at Stanford in France; and Charlotte Morse, Penelope Reed Doob, Glending Olson, Roger Dahood, and Alan Nelson, from graduate studies at Stanford University itself. At the University of Virginia I was privileged to work with Louise (Aranye) Fradenburg, Allen Frantzen, Gail McMurray Gibson, John Bowers, Thomas Reed, Jr., Lisa Kiser, Kathryn Lynch, Roger Hillas, R. James Goldstein, Denise Baker, and Susan Hagen. At UCLA it has been my pleasure to work with Lisa Lampert, Theresa Tinkle, Victor Scherb, and Sarah McNamer, culminating in a brilliant last brigade, whose first books are appearing just as I finish this one, Christina Fitzgerald, Jessica Brantley, Catherine Sanok, Jennifer Bryant, and George Edmondson. As such a roll call makes clear, I have been unusually lucky in my students, and in the medievalist colleagues who guided and taught those students with me.

But I have my own teachers to thank as well, beginning with my parents, whose schooling ended at the eighth grade, but who dreamed of more opportunity for me; two great women at the University of Wisconsin, Ruth Wallerstein and Madeleine Doran, who (at a time when women were rarely found in the highest ranks of the profession) first taught me some ways of thinking about literature; three distinguished men who became my tutors and supervisors at Oxford, Reggie Alton, Nevill Coghill, and J. R. R. Tolkien; and my many colleagues at Stanford, Virginia, and at UCLA whose work has steadily enriched my own. But my most profound teacher has been Larry Luchtel, who has shared his life with me for more than thirty-six years, and kept me from imagining that life is ever simply academic, or to be studied only in the past. This book, like the one before, is dedicated to him.

I thank Charles Russell Stone for his help in readying this book for the press—no easy task, given its diverse printed sources, its many photos, and its related photo permissions—and for his occasional counsel on larger matters. Thanks are due as well to Eric Jager, Robert Yeager, and Rachel Jacoff for reading the new writing on *The Merchant's Tale*, advising me on its needs, and reassuring me (not the least of their services) that it might have some merit. Norris Pope, Director of Scholarly Publishing for Stanford University Press, has been a stalwart friend and supporter of this book, together with Emily-Jane Cohen, Sarah Crane Newman, Emily Smith, and Andrew Frisardi who have seen it through the editorial and production process with patience sometimes sorely tested, good humor, and skill.

Last but not least, I thank the editors and publishers of the volumes in which the following essays first appeared, for permission to republish them here.

Chapter 1: *Chaucer and the Challenges of Medievalism: Studies in Honor of H.A. Kelly*, ed. Donka Minkova and Theresa Tinkle (Frankfurt am Main: Peter Lang, 2003), pp. 31–71.

Chapter 2: *Signs and Symbols in Chaucer's Poetry*, ed. John P. Hermann and John J. Burke, Jr. (University: Alabama University Press, 1981), pp. 130–78, 233–45.

Chapter 3: Biennial Chaucer Lecture (1988), New Chaucer Society Sixth International Congress, University of British Columbia, Vancouver, *Studies in the Age of Chaucer* 12 (1990): pp. 5–46.

Chapter 6: *Poetics: Theory and Practice in Medieval English Literature*, ed. Piero Boitani and Anna Torti, J. A. W. Bennett Memorial Lectures, 7th series, Perugia, Italy, 1990 (Cambridge: D. S. Brewer, 1991), pp. 165–95.

Chapter 7: *New Perspectives in Chaucer Criticism*, ed. Donald M. Rose (Norman, OK: Pilgrim Books, 1981), pp. 137–74.

Chapter 8: Presidential Address, New Chaucer Society Tenth International Congress (1996), University of California, Los Angeles, *Studies in the Age of Chaucer* 19 (1997): 3–59.

Notes to the Reader

THE ENDNOTES to this book are discursive and often lengthy. Though not intended to be read in tandem with the text, they may reward a quick glance at the end of each chapter, for the sake of ideas, qualifications, and further reflections scattered among the scholarly citations.

The earlier essays are published substantively unchanged, though errors, obscurities, and stylistic lapses have been remedied. There is of course much I might do differently now, but time grows short, and revisions made long after the fact are not always for the better. I have chosen instead to present some ambitious new work along with the old. The first chapter, "Looking at the Sun in Chaucer's *Troilus and Criseyde*," the two chapters on calendar art and *The Merchant's Tale*, and the foregoing preface, are all products of the present or the more recent past.

Because there is little overlap between these chapters, each has been left fully annotated, as in its first publication, making a concluding bibliography unnecessary. The Index will guide one to all citations. Three abbreviations occur often: EETS (Early English Text Society); *SAC* (*Studies in the Age of Chaucer*); and *ChauR* (*The Chaucer Review*).

In quotations from early English I have replaced the runic letter *thorn* and the Old English script form *yogh* with their modern equivalents.

Biblical texts are quoted from the Latin Vulgate and its English translation made at Douay/Rheims in 1582/1609.

P.L. in the notes section refers to *Patrologiae cursus completus*, Series Latina, ed. Jacques-Paul Migne, 221 vols. (Paris: 1844–64).

All quotations from Chaucer are from *The Riverside Chaucer*, 3rd ed., ed. Larry D. Benson (Boston: Houghton Mifflin, 1987).

Please note that every manuscript illumination from the Pierpont Morgan Library reproduced or cited in these pages can now be seen in color (and often in enlarged detail) at http://corsair.morganlibrary.org. This valuable new resource became available to me only in writing about *The Merchant's Tale*, but its reach is inclusive.

Telling Images

I. Looking at the Sun in Chaucer's *Troilus and Criseyde*

> What is the sonne wers, of kynde right, (II 862)
> Though that a man, for feeblesse of his yën,
> May nought endure on it to see for bright?
> Or love the wers, though wrecches on it crien?

IN THE first volume of *Chaucer and the Imagery of Narrative*, and in the chapters that follow, I have sought to show, one poem or tale at a time, how the mature Chaucer uncovers within his fictions a range of iconographic images, rich in affiliation, that he and his first audiences knew from other literary works and the visual culture of their time. Passages that can readily be visualized with the "eye of the mind," they are central to the story and distinguished by the force and clarity of their detail. But what makes them most distinctive within late medieval poetic practice is the fact that Chaucer insists so little on their symbolic dimension. That is left for the reader or listener to discover as the tale progresses, and to take thoughtful pleasure in after it is over. Though such images loom large in memory—within any given tale it is rare for more than one or two to emerge in this way—they are subsumed within a narrative style that gives prominence to setting and event, character and conversation, emotion and rhetorical address, adorned by only the occasional metaphor or simile. The prison/garden and the tournament amphitheater in *The Knight's Tale* are examples of this kind, as is the runaway horse in *The Reeve's Tale* and the rudderless ship at sea in *The Man of Law's Tale*.[1] Though embedded in the plot, either as setting or as an action the story moves to or through, the symbolic potential of these images allows the poet to suggest meanings larger and more general than those of the tale's specific narrative.

This chapter will concern two images whose function is as large but whose construction is based on wholly different principles. As images that *insist upon* a nonliteral interpretation, they are woven into the mimetic surfaces of the poem only by the fiction that they have been received in dreams, where the obscure and enigmatic are commonplace. In doing so, they remind us how little the other sort of image, more characteristic of Chaucer's mature practice, conforms to some of the most important teaching concerning images current in his time. That teaching had been passed down through handbooks written by Cicero (*De oratore*) or widely attributed to him (the celebrated *Rhetorica ad Herrenium*), up to and including a treatise on the art of memory (*De memoria artificiali*) we reasonably attribute to Thomas Bradwardine—the fourteenth-century "Bisshop Bradwardyn" Chaucer refers to in *The Nun's Priest's Tale* as an authority on free will (*CT*, VII 3242).[2] We will pay his treatise some close attention here.

In teaching the art of persuasive public speech, Rhetoric, both ancient and medieval, recognized that an orator, beyond skill in arrangement, delivery, invention, and style, needs to remember in proper order the topics of a speech he plans to give in counsel or in forum. And so a fifth branch of rhetoric taught the art of memory, in which certain assumptions about imagery, influential throughout the Middle Ages, are spelled out in precise detail.[3]

Rhetoric taught a way of creating memory systems—first by visualizing in one's mind a well-known place or "background," usually architectural, containing several distinct locations (loci) within it. There, in a sequence natural to the place, usually from left to right, one could place a set of "images" invented to represent the topics of one's speech, making them so memorable as to be readily revisited in the mind. In two magisterial books, Mary Carruthers has shown how memory treatises of this kind reflect cultural practices deeper and more widespread than the training of "artificial" memory on its own.[4] Common to most is the assumption that images competent in this way will exhibit a certain exaggerated quality—as Bishop Bradwardine, like many others before him, makes clear. I quote Carruthers's summary:

> Because the memory retains distinctly only what is extraordinary, wonderful, and intensely charged with emotion, the images should be of extremes—of ugliness or beauty, ridicule or nobility, of laughter or weeping, of worthiness or salaciousness. Bloody figures, or monstrosities, or figures brilliantly but abnormally colored should be used, and they should be engaged in activity of a sort that is extremely vigorous.[5]

Bradwardine chose the zodiac to illustrate how memorial images might best be invented and arranged, linking its star signs to each other through actions that are violent, improbable, and often sexual in kind. "Suppose someone," he writes,

> must memorize the twelve zodiacal signs, that is the ram, the bull, etc. So he should make for himself in the front of the first [memory] location a very white ram standing up and rearing on his hind feet, with (if you like) golden horns. Likewise one places a very red bull to the right of the ram, kicking the ram with his rear feet; standing erect, the ram then with his right foot kicks the bull above his large and super-swollen testicles, causing a copious infusion of blood. And by means of the testicles one will recall that it is a bull, not a castrated ox or a cow.

By this image, Bradwardine claims, we will remember Aries and Taurus. "In a similar manner," Bradwardine goes on, "a woman is placed before the bull as though laboring in birth, and from her uterus as though ripped open from the breast are figured coming forth two most beautiful twins, playing with a horrible, intensely red crab, which holds captive the hand of one of the little ones," making him weep, while the other caresses the crab

> in a childish way. Or the two twins are placed there born not of a woman but from the bull in a marvelous manner, so that the principle of economy of material may

be observed. To the left of the ram a dreadful lion is placed, who with open mouth and rearing on its legs attacks a virgin, beautifully adorned, by tearing her ornate garments. With its left foot the ram inflicts a wound to the lion's head. The virgin truly holds in her right hand scales for which might be fashioned a balance-beam of silver with a plumb-line of red silk, and then weighing-pans of gold; on her left is placed a scorpion wondrously fighting her so that her whole arm is swollen, which she tries to balance in the aforesaid scales.[6]

By these images, the author states, we will remember Gemini, Cancer, Leo, Virgo, Libra, and Scorpio. Bradwardine goes on to fill a second "memory location" in similar fashion, completing the zodiac's divisions. Anyone who holds such images in his mind, he promises, can revisit the whole sequence in whatever order he wants, forward or backward. Carruthers, however, emphasizes something deeper: "What is most surprising, to a puritan-formed sensibility, is the emphasis on violence and sexuality which runs through all the interaction of the figures in each scene."[7] That, she makes clear, is the very essence of the art. A wildly singular image is put in touch with others equally odd, in an interaction or display that can be readily recalled—here to remember the signs of the zodiac in their order, or (quite possibly) to use them as a primary "location system" in which to place other invented images equally startling and bizarre. As the ancients knew, and all experience confirms, what is extraordinary and extreme impresses itself upon the mind.

Whether Chaucer knew such ideas from the handbooks of rhetoric itself, we do not know. But he knew the kind of imagery such teaching produced, for he built two of his dream-vision poems, *The Parlement of Foules* and *The Hous of Fame*, around just such imaginings. In the former, the goddess Nature is described as seated in a glade bounded by green halls and bowers, attended by every sort of bird, arranged according to their kinds. She is imported directly from Alain de Lille's *Complaint of Nature* (*De planctu naturae*), where her description runs to many pages:

> And right as Aleyn, in the Pleynt of Kynde, (316)
> Devyseth Nature of aray and face,
> In swich aray men mygte hire there fynde.

In the second of these poems, Chaucer presents the goddess Fame as one whose size expands and shrinks constantly; whose ears, eyes, and tongues are as numerous as feathers on a bird; and whose feet are adorned with partridge wings, signifying the swiftness of rumor. From within her palace, built on a mountain of ice one side of which melts in the sun, she delivers capricious justice to suppliants who beg for good fame or bad fame, wrong fame or no fame at all. Everything about her is artificial, in the root sense of the word:

> Y saugh, perpetually ystalled, (1364)
> A femynyne creature,
> That never formed by Nature
> Nas such another thing yseye.

Indeed, almost everything about her has been taken from Virgil's *Aeneid* and Ovid's *Metamorphoses*, which provide the details noted above. To visit the dream images in such a poem is to gain entrance to its main attraction, since the allegorical construct is itself, in many ways, the poem.

That however is not the case with the two "strong" images that are my subject in this essay: Criseyde's dream of the eagle, Troilus's dream of the boar. I mean to give them a "strong" reading in turn, noting first their iconic importance, being the kind of extravagant, unnatural image favored in the rhetorical handbooks and memory treatises; and exploring, second, their iconographic affiliations, which invite literary interpretation. Since the poem that encloses them is not allegorical in mode, they function instead like embedded images (but not "covered over" or concealed) as a symbolic means of organizing the action of the poem as a whole. They suggest more than they present; they leave work for the auditor/reader to do.

Some 1,750 lines into his poem—possibly the most leisurely poem about love ever written—Chaucer imagines a critic registering this objection:

> Now myghte som envious jangle thus: (II 666)
> "This was a sodeyn love; how myght it be
> That she so lightly loved Troilus
> Right for the firste syghte, ye, parde?"

Chaucer's answer to the charge is dismissive and urbane: everything, he reminds us, has to begin somewhere. But that is merely an understated way of introducing one of the most beautiful passages in this ravishing poem. In the next 261 lines, Chaucer will enter the consciousness of Criseyde as she thinks about Troilus's proffered love—an inner debate in which concern for reputation and private tranquility sometimes clouds her face as clouds cover the sun (II 764–70). The prospect both intrigues and frightens her, so much so that she can reach no decision: "now hoot, now cold," she chooses instead to put it out of mind, walking in the garden "for to pleye" (II 808, 812). Accompanied by three young women, she wanders up and down, surrendering herself to desultory conversation and the beauty of a "Trojan" song. Chaucer gives us its lyric in full.

Sung by her niece Antigone, the poem within a poem affirms the goodness and worth, majesty and mystery of romantic love: "al this blisse, in which to bathe I gynne . . . /This is the ryghte lif that I am inne" (II 849). Criseyde, choosing to hear it as first-person testimony, asks in an offhand sort of way, "Who made this song now with so good entente?" To which Antigone replies,

> Madame, ywys, the goodlieste mayde (II 880)
> Of gret estat in al the town of Troye,
> And let hire lif in moste honour and joye.

This attribution of authorship is of great importance: though no name is given, the song's maker is known, and its substance is presumed to reflect her life. Composed by someone like themselves—a Trojan woman apparently of similar age ("the goodlieste mayde") and of their own social class ("of gret estat")—it testifies to the pleasure of loving passionately, and to the possibility of doing so without loss of happiness or reputation. Or at least, Criseyde reflects, "so it semeth by hire song." But can there really be such bliss among lovers? she asks. "Ye, wis," Antigone replies, though not everyone is capable of it, and though no one can describe it well. If you want to know about heaven, you must ask a saint. Fiends can only report on the foulness of hell.[8]

The reassurance gained through that oblique exchange, enforced by the beauty and high idealism of the song, imprints itself upon Criseyde's consciousness, leaving her a little less afraid than before, and moving her slowly toward a kind of love adventure she has never known. Soon it grows dusk, when "white thynges waxen dymme and donne," and her women prepare her for bed. There, in a kind of reverie, she will hear a nightingale sing its "lay / Of love." It too works upon her, gladdening her heart, readying her for change, bringing her to sleep.

And then the final persuasion. In a single stanza, Chaucer invents for her a dream so bizarre and violent, so sexual and surreal, that it fastens itself in the reader's memory as forcefully as it plays upon the unconscious of Criseyde:

> And as she slep, anonright tho hire mette (II 925)
> How that an egle, fethered whit as bon,
> Under hire brest his longe clawes sette,
> And out hire herte he rente, and that anon,
> And dide his herte into hire brest to gon—
> Of which she nought agroos, ne nothyng smerte—
> And forth he fleigh, with herte left for herte.

Though situated in a narrative poem rather than a "memory" palace invented for the purpose of remembering, the image is, as the memory treatises recommend, strange and unusual in the extreme. The action it causes us to imagine so starkly—a white eagle sets his claws into Criseyde's breast, tears out her heart, replaces it with his own, and then flies away, heart left for heart—brilliantly plays upon a theme often represented in the medieval art of love: poems and pictures in which a lover offers his lady his (very literal) heart, and she rewards him with a garland or chaplet in return. Most often he does so on his knees in adoration, for this is a religion of love. Chrétien de Troyes' *Cligés*, for instance, written in the twelfth century, includes "extensive heart-swapping"—the phrase is Michael Camille's—with its heroine Fenice at one point declaring that her heart is lodged as a slave in the heart of her lover. But the theme was important in other media too, including manuscript illumination and ivory carvings meant for ladies, all as a way of idealizing (or sometimes satirizing) courtly loving. Figure I.1, from a French writing tablet of the fourteenth century, shows the lover on his knees, offering his heart like a sacred thing in his sleeve-covered hand; she offers him a garland in return. On the right, they walk off together, an arm around each other's

I.1. The lover offers his lady his heart; they go off together. Ivory writing tablet, French, fourteenth century. The Detroit Institute of Arts (42.136), Founders Society Purchase with funds from Robert H. Tannahill. Photo © 1994 The Detroit Institute of Arts.

shoulder, with the falcon on his wrist indicating that masculine dominance has been reclaimed. In both wings of the diptych, she carries a small lapdog, a sign of fidelity in courtly art of the time.[9] As Camille puts it, the gift of the heart symbolizes "the greatest gift of self," and in his book *The Medieval Art of Love*, he reproduces a range of examples from the visual arts relevant to the dream image under discussion here.[10] What is novel in Chaucer's version is the substitution of an eagle for a human lover, the almost surgical violence of the exchange, and (not least) the unexpected emotional response, as Criseyde realizes she has felt neither fear nor pain. Medieval cognitive theory held that the memory stores not only images but their "intentions"—their likely consequence for us—which we sense intuitively, just as animals do. From this alarming yet ultimately benign dream, Criseyde learns, on a level deeper than conscious thought, that there is nothing to fear in love.[11]

We will return to this dream, for it serves other purposes besides preparing Criseyde for "conversion" to love. But before we do, I want to examine Troilus's dream in Book V—another image distinguished by "exceptional beauty or singular ugliness," so much so it is "almost a marvel." But this dream leads to utter despair.[12]

As Troilus's trust in Criseyde is eroded by her failure to return to Troy, we are told in summary fashion that he has bad dreams—"the dredefulleste thynges / That myghte ben" (V 248). He dreams that he is alone in a horrible place, that he has fallen into the hands of enemies, that he is falling from a great height. But then he too is granted a full-scale dream, its shocking detail addressed not just to the mind but to the "eye of the mind," the visual imagination:

> So on a day he leyde hym doun to slepe, (V 1233)
> And so byfel that yn his slep hym thoughte
> That in a forest faste he welk to wepe
> For love of here that hym these peynes wroughte;
> And up and doun as he the forest soughte,
> He mette he saugh a bor with tuskes grete,
> That slepte ayeyn the bryghte sonnes hete.
>
> And by this bor, faste in his armes folde,
> Lay, kyssyng ay, his lady bryght, Criseyde.

The horror of this vision wakes him, leaving him certain the dream is true:

> The blysful goddes, thorugh here grete myght, (V 1250)
> Han in my drem yshewed it ful right.

In that dream he stumbles through a forest, weeping for Criseyde, only to find her in the embrace of a boar who lies sleeping in the sun—a boar she kisses again and again.

Both dreams imagine eros in terms of sex across species—the breaching of a barrier between animal and human most societies hold utterly taboo. Indeed, by the thirteenth century, bestiality was in Europe commonly classified as the most terrible of sins.[13] But Criseyde's dream, paradoxically, is presented as acceptable. By symbolizing something the poem and its readers have come to desire—the sexual union of Troilus and Criseyde—this action, which in real life would elicit horror, can be read *in bono*, as a good and noble thing. The dream of the boar, in contrast, precludes sympathetic response. As readers we understand immediately this boar must be Diomede, whose heartless courtship of Criseyde we have witnessed with some pain. From within the story, however, it remains a dream in need of interpretation. Troilus understands at once that Crisyede has betrayed him. But what is he to make of the boar?

Pandarus is quick to suggest an honorable interpretation: the boar represents Criseyde's father, Calkas, "which that old is and ek hoor," embraced by her as he lies in the sun, waiting to die. "Thus sholdestow thi drem aright expounde!" (V 1288). Forget the dream, he advises. Write her a letter instead, confessing how much you suffer and asking her true intent.

And so a series of letters is exchanged, serving only to make what Criseyde intends ever less clear than before. Troilus meanwhile remains haunted by the dream—it "may never come out of his remembraunce" (V 1444)—

and is convinced of two things in particular: that it was sent by Jove and that "the boor was shewed hym in figure" (V 1449) as a meaningful sign. He finally brings it to his sister Cassandra, the prophetess whose destiny it was always to tell the truth and never be believed. She interprets the dream historically, remembering that the goddess Diana, in anger, once sent a monstrous boar "as gret as ox in stalle," to lay waste the croplands and vineyards of Greece. The slaughter of that boar by Meleager, the Calydonian king, occasioned so much envy and strife it became a major cause of the war against Thebes. In that war, Tideus, a descendant of Meleager and father to Diomede, was killed. The dream's interpretation is therefore simple—"This ilke boor bitokneth Diomede"—and its meaning painfully unambiguous:

> And thy lady, wherso she be, ywis, (V 1516)
> This Diomede hire herte hath, and she his.
> Wep if thow wolt, or lef, for, out of doute,
> This Diomede is inne, and thow art oute.

The exchange of hearts, presented in Criseyde's dream as courtly and noble, is here reprised ("this Diomede hire herte hath, and she his") but with a grotesque change of partners—the white-feathered eagle replaced by a somnolent wild boar—and in language bluntly sexual ("This Diomede is inne, and thow art oute"). The two dream images, as "strong" as any Bishop Bradwardine invented for his zodiac, turn out to be oddly alike: the one is transformed into the other.

This odd likeness is no accident, for Chaucer derived both from a single dream in Boccaccio's *Il Filostrato*, the major source of his poem. There, in Part VII, Troilo, overcome with grief, experiences the following:

> One day, all melancholy because of the broken pledge, Troilo had gone to sleep, and in a dream he saw the perilous sin of her who made him languish. For he seemed to hear within a shady wood a great and unpleasant crashing; at that, when he raised his head, he seemed to see a great charging boar.//And then afterward he seemed to see Criseida underneath its feet, from whom it drew her heart with its snout and it appeared to him that Criseida was not concerned by such a great hurt but almost took pleasure in what the animal did, which made him so strongly indignant that it broke his feeble sleep.[14]

In tears Troilo summons Pandaro, his confidant and friend, to tell him of the dream, which Troilo (unlike Chaucer's Troilus) has fully understood from the beginning: "This boar which I saw is Diomede, since his grandfather slew the boar of Calydon, if we can believe our ancestors, and ever afterward his descendants have carried the swine for a crest. Ah me, bitter and true dream!"[15] Figure I.2, from a manuscript of Boccaccio's poem made in Naples in 1414, shows Troilo in bed dreaming of Criseida lying placidly on her back, mounted by a boar with its snout in the air. In the picture, interestingly enough, no heart is shown.

From this single passage, Chaucer made a dream for Criseyde that would involve an eagle (his singular invention) in a heart-*exchange* wholly different

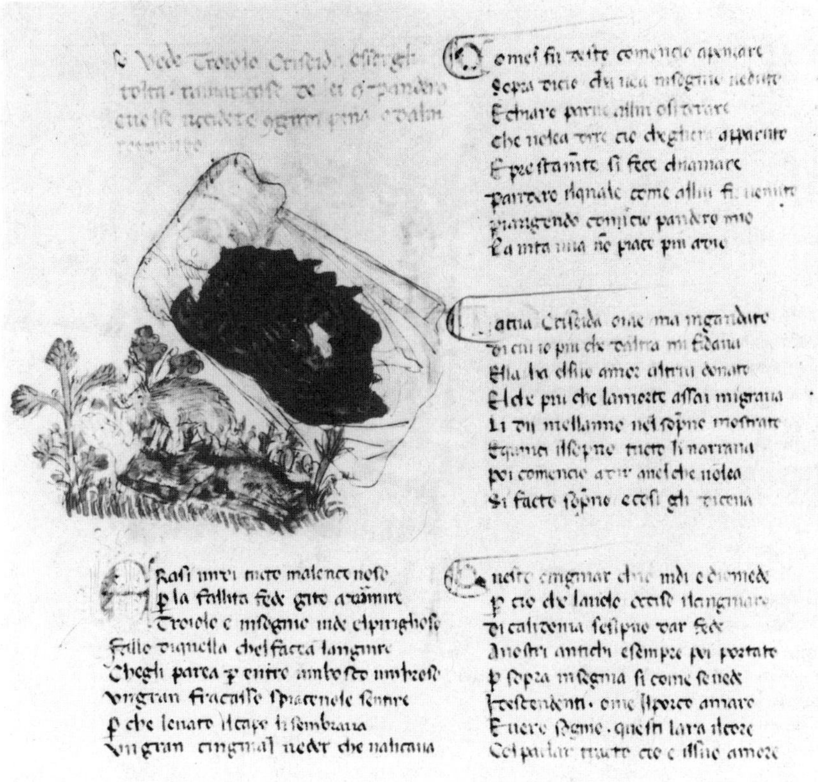

I.2. Troilo's dream of a boar lying with Criseida. From a manuscript of Boccaccio's *Il Filostrato*, Naples, 1414. New York, Pierpont Morgan Library MS M. 371, fol. 48v.

in tone, along with a dream for Troilus, adapting much that the first dream had left unused. But instead of the fierce beast that Troilo sees crashing through the woods before it mounts Criseida to root out her heart, Troilus dreams of a great boar asleep in the sun, with Criseyde lying beside him, "kyssyng [him] ay." It is a toss-up as to whose version of this dream is the more repellent. Both undermine the courtly ethos of their poems.

Boccaccio's original beast presents a genuine threat to hunters and countryside, quite apart from the woman whose heart he rips out—an experience she appears to enjoy. One recognizes in him the wild boar (*aper*) of the Bestiaries, a savage and dangerous adversary. Figure I.3, for example, shows the boar charging a hunter's spear, tossing a dog in the air, and trampling a second hunter, who stabs him in the belly from below. It illustrates a Bestiary made in England in the thirteenth century,[16] whose text says of him, in part:

The boar (*aper*) is so called from its wildness (*feritas*), substituting a *p* for the *f*. . . . The boar signifies the fierceness of the rulers of this world. Hence the Psalmist writes

I.3. A boar hunt. From an English Bestiary, second quarter of the thirteenth century. Oxford, Bodley MS 764, fol. 38v.

of the vineyard of the Lord: "The boar out of the wood doth waste it, and the wild beast of the field doth devour it" [Ps. 80:13]. . . . In the spiritual sense the boar means the devil because of its fierceness and strength. It is said to be a creature of the woods because its thoughts are wild and unruly.[17]

The boar in Troilus's dream has in him some of this danger and wildness—that is why he is called a boar—but in terms of the dream his physical threat is merely potential.[18] It presents him instead as sensual, gross, and in his sleep unwary—a condition more characteristic of the domesticated pig (*porcus*) of the Bestiaries than to its cousin the wild boar. Bartholomew the Englishman, in his great encyclopedia *On the Nature of Things* (*De proprietatibus rerum*, ca. 1230), can describe for us the pig's nature, here in his chapter on swine as Englished by John Trevisa at the end of the fourteenth century:

A swyn hatte *porcus* as it were *sporcus* "vile and defouled", as Isidorus seith *libro xii*. And froteth and walweth in drytte and in fenne and dyveth in slyme and bawdeth himself therwith and resteth in stynkyng place . . . and therefore swyn ben accompted foule and unhoneste . . . some swine ben tame and some wilde. . . . Tame swine . . . grontyn in goynge and in liggynge and in slepynge and nameliche if they be right fatte. And swyn slepen faster in May than in other tyme of the yere.[19]

The emphasis is on filth, sensuality, sloth and sleep, in contrast to the ferocious cruelty Bartholomew describes as characteristic of *aper*, the wild boar:

"He reseth ful spitously ayeins the point of a spere of the hontere. . . . And hath in his mouthe tweye crokede tuskes stronge and scharpe, and breketh and rendeth therewith cruelliche that him withstondeth. . . . The feeld swyn loveth wel rootes and wroteth and diggeth the erthe, and wroteth up rootes and kerveth hem with his tuskes. . . . And whanne that the bore is wroth he freteth and fometh at the mouth; and so he doth whan he gendreth with his wyf. . . . Also boores beth scharpe and most feerse whanne they beeth in loue.[20]

In medieval iconography a boar typically symbolizes wrath, and a pig lechery, though sometimes the boar stood in for the two together.[21] Chaucer drew on both in creating a dream image to stand for Diomede as warrior and lover, perhaps taking his cue from Boccaccio, who merged the wild boar (*gran cinghiar*) of the dream with the pig (*il porco*) on the Calydonian heraldic crest, with that being the sign that unlocks the dream's true meaning. In Troilus's dream, we never see the wildness or ferocity of the boar.

Just as Troilus was puzzled by the fact his dream involved a boar—a creature he believes was shown him "in figure"—so I think we are meant to wonder about Criseyde's dream, why it should involve an eagle. The choice, I repeat, was entirely Chaucer's own. One reason, of course, is that the eagle was thought of as being royal—king of all birds / *rei de oisel*[22]—and Troilus is King Priam's son. For Criseyde to dream of Troilus in these terms is to acknowledge his royal birth and to ensure that the dream remains courtly, even heraldic, in its register.[23] Perhaps that is all that needs to be said.

But Chaucer and his first audiences knew other lore about eagles, potentially relevant here. In the *Parlement of Foules*, for instance, after noting their royal status, he calls attention to something even rarer, the fact that they can gaze at the sun without flinching: "There myghte men the royal egle fynde / That with his sharpe lok perseth the sonne . . ." (330–31). This belief, widely promulgated in Bestiaries and encyclopedias, was confirmed even by Albertus Magnus, whose importance as a naturalist stemmed in part from his willingness to test traditional claims against personal observation. In his *De animalibus* (ca. 1258–62), he writes of the eagle: "Soaring at great heights, it is able to gaze directly at the sun's disk, so great is its power of vision."[24] Bartholomew's encyclopedia, too, affirmed the bird's wondrous ability to behold "the sonne in roundenes of his cercle withouten any blenchinge of yyen."[25]

This unparalleled strength of vision, the Bestiary informs us, provided the eagle a sure means of testing the legitimacy of his offspring:

It is also said of the eagle that it tests its young by putting them into the sun's rays while it holds them in its claws in midair. In this way the young eagle which looks fearlessly at the sun without harming its eyesight proves that it is the true offspring of its race. If it looks away, however, it is at once dropped, because it is a creature unworthy of so great a father.[26]

Figure I.4, illustrating a Bestiary made in the southeast of England, circa 1230,[27] shows the test underway. The eagle with two of his offspring gaze steadfastly at the sun as a third is cast away. T. H. White, in a note to his translation of a Bestiary, suggests these beliefs concerning the eagle may have been based on observation: "The upward glance toward the sun has been noticed by all falconers or austringers, as their captive, cocking his head on one side, gazes upward without a blink, generally at some other raptor."[28]

Being "eagle-eyed" implied other powers as well, confirmed by many texts and observers: "Its sight is so sharp that it can glide over the sea, beyond the ken of human eyes; from so great a height it can see the fish swimming in the sea. It will plunge down like a thunderbolt and seize its prey, and bring it ashore."[29]

From details such as these—the eagle's ability to see from great heights, its unflinching gaze, and the uncanny swiftness of its flight, ascending or descending—further claims could be made.[30] "It is a true fact," the Bestiary continues,

> that when the eagle grows old and his wings become heavy and his eyes become darkened with a mist, then he goes in search of a fountain, and, over against it, he flies up to the height of heaven, even unto the circle of the sun; and there he

I.4. The eagle tests its young against the sun. From an English Bestiary, ca. 1230. London, Brit. Lib. MS Royal 12. F. xiii, fol. 49. © The British Library. All Rights Reserved.

singes his wings and at the same time evaporates the fog of his eyes, in a ray of the sun. Then at length, taking a header down into the fountain, he dips himself three times in it, and instantly he is renewed with a great vigor of plumage and splendour of vision.[31]

Figure I.5, from the same Bestiary as Figure I.3 (MS Bodley 764), means to illustrate all three of these beliefs, showing us, on the left, the eagle as a remarkable catcher of fish; at the upper right, its recourse to the sun, where it purges its sight and singes its wings; and just below, its descent into rejuvenating waters.[32] (In the interests of pictorial economy, the sea here represents not only the domain of fish but the [baptismal] fountain referred to in the text.)[33] The picture begs to be seen in color, for the gold that blazes on the manuscript page, undiminished after all these centuries, announces in its own way the intimate relation a Bestiary eagle bears to the sun.

Chaucer too, in *Troilus and Criseyde*, brings together images of the eagle and the sun. Not only does he ask us to think of Troilus as an eagle/lover, one who will (in the end) be granted an eagle's capacity for vision, he asks us to imagine Diomede as a boar who *sleeps* in the sun—"ageyne the bryghte sonnes hete"—even as he is being loved by Criseyde. This reference to the sun is entirely Chaucer's own, not present in Boccaccio's original poem. I think of it as another primal signifier—like the boar and the eagle, something in need of interpretation—as Pandarus's careful attention to it would suggest: "Hire fader, which that old is and ek hoor, / Ayeyn the sonne lith, o point to dye . . ." (V 1284–85). But Pandarus hasn't a clue. The key to interpreting the sun lies elsewhere, in the song that in Book II led directly/indirectly to Criseyde's dream.

As Criseyde was quick to notice, Antigone sings in first person of the supreme happiness that can be found in love—"And thanked be ye, lord, for that I love! / This is the righte lif that I am inne" (II 850–51). Whoever says otherwise, disparaging love as bondage or sin, she scorns as envious or foolish or impotent, proving only their incapacity to understand or sustain so great a thing:

> What is the sonne wers, of kynde right, (II 862)
> Though that a man, for feeblesse of his yën,
> May nought endure on it to see for bright?
> Or love the wers, though wrecches on it crien?

Shall we hold the sun at fault, she asks, because we cannot look at it directly? Shall we think the worse of love because wretched folk cry out against it? Through two grandly rhetorical questions equating two comparably great powers, Chaucer prepares us for the eagle of Criseyde's dream, an eagle who will (in the end) prove its nature by gazing at the sun, while preparing us also for a boar who sleeps against its light and heat.

Antigone's song, like Criseyde's dream, is something Chaucer added to the plot of *Il Filostrato*, and is an invention mostly his own. Its beauty is peerless, despite the fact it rehearses many themes conventional in the love poetry of

I.5. The eagle purges its sight and descends into rejuvenating waters. From an English Bestiary, second quarter of the thirteenth century. Oxford, Bodley MS 764, fol. 57v.

the time. Indeed, a fair number of its lines are traceable (whether translated or half remembered) to love lyrics by his great French contemporary Guillaume de Machaut.[34] But no one, so far as I know, has found a source for Antigone's equation of romantic love and the sun. For that, Macrobius's influential *Commentary on the Dream of Scipio*, written at the end of the fourth or early fifth century, will prove more suggestive by far. (This is the book Chaucer "reads" and summarizes at the beginning of *The Parlement of Foules*, lines 29–84.) Macrobius there explains that when philosophers aspire to talk about "the Highest and Supreme of all the gods"—that which the Greeks called the Good (*tagathon*) and the First Cause (*proton aition*)—or when they wish to treat of the Mind or Intellect (*nous*), which holds "the original concepts of things" otherwise called Ideas (*ideai*), they deliberately reject fables and fictions. To discuss things that "not only pass the bounds of speech, but those of human comprehension," they resort to similes and analogies: "That is why Plato, when he was moved to speak about the Good, did not dare to tell what it was, knowing only this about it, that it was impossible for the human mind to grasp what it was. In truth, of visible objects he found the sun most like it, and by using this as an illustration opened the way for his discourse to approach what was otherwise incomprehensible."[35] Cicero's *Dream of Scipio*—on whose relatively brief text Macrobius erects his encyclopedic commentary—had used the same comparison in commenting on our inability to hear the music of the spheres: "The sound coming from the heavenly spheres revolving at very swift speeds is of course so great that human ears cannot catch it; you might as well try to stare directly at the sun, whose rays are much too strong for your eyes."[36] Until its last eighty lines or so, the subject matter of *Troilus and Criseyde* is nowhere near as grand as the Supreme Good, the First Cause, or the Divine Intellect. But if a poem can be said to have a desire—an intention so deep that it animates all the rest—then the desire of this poem is to know the truth about love. It invests in that experience so much idealism and faith, grants it such ample scale, subjects it to such extreme pressure, and demands of it so many kinds of good, that it becomes a kind of testing ground for love, in which the earthly and the transcendent, the false and the true are first mixed together and then separated out, in devastating and deeply tragic ways. From its opening verses, heavy with liturgical language, in which the poet presents himself as a priest of love and addresses his audience as a congregation of lovers,[37] the poem does everything it can to elevate romantic love to the stature not just of religion but of those great philosophical subjects named by Macrobius—despite his warning that they cannot be addressed directly and should not be approached through invented fictions (fable). From within the boundaries of its fiction, the poem does indeed end badly. But in its final stanzas, where *Il Filostrato* is overwritten by Dante's *Divine Comedy*, Chaucer shows how the failure of romantic love, seen clearly, may give way to a view of something grander and more grounded in the real. First Troilus as a pagan, and then Chaucer as a Christian, will show us what it is like to look directly at the sun.

Before we reach those final moments, let me briefly allude to some of the ways the poem attempts to bring erotic love and the highest good together, as though they were, or could become, one; and how it does so in terms of vision, both metaphoric and literal, accurate and grossly deceived. In its desire to uncover the full truth about love—an intention far outstripping Boccaccio's apparently more personal and self-limiting poem—the *Troilus* places a premium upon the act of seeing, beginning with what feminist critics, with reference to film, have taught us to call "the gaze."[38]

We first meet Troilus in a temple at a feast honoring the Palladion, a sacred statue whose innate power guarantees the security and continuance of Troy. Callow and immature, he strolls about the temple with a group of young knights

> Byholding ay the ladies of the town, (I 186)
> Now here, now there; for no devocioun
> Hadde he to non, to reven hym his reste.

Inexperienced in love, he sees only its power to make fools of those caught in its snare—a vision and a judgment he will reaffirm some eight thousand lines later, near the poem's end. But first the poem must transform him into an instrument capable of testing love's limits; and for that, as with Criseyde a little later, nothing less than a conversion experience will do. She will need to gaze on him twice, from her window, for the process even to begin: first without his knowledge, as he returns victorious from battle (II 610–51); and later, as he rides by in a dumbshow stage-managed by Pandarus (II 1009–22, 1247–74). (In this poem the erotic "gaze" is not inevitably gendered male.) But Troilus, in the temple, was converted the instant he laid eyes on her—a beautiful young woman, dressed in widow's black, whose bright glances gladden all the crowd. "Nas nevere yet seyn thyng to ben preysed deere,/ Nor under cloude blak so bright a sterre" (I 174–75).

This image, comparing Criseyde to a star covered by black clouds, is recalled near the end of the poem in a despairing song, the "Canticus Troili" of Book V (638 ff.), where he addresses her as a "sterre, of which I lost have al the light," and sees himself as a shipman sailing in darkness toward his death. But throughout the first three books of the poem, Criseyde is likened to the sun, in its power to illumine, to quicken and excite. Her "sonnyssh" hair (IV 736, 816) betokens the role she plays in the "hertes day" of her lover (V 1405), just as the consummation of their love at the center of the poem, "whan lightles is the world" (III 550) on a night of "smoky reyn" (III 628), provides on its own all the light they need. At that night's end, Criseyde swears that the sun will fall from its sphere and eagles will mate with doves before she will ever prove unfaithful in love (III 149).[39]

Troilus, of course, *is* the eagle of her dream, just as she for him embodies the power and mystery of love, equated with the sun in Antigone's song. And Chaucer, for a time, will sustain that symbolic equation with the full force of his poetry, steadily increasing the eagle's acuity of sight, allowing him to peer deeper into the real nature of things. Near the end of Book III, Troilus expresses in song the full dignity of their desire, the place of their love in the structure of the universe. The hymn to love assigned him there is, in fact, the third such hymn in Book III. The first, a proem in seven stanzas spoken by the poet, celebrates the power and benevolence of Venus, as both goddess and planet, but with the planet chiefly in mind: "O blissful light," it begins, "of which the bemes clere / Adorneth al the thridde heven faire!" (III 1–2). Though Venus's light may pale in comparison to the sun's, its astrological influence is universal: "In hevene and helle, in erthe and salte see / Is felt thi myght, if that I wel descerne" (III 8–9). Forging a universal law out of attraction and desire, she holds together not only the cosmos itself but kingdoms and households and the union of true friends. The second hymn to love, three stanzas long, is given to Troilus when he first holds Criseyde in his arms, caressing her every limb and finding his "hevene" there (III 1251). In that song he praises Venus as goddess ("Citherea the swete") as well as planetary force ("the wel-willy planete!"), together with Hymen, god of marriage. Goodness, harmony, and cohesion are here derived from "benigne Love," the "holy bond of thynges," identified in the first line as "Charite" itself, a word the Palinode will redefine at the very end of the poem, though its status as a virtue was certainly honored in the pagan world. The third hymn (III 1744 ff.) bookends the first, repeating and amplifying many of its claims. It is sung by Troilus to Pandarus as part of his perpetual praise of Criseyde:

> And by the hond ful ofte he wolde take (III 1737)
> This Pandarus, and into gardyn lede,
> And swich a feste and swich a process make
> Hym of Criseyde, and of hire wommanhede,
> And of hire beaute, that withouten drede
> It was an hevene his wordes for to here;
> And thanne he wolde synge in this manere:
>
> "Love, that of erthe and se hath governaunce,
> Love, that his hestes hath in hevene hye . . . "

This goes on at considerable length, in verses that deepen their original—Troilo's hymn to love in the *Il Filostrato* also (oddly enough) sung to Pandaro.[40] In Chaucer's version, Love has brought Troilus to "so heigh a place / That thilke boundes may no blisse pace" (III 1271), and he tells us what the view is like from there. The erotic "gaze" has become philosophical, and what Troilus sees in these moments is too deeply derived from Boethius's *Consolation of Philosophy* ever to be thought ironical or subtly repudiated by the poet. In Book III Troilus's experience of love leads to something like mystical contemplation—we might think of it as the first "soul journey" in the poem—and from its great height he sees many things truly.

But the light that is cast there comes not from the sun but from Venus, planet and goddess, whose light we can gaze on without anything like the same danger. And at the center of what he thinks he sees is a dangerous confusion of categories. In his eyes, Criseyde is love, Criseyde is the sun. But Criseyde is also human and vulnerable; Criseyde is Criseyde.

When Troilus, in his ecstasy, praises love as a principle of order, he offers as proof the way the sun each day brings forth the dawn—"his rosy day"—just as every night the moon holds romantic lordship over night: "Al this doth Love, ay heried be his myghtes!" (III 1755–57). But as the lovers quickly discover, within the "hevene blisse" of their secret sexual affair, the diurnal cycle of the sun—at the heart of any idea of cosmic order—has no place at all. When "cruel day" breaks in on their first night of love, the lovers complain bitterly against the night for ending too quickly, and rail against the sun for rising at all (III 1422–70). Criseyde indeed calls for endless night, and Troilus curses the sun, wishing its light might be quenched forever: "We wol the nought, us nedeth no day have" (III 1463). Extravagant emotion of this sort is well known within the dawn-song (aubade) tradition, but set against the cosmic idealism of Book III it sounds a discordant note, becoming their characteristic response even after other perfect nights of love:

> And day they gonnen to despise al newe, (III 1699)
> Callyng it traitour, envious, and worse,
> And bitterly the dayes light thei corse.

Books I through III, it has often been noted, are structurally modeled upon Dante's *Divine Comedy*. Book I offers a lover's version of the *Inferno*; Book II, the book of hope, begins with verses translated literally from the *Purgatorio*; and Book III presents an erotic version of the *Paradiso*—but with a troubling difference. Book III's lovers cannot bear to look at the sun, not even as it rises on an ordinary day. Their "insight" into love requires darkness.

In the Books that follow (IV and V) the lovers' ability to see clearly weakens, dimmed for both by confusion and error, fear and fantasy. Criseyde, in the Greek camp, regretting her refusal to run off with Troilus, blames herself for lacking Prudence's three eyes. She understands the past well enough, she thinks, and she can take the measure of the present. "But future tyme, er I was in the snare,/ Koude I nat sen; that causeth now my care" (V 744–49). Even in that, however, she is self-deceived: it is her anxiety about the future, so obsessively "foreseen," that bleers her sight in the present. Gazing across the no-man's-land between her and the high towers of Troy, she makes a fundamental misjudgment, asking herself whether Troilus thinks of her—remembers her—at all.

We know, of course, that he thinks of nothing else. As hope gives way to despair, he turns again to philosophy—to the Boethian text that underlay his vision of love as the source of all order, harmony, and integrity in the universe. But this time it is to put an urgent question concerning destiny and free will, and this time he gets the answer wrong. The mind has wings, Philosophy taught Boethius, with which it can fly to the stars, join the sun in its path, ride with Saturn in his sphere. And then, when it has seen enough, it can fly "beyond the farthest sphere to mount the top of the swift heaven and share the holy light.//There the Lord of kings holds His scepter, governing the reins of the world. With sure control He drives the swift chariot ["that is to seyn, the circuler moevynge of the sonne"], the shining judge of all things."[41] But in Chaucer's present adaptation of Boethius's Book IV, Philosophy's wings—"swifte fetheris that surmounten the heighte of the hevene"—fail to raise Troilus out of his darkness. In the course of a long and tortuous meditation (IV 953 ff.), he proves to himself that everything happens by necessity—that there is no free will.

As Criseyde's absence from Troy is prolonged, what Troilus sees, like the eyes with which he sees, grows ever more clouded and dim. He visits her palace, only to find the doors barred and the windows covered over, like a lantern whose light is quenched ("queynt is the light") (V 543), or like a shrine whose saint is missing. Increasingly he lives in the past, retelling its joys to Pandarus and renewing his memory in places made numinous by their love:

> Lo, yonder saugh ich last my lady daunce (V 565–75)
> And yonder have I herd ful lustyly
> My dere herte laugh; and yonder pleye.

And on and on. His own life becomes unreal to him—a fiction, he thinks, from which a book might be made (V 585). And often he stands at the city gate, gazing at the Greek camp and reliving the moment when she was led away. In a "fantasie" born of "malencolie" (V 622), he becomes morbidly self-conscious, imagining himself diminished and disfigured, an object of curiosity or pity to passersby. As evening falls on the tenth day, the day of her promised return, he stands again at the city gate, straining to catch sight of her in the dimming light—and, in one of the most painful passages in the poem, he is suddenly convinced he does:

> And Pandarus, now woltow trowen me? (V 1157)
> Have here my trouthe, I se hire! Yond she is!
> Heve up thyn eyen, man! Maistow nat se?

What you see, Pandarus tells him sharply, is only a field cart.

To mistake a field cart for one's mistress marks a low point, somewhere between the tragic and the comic, in a poem that has invested so much in the faculty of vision, the power of the gaze. Troilus's capacity for hope has blinded him—"his hope alwey hym blente" (V 1195)—as has his increasing despair: "He kan now sen non other remedie / But for to shape hym soone for to dye" (V 1210). It is in that condition that he dreams of Criseyde in the arms of a wild boar.

The dream-vision, for all its horror, does not fully restore his sight, not even after Cassandra's brutal interpretation. Nor do Criseyde's evasive replies to his letters, each more temporizing and equivocal than the last. Something more is needed, powerful enough to clear his eyes and force him to see the truth: "men seyen that at the laste, / For any thing, men shal the soothe se" (V 1639–40).

It comes in the form of a golden brooch, pinned to a coat Deiphebus one day strips from Diomede in battle, and then proudly displays in the streets of Troy. For Deiphebus it is a token of victory, but for Troilus a token of defeat—being the brooch she gave him on the night they first made love (III 1370). He returned it to her, to remember him by, on their last morning in bed together, just before her departure from Troy. She had promised to keep it forever; seeing it pinned to Diomede's coat-armor, Troilus knows at last that he has lost her: "Of Diomede have ye now al this feeste!" (V 1677). The brooch is pictured large and resplendent in Figure I.6, illustrating a French prose translation of Boccaccio's poem, made circa 1455–56 for the wife of Charles d'Orléans.[42]

This brooch—"gold and azure, / In which a ruby set was lik an herte"—serves Troilus as the sun does the Bestiary eagle: it purges his clouded vision and shows him the truth, reducing the mutual rapture experienced in Book III to little more than a dream of love, a brief episode in a history of obsession and self-deception. And it teaches him something even harder to bear, that he cannot stop loving her, despite this knowledge and all this pain:

> Thorugh which I se that clene out of youre mynde (V 1695)
> Ye han me cast—and I ne kan nor may,
> For al this world, withinne myn herte fynde
> To unloven yow a quarter of a day!
> In corsed tyme I born was, weilaway,
> That yow, that doon me al this wo endure,
> Yet love I best of any creature!

Whether one thinks of Troilus's continuing fidelity as abject or noble—or some awful combination of the two—it is part of the mystery of love as sounded in this poem. It is both possible and terrible to love as Troilus has loved and cannot help but go on loving. The brooch turns out to be as blinding as the sun in its destructive power. By looking at it directly, Troilus frees himself from illusion—a good thing, no doubt—but the view comes at a price. He is left desiring nothing but death. Caring nothing for this world, he fights ferociously, killing many a Greek in seeking out Diomede, to kill him or be killed. But Fortune, in a final cosmic joke, denies him even that small symmetry. In a single line of verse, "Despitously hym slough the fierse Achille" (V 1806).

Troilus's eye of the flesh has seen as much as it can bear. Rewarded for his loyalty in love, or more likely (following Cicero's dream-vision lead) for his service to the state,[43] Troilus's soul, released from his body, ascends the heavens, *passing* the sun, to the hollowness of the eighth sphere—the sphere of the fixed stars.[44] Figure I.7, illustrating Scipio's dream in a manuscript of Macrobius's *Commentary*, makes graphic the distance and liberation involved. At its center it shows the earth, with the warring cities of Carthage and

I.6. Diomede's battle coat, with broach, being displayed in Troy. From a French prose translation of *Il Filostrato*, ca. 1455–56. Paris, Bibl. Natl. MS fr. 25528, fol. 89v.

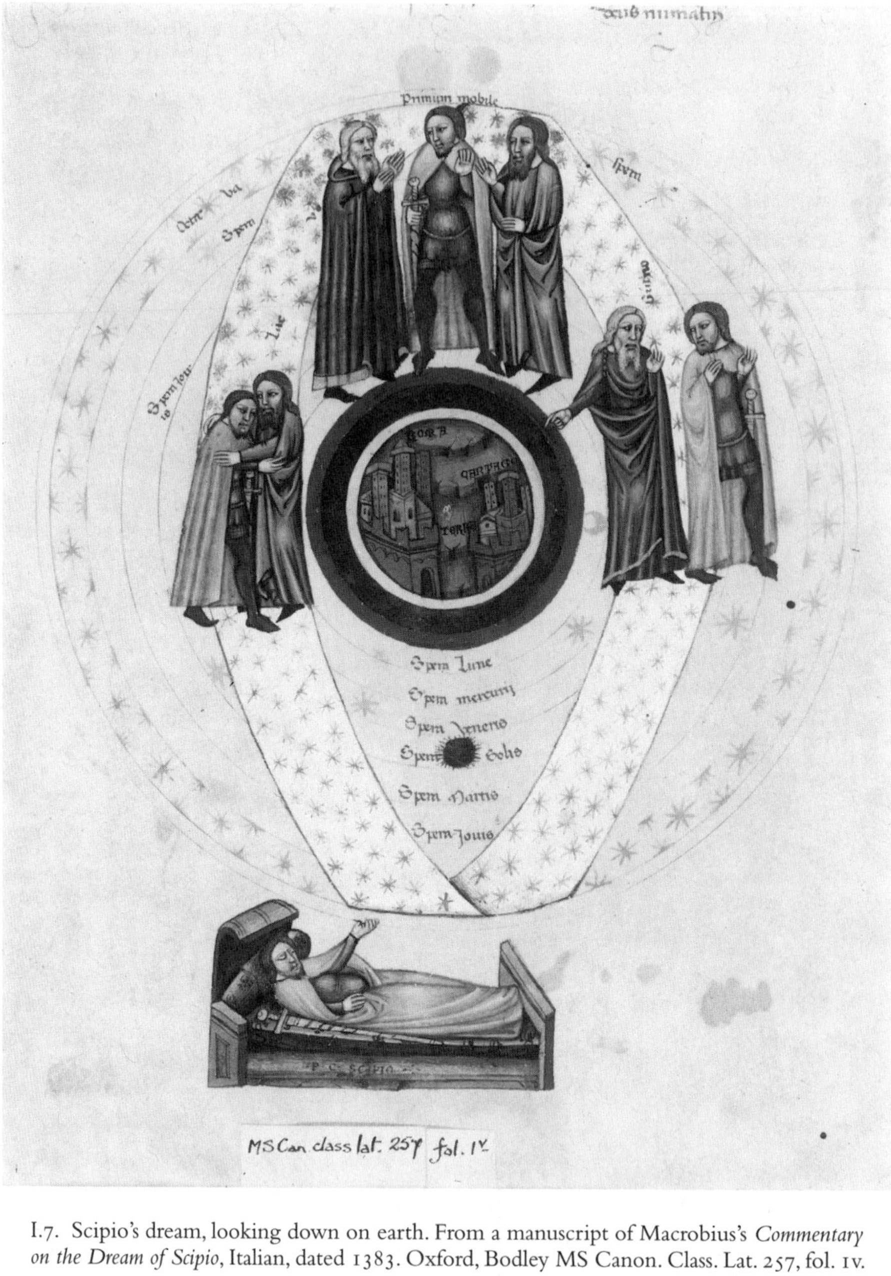

I.7. Scipio's dream, looking down on earth. From a manuscript of Macrobius's *Commentary on the Dream of Scipio*, Italian, dated 1383. Oxford, Bodley MS Canon. Class. Lat. 257, fol. 1v.

Rome; on the left, Scipio Africanus the Younger, who will destroy Carthage, is embraced by Masinissa, King of Numidia; at the top, they are joined by Scipio Africanus the Elder, his grandfather, who once subjugated Carthage; at the right, Scipio the Elder points to the earth; and at the bottom, Scipio in bed dreams his prophetic dream. The sun (*Solis*) is shown ablaze in the fourth sphere, counting from the center, above the spheres of the Moon, Mercury, and Venus. Scipio dreams he is in the eighth sphere, here a kind of belted oval, the sphere of the fixed stars. From that place Troilus, like Scipio before him, sees the seven planets in continual motion, hears the ravishing music of the spheres, and looks down upon

> This litel spot of erthe that with the se (V 1815)
> Embraced is, and fully gan despise
> This wrecched world, and held al vanite
> To respect of the pleyn felicite
> That is in hevene above.

The journey of his soul (V 1807–27), like the flight of an aged eagle to the sun, grants him a new acuity of vision. Gazing on the brooch in Troy cleared his eyes to the particular. Now he sees everything at its most universal, and (to our discomfort) laughs at those who mourn his death, condemning all who seek love below (now named "blynde lust") instead of raising their hearts to heaven. Everything reduces to vanity in a world "that passeth soone as floures faire." Though Troilus's soul journey and backward glance are hardly a triumph or a happy ending, they do constitute a reward of sorts—a clarification if not a consolation—worthy of a pagan hero. Diomede, in contrast, "sleeps" against such knowledge even as he embraces Criseyde. Diomede's inability to invest his heart both protects and limits him. It is not in his nature to look at the sun.

Chaucer takes leave of Troilus's soul in two carefully noncommittal lines of verse:[45] "And forth he wente, shortly for to telle,/Ther as Mercurye sorted hym to dwelle" (V 1826). But he is not finished with his poem. There was theological uncertainty about the destiny of virtuous souls born before the incarnation of Christ, and so the "hevene" Troilus experiences, possibly only briefly, is one of "pleyn felicite" (complete happiness), based solely upon distance and freedom from earthly cares. It is not the heaven of Christian salvation. Bestiary lore saw in the aging eagle's restorative flight an image of redemption, whose basic outline we have already noted: "When it grows old, its wings grow heavy and its eyes cloud over. Then it seeks out a fountain and flies up into the atmosphere of the sun; there its wings catch fire and the darkness of its eyes is burnt away in the sun's rays. It falls into the fountain and dives under water three times: at once its wings are restored to their full strength and its eyes to their former brightness." But this passage from the Bestiary concludes with a further teaching, unavailable to the world of Troy: "So you, O man, whose clothes are old and the eyes of whose heart are darkened, should seek out the spiritual fountain of the Lord, and lift the eyes of your mind to God, who is the fount of justice; and then you will renew your youth like the eagle."[46] It speaks of a redemption ready all along, outside the boundaries of the Troilus story.

Having formally dismissed Troilus from the poem—"Swich fyn hath, lo, this Troilus for love!" (V 1828)—with or without sympathy, it is hard to tell—Chaucer advises his audience to "look up" and see an even greater mystery at the heart of love: the love of the god who made us, who for the sake of love redeemed us, and who, unlike an earthly lover, will never betray us.

> For he nyl falsen no wight, dar I seye (V 1845)
> That wol his herte al holly on hym leye.
> And syn he best to love is, and most meke,
> What nedeth feynede loves for to seke?

A paradigm shift has taken place, and the eagle whose "sharpe lok perseth the sonne" (*Parlement of Foules*, 331) is crucial to this strategy, a poetic program in which Dante's great poem also plays a part. The *Paradiso* opens powerfully in a blaze of noon—it is the spring equinox, with the sun directly over the equator—when Dante, still in the earthly paradise, discovers that Beatrice has turned around and raised her eyes to the sun: "no eagle ever / could stare so fixed and straight into such light" (*Par.*, I 46–48).[47] Inspired to imitate her gaze, he too stares "straight at the sun as no man could," though only briefly:

> I could not look for long, but my eyes saw (*Par.*, I 58)
> the sun enclosed in blazing sparks of light
> like molten iron as it pours from the fire.

Though Beatrice is able to gaze at the sun continually, he is better suited to gaze upon her, until he is drawn heavenward through the sphere of fire with her at his side. Figure I.8, from a manuscript made circa 1445 for the King of Naples and illustrated by Giovanni di Paolo, shows Dante and Beatrice leaving the heaven of Venus and moving upward toward the heaven of the sun.[48] Their further journey, detailed in the cantos that follow, will reveal truths deeper than the soul journey awarded Troilus. In medieval belief, a Trojan prince, living before the time of Christ, could not expect as much. But when Troilus looks down on the earth from the sphere of the fixed stars, it is the Italian poem that directs his gaze and purpose, just as Beatrice had directed Dante's gaze before. From that same eighth sphere, in preparation for "the final blessedness," she had ordered Dante to look down at the vast universe beneath his feet, as a way of keeping his eyes unclouded and his vision keen:

> My vision traveled back through all the spheres, (*Par.*, XXII 133)
> through seven heavens, and then I saw our globe;
> it made me smile, it looked so paltry there.
> I hold that mind as best that holds our world
> for least, and I consider truly wise
> the man who turns his thoughts to other things.

All seven [planets] become visible at one time: (*Par.*, XXII 148)
 I saw how vast they were, how swift they spun,
 and all the distances between the spheres;
as for the puny threshing-ground that drives
 us mad—I, turning with the timeless Twins,
 saw all of it, from hilltops to its shores.
Then, to the eyes of beauty my eyes turned.

With these lines, closing Canto XXII, Dante turns back to Beatrice and opens himself to all the revelations to come, culminating (at the poem's conclusion) in a sublime vision of light emanating from the Love that *moves* the sun and the other stars: "l'amor che move il sole e l'altre stelle" (*Par.*, XXXIII 145).

The very last stanza of Chaucer's poem, translated directly from Dante's *Paradiso*, addresses the Trinity in language comparably sublime—at once veiling and making manifest the power and mystery of the Christian God:

Thow oon, and two, and thre, eterne on lyve, (V 1863)
That regnest ay in thre, and two, and oon,
Uncircumscript, and al maist circumscrive . . .

Quell' uno e due e tre che sempre vive (*Par.*, XXIV 28–30)
 e regna sempre in tre e 'n due e 'n uno,
 non circunscritto, e tutto circunscrive . . .

Language of this kind shields us from the power of the thing it signifies, gesturing toward something beyond our capacity to see or name directly. But two previous stanzas, in which Chaucer addresses his audience as "yonge, fresshe folks, he or she," are far more characteristic of his poem

I.8. Dante and Beatrice move toward the heaven of the sun (*Paradiso* XXII). Painted by Giovanni di Paolo, Italian ca. 1445. London, Brit. Lib. MS Yates Thompson 36, fol. 146. © The British Library. All Rights Reserved.

(V 1835 ff.). Those stanzas too evoke God, but in the person of the Son, as the culmination of the poem's quest to understand the full mystery of love. The second of them discovers love's highest manifestation in the death and resurrection of Christ, who "upon a crois, oure soules for to beye, / First starf, and roos, and sit in hevene above" (V 1843). The mystery of love—the poem's greatest subject—is here absorbed into the mystery of God, as mediated by Christ's flesh and adjusted to the weakness of our human vision. The false heaven celebrated in Book III is replaced by the prospect of a paradise more true, and the reader-listener is invited to see with greater clarity than has been allowed (from within the poem) before.

The view from the eighth sphere is the longest view in the poem. But it is not (to the poem's advantage) the most important. It is from *this* world that Chaucer bids us "cast up" the "visage of our hearts" to see the Son on the cross. And it is in this world that charity emerges as the highest kind of human love. In this world at least, Troilus knows that he cannot stop loving Criseyde, even after she has betrayed him. And Chaucer, from out of the same human condition, cannot bring himself to condemn her either: "Men seyn—I not—that she yaf him hire herte" (V 1050). (In Chaucer's English, "I not"—a contraction of "I ne wot"—means simply and abjectly "I do not know.") Though in the end he will abandon her to what the books tell us is her story, he knows that in the chaff rising from the threshing ground of this earth not everything can be seen or known clearly, least of all the intentions of the human heart. Unlike Dante, who judges the illustrious dead with a God-like rigor, Chaucer, in the soul journey he grants the pagan Troilus and in his reluctance to judge Criseyde, enacts a special form of Christian charity—that of a poet toward the characters of his poem. And that may be deemed exemplary in its own right. John Wycliffe, for instance, compared the works of charity to the strong wings of an eagle, capable of carrying us to heaven where we shall look on a sun that "nevere schal have settinge."[49] The link between *sun* and *Son*, commonplace in English religious writing of the time, may furnish the deepest logic for the way Chaucer ended his poem.

Thinking about the poem in these terms reveals a structural unity that brings it closer to the *Divine Comedy* than has perhaps been noticed before: the concluding stanzas, including the soul journey and the turn to Christ, are not, as some have claimed, a pious afterthought, a conventional literary reflex, or (as one distinguished critic from the 1950s suggested, only half in jest) the equivalent of a poetic nervous breakdown. They are made necessary by the lovers' "liturgy" that opens Book I, by Antigone's song, and by the dream of the eagle and the dream of the boar, all of which Chaucer invented or made significantly his own. Their resolution, outside the bounds of the Trojan story, owes much to Dante's *Divine Comedy*. To see the Palinode as part of the poem's trajectory from the very beginning is to see the poem whole. But the differences between the two are equally important. Whereas Dante ends his poem at the greatest possible distance from earth, contemplating a light infinitely greater than the sun, Chaucer returns us from the eighth sphere to the light of ordinary day, a light in which we can look about us without presumption or danger.[50] The *Troilus* ends in devotion rather than ecstatic vision, praying to Jesus and his mother out of humankind's need for mercy. Its last word is *Amen.*

For those of us not Christian, the truth component of the Palinode—these verses invoking the redemptive love of Christ—must seem as wishful, as invented, as anything that goes before. But it is an invention (if I may) of a wholly different kind, bearing the richness and authority of an entire civilization, and it contributes something very important to the poem. I do not think Chaucer meant it to overshadow and erase everything that has brought us to this point. Proportion alone can tell us that: this immensely ambitious poem has not been suppressed or unwritten. Its interest in character and contingency, in lyric grace and urbane sophistication, together with its rich representation of the human comedy, remain valuable even after their "correction," though for lack of space such qualities have gone largely unmentioned in this chapter. But the soul journey and the Palinode must also be given their due. They contribute a gravitas sufficient to transform Boccaccio's youthful and far less searching work into something philosophic and profound. *Il Filostrato*, enclosed by a cautionary prose proem addressed to Boccaccio's own "absent lady," became in Chaucer's hands an epic poem on love.

Because Chaucer was interested in exploring love as a whole, he could not end it "small" as Boccaccio does, advising young men against the vanity of young women and urging them to choose lovers more prudent and mature: women who take delight in loving; women who will keep the promises they make. Nor could Chaucer send it off as Boccaccio does, with a concluding envoy, as though it were a letter to his lady—a Troilus kind of letter—begging her either to "return here now" (his highest hope) or to command him to die. In Boccaccio's early poetic, only the lady's "high worth" (*alta sua virtute*) can grant salvation: "mi puó render salute."[51]

Because Chaucer's poem has asked more of love than that, it cannot end in advice so merely pragmatic, emotion so narrowly personal, and metaphysical confusion so great. But neither can it reasonably end in cosmic distance, disillusion, and disembodied laughter,[52] though its end it will move to and through those things. In Chaucer's time there lay ready, beyond the boundaries of (imagined) Troy, the redemptive love of Christ—the only truth that fully could prevail over medieval "contempt for the world." Though for some of us it is a truth culturally contingent, Chaucer and his first audiences took it to be the very ground of the real. And so it functions beautifully here, bringing to a worthy end a very great medieval poem.

II. From Cleopatra to Alceste

An Iconographic Study of *The Legend of Good Women*

It is a truth universally acknowledged that Cleopatra is an odd candidate for inclusion in a *Legend of Good Women*; as is Medea, whose larger fame includes the slaughter of her own children; and as would have been such other virtuous ladies as Helen of Troy, Tristan's Yseult, and Canace, who "loved hir owene brother sinfully" (*CT*, II 79), had the poem been finished.[1] Chaucer promises us the stories of them all. But before we rush to conclude that his choices are ironic and the *Legend* an elaborate parody, we notice among this company other ladies whose fame is of a different kind. Thisbe, Dido, Lucretia, Philomela are there as well—love's victims, not love's criminals—to say nothing of Alceste, the Prologue's queen, whose legend was meant to conclude the whole. No irony attends these latter choices, and Chaucer reserves no parodic modes specifically for the former, though their claim to place is problematic indeed. The moral heterogeneity of this company of Love's saints constitutes the greatest of the many puzzles intrinsic to the poem, and in this chapter I wish to think about it in some new ways, by attending closely, first of all, to the *Legend of Cleopatra*. Though her credentials are as dubious as any, her story is given structural as well as thematic importance by a strict command from the God of Love: "At Cleopatre," he says to Chaucer, "I wol that thou begynne" (F Prologue, 566). If that is a directive few critics have followed, perhaps it is because in our age the Prologue has effectively become the poem. Cut free from the legends it was meant to introduce, it is read as though it were likely to contain within itself the completion of all its meanings.[2] A closer look at the *Legend of Cleopatra* can serve not only as a case study in the iconographic mode of Chaucer's literary imagination, but can also lead us—after a survey of the materials available to Chaucer for his projected legend of Alceste—to some more appropriate ways of regarding *The Legend of Good Women* as a whole.

We do not know the exact source or sources from which Chaucer derived his knowledge of Cleopatra's history. His version of her life is so brief (124 lines) and so much occupied with inventions apparently his own (including a vivid description of the sea battle at Actium) that there are insufficient grounds on which to judge. A few textual details, none substantive in importance, suggest that the *Epitome rerum Romanorum* of Florus, written in the second century A.D., or its thirteenth-century redaction in the *Speculum historiale* of Vincent of Beauvais, may have been at hand. Boccaccio's *De claris mulieribus* remains a possibility as well, not for any influence that can be demonstrated upon Chaucer's opening legend, but because, as a collection of lives of famous women, it offers the closest formal antecedent in medieval literature to *The Legend of Good Women* as a whole, and because it too makes room for Cleopatra. But the search for sources is unlikely ever to approach the vital center of the poem, for it is clear that Chaucer deliberately suppressed most of Cleopatra's history, what we may call in sum "the Cleopatra tradition," and significantly altered almost every part that he retained.[3] The passionate, fickle, and ambitious queen familiar to us from the historians, Boccaccio, and Shakespeare is missing from Chaucer's verse, as is any detailed notice of her life prior to her love for Anthony. His alterations, indeed, are as important as the omissions: Chaucer's Cleopatra is wife to Anthony rather than mistress, and she follows rather than leads him in the flight from Actium that confirms their defeat and occasions their deaths. Wherever Chaucer may have found his Cleopatra among the several possible sources, and whatever he may have found her there to be, she enters English literature as a "good woman"—in the special sense that term acquires in this poem, a sense initially defined by her legend, where the series begins.

If our interest, then, is in Chaucer's poem rather than in the Cleopatra of other books, these changes and omissions are of the first importance. But they do not contain their own explanation. They offer no clue as to why Chaucer should have gone to such lengths in order to include her in his legendary.[4] For that, I think we must look to Chaucer's largest single departure from the tradition: his version of her death. From a single detail recounted in all the sources, the tradition that Cleopatra killed herself with an asp, or with two, Chaucer invented a death scene that is wholly original and stunning in its power. It occupies the full final third of Cleopatra's legend and, if my reading is correct, offers one of two essential images meant to establish the meaning of the poem as a whole—a poem unfinished but conceptually complete, a poem whose larger "idea" (in the sense that Donald Howard has used the term) can still be reconstructed.[5]

So let us begin with what earlier texts had to offer concerning Cleopatra's death, and then look at that death within an associated tradition—its illustration in the medieval visual arts. For this is an example of "narrative imagery," as I define it in my first book about imagery in *The Canterbury Tales*: a setting, or an event, or a property which Chaucer invites us first to visualize as part of the poem's literal action, and afterward to recognize as bearing a suggestive likeness to (as displaying iconographic kinship with) certain other images known from elsewhere in medieval literature and the visual arts, some of which carry meanings that are stipulated and exact, generalized in their address, unmediated by the ambiguities of fiction or the accidents of history. Chaucer discovered within the Cleopatra tradition certain materials that could be made to address a truth larger than the particulars of chronicle or legend, and he worked them into a memorial center of meaning and meditative suggestion for the entire poem.[6] Cleopatra's death, in the Chaucer version, must be thought about iconographically if it is to be understood at all.

The tradition that he worked out of (but ultimately counter to) can be represented in its essentials by the Roman historian Florus:

> Despairing of winning [a portion of her kingdom] from Caesar and perceiving that she was being reserved to figure in his triumph, profiting by the carelessness of her guard, she betook herself to the Mausoleum, as the royal sepulchre is called. There, having put on the elaborate raiment which she was wont to wear, she placed herself by the side of her beloved Antonius in a coffin filled with rich perfumes, and applying serpents to her veins thus passed into death as into a sleep."[7]

Boccaccio's *De claris mulieribus* tells a similar story. "Cleopatra, dressed in royal garments, followed her Anthony. Lying down next to him, she opened the veins of her arms and put two asps in the openings in order to die. Some say that they cause death in sleep."[8] Only in the same author's *De casibus virorum illustrium* does one find even a hint of the nakedness with which Chaucer's Cleopatra will confront her death. There, again "anointed with perfumes and decorated with all her royal insignia," "she bared her breasts, and after placing serpents next to them, she lay down to die. As if in a quiet sleep her spirit was released."[9]

Renaissance engravings of Cleopatra's death, responsive to her full amorous history and perhaps specifically to this latter text, customarily show her dying naked. An engraving by Barthel Beham, for instance (Figure II.1; made ca. 1524), shows an asp coiled around her arm almost like a bracelet, allowing the beauty of her body to speak more expressively than any suggestion of its mortality.[10] An engraving by Augustin Hirschvogel (dated 1547) uses a recumbent pose to create a languorous mood, in which the frontal display of her body and the seductive rebuke of her glance suggest that the viewer has intruded upon her privacy rather than her death (Figure II.2). The head of the asp moving toward her breast unmistakably highlights the picture's true subject—the female body as erotic icon. Cleopatra's death serves only as pretext, as presumptive occasion; it is not what the picture is chiefly about.[11] A fine engraving by Hans Sebald Beham (ca. 1529) is unusual in showing Cleopatra in a prison and at the moment of the serpent's sting: her face and body, contorted in anguish, suggest a heroic death (Figure II.3).[12] But even here she dies semidraped and voluptuous. That is true as well of an engraving by Agostino Veneziano, dated 1528 (Figure II.4), which locates her death within a classical setting, and aims at a tragic, elegiac mood. Cupid weeps before a flaming altar as Cleopatra, resting against a pillar, slumps forward in death. The asp, twined round her arm, bites at the nipple of her breast.[13]

II.1. The death of Cleopatra. Engraving by Barthel Beham, ca. 1524. Photo: The Warburg Institute, London.

II.2. The death of Cleopatra. Engraving by Augustin Hirschvogel, 1547. Photo: The Warburg Institute, London.

II.3. The death of Cleopatra. Engraving by Hans Sebald Beham, ca. 1529. Photo: The Warburg Institute, London.

II.4. The death of Cleopatra, with Cupid weeping. Engraving by Agostino Veneziano, 1528. Photo: The Warburg Institute, London.

The medieval visual arts, in contrast, generally illustrate these texts with a strict decorum, avoiding nudity of any kind. They do so even with the *De casibus,* whose text specifies a baring of her breasts. Figures II.5 and II.6, however, present two exceptions: I know of only three. The first one, illustrating a French translation of the *De casibus,* painted circa 1470–83, shows Cleopatra in a fur-trimmed gown lowered to her waist. The second (Figure II.6), illustrating an *Hystoire tripartite,* was made in Flanders in 1473.[14] They both seem startled by what they have done: rulers in control no longer. I call attention to them here because, unlike these but like the heroine of the later Renaissance engravings, Chaucer's Cleopatra will go to her death stripped naked. Though her nakedness will have another meaning, it is another of the ways that distinguish her from the Cleopatra of tradition, including the *De casibus* tradition. For elsewhere in medieval art Cleopatra typically dies clothed, in royal robes and wearing a crown. In Figure II.7, a miniature made in 1410 illustrating *Des cleres et nobles femmes* (a French translation of *De claris mulieribus*), a beautifully gowned Cleopatra dies seated on a throne with serpents at her arms, while Anthony lies dead before her in an ermine-lined robe, his hands still gripping the sword he has lodged in his breast. The image is elegant and rather moving—tragic even—in depicting the fall of great ones. But it is without moral resonance of any other kind.[15] Like Figure II.8 (also illustrating a French translation of this text), it presents the minimum visual information necessary for us to identify and remember these personages.[16] In a manuscript of the French *De casibus,* made circa 1410, the lovers lie side by side in (or

II.5. The deaths of Anthony and Cleopatra. An illustration from Boccaccio, *Des cas des nobles hommes et femmes,* trans. Laurent de Premierfait, ca. 1470–83. London, Brit. Lib. MS Royal 14 E. v, fol. 339.

II.6. The deaths of Anthony and Cleopatra. *Hystoire tripartite,* Flanders, dated 1473. London, Brit. Lib. MS Royal 18. E. v, fol. 363v.

II.7. The deaths of Anthony and Cleopatra. From Boccaccio, *Des cleres et nobles femmes*, manuscript dated 1410. Paris, Bibl. Natl. MS fr. 12420, fol. 129v.

II.8. The deaths of Anthony and Cleopatra. Same text as Fig. II.7, manuscript dated 1404. Paris, Bibl. Natl. MS fr. 598, fol. 128v.

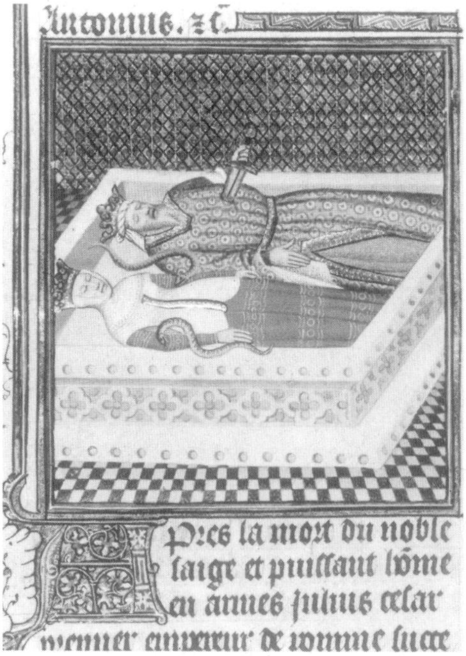

II.9. The deaths of Anthony and Cleopatra. From Boccaccio, *Des cas des nobles hommes et femmes*, ca. 1410. Paris, Bibl. de l'Arsenal MS 5193, fol. 272v.

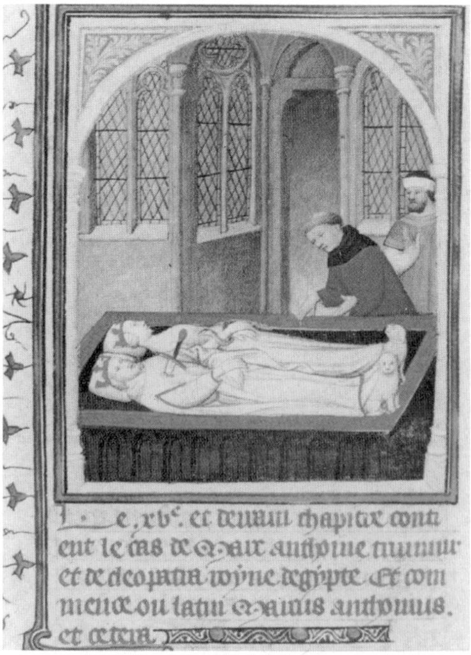

II.10. The tomb of Anthony and Cleopatra. Same text as Fig. II.9, ca. 1415. New York, formerly Coll. Francis Kettaneh, no pagination.

on) a tomb of precious stones (Figure II.9). Once again they are fully and royally dressed, with the sword at his breast and the serpents at her arms.[17] They look like funeral effigies, which is indeed how they are painted in Figure II.10, an illustration to the same text, made circa 1415. Here two men, one of them a sacristan or monk, are shown visiting the lovers' tomb, a massive Gothic monument of black stone adorned with a golden rail. Their images are carved of alabaster or white marble, with gilded crowns and dagger; the single serpent is tinted a pale gray-blue, and a lion and dog are carved at their feet.[18] In Figure II.11, also illustrating the French *De casibus*, Anthony lies dead within a simple tomb or coffin, open to the sky, with Cleopatra dead on the ground beside him, flanked by two fat serpents feeding at the veins of her arms.[19] This picture, in distinguishing Anthony's final resting place from hers, comes a degree nearer to Chaucer's version of the lovers' ending than any illustration examined so far. But here the distinction signifies nothing beyond itself. If as critics we would accurately illustrate Chaucer's poem, or as readers accurately imagine it in our mind's eye, neither this nor any other image from the Cleopatra tradition will serve. Such images convey at most the essential elements of the tradition: a royal setting, whether throne or tomb; the dagger; the serpents. But knowing such images can help us to estimate better the brilliance and audacity with which Chaucer transformed that tradition in the first of his legends of good women.

II.11. Anthony and Cleopatra dead. Same text as Fig. II.9, ca. 1415–20. Paris, Bibl. Natl. MS fr. 226, fol. 183v.

The scene is so important to the poem as a whole that I must quote it here entire, and urge that it be read in its full detail. After briefly noting Cleopatra's first grief over Anthony's death—"This woful Cleopatre hath mad swich routhe / That ther is tonge non that may it telle" (669–70)—Chaucer narrates her own death so:

> But on the morwe she wolde no lengere dwelle, (F 671)
> But made hire subtyl werkmen make a shryne
> Of alle the rubyes and the stones fyne
> In al Egypte that she coude espie,
> And putte ful the shryne of spicerye,
> And let the cors enbaume, and forth she fette
> This dede cors, and in the shryne it shette.
> And next the shryne a pit thanne doth she grave,
> And alle the serpentes that she myghte have,
> She putte hem in that grave, and thus she seyde:
> "Now, love, to whom my sorweful herte obeyde
> So ferforthly that from that blisful houre
> That I yow swor to ben al frely youre—
> I mene yow, Antonius, my knyght—
> That nevere wakynge, in the day or nyght,
> Ye nere out of myn hertes remembraunce,
> For wel or wo, for carole or for daunce;
> And in myself this covenaunt made I tho,
> That ryght swich as ye felten, wel or wo,
> As fer forth as it in my power lay,
> Unreprovable unto my wyfhod ay,
> The same wolde I fele, lyf or deth—
> And thilke covenant whil me lasteth breth
> I wol fulfille; and that shal ben wel sene,
> Was nevere unto hire love a trewer quene."
> And with that word, naked, with ful good herte,
> Among the serpents in the pit she sterte,
> And there she ches to have hire buryinge.
> Anon the nadderes gonne hire for to stynge,
> And she hire deth receyveth with good cheere
> For love of Antony that was hire so dere.
> And this is storyal soth, it is no fable.

Chaucer imagines for his Cleopatra a death far more strenuous and self-conscious than anything provided in the Cleopatra tradition. Instead of entering a mausoleum to put serpents to her veins and die beside her lover as in a sleep, she creates a magnificent shrine for Anthony alone, building it of precious stones (not corruptible as the flesh is corruptible), filling it with spices, and placing his embalmed corpse within it. Having thus arranged for him what Petrarch would have called the Triumph of Fame over Death, she "graves" for herself a pit beside that monument, fills "that grave" with all the serpents she can obtain, and descends into it "naked, with ful good herte." It reads as a powerful ending in its own terms, even if one has little idea what it may have meant in its own time. But read iconographically, with an exercise of the historical imagination, it is more powerful by far. Although modern critics have had difficulty in perceiving the intrinsic logic of this double image,[20] I think the attentive parish Christian of the fourteenth century would have understood it with ease.

Chaucer's invention is based on the fact that the words *pit* and *grave* in medieval English could be exact synonyms, as could *serpent* and *worm*—with the latter including not only earthworms and maggots, but snakes, dragons, toads, scorpions, and everything reptilian in between.[21] Cleopatra in her death dramatizes the medieval commonplace that man's flesh was eaten by worms and serpents in the grave—a truth she accepts with fiercely stoic courage.

Some ancient pseudoscience lay behind this view of the body's corruption, as the medieval Bestiary reveals in its discussion of snakes:

> Pythagoras says: "Serpents are created out of the spinal marrow of corpses"—a thing which Ovid also calls to mind in the books of the Metamorphoses, when he says:
>
> "Some there are who believe that sealed in the grave, the spine rotting, / Marrows of humankind do turn themselves into serpents."
>
> And this, if it is to be credited, is all very appropriate: that just as Man's death was first brought about by a Snake, so by the death of man a snake should be brought about.[22]

Hans Sebald Beham may have drawn on this tradition in depicting the temptation of Adam and Eve.[23] In an engraving dated 1543 (Figure II.12), he shows the Tree of Knowledge, whose fruit will bring death into the world, as a human skeleton along whose spine there climbs the body of the serpent-tempter himself.

II.12. The temptation of Adam and Eve. Hans Sebald Beham, engraving on paper (1543), 8.2 × 5.7 cm. Gift of Mr. and Mrs. Potter Palmer, Jr., 1921.316. Art Institute of Chicago. Photography © The Art Institute of Chicago.

For reasons I shall soon explain, I do not think that Chaucer invented his version of Cleopatra's death in order to invite a specifically Christian interpretation, in which (let us say) the serpents that kill her are to be identified with the serpent of sin, or with sin's mortal consequence. Instead, I think Chaucer was interested in and sought to go no further than a formulaic truth that medieval men and women heard all their lives long, and often saw depicted in funerary art: the fact that the human body ends up as nothing but food for worms. Among the traditional medieval meditations on death, no Warning from the Grave is more confident than "wermes fode thu salt be"; "wormes fode / is fyne of owre lyuynge."[24] Paintings that show the meeting of the Three Living and the Three Dead, for instance—a subject found on church walls as well as in illuminated manuscripts—most often depict those personages as kings: three still alive and crowned, met by three others who confront them in the full, mocking beggary of death.[25] In the De Lisle Psalter version (Figure II.13; English, ca. 1330–45), the living say in turn, "Ich am afert. Lo whet ich se. Me thinketh hit beth deueles thre," and the dead kings reply, "Ich wes wel fair. Such scheltou be. For godes loue be wer by me."[26] In this archetypal scene, the living kings meet themselves, so to speak, in death: they encounter what they will become. Note that the first of the dead kings is being eaten by a carefully rendered company of maggot-worms.

But we are still at some distance from Chaucer's invention, though these are traditions he surely knew and on which he depended for its legibility and cultural authority. A fifteenth-century debate poem entitled "A Disputacioun Betwyx the Body and Wormes," richly illustrated in its single extant

II.13. The Meeting of the Three Living and the Three Dead, English, ca. 1330–45. London, Brit. Lib. MS Arundel 83, fol. 127. © The British Library. All Rights Reserved.

manuscript (ca. 1460–70), can take us directly to the scene's thematic center. Its narrator, moved to go on pilgrimage during a period of plague ("In the ceson of huge mortalite"), stops at a church to pray. As he kneels "to ane ymage with gret deuocione"—an image depicting Christ on the cross (Figure II.14)—he notices alongside a newly made "towmbe or sepulture" (Figure II.15), adorned with "a fresche fygure fyne of a woman / Wele atyred in the moste newe gyse."[27] He is so struck by this image that he falls into a slumber or swoon, and dreams he hears a debate between the woman's body and the worms that are eating away at her—"betwyx this body and wormes hyr fretynge." As her monument with its heraldic blazons, crown, and ermine robe clearly testifies, and as she herself is quick to remind the worms, the woman whose body speaks was nobly born: alive, she reminds them, she was called "Lady and soferayne."[28] The worms, boastful in turn, claim to have eaten "alle that wer myghty passed forth and gone"—including emperors, kings, and conquerors, along with women of great beauty and renown: Helen, Polyxena, Lucrece, Dido of Carthage.[29] Our lady of the debate is not the first to find her beauty mortal. Her figure is made unmistakably royal above, as so often in medieval death imagery, in order that its lesson may encompass all ranks, degrees, and conditions. Whatever the grandeur of her funeral effigy, the truth of her present estate is imaged by the cadaver wrapped in a shroud below, devoured by snakes and worms, toads, scorpions.[30] In the pages that follow, a series of marginal drawings, represented here by Figure II.16, depict over and over again the parties to the debate in their naked confrontation. Only the lady's headdress remains to indicate her body's gender and rank; all other lendings have been lost. This manuscript includes as well the story of the Emperor Antiochenus and his son—another warning from the grave—in which the son, surpassing even his father in wickedness, is led by a good steward to his father's golden tomb, where the corpse speaks to warn his son of what he will become in death, and how he ought to live in preparation for that end. Figure II.17 reproduces the illustration to that story, in which (once again) a magnificent monument is set in didactic relation to a grave and its serpent company.[31]

Chaucer, of course, could not have known the poems in this manuscript; it was made too late for that. But I wish to suggest that these poems and pictures, along with his version of Cleopatra's death, grow out of a common tradition. Chaucer has simply apportioned to Anthony the customary pomp and splendor of the tomb, and to Cleopatra herself the enactment of death's grimmer meaning. In the speech she makes to Anthony's corpse just before her own descent into the grave, she recalls to him her marriage promise—"ryght swich as ye felten, wel or wo / . . . The same wolde I fele, lyf or deth"—thereby declaring their two ends essentially the same. The splendor of Anthony's tomb makes visible their fame, while the horror of Cleopatra's serpent-ridden grave embodies that other truth, which fame can disguise or cover over but never alter or deny. The two parts of the image are inseparable.

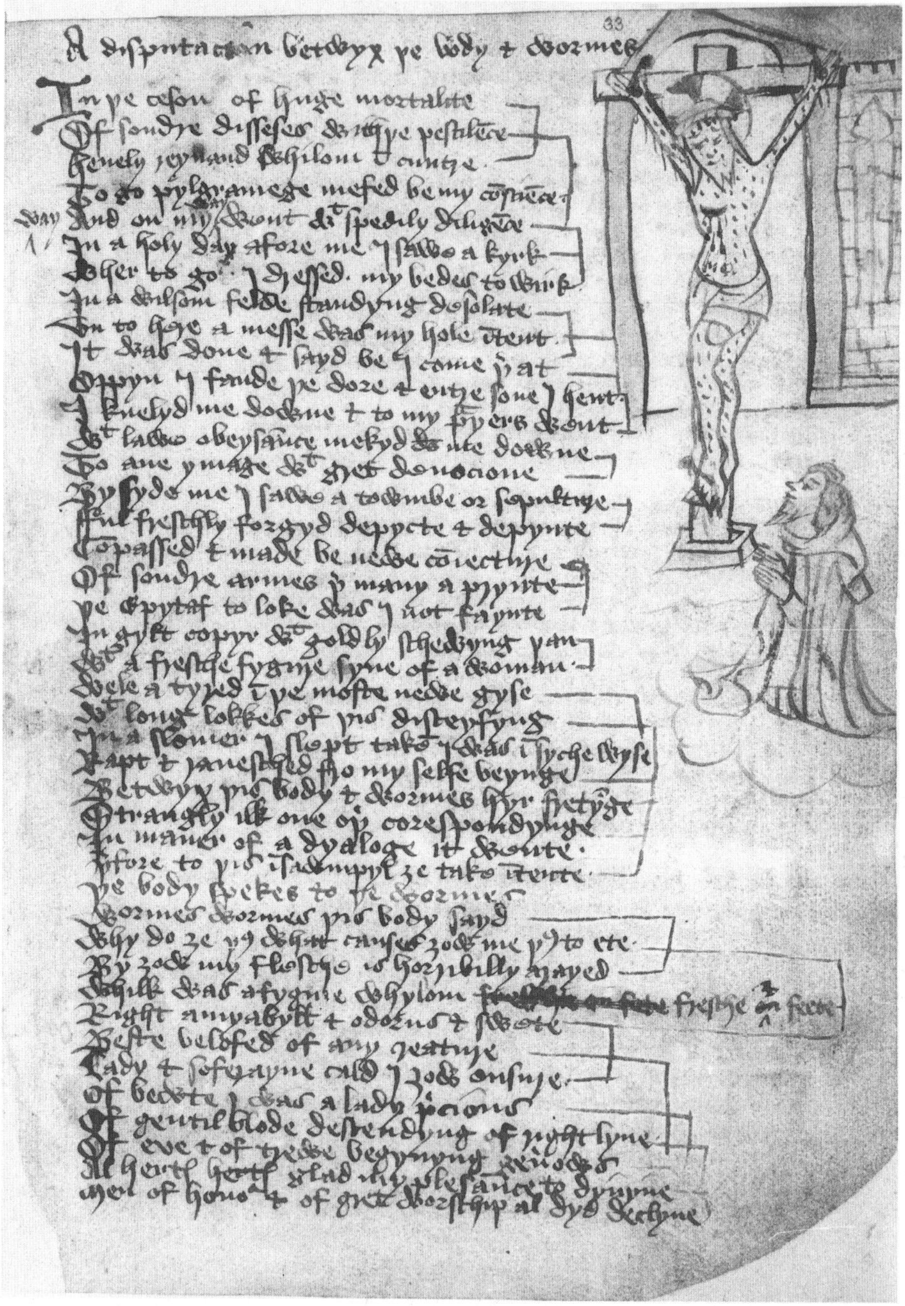

II.14. The narrator of "A Disputacioun Betwyx the Body and Wormes" at prayer in a church. English, ca. 1435–40. London, Brit. Lib. MS 37049, fol. 33. © The British Library. All Rights Reserved.

II.15. Tomb image illustrating the same poem. London, Brit. Lib. MS 37049, fol. 32v.

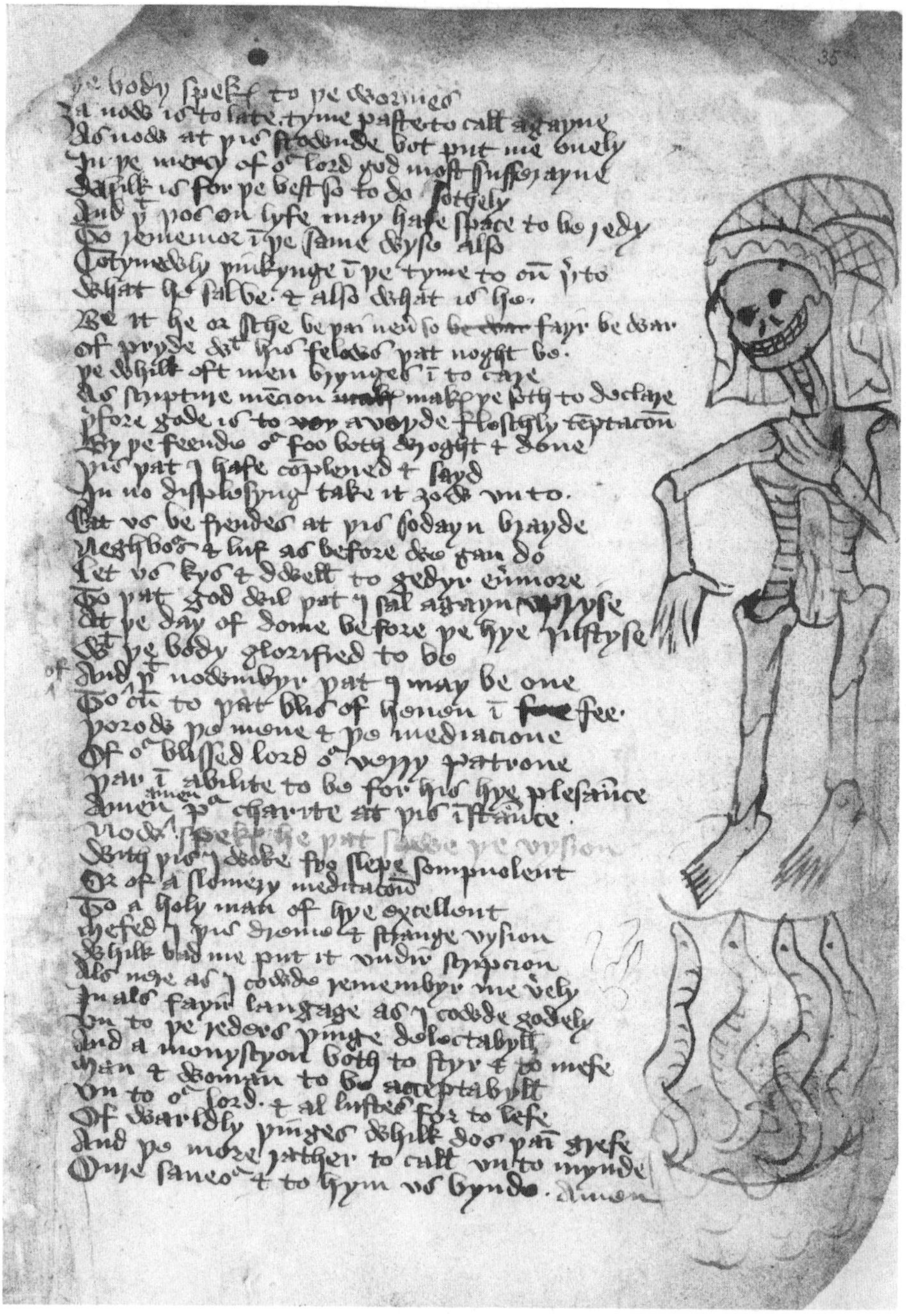

II.16. A woman's body debates with worms. London, Brit. Lib. MS 37049, fol. 35.

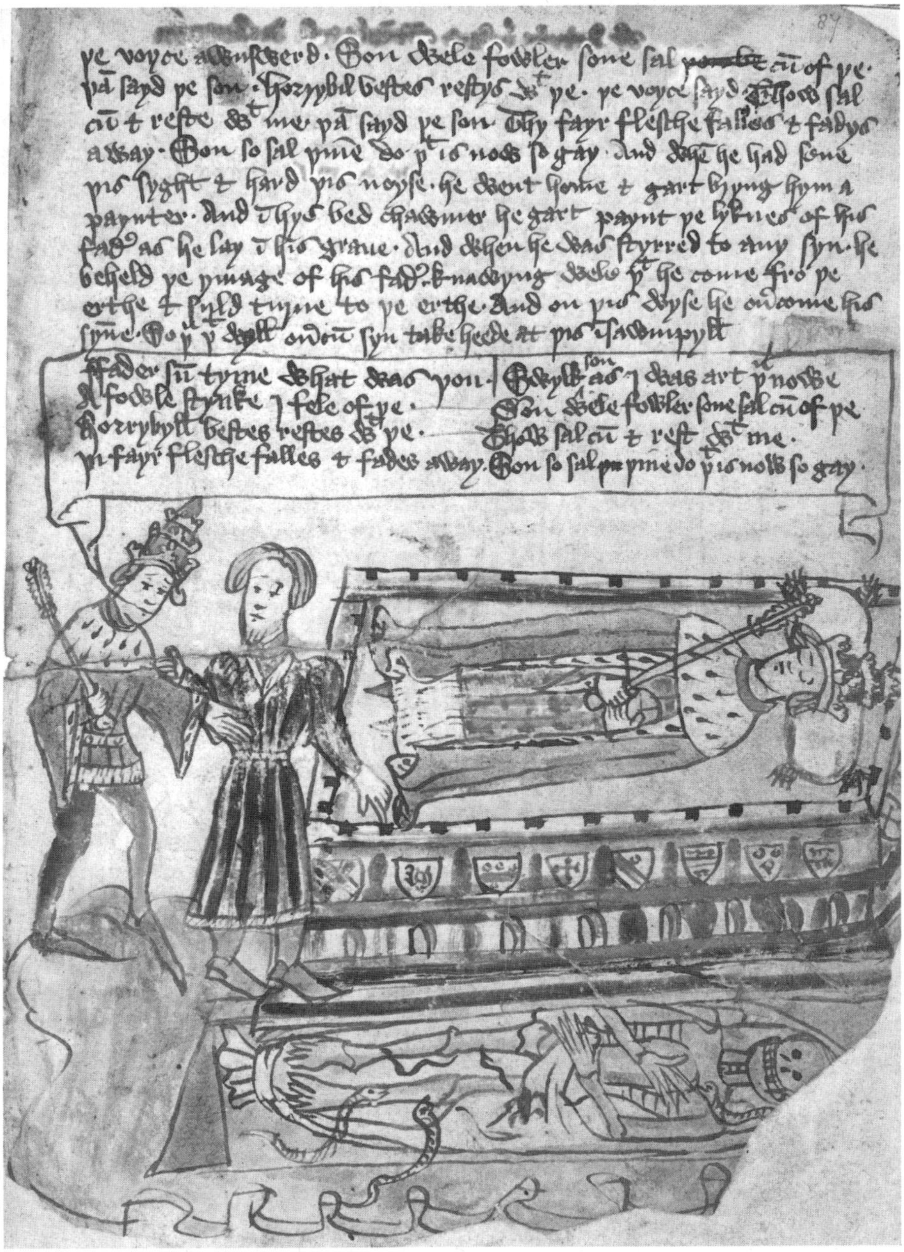

II.17. A warning from the grave; the tomb of the Emperor Antiochenus visited by his steward and his son. London, Brit. Lib. MS 37049, fol. 87. © The British Library. All Rights Reserved.

These starker aspects of death were often depicted in tomb sculpture of the fifteenth century, most powerfully in the so-called *transi* tombs, which represent the deceased as a corpse, naked or wrapped in a shroud, withered by death and often eaten by worms. The grandest of these are double tombs, showing (above) the effigy of the departed as he or she was in life, lying in state, hands often folded in prayer, and (below, at floor level) the effigy of that same person in death.[32] The earliest known double tomb was commissioned by Cardinal Jean de Lagrange just before his death in 1402 (Figure II.18). His epitaph, carved above the *transi* figure, spells out the public purpose of such an image: "We have been made a spectacle for the world so that the older and the younger may look clearly upon us, in order that they might see to what state they will be reduced. No one is excluded, regardless of estate, sex, or age. Therefore, miserable one, why are you proud? You are only ash, and you will revert, as we have done, to a fetid cadaver, food and tidbits for worms, and

II.18. The tomb of Cardinal Jean de Lagrange, 1402. Avignon, Musée du Petit Palais. Photo: © Archives Photographiques, Paris. S.P.A.D.E.M.

ashes."[33] (The debate poem whose pictures we have just examined may represent a meditation upon just such a tomb.) Henry Chichele, archbishop of Canterbury, commissioned for himself a similar tomb in 1424 (Figure II.19), and lived in the presence of his double effigy for nearly twenty years—a most personal *memento mori*, instructive to other worshipers as well.[34] Another such tomb (Figure II.20), was built in Lincoln Cathedral by the Bishop Richard Fleming, who died in 1431.[35] The only surviving *transi* tomb that may have

II.19. The tomb of Archbishop Henry Chichele, 1424. Canterbury Cathedral. Photo: National Monuments Record, London. Reproduced by permission of English Heritage, NMR.

II.20. The tomb of Bishop Richard Fleming, before 1431. Lincoln Cathedral. Photo: National Monuments Record, London. Reproduced by permission of English Heritage, NMR.

II.21. The tomb of François de la Sarra, ca. 1370–1400. Vaud, Switzerland. Lausanne, Musée d'Elysée. Photo: Archives de Jongh, Lausanne.

been built before Chaucer's own death in 1400 is that of François de la Sarra in Vaud, Switzerland (Figure II.21). It has been variously dated from circa 1370 to circa 1400, although François died in 1363. Its single effigy—among the most remarkable in all medieval funerary sculpture—has toads at its eyes and at the corners of its mouth, with another covering its genitals; the entire body is eaten by long, thin, serpentlike worms (Figure II.22, detail).[36]

It is unlikely we will ever know whether Chaucer's double tomb for Anthony and Cleopatra anticipates this kind of tomb, soon to become fashionable in funerary art, or if it simply works a brilliant variation upon the same materials. Too much has been lost or destroyed, both in manuscripts and church sculpture, to allow a confident guess.[37] But as Kathleen Cohen has remarked in her learned study of the *transi* tombs, the motifs from which such tombs and their characteristic epitaphs were invented had been commonplace in literature for several centuries. She cites, for instance, this passage from Innocent III's *De contemptu mundi* (1195), a work we know Chaucer himself had translated: "He who just now sat glorious

II.22. The tomb of François de la Sarra (detail of Figure II.21).

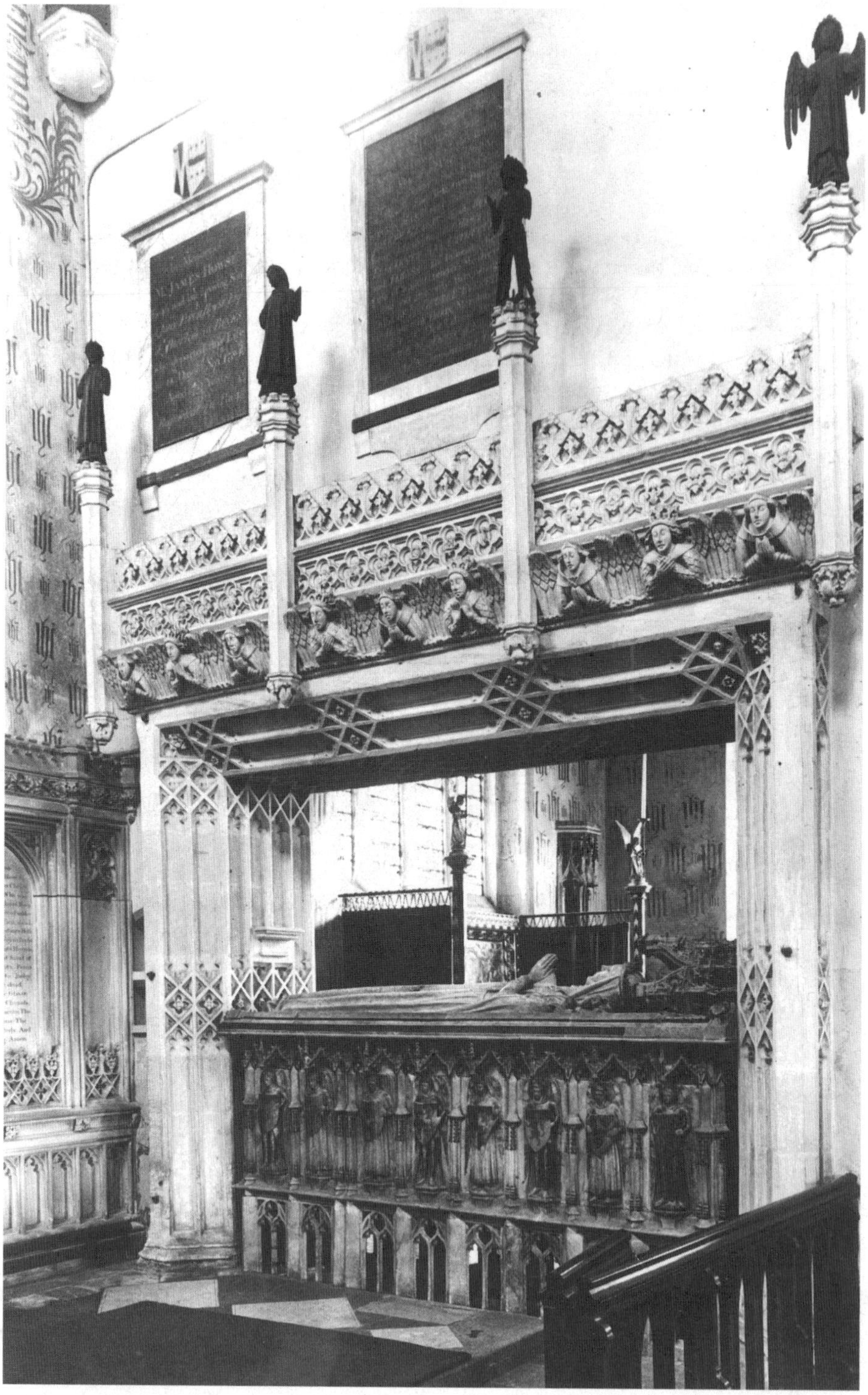

II.23. The tomb of Alice de la Pole, Duchess of Suffolk, granddaughter of Geoffrey Chaucer, 1475. Ewelme. Photo: National Monuments Record, London. Reproduced by permission of English Heritage, NMR.

on his throne, now lies in his tomb, looked down upon. Who just now was decorated with gleaming gold, now lies naked in the tomb. The man who just now dined upon delights in his living room, is now being dined on by worms in his grave."[38] If Chaucer's *Legend of Cleopatra* did indeed anticipate the art of the tomb sculptor in this matter, it is doubly worthy of note that his own granddaughter, Alice de la Pole, Duchess of Suffolk, was buried at Ewelme in 1475 in an alabaster tomb of just this kind (Figure II.23). The beauty of her effigy above (Figure II.24, detail) establishes a relationship at once dialectical and elegaic with the *transi* that can be seen, though not effectively photographed, through the gallery of arches at floor level below.[39] There her emaciated corpse, its hair loose about its shoulders, offers its separate truth. The duchess's actual remains are interred in the chest that separates the two effigies and links their meaning.

Thus Cleopatra's death in *The Legend of Good Women* bears a clear iconographic relationship to these Christian themes and images. But the intention of Chaucer's image is not primarily the lesson of *memento mori*, as represented, say, by the royal lady whose body is eaten by worms: "se what thou art and here aftyr sal be."[40] Nor does Chaucer invoke the image of a decaying corpse in order to persuade man to avoid the Seven Deadly Sins, as does his friend John Gower (near the end of the *Vox clamantis*), who devotes brief chapters to the mockery the grave makes of each.[41] Chaucer might have drawn upon the Cleopatra tradition to point to either lesson—the admonitory horror of death or the grave's rebuke to sin, here most probably the sins of pride and lechery—for the Middle Ages valued such lessons in literature, and in other places Chaucer too does not disdain their use. But his purpose here is clearly different. As noted earlier in this chapter, his Cleopatra is no figure of lechery but is instead Anthony's wife, faithful to him even unto the grave. She builds for herself no prideful monument and is not appalled by death, not even in

II.24. The tomb of Alice de la Pole (detail). Conway Library, Courtauld Insitute of Art. Photograph by the late F. H. Crossley.

its most horrible aspect. She goes into the grave alive and by her own will, to enact—in advance, and by fierce analogy—the full horror and meaninglessness of the body's corruption in the grave. She creates and confronts that death "with ful good herte" and "with good cheere," as a means of *affirming* her life and love, not as a means of revaluing them.

As I shall soon explain, I think *The Legend of Good Women* is significantly Christian in its meaning, but in ways more subtle and interesting than the formulaic moral lessons that Chaucer here passes over. He allowed Cleopatra, along with Dido, Medea, and all the other "good women" of his poem, lives essentially free of Pauline and Augustinian interpretation, in part because such standards are inappropriate to a fiction concerning a company of pagan women, "hethene al the pak." Their virtue, though real, was limited by their moment in history. But (if my argument proves persuasive) he did so also because his program for the poem as a whole provided a way of honoring Christian truth in a manner more tactful, humane, and ultimately more profound in the legend intended for its conclusion. Just as the legends themselves are experiments in plain and brief narration—"the naked text in English to declare / Of many a story, or elles of many a geste" (G Prologue 86)—so too his larger purpose, related to but not identical with the goals of Boccaccian humanism,[42] seems to have been to present the lives of pagan women "martyred" for love in a fashion free of extraneous moralization. As the God of Love's commission would lead us to expect, Chaucer's image of Cleopatra's death is heroic rather than didactic: "For lat see now what man that lover be, / Wol doon so strong a peyne for love as she" (F 568–69). She strips for the grave like an athlete preparing for a contest. Unlike the nudity celebrated in the Renaissance engravings of her death, the nakedness of Chaucer's Cleopatra is austere—the nakedness of a corpse not a courtesan. We hear from her, at the end, nothing comparable to the sonnet with which Sir Philip Sidney concludes his *Astrophel and Stella*, "Leave me, O love, that reachest but to dust." Chaucer's Cleopatra goes to ground with Anthony in proof that love and courage can coexist with despair.

In Chaucer's vision of the pre-Christian world there are tombs in plenty, but no answering image of Christ on the cross to whom one may pray in hope of heaven (as does the narrator of the "Disputacioun Betwyx the Body and Wormes"). Cleopatra's death, which the "God of Love" chooses to begin this pagan legendary, offers a spectacle of courage, self-awareness, and self-definition, untouched by authorial irony; but her martyrdom is also limited to those values. That her death has no meaning beyond itself *is* its essential meaning.

It is in this sense that Cleopatra's death offers a preliminary discreet gloss on the "naked text" of all the legends that follow. They end either in the creation of a death spectacle, subtly varied for each, as in the case of Thisbe, Dido, Lucrece, and Phyllis; or in the bodiless reproaches of a letter (derived from Ovid's *Heroides*) written without expectation of an answer, as in the case of Hypsipyle, Medea, and Ariadne; or in no ending at all, just bleak continuance, as in the case of Philomela and Hypermnestra.[43] Their deaths and their suffering address no values higher than fame, the avoidance of shame, the preservation of good name—to echo a threefold rhyme vital to the verbal matrix of the poem. Cleopatra's death scene, in which the asps of historical tradition become the mordant worms of the grave, becomes in retrospect paradigmatic: it expresses the naked truth those other destinies bear at their center. Chaucer displays the "good women" of his poem locked in a mortal coil in which dust embraces dust, whether in the marriage bed, through rape, or in a descent into the grave. Within such limits a poet can "make of sentement" (make verses about feelings) and no more (F 69), for the suffering that is Chaucer's present subject redeems nothing and is redeemed by nothing: it yields emotion, not meaning.

Although they were painted in the late fifteenth century, two French illuminations of the death of Dido can express in visual terms what I take to be the essential ethos of those legends that Chaucer completed for his poem. In Figure II.25, a crowd of men watch solemnly and at a distance as Dido, high on a mountain path, falls forward upon a sword, impaling herself and ending her life. One spectator, his arm draped casually around

II.25. The death of Dido. An illustration from Boccaccio, *Des cas des nobles hommes et femmes*, fifteenth century. London, Brit. Lib. MS Add. 35321, fol. 43. © The British Library. All Rights Reserved.

the shoulders of a friend, points to her suicide; another makes a gesture expressing wonder; others simply stare. Something is happening; nothing is happening; such suffering causes nothing to happen. Figure II.26 shows Dido stabbing herself as she falls forward into a sacrificial fire, while her sister Anne supports (or restrains) her, and as a company of men make gestures expressing grief. Here the distance between Dido's death and those who observe it is closed up both spatially and emotionally, but the difference is of no great consequence. Dido's self-sacrifice, with or without a ceremonial fire, is to no god more real than the god of earthly love, and her death is meaningless outside his secular theology. While responsive to the courage and pathos of her death, these painters also imagined it in terms of the traditional iconography of despair: suicide with a sword or dagger.[44] Figure II.27 projects the death of Lucrece against the same archetype,[45] as do several of the miniatures we examined earlier that show Anthony dying by his own hand. Like the martyrdom of Virginia in *The Physician's Tale*—the single Canterbury tale that bears any thematic or generic relationship to these

II.26. The death of Dido. Ca. 1470–83. London, Brit. Lib. MS Royal 14 E. v, fol. 77v. It illustrates the same text as Figure II.25.

legends of good women—such suffering is without purpose and without redemptive potential: such is tragedy in a pagan world.[46]

And so it goes, in our present poem, from Legend to Legend; and so the pressure grows, for poet and audience alike, to find escape from these topoi, these commonplace truths that declare women can be faithful in love, but men are deceivers ever; that erotic love (even when mutual, as with Anthony and Cleopatra, or Pyramus and Thisbe) ends only in the monument and the grave. Whatever the statistical claims of these topoi to comprehensive truth (the twenty thousand women of the Prologue stand ready to furnish further example), that truth seems finally incomplete, no matter how dispiriting.[47] Yet the poem as we have it seems locked in a pattern from which there is no release. This becomes particularly clear in the *Legend of Phyllis*, where the history of men false in love is declared not only commonplace but lineal. Having learned "of Theseus the grete untrouthe of love" (1890), just two Legends earlier, where he betrayed Ariadne for her sister Phedra, we are now introduced to Demophoon, his son,[48] although Demophoon's history

II.27. The death of Lucrece. Same text and manuscript as Figure ii.26, fol. 121v.

can yield nothing new: "the same wey, the same path" (2463) for both. The poet's discontent rises to its greatest intensity at this moment, as he declares himself surfeited with such stories—"I am agroted herebyforn / To wryte of hem that ben in love forsworn" (2454)—and tired of Demophoon (and his father) in particular:

> Me lyste nat vouche-sauf on hym to swynke, (F 2490)
> Ne spende on hym a penne ful of ynke,
> For fals in love was he, ryght as his syre.
> The devil sette here soules bothe afyre!

Chaucer ran a certain risk in choosing this technique—a risk Yvor Winters termed, in another context, "the fallacy of imitative form"—and he pays a substantial price. In suggesting a personal antipathy to his subject and in recording an increasing weariness with its intrinsic limitations and its sameness, Chaucer offers a model of response difficult not to emulate: we become fretful and distanced in our turn. But the technique is not uncalculated, and it cannot be explained simply as a variation upon the rhetorical figure of *occupatio*, or as a further experiment in the rhetorical technique of *abbreviatio*. Though I do not claim that an understanding of Chaucer's larger purpose can redeem in full the great unfinished middle of the poem—its interest varies, its tone often puzzles—yet we must not judge the idea of the poem without paying some attention to where it was going. Its destination, quite simply, was Alceste.

It is a curious fact that although hundreds of pages have been written concerning Alceste as a daisy figure (her identity in the Prologue), virtually nothing has been said about her legend, although it is her legend that has earned her that flowery metamorphosis (apparently unique to this poem), and though it is her legend that is meant to bring the poem to its end. In the words of the God of Love:

> But now I charge the upon thy lyf (F 548)
> That in thy legende thou make of thys wyf
> Whan thou hast other smale ymaad before.

We shall later have cause to note one honorable exception to this description of the extant criticism: in this matter, as in many others, D. W. Robertson, Jr., has adduced the information necessary to a fuller understanding of the poem.[49] But the essentials are furnished by Chaucer himself, in the God of Love's four-line abbreviation of her life:

> She that for hire housbonde chees to dye, (F 513)
> And eke to goon to helle, rather than he,
> And Ercules rescowed hire, parde,
> And broght hir out of helle agayn to blys.

On the authority of these lines, and as the final argument of this paper, I wish to suggest that the poem as a whole, like the Prologue that introduces it, is essentially a quest to discover the identity and meaning of Alceste.

The Prologue's action begins with Chaucer's worship of a daisy in a field and makes of that fiction, so comically literal, a devotion simultaneously preposterous and charming. The flower seems to elicit both his erotic love and his religious adoration:

> That blisful sighte softneth al my sorwe, (F 50)
> So glad am I, whan that I have presence
> Of it, to doon it alle reverence,
> As she that is of alle floures flour.

His obsession with the daisy leads him to sleep outdoors in a turfed arbor, where he dreams of the God of Love's queen dressed and crowned in such a way (green, gold and white) that she looks like that flower. In the action that follows she will stand between the poet, guilty of having written the *Troilus*, and the anger of the God of Love, just as in her life (we remember, once we know who she is) she had stood between her husband, Admetus, and the god Apollo, when the god demanded her husband's death. But for a long while we have no more idea than Chaucer-the-dreamer who she might be: though moved by her beauty and grateful for her intervention, he sees in her only a deification of the daisy he worships in the field. When the God of Love identifies her, and when Chaucer echoes her name—"And is this good Alceste, / The dayesie, and myn owene hertes reste?" (F 518)—the Prologue's quest on its most elementary level, the level of identification, is over. But the poem's larger quest—to realize *the meaning* of Alceste, to estimate properly the great difference between her and the twenty thousand other "good women" present, a difference that has made her the God of Love's queen—that quest was meant to include the legends of nineteen other women who also died for love. I think it possible that Chaucer himself grew weary of the numbing repetition, the despair, the partial and (for Christians) superseded truths that characterize that preliminary series. But his program for the poem had him moving toward a death that had served an end beyond its own fame: the legend of a lover willing to die so that another might live, and who earned her own release from death thereby.

Chaucer was not the first to put the legend of Alcestis to that use. It had served in the sarcophagus art of late pagan Rome to suggest the promise of a blessed afterlife,[50] and it had found occasional place in early Christian iconography as well. The fourth-century catacombs beneath the Via Latina in Rome include a notable chamber dedicated to *Hercules soter* (Hercules the Savior), which includes a painting of Admetus on his deathbed surrounded by family and friends, as Alcestis offers to die in his place, and another in which Hercules leads Alcestis back to Admetus, with Cerberus, the three-headed dog of hell, on a leash in his other hand (Figure II.28).[51] These are scenes associated with the Labors of Hercules, a cycle depicting the exploits of a mortal son of a god, and thus acceptable in a setting explicitly Christian in motif and intent. Such paintings of Alcestis represent a transitional use of myth, a gesture of accommodation; but they were rare, and had no long-term presence in Christian iconography. So far as I have been able to discover, her legend survived into the later Middle Ages through mythographic handbooks only. Because the importance that Chaucer assigns to Alceste is otherwise without parallel in medieval art and literature, it is to those handbooks and their illustrations we must turn, if we would guess usefully at what Chaucer might have made of her story.

He would have known, at a minimum, the bare bones of the story, here as narrated by Fulgentius in his *Mythologiae*: "When Admetus fell ill and discovered he was dying, he sought to avert it by entreating Apollo, who said he could do nothing for him in his sickness unless he found one of his relatives who would voluntarily accept death in his place. This his wife undertook; and so Hercules, when he went down to drag away the three-headed dog Cerberus, also freed her from the lower world." Fulgentius, a Christian writing in the late fifth or early sixth century, interprets the story chiefly in terms of Admetus, explicating it as an allegory of mind: the test by which Admetus won Alcestis in marriage—the successful yoking of a wild lion and a wild boar to a chariot—signifies a marriage between "strength

II.28. Hercules, with Cerberus on a leash, restores Alcestis to her husband, Admetus. Catacomb painting, fourth century. Rome, Via Latina. Photo: Pontifical Institute of Christian Archaeology, Vatican City.

of mind" and "strength of body" that can win one succor (*alce*) in the end, even from peril of death.[52]

This interpretation is repeated in essence by the three so-called Vatican mythographers, and again (with some variation) by Boccaccio in his *Genealogie deorum gentilium libri* (*Genealogy of the Pagan Gods*).[53] But it is not the kind of idea from which Chaucer was making his *Legend*. On the basis of the 2,723 lines that he finished, I think we must judge wholly unlikely any movement into psychological allegory at the poem's end; his focus, furthermore, is upon the wife rather than the husband. I think Chaucer trusted the superior dignity of Alceste would emerge even in a text as "naked" as that of the other legends, because her story possesses a special kind of suggestiveness. As Pierre Bersuire noted in his introduction to the *Ovidius moralizatus*, written in the early fourteenth century, Alceste may be seen as a type of those "good women who love their husbands perfectly so that on account of their love they will if necessary expose themselves to death. They are worthy that Hercules, or Christ, rescue them from Hell, or Purgatory, because of the conjugal faith they maintain."[54] Professor Robertson would follow Bersuire in putting his emphasis on that last clause—on Alceste's conjugal fidelity—and there is indeed evidence in the text that such emphasis is not inappropriate:

> For she taught al the craft of fyn lovynge, (F 544)
> And namely of wyfhod the lyvynge,
> And al the boundes that she oghte kepe.

But Cleopatra too is a "faithful wife" within the boundaries of the *Legend*, as are others whose fate is equally unhappy; and pagan marriage does not normally carry sacramental value for a medieval poet. Because I think Chaucer was attracted to the legend of Alceste chiefly in its typological dimension, I would emphasize instead the "Hercules, or Christ" equation in Bersuire's commentary. The death Alceste dies so that her husband might live can be seen as adumbrating the sacrificial history of Christ, just as her rescue from Hades adumbrates the history of virtuous souls rescued from hell *by* him. Even "in naked text," the configurations of her story would have offered an implicit commentary on every story that had gone before.

Her legend became so rare in later Christian centuries that I have been able to discover only two medieval pictures based on it. The first is a line drawing from about 1420 illustrating the *Libellus de imaginibus deorum*, an abridged version of the first part of Bersuire's *Ovidius moralizatus* (Figure II.29).[55] It shows Hercules leading Alcestis from hell (represented as a rocky landscape), with Cerberus on a leash going before. The picture reveals a clear iconographic affinity with images of Christ leading the patriarchs out of limbo, even though no typology (in the sense of an authoritative theological tradition) existed to support such a reading. The second picture, painted in 1420, is more difficult to interpret, for it depicts several scenes simultaneously, and possibly conflates two of them into one

II.29. Hercules rescues Alcestis from Hell. An illustration from the *Libellus de imaginibus deorum*, northern Italian, ca. 1420. Vatican City, Bibl. Apostolica Vaticana MS Reg. Lat. 1290, fol. 5a v. Photo © Biblioteca Apostolica Vaticana.

(Figure II.30). It illustrates the *Fulgentius metaforalis*—Fulgentius revised and further moralized by John Ridevall—and shows two persons seated together, whom I take to be Alcestis and Admetus, their hands joined in wedlock. On the right, Alcestis is shown twice, once just after her death, as she prepares to enter hell, and again as she is being rescued from Hell-Mouth by Hercules, who drives a cart harnessed to a lion and a wild boar—the very feat that won Alcestis to Admetus as his wife. This Hell-Mouth is identical with that depicted on another page of this manuscript, where Pluto and Prosperina reign as king and queen, with Cerberus at their feet.[56] Whatever the picture's obscurities, the foreground action is surely intended to depict the event that the God of Love describes in these lines: "And Ercules rescowed hire, parde, / And broght hir out of helle agayn to blys" (F 515–16).

The larger shape of the poem, as predicated in the Prologue and begun by the *Legend of Cleopatra*, implies (I suggest) a progress from *topos* to *typos*, from a commonplace "topic" nineteen times rediscovered to a typological adumbration of release and transcendence. When the twenty thousand ladies

II.30. Hercules rescues Alcestis from Hell-Mouth; Alcestis and Admetus (?) enthroned. An illustration from Ridevall, *Fulgentius metaforalis*, 1420. Vatican City, Bibl. Apostolica Vaticana MS Palat. 1066, fol. 228. Photo © Biblioteca Apostolica Vaticana.

who follow in Alceste's train kneel to do her honor as the one who "bereth our alder pris in figurynge" (F 298), they mean, I think, something quite technical and precise. They are saying she surpasses them all in what she "figures"—in what she is a sign for.[57] Though her legend is myth rather than history, and though the Christian patterns of salvation discernible within it constitute a poet's or mythographer's figure rather than a theologian's "type," she alone among this vast company may be said to point toward Christ. The pattern of her loving traces a possibility of release that Christ would later make real—to any who would be, in this new and deeper sense, "trewe in love": "Ne shal no trewe lover come in helle" (F Prologue 553).

Thus the "Legend of Alceste," had it ever been written, seems destined to produce a pattern not of courtly loving but of the love that is charity. Ovid's *Heroides* would find no place in it. The formal *balade* that ushers her into the Prologue's action is virtually an advent lyric, summoning to memory the most famous and most beautiful ladies of the past, only to declare them dimmed by her radiance: "My lady cometh, that al this may disteyne," in the words of the refrain that closes each of the three stanzas (F 255, 262, 269).

Chaucer glosses that line immediately thereafter—"For as the sonne wole the fyr disteyne,/ So passeth al my lady sovereyne" (F 274)—because he is talking of something deeper than beauty and grace alone.[58] In the words of the God of Love:

> "Madame," quod he, "it is so long agoon (F 443)
> That I yow knew so charitable and trewe,
> That never yit syn that the world was newe
> To me ne fond y better noon than yee."

Her beauty and her deeds are at one: "she kytheth [makes known] what she ys" (F 504). Among the twenty legends originally intended, hers alone bears the impress of Christian charity and even of martyrdoms to come. As the Prologue itself makes clear, her legend is meant to end in restoration, transcendence, and joy.

If I have succeeded in these pages in reading the "idea" of the projected poem correctly, then that idea should cast back upon the Prologue itself some useful light. It would confirm, first of all, what any attentive reading of the Prologue must suggest on its own: that Chaucer inhabits it from the beginning in the character of a poet, not a lover, and that his worship of the daisy represents a poet's metaphoric choice of subject and muse rather than a lover's choice of carnal mistress. When Alceste assigns him a poet's penance, she distinguishes him from those who serve love *paramours*: "Thogh the lyke nat a lovere bee,/ Speke wel of love; this penance yive I thee."[59] Indeed, the extravagance of Chaucer's praise of the daisy near the poem's beginning has already established his identity as a poet, for he casts his "service of the flour" (F 82) in the form of an invocation to his muse, hailing her first as "the clernesse and the verray lyght/That in this derke world me wynt and ledeth" (F 84–85); then as "the maistresse of my wit, and nothing I" (F 88); and finally as one who plays on him as a hand might play upon a harp, drawing forth whatever sound it chooses:

> *My word, my werk* ys knyt so in youre bond (F 89)
> That, *as an harpe* obeieth to the hond
> And maketh it soune after his fyngerynge,
> Ryght *so mowe ye* oute of myn herte *bringe*
> *Swich vois*, ryght as yow lyst, *to laughe or pleyne*.
> Be ye *my gide* and *lady sovereyne!* (italics mine)

Though the so-called Portrait with a Daisy would fix Chaucer forever in relationship to a literal flower (Figure II.31),[60] in fact he uses the daisy in his poem to point beyond itself, as a means of reassessing the goals of his earlier poetry, wittily acknowledging its limitations and recognizing the possibility of new poetic directions. The poet's fanciful devotion to the flower epitomizes (in a figure of synecdoche) his love of springtime and the natural

II.31. Geoffrey Chaucer: portrait with a daisy. Sixteenth century. London, Brit. Lib. MS Add. 5141, fol. 1.

world, its beauty reborn annually in seasonal cycle. The praise of the daisy with which he begins grows into a greater poem, more than fifty-five lines long and virtually detachable from the rest of the dream-vision: a poem celebrating the season that has ended winter and all its cares.

Forgeten hadde the erthe his pore estat (F 125)
Of wynter, that hym naked made and mat,
And with his swerd of cold so sore greved;
Now hath th'atempre sonne all that releved,
That naked was, and clad him new agayn.
The smale foules, of the sesoun fayn,

. . .

. . . for the newe blisful somers sake,
Upon the braunches ful of blosmes softe,
In hire delyt they turned hem ful ofte,
And songen, "Blessed be Seynt Valentyn,
For on this day I chees yow to be myn,
Withouten repentyng, myn herte swete!"
. . . And Zepherus and Flora gentilly
Yaf to the floures, softe and tenderly,
Hire swoote breth, and made hem for to sprede,
As god and goddesse of the floury mede.

As Chaucer celebrates in these lines the beauty of spring, the love we attribute to birds, the generative power of nature, and the feast day of St. Valentine, he evokes memories of several earlier poems, most especially *The Parliament of Fowls*, in their essential ethos. (*The Canterbury Tales* will begin with just such a poem, eighteen lines long, as part of its dialectical design.)

But Chaucer uses the daisy to point toward a part of his own autobiography as a poet—toward the love poetry of fourteenth-century France, explored so brilliantly in his early poems from *The Book of the Duchess* forward. Again the figure is one of synecdoche: a whole body of poetry is here represented by one part, by the "marguerite" poems—using the French word for daisy—in which that flower is used to signify and (by convention) disguise the identity of the courtly lady whom the poet-lover serves.[61] This usage points toward a different sort of flower altogether: a flower not literal, but no less mortal for that, no less bound to a natural cycle that moves from birth to death. Chaucer calls on his French contemporaries (poet-lovers who know how to make poems out of feelings) to help him praise the daisy suitably:

Allas, that I ne had Englyssh, ryme or prose, (F 66)
Suffisant this flour to preyse aryght!
But helpeth, ye that han konnyng and myght,
Ye lovers that kan make of sentement;
In this cas oghte ye be diligent
To forthren me somwhat in my labour,
Whethir ye ben with the leef or with the flour.

He disclaims any interest in the more fanciful part of their courtly games—the poetry of "the flour agayn the leef" (F 189)—for he has other purposes in mind: "this thing is al of another tonne,/ Of olde storye, er swich stryf was begonne" (F 195–96).[62]

In his bold identification of the daisy with good Alceste, a metamorphosis otherwise unrecorded in literature or myth, Chaucer (even in the Prologue proper) bypasses the ordinary use of that poetic figure among the French poets to whom his early poetry owes so much. *The Legend of Good Women* not only redresses the account of love offered in *The Romance of the Rose* and the *Troilus*—the two poems about which the God of Love specifically complains—but the versions offered in *The Book of the Duchess* and *The Parliament of Fowls* as well. Indeed, it is quite possible that the *balade* at the Prologue's center, "My lady cometh, that al this may disteyne," is an earlier poem by Chaucer interpolated here, much as Dante incorporated his own early poems into the *Vita nuova*, creating for them a context in which their true meaning could be read for the first time, a revealed meaning unclear even to Dante at the time of their composition. I think Chaucer's larger plan may have been meant to complete his otherwise conventional *balade* in a similar way. While gracefully fulfilling the exigencies of a royal commission, he moves his fiction steadily toward the figure and the legend of Alceste, and through her toward patterns of dedication and release outside the poem.

As a result, Chaucer's praise of "good women" from before the time of Christ is never in any sustained way satiric. Though he is sometimes amused, permitting himself jokes that are tonally incongruous—"Be war, ye wemen, of youre subtyl fo, . . . /And trusteth, as in love, no man but me" (2559)—and though he grows weary at times of the lessons in suffering these legends yield, it is the men in them that he holds at a distance. He knows, of course, that the story of Alceste is no more than a myth concerning self-sacrifice and resurrection. Yet I think he might have said, as Boccaccio did in the Dedication to *De claris mulieribus*, "Whenever you read of a pagan woman having qualities which are worthy of those who profess to be Christians, if you feel that you do not have them, blush a little and reproach yourself that although marked by the baptism of Christ you have let yourself be surpassed by a pagan in integrity, chastity, or virtue." And I think he might have defended the strategic exclusions of his poem in the manner of Boccaccio's Preface to the same work: "I have neglected to include almost all Hebrew or Christian women among these pagans . . . because it seemed that they could not very well be placed side by side and that they did not strive for the same goal."[63] Yet at the end of the *Legend of Lucrece*, Chaucer praises her (and all "these wymmen" like her) for their great fidelity in love; Christ himself, he says, prized women for that very quality:

> For wel I wot that Crist himselve telleth (F 1879)
> That in Israel, as wyd as is the lond,
> That so gret feyth in al that he ne fond
> As in a woman; and this is no lye.

And as of men, loke ye which tirannye
They doon alday; assay hem whoso lyste,
The trewest ys ful brotel for to triste.

In all the land of Israel, Christ found no greater faithfulness than that shown by a woman. A comparable virtue, possible even for pagan women, causes the God of Love to value (and disvalue) the "good women" of the poem in two distinct ways, both exemplary to the reader: "men schulde sette on hem no lak;/And yit they were hethene, al the pak" (G Prologue 298). Where Chaucer most differed from Boccaccio was in his wish to give the formal shape of the work a meaning. Out of a profound sympathy for the pagan past, and for the dignity of women as fully human beings, Chaucer saw the shadow of a new dispensation to come, in which *ave* would reverse *eva*, and Mary Magdalene would see the resurrected Lord before any of the twelve apostles. If I am right, Chaucer found a shadow of that "something-to-come" within the legend of Alceste, and intended to conclude with her for reasons as formally decisive as those which led him to begin with Cleopatra. He meant his poem to locate within pagan history certain possibilities of human loving that Christian history would later confirm and redeem.

The quest for a truer poetry begins or ends virtually all of Chaucer's major poems. It is provisional and strategic, and in *The Canterbury Tales* successive as well, marking several critical moments in the telling of the tales. At opportune moments, a kind of self-criticism takes place, with tales brought forward that promise (if only for their own duration) a new and more "worthy" direction—a promise never wholly intended, and never wholly kept, until Chaucer's "Retraction" silences the pilgrim voices and declares the literary game at an end. (I have argued the case for this in the concluding chapter of my earlier book *Chaucer and the Imagery of Narrative: The First Five Canterbury Tales*.)

In the version of this quest that begins *The Legend of Good Women*, Chaucer looks back upon much of what he has previously written, and presents himself (a few works excepted) as absurdly self-cast in the worship/service of that which is mortal and can only die. To the extent that his poems celebrate the coming of spring, the beauty of nature, and the potency of natural generation, they themselves are part of an order that ends in decay and corruption, cycles of birth and death, tears for what is mortal. And in those of his poems that praise the lady for being beautiful as a flower—worshiping her, *fin amors*, for that beauty's sake—he sees that error compounded. For the flesh *is like* a flower, and in another of the commonplaces central to the poem, both flesh and flower end as food for worms. Cleopatra, dying first in the sequence of legends, establishes that fact both literally and symbolically. The disdain expressed by the God of Love when he first sees the poet kneeling alongside the literal flower—"Yt were better worthy, trewely,/A worm to neghen ner my flour than thow" (F 317)—intends no insult to worms. A literal worm approaching a literal daisy would draw no such rebuke. But that a poet should find his highest muse in the order of nature or the beauty of woman—that a rational creature possessed of an immortal soul should *worship* either flesh or flower—that he judges monstrous indeed. Behind the God of Love's comic misreading of Chaucer's prior texts, I think we are meant to hear the voice of the poet himself, rendering a deeper and more mordant judgment on his poetic career. It is spoken strategically, as part of a poem meant both to substantiate and ultimately to remedy that charge: a poem meant to move from the legend of Cleopatra, "fayr as is the rose in May" (613), through the legend of Dido, "of alle queenes flour" (1009), to Alceste, apotheosis of the daisy, only apparently and for a time mortal. Her body does not feed the worms, and her destiny transcends the grave. Whatever Chaucer's technical interest in the art of abbreviated narrative, so interesting to rhetorical critics, it is the quest for Alceste, *in her deepest meaning*, that furnishes the essential narrative impulse of the poem. "Madame," the poet beseeches her, "yeve me grace so longe for to lyve, / That I may knowe soothly what ye bee" (F 459).

We do not know what Chaucer might have made of the *Legend of Alceste*, line by line, had he finished the poem, nor how he would have handled its typological potential: a death undertaken so that another might live. But since her story was the poem's intended conclusion, the way it was understood in medieval culture properly invites speculation as to what it might have become, whether or not one regrets the other legends missing in between. This much, I think, can be safely assumed: Chaucer would have approached the typological Alceste with tact and discretion, respecting the limits of his poem's declared subject (the virtue, fidelity, and suffering of illustrious pagan women), the classical parameters of their world, and the integrity of their own value systems, transmitted to him by the classical poets he revered the most. But here are some speculative possibilities, based on his practice elsewhere. He might have made only a passing allusion or two to Christ, as he did in the *Legend of Lucrece*, noted above—an allusion notable for the sympathy, the nondogmatic judgment there expressed. Or he might have alluded to the Christian story of salvation in a veiled, enigmatic way, as he does at the end of *The Book of the Duchess*, where nothing is said of Christ, but symbolic numbers and a few mysterious phrases hint at Last Things and eternal salvation. Or, in a brief coda separate from the rest of the poem, he might have cast a retrospective eye over the whole of it, unmediated by classical decorum or dream-vision convention, as he did in the Palinode to *Troilus and Criseyde*, examined in the preceding chapter.

What exactly Chaucer might have done with Alceste remain an unanswerable question. But it is also, I submit, a most relevant question for anyone wanting to think about the poem as a whole. Its Prologue announces the poem, unequivocally, as a quest to discover her meaning: "that I may knowe soothly what ye bee." By working as Chaucer did, from Cleopatra to Alceste, this chapter, whatever its success or failure, has attempted to do the same.

III. Man in the Middle

Art and Religion in *The Friar's Tale*

SOMETHING very odd has happened to *The Friar's Tale* as it is read in the pages of contemporary criticism.[1] Though widely celebrated as one of Chaucer's most brilliant achievements in short fiction, it has somehow lost its identity as a religious tale: a tale that communicates an explicitly religious view of human life. So brilliantly is it integrated into a roadside quarrel between pilgrim Friar and pilgrim Summoner that we read it chiefly as satire—as an exercise in rhetorical aggression, smooth, accomplished, seamlessly ironic.[2] Antagonism and greed are declared its major subjects, the former being discovered on many levels, including that of profession and social class. The tale is read in this manner, to name a persuasive recent instance, in H. Marshall Leicester's sophisticated redaction of Kittredge's view of the poem as a "roadside drama."[3] The tale emerges so in scholarly accounts of the way actual bishops' and archdeacons' courts abused their power over ordinary medieval parishioners, a form of abuse powerfully dramatized in the tale itself.[4] And Marxist interpretation registers the conflict in still other terms. David Aers, for instance, finds in the Friar-Summoner antagonism a working over of "deep divisions in the Church, the self-styled body of Christ." Stephen Knight discovers in *The Friar's Tale* "a powerful analysis of socioeconomic reality and change," exposing a conflict between a new "world of exchange values" (represented by the entrepreneurial, money-seeking summoner) and the older "manorial world of use value" (represented by the devil, a bondsman in strict feudal relationship to both Satan and God).[5]

The focus almost everywhere is on the quarrel and its social setting. Though we may disagree on who emerges as victor, each pilgrim delivers a scathing satire on the profession of the other, and each undermines his own ethical authority in the course of it. In the 1970s, R. T. Lenaghan noted that an unusual consensus characterized published interpretations of *The Friar's Tale*, and his claim still remains largely valid.[6] Reading the tale as part of a mutually destructive quarrel, we declare even the concluding morals immoral, expressive simply of the hypocrisy of the Friar and his hatred of the Summoner.

When we seek to specify the tale's genre, this emphasis on a conflict between two narrators (or even between two socioeconomic systems) gives birth—symptomatically—to some confusion.[7] Many critics have labeled the tale a fabliau or a comedy, despite the fact that, in the real world of medieval author and audience alike, its central concerns were no laughing matter: excommunication was serious, the devil real, and the summoner's fate (eternal damnation) the greatest, indeed the only, Christian tragedy. Exclusion of the tale on generic grounds sometimes tells the same story, as when Roger Ellis omits it from his *Patterns of Religious Narrative in the "Canterbury Tales,"* published in 1986. Limiting himself to stories in which "the narrator's identification with [a Christian] point of view can be taken for granted," Ellis dismisses the Friar's contribution as a tale used simply "to score points against an opponent."[8] Another instance of this kind: in a symposium paper presented at the conference where this chapter first took public form, C. David Benson, an excellent reader of Chaucer, proposed "a reevaluation of what have been for most of this century the most neglected and marginalized of Chaucer's works: the religious poems in *The Canterbury Tales*." But again *The Friar's Tale* was missing, excluded even from the list of tales potentially relevant but passed over for lack of time. In that paper, Benson chose to limit "religious tales" to "poems that directly celebrate the triumph of faith"—a definition that might easily have embraced the old widow's victory over the summoner.[9] The omission, Benson told me later, was inadvertent, and I mention it only as symptomatic of something more general: when Chaucer's religious tales are thought on, *The Friar's Tale* seems rarely to come to mind.

Granted the combination of tale and teller, this uncertainty about genre is easy enough to understand: irony and religion make uncomfortable bedfellows, hypocrisy and religion even worse. "When churchmen like these come together with a devil," as Lenaghan wittily noted, "the devil is the only one you can trust. . . . The only major voice left uncompromised at the end of the tale is the fiend's."[10] But I believe the criticism that has grown up around this tale, for all the brilliance of its response to the Friar-Summoner quarrel and its reconstruction of late-medieval ecclesiastical corruption, is radically deficient. We have paid too little attention to the tale as tale—subordinating the text to a dramatic subtext—when it is Chaucer's special genius to have provided both. The contribution *The Friar's Tale* makes to *The Canterbury Tales* as a whole has been misunderstood and seriously underestimated.

For *The Canterbury Tales* is of course a *collection* of stories—a *compilatio*—as well as a story *about* a collection of stories, and in the case of *The Friar's Tale* there is a balance to be redressed.[11] It is the vision of the tale, not the voice of the Friar, that will be my subject in this chapter. In his survey of the relevant criticism, Lenaghan noted that "the *Friar's Tale* is usually bypassed by recent writers seeking to define a Chaucerian poetic or aesthetic."[12] But I propose to look at it in just that way, taking the episode of the carter, who curses and blesses his horses, as its imaginative center. I hope to persuade the reader that the carter is as important to the tale's design, in ethical terms, as those larger figures that carry its major action—the summoner, the devil, Christ, and the widow. And I hope to work out in those terms a provisional answer to that deepest of all questions about Chaucer as a medieval poet, the relation of secular and religious vision in his art. My larger subject is once again Chaucer and the imagery of narrative.

Chaucer's fictions characteristically exceed generic expectations—that is a given—but to think of *The Friar's Tale* as an exemplum—the kind of story preachers used to illustrate matters of faith or doctrine in sermons—is obviously where we must begin. With one exception, possibly the earliest,[13] every medieval analogue of the tale, from the early thirteenth through the fifteenth centuries, is found in a sermon or in a collection of exempla intended for sermon use.[14] The version most similar to Chaucer's tale was written by Robert Rypon, an English Benedictine monk, as part of a sermon for the fourth Sunday of Lent. (Its unique manuscript refers, a few folios later, to a comet that appeared in 1401, furnishing an approximate date for the manuscript as well.) At the story's end Rypon acknowledges its comic potential, but carefully subordinates it to his larger homiletic purpose: "This story," he says, "though in part humorous [*in parte iocosa*], is also a summoning away from certain evils," four of which he names. It teaches man not to call on the devil "out of negligence or rancor," nor to "commend anything to him"; it teaches "the officers of lords" not to be "too greedy," and not to "do injury to the poor or others," lest, like the bailiff of the story, they be taken off for punishment in hell.[15]

I am by no means the first to think the tale essentially an exemplum.[16] But its use to *The Canterbury Tales* as a whole goes well beyond the simple moral teaching of Robert Rypon's sermon, or of a 1493 woodcut illustrating a related story in a German translation of the immensely popular *Livre du Chevalier de la Tour*, written in 1371–72 (Figure III.1). In that story two angry parents curse their child and see the devil lay hold of him; the child loses his hand and lives the rest of his life in constant peril of the devil. The moral (in Caxton's English version of 1484) reads so: "And therfor there is grete daunger in cursynge of his owne children And wysshyng to them ony euylle and yet gretter perylle is to gyue them by ony yre or wrathe to the deuyll And therfor haue ye this ensample in your memorye."[17] It is a child-rearing tale with a straightforward moral: don't curse your children, and don't give them to the devil in anger. Chaucer will do something far more subtle and far-reaching, intending more by "religious tale" than simply a Christian moral exemplum. The claims I shall make for it have not (to my knowledge) been made before.

Compared to its analogues, the episode involving the carter, though a mere thirty-three lines of verse, is leisurely in narration (elsewhere two or three lines of prose suffice) and rich in circumstantial detail. The carter enters the story at the point where the summoner and the devil, having

III.1. Angry parents curse their child. Woodcut from Geoffrey de la Tour Landry's *Ritter vom Turn*, Basel, Michael Furter, 1493. Reproduced with permission from Ernest and Johanna Lehner, *Picture Book of Devils, Demons, and Witchcraft* (New York: Dover Books, 1971), fig. 23.

sworn an oath of brotherhood and having promised to share equally their winnings, ride forth upon their way:

> And right at the entryng of the townes ende, (III 1537)
> To which this somonour shoop hym for to wende,
> They saugh a cart that charged was with hey,
> Which that a cartere droof forth in his wey.
> Deep was the wey, for which the carte stood.
> The cartere smoot, and cryde as he were wood,
> "Hayt, Brok! hayt, Scot! what spare ye for the stones?
> The feend," quod he, "yow fecche, body and bones,
> As ferforthly as evere were ye foled,
> So muche wo as I have with yow tholed!
> The devel have al, bothe hors and cart and hey!"
> This somonour seyde, "Heere shal we have a pley."
> And neer the feend he drough, as noght ne were,
> Ful prively, and rowned in his ere:
> "Herkne, my brother, herkne, by thy feith!
> Herestow nat how that the cartere seith?
> Hent it anon, for he hath yeve it thee,

Bothe hey and cart, and eek his caples thre."
"Nay," quod the devel, "God woot, never a deel!
It is nat his entente, trust me weel.
Axe hym thyself, if thou nat trowest me;
Or elles stynt a while, and thou shalt see."
This cartere thakketh his hors upon the croupe,
And they bigonne to drawen and to stoupe.
"Heyt! now," quod he, "ther Jhesu Crist yow blesse,
And al his handwerk, bothe moore and lesse!
That was wel twight, myn owene lyard boy.
I pray God save thee, and Seinte Loy!
Now is my cart out of the slow, pardee!"
"Lo, brother," quod the feend, "what tolde I thee?
Heere may ye se, myn owene deere brother,
The carl spak oo thing, but he thoghte another.
Lat us go forth abouten oure viage;
Heere wynne I nothyng upon cariage."

It is worth setting these lines side by side with an image from the borders of the Luttrell Psalter, made in East Anglia about 1340, an image meant to illustrate a scene from ordinary peasant life (Figure III.2). It shows a carter and three horses ("caples thre") trying to move a cart of hay as three other peasants push and shove; a steep hill is to be inferred. All available energy and attention, from man and beast alike, is concentrated on that task. The

III.2. A carter and three horses try to move a cart of hay as three other peasants push and shove. From Luttrell Psalter, English, ca. 1340. London, Brit. Lib., MS Add. 42130, fol. 173v. © The British Library. All Rights Reserved.

picture bears no discernible relation to the psalm text around which it moves, and it invokes no moral or theological context. Like many other scenes in the borders of this manuscript—those, for instance, that show the preparation of a meal in a castle kitchen and the manner of its serving in a castle hall[18]—this image of an ordinary harvest event records medieval life free of transcendent system, fitted catch-as-catch-can into the uncommitted space of the manuscript's borders.[19] Sacred text (sometimes including framed paintings of sacred subjects) confidently fills the privileged center.

By dramatizing at such length the difficulties of his fictional carter, Chaucer moves a comparably ordinary event into a moral and theological context and gives it a full, colloquial voice: the air is alive with shouted commands, horses' names, terms of endearment, vernacular curses and blessings. By moving the "image" of that event to center page, so to speak, and relegating the devil and the summoner to the margin, Chaucer for a moment reverses the spatial hierarchies of the psalter format. From the margin they listen to the words of an ordinary man. Everything depends on what that carter will say and mean.

The incident Chaucer narrates differs in important details from anything found in the analogues—and thus quite likely from anything Chaucer might have found in his source, which has not survived. None of the analogues involve a carter, and none is content with just a single insincere curse. Instead of Chaucer's grandly circumstantial, richly elaborated scene, we are offered two, sometimes three, such curses, none more than minimally detailed. In the earliest preacher's exemplum version, that by Caesarius of Heisterbach, an *advocatus* and the *diabolus in specie hominis* (a lawyer and the devil in the former of a man) first meet a poor man having trouble leading a pig by a rope, and after that a mother whose baby won't stop crying. Both curse the source of their trouble—"May the devil take you!" (*Diabolus te habeat!*). But the devil is unable to act, explaining to his companion: "He did not give it to me from the bottom of his heart, and therefore I can't take it," and again: "But she did not give it to me from her heart; this is just the way people talk when they are angry."[20] The story as written by Johannes Herolt, a Dominican friar at Basel in the early fifteenth century, specifies the exact same encounters.[21] In other versions the devil and his companion meet a farmer with a sheep and a mother with an unruly child,[22] or a farmer with a calf that strays and a mother angry at her son[23]—never a carter cursing his horses. The version closest to Chaucer's tale, that of the English Benedictine Robert Rypon, can represent the characteristic speed and economy of the scene in exemplum form, while introducing yet another variant first encounter:

> Proceeding thus they came near to the said village, and they saw coming towards them some nearly untamed oxen on a plough, which the farmer, (since they were) going more often crookedly and off the track, commended to the devil. "Here," said the bailiff, "these are yours." "No, because they are by no means given from the heart." Then coming into the village they heard a baby cry, and the angry mother,

not able to pacify it, said, "Be quiet or let the devil take you." Then the bailiff said, "This is yours." He replied, "Not at all, because she does not wish to lose her child."

Finally they come upon a poor widow whose only cow had been seized by the bailiff the day before. Her heartfelt curses (in a swift sentence or two) damn him to hell and end the story.[24]

The choice of a carter seems to be Chaucer's alone, as is the rich, anecdotal detail of his struggle with horses and cart. But Chaucer criticism has treated the carter in summary fashion, content to mention him simply as proof that effective curses must come from the heart. Some critics add a measure of praise for the realism with which Chaucer has imagined the scene, or for the narrative economy he achieved by reducing two such examples to one. I wish to go well beyond that, to suggest that Chaucer shaped this scene into the moral and doctrinal center of the tale. And I shall further claim that in doing so he found a way to confront and defend what is most distinctive and problematic about the poetic of *The Canterbury Tales* as a whole.

The difference between the tale and its analogues that interests me most is not the reduction of insincere curses from three or two to one but instead an expansion that is quite likely Chaucer's own: he makes time for a blessing as well as a curse.[25] In the analogues the curses find resolution only when the devil announces that they were not sincerely meant. Chaucer instead allows the action its own closure: it begins *and ends* independently of the summoner-devil story. The carter curses and blesses as naturally as he breathes or sweats—it is a reflex of his ordinary humanity, not an active intention of his will—and in that moment of workaday crisis (this is the great brilliance of the image) the Christ of his blessing is no more real to him than the devil of his curse. Only the horses, and the success or failure of his immediate "entente"—getting his cart out of the rut—engage his attention. By balancing a casual curse with an equally casual blessing, Chaucer delineates the metaphysical boundaries of a world and places inattention and unawareness at its center. Or to put it another way, by denying language these references, Chaucer (through the carter) creates a world all "middle"—self-engrossed, distracted, careless of beginnings and endings, ontologies and teleologies. It is a daring and original image, anchored in the moral truthfulness of great art rather than in the dogmas of received religion—and Chaucer surely meant for his audience to see their own lives reflected in it. The carter's action is emblematic of life lived in easy, unthinking forgetfulness of eternity, and its representation here one of the places where medieval art comes nearest to imagining an idea nearly unthinkable in that culture: life in a wholly secular world. From out of a chaos of noise and activity two symmetrical speech acts create a moral and theological space, with man at its center, intending nothing, thinking about neither. The carter exemplifies man's ordinary relation to blessing as well as to cursing: his *forgetful* relation, that is, to God as well as the devil, to heaven as much as to hell. There is, in fact, a theological topos concealed beneath the richly imagined specificity of this scene, whose long life in medieval culture, both before and after Chaucer, is interesting in its own right and can help us understand this aspect of the tale better. St. Augustine expressed it succinctly in a phrase: "man in the middle."[26]

Though I shall explore that tradition chiefly through texts and pictures contemporary with Chaucer, I want to begin with a northern Renaissance example that similarly opts for a cart laden with hay as its central image: Hieronymus Bosch's *The Hay Wain*, dated about 1485–90 (Figure III.3).[27] Much of the picture's detail—and the resolution of controversies concerning the meaning of that detail—is mercifully not germane to my argument.[28] But the larger theme of the triptych is not so hard to read, and it is that theme alone that casts a retrospective light on Chaucer's tale.

For this much at least can be confidently said: the large central panel offers a moralized image of life in this world, framed on its two sides (the outer panels of the triptych) by an image of paradise and an image of hell. That on the left shows the earthly paradise as a parklike space with trees, in which a prior event (the fall of the angels) is visible in the sky above, and the creation and the Fall of Adam and Eve, along with their expulsion from the

III.3. *The Hay Wain*, by Hieronymus Bosch. Madrid, Prado Museum. Triptych open: paradise on the left wing, hell on the right. Dutch, ca. 1485–90. Photo: Erich Lessing/Art Resource, NY.

III.4. *The Hay Wain*, by Hieronymus Bosch. Madrid, Prado Museum. Central panel: the world as a cart of hay, from which everyone takes what he can. Photo: Erich Lessing / Art Resource, NY.

garden, can be seen below. Hell is shown on the right as a place of fire, incarceration, and fiendish torment. But in the central panel we are shown what Langland would have called a "field full of folk," from peasants to prelates, struggling, sinning, living out their obsessions, following a cart stuffed with hay. It is of course an allegorical cart, as evidenced by the strange creatures who pull it forward—nightmare replacements for Chaucer's three horses, or "caples thre" (Figure III.4).[29] This panel is thought to illustrate a Flemish proverb, "The world is a haystack and each man grabs from it what he can,"[30] or else another in that genre, "Al hoy" (Everything is hay), an expression equivalent to "All flesh is grass" or "All is vanity."[31] The frenzied greed with which each person struggles for his own handful of hay—some even kill for it—is powerfully registered, as is another kind of devotion to things of this world, the cavalcade of prelates and princes following the wagon in stately procession. This central panel is itself full of life and horror, but what

III.5. *The Hay Wain*, by Hieronymus Bosch. Detail of central panel: lovers and music makers between angel and devil, with Christ above. Photo: Erich Lessing / Art Resource, NY.

makes it particularly potent as a moral image is its placement between the peripheral paintings of paradise and hell, and the way the cart and its followers advance enthusiastically from the one toward the other, careless and unaware of the direction in which their lives lead them. The picture presents us with a company in which the summoner of *The Friar's Tale* would be right at home, and (though his ultimate destiny is less certain) the carter of that tale as well. Christ is visible in the sky above, showing his wounds, as he will, when he appears as Judge (Figure III.5). Doomsday is implied, and possibly near.[32]

The eschatological structure of the triptych as a whole is mirrored within it by the group on top of the hay wagon, directly below Christ. One couple, elegant and courtly, makes music together, while another pair, their rustic equivalent, makes furtive love in the bushes—perhaps as a gloss on the energies and intentions concealed beneath the music making (the "old song," whether courtly or rustic).[33] Both pairs ride comfortably on this wagon headed toward hell, accompanied by a musical friend and a secret voyeur. This imbedded image of leisure, lust, and insouciance is likewise situated "in the middle," but here in psychological terms, with a guardian angel on one side and a demon on the other.

In this painting, then, the social world and the individual human soul occupy an analogous theological space. And that is surely the reason why Bosch chose to paint the image of a wanderer or wayfarer on the back of the triptych's two wings (Figure III.6). When those wings are closed—paradise, middle earth, and hell no longer visible—they show us instead a solitary figure on a road (*in via*), impoverished and emaciated, moving with some pain through a world of lust, violence, and greed. He is mirrored by the man fallen among thieves (visible in the middle distance), and he moves in the same direction as the hay wagon within, from creation to damnation, from paradise to hell. The painting within and the painting without interpret each other. I take the wayfarer-wanderer to be a late-medieval everyman, inviting our recognition in a manner both tragic and admonitory.[34]

There is in Bosch's painting, here as elsewhere, a profound pessimism about humankind and its destiny. But its representation of the world is, for all that, ethically ambiguous, torn between attraction and repulsion, desire and despair. Chaucer's representation of a similar theme, some ninety years earlier, differs in both mood and meaning, in ways Bosch's masterpiece can help us isolate and define. For the pilgrim company of *The Canterbury Tales*, fully as diverse in status and in moral intention, is headed instead toward a saint's shrine and a cathedral. The work ends with a treatise on the efficacy of penance and a retraction (in the poet's own voice) that affirms the hope of heaven. "Roadside drama" and social-context critics having had their say, it is time to acknowledge one other major concern that animates *The Friar's Tale*. Chaucer uses it to create an explicitly theological image of the world in which the Canterbury pilgrimage takes place—a world defined by real supernatural *powers*—in which his pilgrims (both in the tales they tell and in

III.6. *The Wayfarer*, by Hieronymus Bosch. Madrid, Prado Museum. *The Hay Wain* triptych, outer wings closed. Dutch, ca. 1485–90. Photo: Scala / Art Resource, NY.

the framing fiction they inhabit) move and speak and intend and determine their eternal destiny.

In a fuller version of this argument much might be said about the explicit theology of the tale—for that too is without parallel in the analogue versions, an addition almost certainly Chaucer's own. One would wish to explore the doctrinal explanation of diabolic power, its privileges and its limits, which the demon offers the carelessly inquisitive summoner. And one would wish to think hard about the issues concerning intention and possible repentance that are examined in the widow-summoner confrontation. Not all of that would be new to Chaucer criticism,[35] but it is part of what *The Friar's Tale*, read as a religious tale, brings to *The Canterbury Tales* as a whole.

Yet what interests me above all is the implicit theology of the carter episode. For it is there, and in the morals that bring it once again to mind at the tale's end, that one finds the center and the sanity of the tale: the image of man in the middle. The medieval topos is both honored and made his own in the "comedye" that is Chaucer's final and most characteristic work.

The carter episode is an intensely imagined event, though it goes nowhere and seems as ordinary as daily life itself. The carter is brought before us, lost in a world of language and will, oblivious to everything but the cart and the mire, the horses and the hay. The image it creates in the mind's eye, imagining the scene, is resolutely literal. But the speech acts, full of affection, irritation, triumph, and joy, evoke the larger theological landscape within which, for the Middle Ages, all human activity is played out and ultimately judged. The rhetorical address is from the worldly center to the margins, where real power resides:

> The cartere smoot, and cryde as he were wood, (III 1542)
> "Hayt, Brok! hayt, Scot! what spare ye for the stones?
> The feend," quod he, "yow fecche, body and bones. . . .
> The devel have al, bothe hors and cart and hey!"

After a few thwacks on the horses' rumps he changes both the tone and the address of his language:

> "Heyt! now," quod he, "ther Jhesu Crist yow blesse, (III 1561)
> And al his handwerk, bothe moore and lesse!
> That was wel twight, myn owene lyard boy.
> I pray God save thee, and Seinte Loy!
> Now is my cart out of the slow, pardee!"

The lesson the devil draws from this is clear and succinct, no more subtle here than in the analogues: "The carl spak oo thing, but he thoghte another." But the lesson Chaucer intended for the reader or listener surely goes beyond that. It is equivalent, I suggest, to the grand lesson of the Prologue to *Piers Plowman*, which creates in some eight hundred lines of rich, panoramic detail the portrait of a "field full of folk"—bounded on one side by the

Tower of Truth, where God has his dwelling, and on the other by the Dungeon of Falsehood, where the devil has his. Heaven and hell are projected, as it were, on to the landscape of the Malvern hills. The moral meaning of that scene—an allegorical landscape within which the whole action of the *visio* section of the poem takes place—is similar to that implied by the carter's careless oaths and by Bosch's devotees of hay. Men and women live, work, and play as though the Tower and the Dungeon were unreal:

> A fair feeld ful of folk fond I ther bitwene
> Of alle manere of men, the meene and the riche,
> *Werchynge and wandrynge as the world asketh.*[36] (italics mine)

The carter's symmetrical curse and blessing evoke as well the stage settings of medieval drama, with pageant wagons or scaffold "houses" spread out (in stationary performance) between Heaven-Tower and Hell-Mouth. Those outer mansions, charting the cosmos and its moral coordinates, defined the ultimate meaning of everything that took place in between.[37] A famous miniature by Jean Fouquet, showing a saint's play in performance (the martyrdom of St. Apollonia) records scaffolds for actors and for spectators alternating in a circle around the playing space, theologically defined by angels seated high on the left, their wings diaphanous and gilded, while hairy devils fill hell's scaffold on the right, both above and below.[38] Morality plays staged "in the round" offered a no less striking image of man in the middle, as Figure III.7 can make clear. A stage diagram accompanying *The Castle of Perseverance* (a play dated ca. 1425, its manuscript ca. 1440), it calls for a bed under the castle tower, in the middle of the circle. There "Mankind" will be born; there he will retreat, for a time, to a life of virtue; there he will die. His life (which constitutes the play's action) will move him here and there throughout the surrounding space (the "place," in English, or *platea*, in Latin), whose circumference is charged, like a magnetic field, with moral meaning: God's scaffold is located on it to the East, World's scaffold to the West, the Devil's (Belial's) to the North, and that of Flesh to the South. The "place" (save for the central Castle of Perseverance itself) is morally ambiguous: the ultimate meaning of what happens there depends on alliances made with the circumscribing powers.[39]

But the carter's linked curse and blessing seem to me, above all, a variant on the tradition already encountered at the top of Bosch's *Hay Wain* (Figure III.5): the belief that every human being is attended by two spirits—a good angel and a bad—who from birth to death will battle over his soul, one urging him along the road to salvation, the other tempting him to deadly sin and eternal punishment. In an English poem (ca. 1435–40) on the Seven Ages of Man's Life, crude but vigorous drawings illustrate the way those opposing spirits counsel him as he grows from infant (in the cradle at the top) to "childe" (standing between them) to "youthe" to "man" to "age" to "the crepil" to "the last old age," where the good angel, finally victorious, receives his soul at his deathbed (Figures III.8, III.9).[40] A related tradition

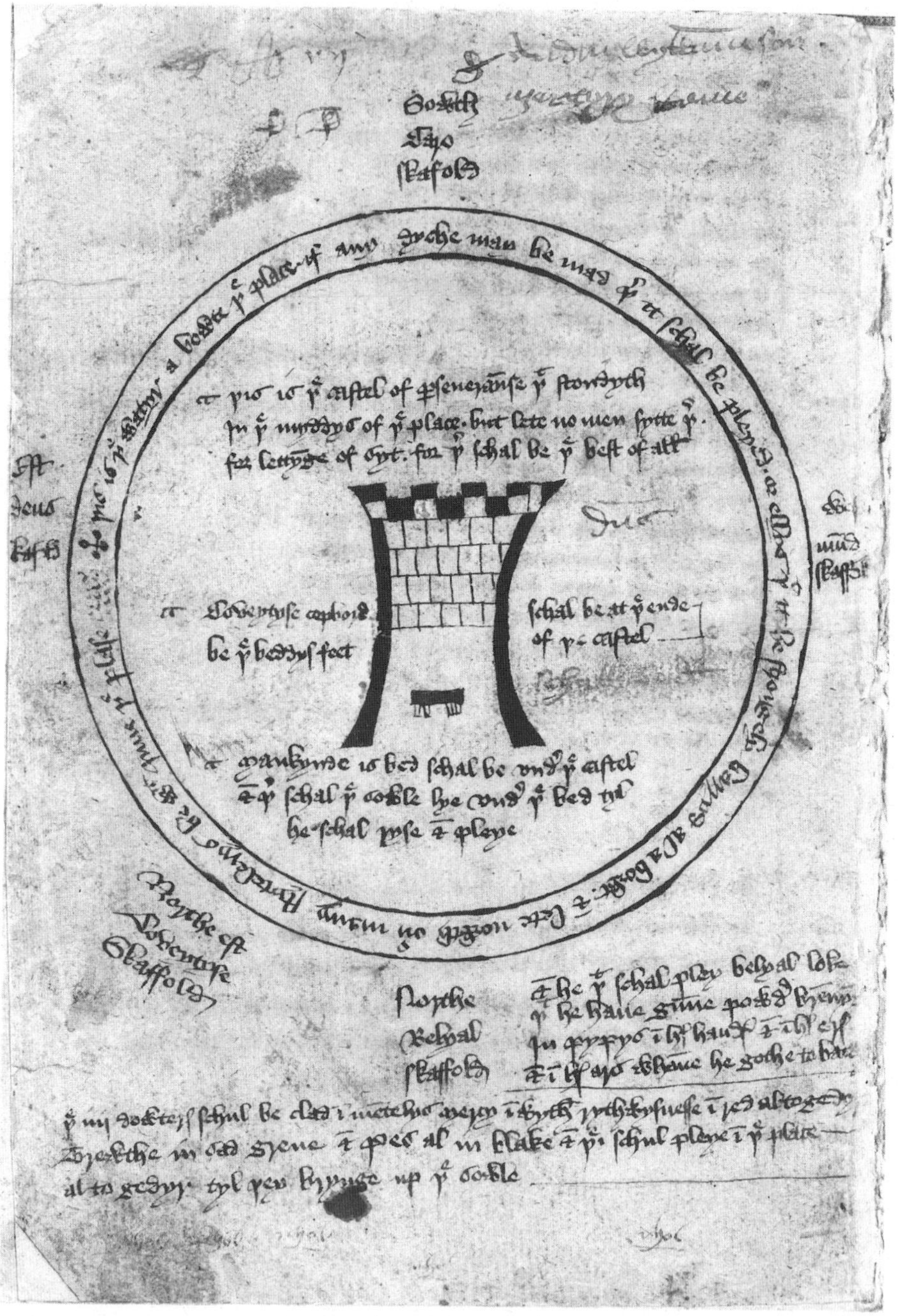

III.7. Staging diagram for *The Castle of Perseverance*. Ca. 1425–40. Washington, DC, Folger Shakespeare Library MS V. a. 354, fol. 191v. By permission of the Library.

III.8. An illustrated poem of the Seven Ages of Man's Life, with good angel and bad angel in attendance. English, ca. 1435–40. London, Brit. Lib. MS Add. 37049, fol. 28v. © The British Library. All Rights Reserved.

III.9. The Seven Ages of Man's Life (continued). English, ca. 1435–40. London, Brit. Lib. MS Add. 37049, fol. 29.

in the drama extends across the medieval centuries. The twelfth-century Benediktbeuern plays, for instance, employ the convention twice, once in the Christmas play, where a devil urges the shepherds to doubt and disregard the angel who announces Christ's birth, and again in the Passion play, as a means of dramatizing Mary Magdalene's life in sin.[41] Early fifteenth-century audiences of *The Castle of Perseverance* likewise saw those two spirits accompany Mankind from his very first entrance into the "place":

Of erthe I cam, I wot ryth wele,
And as erthe I stande this sele.
Of Mankende it is gret dele.
Lord God, I crye thyne ore!

To aungels bene asynyd to me:
The ton techyth me to goode;
On my ryth syde ye may hym se;
He cam fro Criste that deyed on rode.
Anothyr is ordeynyd her to be
That is my foo, be fen and flode;
He is aboute in euery degre
To drawe me to tho dewylys wode
That in helle ben thycke.
Swyche to hath euery man on lyue.[42]

The manuscript's list of players treats the trio as an inseparable unit, naming its central figure in a compound phrase: "Humanum Genus et cum eo Bonus Angelus et Malus Angelus" (Mankind, and with him the Good Angel and the Bad Angel).[43] A contemporary English lyric rhymes that relationship so:

I saw a child moder nakid
New born the moder fro.
Al aloone, as god him makid,
In wildernesse he dide goo,
Til two in governaunce it takid,
An aungel freende, an aungil foo.[44]

Figure III.10, illustrating Guillaume de Deguileville's *Pèlerinage de l'Ame* (early fifteenth century),[45] depicts the beginning of the soul's death-journey as it stands naked and afraid between angel and devil, claimed by both and soon to be judged by God. In a similar arrangement from the Book of Hours of Catherine of Cleves (Figure III.11; Dutch, ca. 1440), they quarrel over a man's book of accounts (his mortal reckoning) as his grave is dug below: here St. Michael, the angel of the Judgment, has replaced the personal good angel, but man is in the middle still.[46] The most common images of this kind, however, show the soul of a dead man as an object of continuing contestation between angel and demon even as it flies upward to God's judgment: "man in the middle" until the very end, awaiting the curse or blessing of his maker.[47]

III.10. The pilgrim's soul between devil and angel. An illustration from *Le pèlerinage de l'âme*, by Guillaume de Deguileville, early fifteenth century. Paris, Bibl. Natl. MS fr. 376, fol. 89.

We should not think of the Good Angel–Bad Angel tradition as representing a simple folk belief only. As early as Plato and Xenocrates the contradictory impulses of the soul and the various *daemones* of the world were seen as somehow linked together. In the first century B.C., Posidonius claimed two daemonic powers for every soul, one good, one evil—an idea developed in the early Christian centuries by Philo, Plutarch, Apuleius, the Gnostics, and Origen, among others, and taking narrative form in the legends of the Desert Fathers.[48] Bartholomaeus Anglicus, in his great thirteenth-century encyclopedia, *De proprietatibus rerum* (*On the Properties of Things*), included articles on the good angel and bad angel that constantly attend us,[49] Bartholomaeus being as confident of their existence as the friars and preachers who spoke of them in poems and sermons intended to instruct the laity and move them to devotion.[50]

I have brought forward a number of variations on this theme, not because I expect it to be unfamiliar to my readers, but because I want to suggest its weight and range in medieval iconographic tradition and because Chaucer's carter (so far as I have been able to discover) has not been seen as having a place within it. Augustine expressed the topos so: "Man is always in the middle between heaven and hell, between the good and the damned, between the stars and the beasts, between the superior and the inferior. This is

III.11. St. Michael and the devil argue over a dead man's book of reckoning. From the Book of Hours of Catherine of Cleves, Dutch, ca. 1440. New York, Pierpont Morgan Library MS M.917, p. 206.

his place."[51] "Man in the middle" was one of the foundational paradigms of medieval culture: an explanation not only of the cosmos in relation to this world, but of the ethical conflict medieval men and women sensed within their own souls.

That the paradigm still lives on was amusingly demonstrated, shortly before this chapter was first written, in an issue of *Time* magazine that devoted its cover story—"Through the Eyes of Children"—to life as young people in America perceived it in those days. Among the five it interviewed at length, a boy named Josh Maisel, from Belmont, Massachusetts, expressed the mysteries of moral choice in these terms: I've got "a little angel and a little devil" inside my head, he told the interviewer, but "I usually don't do what the devil tells me." Josh is not the son of Christian fundamentalists, as such language might suggest; he celebrated his bar mitzvah just before being featured in *Time*.[52] The figure of contrary counselors remains a convenient psychological topos, whatever may have happened to the theology that once declared it literally true.

With that to represent both the longevity and the tenacity of the tradition, let us return now to Chaucer's tale and the fact that he brings the carter's curse into suggestive register with it. I think he did so for this reason: without the self-enclosed episode of the carter at its center, we might read the tale of the summoner and the devil too comfortably, separated from them by our distance, our difference, our finer ethical and intellectual understanding. Thomas Hahn and Richard W. Kaeuper, in an exhaustive study of the records of English ecclesiastical courts in the fourteenth century, find many summoners whom they describe as "imperfect or vicious officials," but none of them the equal of Chaucer's summoner, none of them "figures of evil surpassing even the Prince of Evil."[53] Their scholarship enforces a simple critical perception: absent the carter, Everyman-with-a-capital-*E* (an inclusive Everyman, you and I, he and she) might look in vain for his image in this tale. The devil, by definition, is not our kind or kin. The summoner won't do for us either, for he has moved so far into diabolic likeness that his damnation is already implicit: he would *teach* the devil. Nor, finally, I think, will the widow sufficiently serve. Though she, like us, is neither saint nor conspicuous sinner, she is too old, too poor, too vulnerable (in terms of sex and age and estate) to offer a capacious image of the Active Life, and in that sense excludes too many. The need is for a character who can inhabit the poetic center fully and vigorously—and in Chaucer's tale that space is filled by the carter alone, confidently inviting our self-recognition, our creaturely regard.

But that act of recognition is not entirely comfortable—not even within the limits of the carter episode—and it grows still more disturbing later, when we realize that, if the carter is a trope for Everyman (an image sufficiently capacious to include us all), he is also a trope for the story's summoner, who is carried off to hell, utterly oblivious of his destiny. At that moment three images, not two, come into moral alignment. Mediated by the carter, the summoner himself greets us in family fashion.

As best we can tell from the analogues that have come down to us, not only the large-scale expansion of the episode but the choice of a carter as its protagonist was Chaucer's own—a choice (I have argued) that invites us to read him as a version of the medieval Everyman. For this is not the first time that Chaucer has used a carter to exemplify a human preoccupation with ordinary circumstance so intense as to exclude higher and more important concerns. In *The Parliament of Fowls* a carter shares that dubious distinction with others (the weary hunter, the judge, the knight, the sick man, the lover) who dream at night about their daily cares: "The cartere," he tells us, "dremeth how his cart is gon" (*PF* 102).[54] The road a carter drove his cart along became itself a proverbial expression for the ordinary, the commonplace, as when Conscience in *Piers Plowman* (B.3.131) says of Lady Mede (Lady Lucre / Lady Reward):

> She is tikel of hire tail, talewis of tonge,
> As commune as the Cartwey to knaue & to alle,
> To Monkes, to Mynstrales, to Meseles in hegges.[55]

Yet John Lydgate, in two of his poems, made plowmen and carters representative of the commons—the laboring class charged with bearing up church and state.[56] Both Chaucer and Langland before him had used the figure of a plowman (as one of the pilgrims, and as Piers the Plowman) in a similarly representative way. That is well known. My purpose here is to suggest that the figure of a carter possessed (*in potentia*) a similar status, available for appropriation within a moral tale.

One further text (beyond evidence from the tale itself) leads me to attribute this importance to the carter in Chaucer's tale. It can be found in his translation of Boethius, prose 4 of the fifth and final book, where Lady Philosophy uses the example of a carter guiding his carts as proof of man's free will. Boethius's own Latin speaks of a charioteer driving four horses, but Chaucer's English uses an image more accessible in medieval experience, the carter that is our subject here. At this point in the argument, Lady Philosophy is explaining how God can foresee things that happen without necessarily causing them to happen. She proves it by an analogy:

> "For we seen many thingis whan thei ben don byforn oure eyen, ryght as men seen the cartere worken in the tornynge and in atemprynge or adressynge of his cartes or chariottes. And by this manere (*as who seith, maistow undirstonden*) of alle othere werkmen. Is ther thanne any necessite (*as who seith, in our lookynge*) that constreynith or compelleth any of thilke thingis to be don so?"

To which Boethius replies:

> "Nay," quod I, "for in idel and in veyn were al the effect of craft, yif that alle thingis weren moeved by constreynynge (*that is to seyn, by constreinynge of our eyen or of our sighte*)."[57]

What Boethius agrees to is the fact that we are able to observe a carter driving his cart without limiting, or preventing, his freedom to do otherwise.

The carter in this text (translated by Chaucer himself) stands unmistakably for any man—every man—engrossed in his daily affairs and the work before him, yet *free* to choose and be held responsible for that choice. The carter's credentials are as humble and commonplace as can be—Figure III.12 illustrates this passage in a French translation of Boethius made about 1406—but that is precisely why he has been chosen. Chaucer and Boethius alike locate our deepest human dignity within his example, for even a carter is free.[58]

The uses to which Chaucer's carter puts that freedom are trivial—an extravagant outburst of emotion and language that inadvertently acknowledges the powers of heaven and hell. But he is permitted that freedom all the same. Though the carter's conduct may lack wisdom and high seriousness, the moral universe in which he moves is neither a prison nor a high court in perpetual session. The creaturely fullness of our lives within it is acknowledged, and is thereby (artistically at least) affirmed.

The real nature of that universe is addressed one final time in the moral teaching that concludes the work: "Waketh," the Friar cries:

> . . . and preyeth Jhesu for his grace (III 1654)
> So kepe us fro the temptour Sathanas.
> Herketh this word! Beth war, as in this cas:
> "The leoun sit in his awayt alway
> To sle the innocent, if that he may."
> Disposeth ay youre hertes to withstonde
> The feend, that yow wolde make thral and bonde.

III.12. A carter and his horse. From a French translation of Boethius's *De consolatione*, ca. 1406, illustrating Book V, prose 4. Cambridge, Trinity Hall MS 12, fol. 81 b. By kind permission of the Master and Fellows.

> He may nat tempte yow over youre myght,
> For Crist wol be youre champion and knyght.
> And prayeth that thise somonours hem repente
> Of hir mysdedes, er that the feend hem hente!

In the last two lines above—lines that conclude the tale—the Friar clearly has the pilgrim Summoner he hates foremost in his mind—and the sincerity of his request that we pray for all such may well be doubted. But for the rest, as several critics have noted, these morals fit the summoner of the tale rather poorly.[59] No one would describe him as an "innocent," whom the lion (read "devil") must watch over patiently, in hope to slay. The morals fit the old widow somewhat better, particularly the line that promises Christ's aid as champion, but she is not among those the devil is seen to tempt.

It is only when one accords the carter a central place that the entire tale becomes coherent, for it is surely through him, engrossed in the world, obsessed with the moment and its circumstance, that the great exhortations, "Waketh!" and "Beth war!" echo down to the pilgrim audience and those who come after. "Wake up! Watch out! Be aware!" Though *The Friar's Tale* ends in the damnation of a soul, its concluding morals serve above all to confirm the ethical structure of the universe in which that event has transpired.[60] You yourself have power to resist the fiend, the Friar tells us, and Christ himself, your champion and knight, will bring to your defense whatever else may be needed. These morals at the end, like the carter's earlier coupling of curse and blessing, situate man "in the middle," between Christ and devil, with all that is evil under God's control (the fiend himself testifies to that), and all that is *not evil* (however imperfectly it may be good) in God's power and care.[61]

For as important to the tale's ethos as the summoner's damnation is the outcome of the carter episode, which can be stated simply: God has patience with him. The *eschaton* is not yet; ethical change remains possible, however rare any signs of movement in that direction; man may yet perfect his "entente" and begin consciously to mean what God would have him mean. Christian belief is rooted in certain absolutes, chief among them the opposition of God and Satan, angel and devil; but I think we can see Chaucer here—and I take this to be central to his poetic—seeking to evade a simple, binary opposition between good and evil in human affairs.

In the voice of his Friar, he disdains to describe "Swiche peynes that youre hertes myghte agryse," the "peynes of thilke cursed hous of helle." He *could indeed do so*, he tells us (l. 1645), but he will not. Such descriptions, both verbal and visual, had, of course, an honored place in medieval preaching, literature, and art.[62] Figure III.13, a page from a London psalter of about 1220–30, showing twelve of the torments, can represent the power and specificity with which this theme was depicted visually.[63] The Taymouth Book of Hours, made in England about 1325–40, testifies to the continuity of that tradition, devoting most of the bottom borders of twenty-six consecutive manuscript pages to picturing the pains of hell; Anglo-Norman

III.13. The pains of hell. From a London psalter, ca. 1220–30. Cambridge, Trinity College MS B. 11. 4, fol. 11v. By kind permission of the Master and Fellows.

inscriptions expand on their meaning.[64] And just before *The Canterbury Tales* reaches its end, Chaucer too, in the voice of the Parson, offers a lengthy description of hell's pains (*ParsT*, 158–230), as part of a sermon on penance: "The thridde cause that oghte moeve a man to Contricioun is drede of the day of doom and of the horrible peynes of helle."[65] But that is preached in the voice of the Parson, not the poet, and it is spoken only after the pilgrim Parson has rejected both fiction and art poetical out of hand.

Dante found in such infernal material the "matter" of a great poem, but in *The Friar's Tale*, Chaucer decisively separates himself from the influence of the man he thought the greatest poet of his age. It is the devil who promises us that if we get to hell we shall learn there (in company with the tale's summoner) all we need to know of its grisly secrets, its gruesome science—more even "than Virgile, while he was on lyve,/ Or Dant also." In this, the most explicitly theological of his versified tales, Chaucer declares his preference for a very different kind of subject, and a different poetic.[66] Just as Dante, uncertain as to why he has been chosen, says to Virgil, "I am not Aeneas, I am not Paul" (*Inf.*, II 32), so Chaucer might have written, in this regard at least, "I am not Dante"—*Io non Dante sono.*

For although Dante begins his poem "in the middle of our life's journey" (*Nel mezzo del cammin di nostra vita*), he uses the conventions of visionary poetry to swiftly leap beyond it, into a journey through hell, purgatory, and heaven. The carter's "metaphysical" space, if I may so style it, remains to the very end "on the road" and "in the middle." And that, theologically and imaginatively, is Chaucer's favored space as well: a rhetorical space, the central playing field of his art. To read *The Friar's Tale* correctly, we must think of the carter as neither damned nor saved, nor even as tending more toward the one than toward the other. We must suspend our judgment—hold it in suspense—as the devil does in the tale, and as Chaucer does in shaping the fiction so. The time is "not yet." Our creaturely distraction may even be salvific, at least in the short run, as word and intention fail to coalesce—fail to become signally and forever (for good or ill) one.

At the core of this intensely doctrinal and cautionary story, Chaucer's Christian humanism allows a carter to speak "in game," not earnest, and shows the universal, sacral order as making allowances for that mode. The Creating Word (the Logos) hears the demotic word (the insincere curse, the insincere blessing) with discrimination and patience. I think it not too much to say that Chaucer here shows God underwriting the play-and-game mode of *The Canterbury Tales* as a whole, whose first article of faith is that neither God nor man will make earnest of game. The carter episode is to *The Friar's Tale* as *The Friar's Tale* is to *The Canterbury Tales* as a whole, with *The Parson's Tale* structurally equivalent to its moral imperatives, "Waketh!"/"Beth war!" and with *Chaucer's Retraction* its acknowledgment that the privileged time of play and game will not last forever. Repentance there becomes as crucial for the poet/pilgrim as it had been for the tale's summoner in his last moments as a free man, not yet bound to the devil.

By shaping the carter's action so, Chaucer clears a space for an art at liberty to evade (until it is necessary) definitive closure, unqualified truth. But he does so within the bounds of a tale that names precisely those limits: God and Satan, heaven and hell. The genius of his last great work, *The Canterbury Tales*, was to find structural ways of holding back order, of privileging *until the very end* the nearly chaotic, the merely phenomenal, over the deeper truths. He found a way to give the *saeculum* its own space and time, while acknowledging its limits and their ultimate authority.

And so we have at the middle of *The Friar's Tale* an action that leads nowhere—an action complete in itself, serving as an emblem and an extension of the plot that carries it—in order that that plot might implicate us all. Nowhere else in *The Canterbury Tales* will Chaucer discuss the powers of hell with such precision or broach so directly the dynamics of damnation; and nowhere else will he affirm with such power the protection of Christ available to the innocent and faithful. There is nothing suspect or unorthodox about the theology of this tale—that part of it could have been assigned the Parson, or (let us say) a second of the Nun's priests, without for a moment inviting ironic readings. And so I have tried to do for the Friar what most of us do for the Pardoner, and what some of us would do for the Man of Law: namely, to admit (with Chaucer) that a wicked man, or a less than virtuous man, can nevertheless tell a true story, potent to teach one about evil and redirect one toward the good. A pilgrim through his choice of story may tell us more about himself than he intends, but he will also (if the art is non-parodic) tell us what the story intends. The friars were the greatest preachers of their age, and this may be the finest sermon, in verse or prose, ever invented for one of their number. Like the "gentilesse" lecture in *The Wife of Bath's Tale*, it brings into the total discourse of *The Canterbury Tales* important matters not limited to, or undercut by, the character of its teller.[67]

Professing not to know with certainty the inner condition of any man's soul—perhaps not even that of his flattering Friar Huberd—Chaucer nevertheless has much to say about everyman "on the road" somewhere between a tavern and a cathedral. It is a humane as well as religious vision. Pilgrims and carters were they all.

IV: Of Calendars and Cuckoldry (1)

January and May in *The Merchant's Tale*

THE MERCHANT'S TALE ends in a carefully staged scene of cuckoldry: a blind old man, clinging to the trunk of a tree, fails to prevent his beautiful young wife and his youthful squire from making love in its branches. I take this to be the tale's "governing image"—the first image likely to come to mind as readers or listeners think back on what they remember of the tale. In this chapter and the next, I propose to investigate the interest and logic of that image as it would have been understood within the visual culture of Chaucer's time. But I begin with a German woodcut copied and published by William Caxton, England's first printer, in 1484, just six years after he first published *The Canterbury Tales* and the very year in which he printed a revised edition of that work (Figure IV.1).[1] I do so because it illustrates that memorable scene of cuckoldry better than any other image we have.

Caxton did not, however, publish it with his *Canterbury Tales*, but in his *Book of the Subtle Histories and Fables of Esope* [*Aesop*], a work he translated from a French *Esope* by one Julien Macho, first published in 1480, which includes a fable analogous to this tale. Macho's work had been illustrated in turn with 186 woodcuts traced from a German edition of his Latin source, Steinhöwel's *Aesop*, published a few years earlier in 1476–77. The mind-numbing complexity of even that little bit of textual history can introduce, all on its own, the widespread dispersion of the "pear tree tale" in fourteenth- and fifteenth-century Europe. But in fact the essential story goes back even further. A version known as the *Comoedia Lydiae* (or Comedy of Lydia), in some 550 lines of Latin verse, dates from the second half of the twelfth century; a *Novellino* version in Italian is provisionally dated ca. 1280; and Boccaccio told a similar story in his *Decameron* (VII 9) sometime after 1349. The analogues that postdate Chaucer's death are more numerous still.[2] Our present business, however, is with the woodcut before us, and the certain fact that Caxton would have recognized his Aesopic "fable of a blynd man and of his wyf" as a cousin to *The Merchant's Tale*, reprinted by him in that same year, despite the fact that his "fable" requires only a page

vt te sanarez.Munera g° mihi debes ob tale meritū cum tibi vi-
sum iam restituerim •Cecꝰ vxoris dolo z fraudibus fidez adhi-
buit ac nephas omne remisit et muneribꝰ ipsam reconciliat q̄si
corruptam inique et inuoluntarie.

IV.1. The climax of the pear-tree story, illustrating Aesop, *Vita et fabulae*, printed by Heinrich Knoblochtzer, Strasbourg, ca. 1481, and copied by William Caxton for his own Aesop (*Esope*; 1484). New York, Pierpont Morgan Library MS PML 50, fol. qiij.

of printed prose, while Chaucer's tale (at 1,173 lines of verse) is one of the longest in the *Canterbury* collection. In Caxton's version the cuckoldry is described as "that pagent vpon the pere tree"—as though it were a sort of spectacle set before January's newly opened eyes, inviting his and our close attention. And so it does. Whatever else a reader or listener sees "with the eye of the mind" at the end of the tale, it is likely to bear some close relationship to this woodcut: a narrative image stripped to its bare details. And that, I shall suggest, would have called to mind a set of other images, once widely familiar, whose likeness to this one, or to essential elements within it, invites recognition and pleasurable thought.

Helen Cooper, in her admirable *Oxford Guide* to *The Canterbury Tales*, noticed an important fact: "Almost the entire action of the analogues is contained within Chaucer's last eighty lines—barely a twelfth of the whole tale. The rest provides a context that transforms one's reading of this final section."[3] Because there is a lot I wish to say about those last eighty lines—and the sense they make of the whole—I shall have to pass over a good deal that matters elsewhere.[4] But before I begin this investigation, let me acknowledge what may seem for a time its most notable lack. Until the final pages of the next chapter, I shall have little to say about the way the ending to this tale "replays" the Fall of Man, showing us a man and his wife in a walled garden, seduced by a third (a traitor) into tasting fruit from a forbidden tree—fruit that will open their eyes to knowledge of good and evil, of nakedness and shame. A reflex of that story can indeed be discovered within the tale's concluding action, and for many years I expected to write at some length about it. But two critics, in particular, have already said most of what needs to be said, or so it seems to me: Kenneth Bleeth, succinctly but with considerable learning; and Eric Jager, at considerable length and with impressive intellectual scope. Both draw upon a pioneering essay by D. W. Robertson, Jr., and go well beyond it.[5]

In these pages I shall propose instead a very different way of accounting for lovers up in a tree, with an old man below inadvertently assisting the lovemaking taking place in its branches. This account, I shall argue, is more deeply implicated than the Fall in the tale's major characterizations, its deepest logical structures, and (perhaps above all) the curiously conflicted feelings evoked by the tale's conclusion. And I shall trace its origins to a richly documented visual milieu: representations of January and May and the astrological sign of Gemini on the calendar pages that open every deluxe medieval psalter and Book of Hours. Taken together, these iconographic traditions throw unexpected cultural light on the tale's germinal disruption—old January wedded to young May—as well as on its apparently inevitable resolution: Damian and May, under the sign of Gemini, making love in a tree. Almost everything I shall use to establish this view of the tale's conclusion—alternative not only to the Fall of Man but even to ordinary fabliau justice—will be drawn from the calendars of these widely owned medieval books.

> Kalenderes enlumnyed ben thei
> That in this world ben lighted with thi name.

These verses by Chaucer, from an "alphabet poem" honoring the Virgin that he translated early in his career, refer to the fact that medieval calendar pages typically begin with a capital *K* (or *KL*) for *Kalends*, the Roman word for the first day of a month.[6] That simple initial, typically the largest on the every calendar page, was often limned in burnished silver or gold, "illuminating" (throwing light on) the rest. Calendars of this kind played an essential role in medieval devotion, listing month by month the feast days of the liturgical year—those honoring the saints—along with others grander still, commemorating the Incarnation, Passion, and Resurrection of Christ. The annual round of prayer and praise offered up by monastic or cathedral clergy, known as the Opus Dei, or Divine Office of the Church, was structured day by day according to these calendars, and devout lay persons were invited to join themselves to it in a coordinated series of private devotions. The psalter, so-called—the Book of Psalms marked and supplemented for liturgical use—was the first text authorized to serve this dual purpose. As it was chanted by the clergy each week, in its entirety, as part of the Divine Office, it was being read privately by devout laypersons, as the only biblical text the Church was willing to entrust to the them. In the fourteenth century, its place would be taken by the Book of Hours, appealing to a much wider public and marking a time of great devotional change.

The verses by Chaucer quoted above translate a French poem honoring the Virgin Mary, the figure most central to this new devotion. Written by Guillaume de Deguilleville in 1331, these specific lines, in praise of her purity, goodness, and mercy toward sinners, are attached to the letter *K*, and declare her name to be the "light" that illuminates these (k)alendars, like the burnished gold initial that heads each calendar page.

There was good reason for this. At the heart of every Book of Hours was the "Little Office" of the Blessed Virgin, a collection of prayers to be recited at the canonical (cathedral) hours of the liturgical day. (Hence their other name "Hours of the Virgin," or more simply "Book of Hours," from *Horae* in Latin.) Though the Office can be traced back to the ninth century, it did not achieve wide popularity until the mid-thirteenth, first among the clergy in their private devotions and then as a book used and treasured by devout lay people, most especially perhaps by women. It played an essential role in the Marian devotion that would dominate late medieval piety. To the "Little Office" itself, the typical Book of Hours added a brief selection of other texts and prayers—four Gospel lessons, seven Penitential Psalms, a Litany of the saints, the vigil Office of the Dead, and so on—creating a textual miscellany (and program for visual decoration) perfectly positioned to surpass the psalter in popular esteem. In the fourteenth and fifteenth centuries, Books of Hours were produced in far greater numbers than any other manuscript class, and many of them were illustrated, some by the greatest artists of the age. As Roger Wieck has noted, such books were "often the only form of art owned by the middle class," and pious folk with sufficient means sometimes possessed several in that kind.[7] (The great bibliophile Jean, duc de Berry, is thought to have owned fifteen.) Christopher de Hamel, in his comprehensive and learned *History of Illuminated Manuscripts*, after devoting separate chapters to "Books for Missionaries," "Books for Emperors," "Books for Monks," "Books for Students," and "Books for Aristocrats," introduces this more recent and most popular kind as "Books for Everybody." Compact, easily carried, and often handsomely illustrated, they were the first "devotional book for ordinary households as well as the aristocracy." A remarkable number of them survive.[8]

What most matters to this chapter is the fact these calendars did more than list in order the festival days of the liturgical year. They charted as well the course of "worldly" (i.e., secular) time, marking its passage on those same calendar pages with images showing the twelve labors of the months and the twelve signs of the zodiac year. It is this "worldly" time, and its distinctive iconography, that will interest us in these pages. The first of these cycles records the occupations and rhythms of the agricultural year; the other (reflecting the medieval understanding of the cosmos) tracks the annual "movement" of the sun across regions of the sky mapped by constellations of stars. As every high school student used to know by heart, Chaucer, in the opening lines to *The Canterbury Tales*, dates his fictional pilgrimage with reference to both. These independent but complementary cycles brought to the calendar page two profound kinds of knowledge, one of them scientific, based upon astronomy, and the other humanistic, reflecting man's life on earth. In the words of an early scholar, James Carson Webster, they contributed to the medieval worldview a reassuring sense of order, of "commemorate recurrence" within that "ocean of time" in which the round of our daily activities might otherwise sink without trace.[9] By naming his badly matched couple January and May, and at the tale's end, sending his young lovers up a tree under the sign of Gemini, Chaucer clearly invites us to think about his characters—and the forces that move them—in calendar terms. In the belief that some knowledge of how they are depicted in calendar art will deepen our pleasure in both the lust and the logic of Chaucer's story, I propose to sketch the history of these traditions and explore their variants with deliberate care.

JANUARY

"January," to begin with, is wholly implausible as a personal name. Children were not named January, then or now. But by referring us to a month, and to its wintry associations, it grounds his character in a traditional iconography, which the January page from the Peterborough Psalter, a sumptuous manuscript made in England sometime before 1318, can suitably introduce (Figure IV.2).[10] Alongside the requisite calendar of liturgical days, it shows January personified as a king with two faces, feasting at table within a structure like a throne. Aquarius (the zodiacal sign of the month) pours water from a jug in the space below, symbolizing the winter rains. We will return to this picture, and to others like it, because a man with two or three faces (sometimes two or three heads), feasting at table, will turn out to be the most common calendar "occupation" of that month.[11]

But feasting, as an "occupation," came later. The earliest calendar pages pictured a man with two faces, to be sure, but showed him instead standing between two doors, one open, one closed. Figure IV.3 (and Figure IV.3a, detail), from a psalter made in the north of France, circa 1230, offers an example,[12] reminding those schooled in such things that January (Januarius) is named after a two-faced deity (Janus bifrons), the Roman god of gates,[13] who presided over beginnings and endings. Occasionally he was imagined as a god with four faces (Janus quadrifrons), presiding over the four directions and the four seasons of the year. But he was especially linked to winter, when the old year went out and the new one came in.[14] Because the sun had been worshiped in his name in early Rome, some think his two faces originally symbolized the alternation of day and night. In any case, Romans were taught to hold him in high honor, naming him first in their prayers to the gods, even before Jupiter himself.[15]

But the euhemerist explanation of his dignity is more detailed. According to Euhemerus, a Greek writer of the late fourth century B.C., those we honor as gods were human beings, first of all—heroes, conquerors, benefactors—venerated during their lifetime and declared gods after their deaths. The myths that grew up around them, affirming that high status were based upon things they did. Janus, for instance, was remembered as a powerful

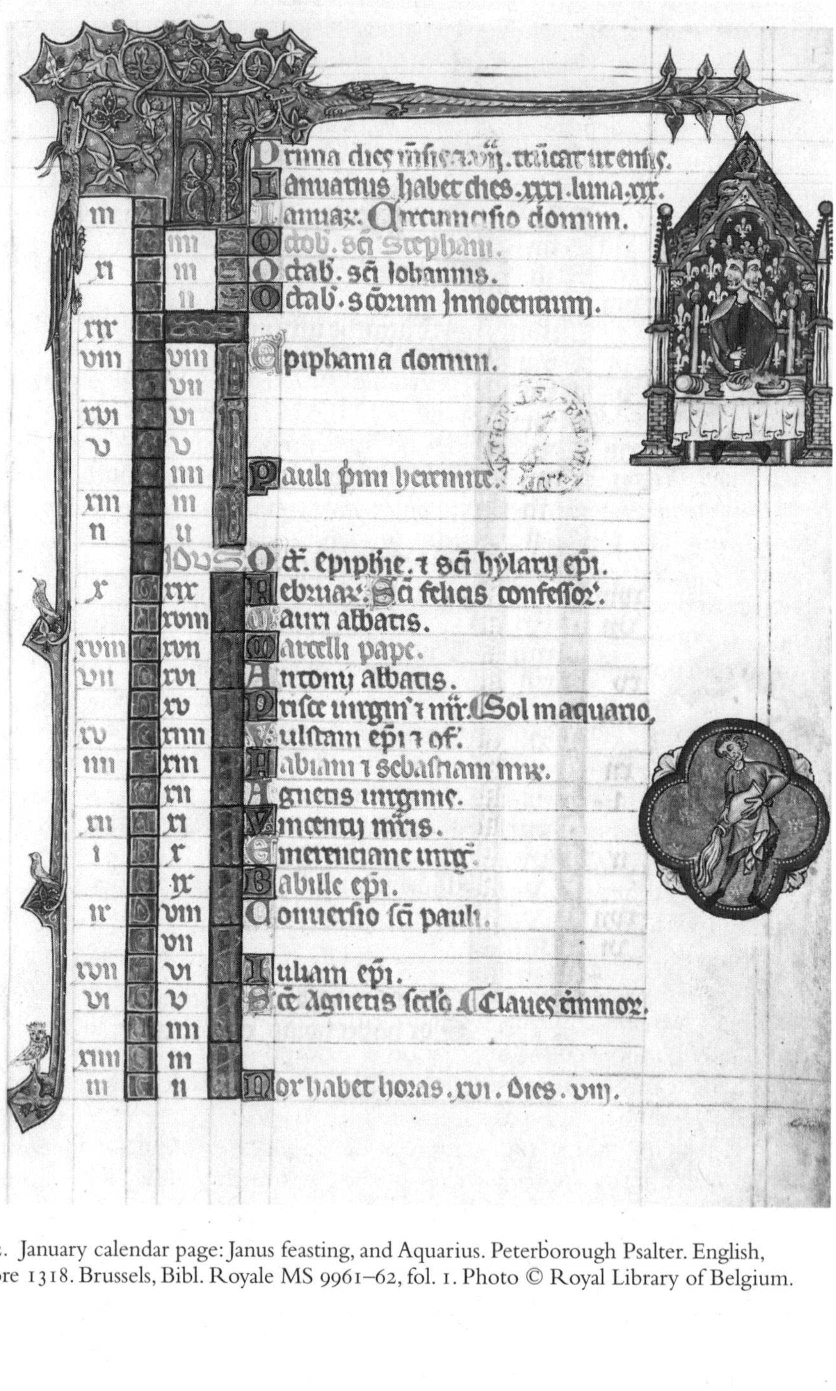

IV.2. January calendar page: Janus feasting, and Aquarius. Peterborough Psalter. English, before 1318. Brussels, Bibl. Royale MS 9961–62, fol. 1. Photo © Royal Library of Belgium.

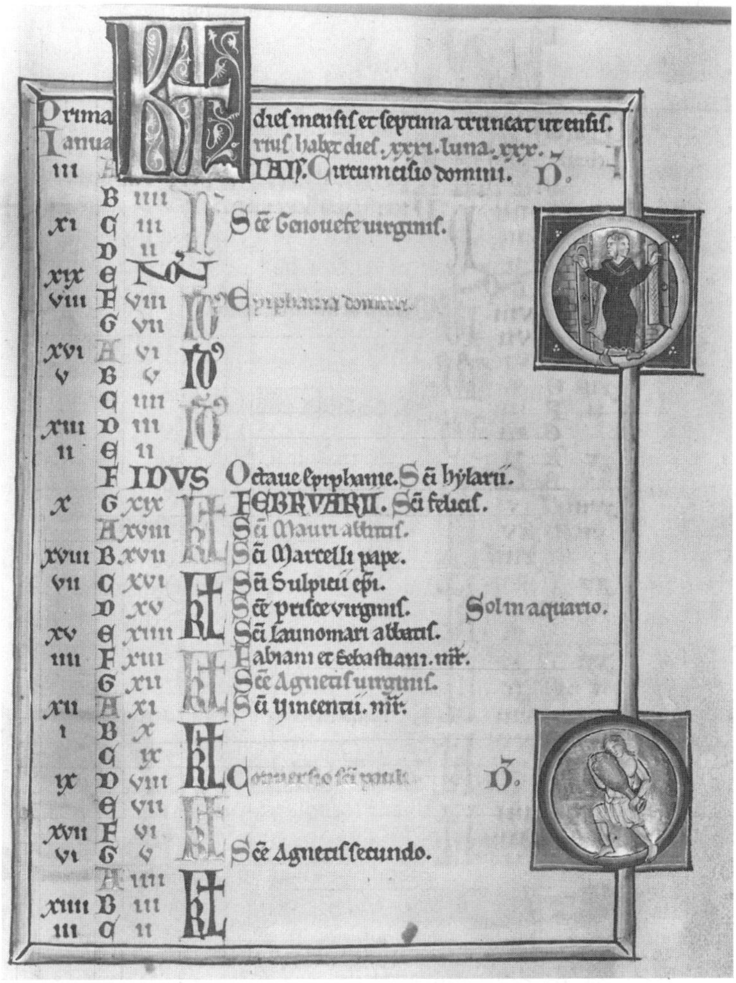

IV.3. January calendar page: Janus between two doors. French, ca. 1230. Paris, Bibl. de l'Arsenal MS 1186, fol. 2.

IV.3A. January calendar page: Janus between two doors (detail from Figure IV.3).

ruler who built a citadel on a hill—called to this day the Janiculum—from which he reigned over the kingdom of Latium, whose capital would become Rome. He shared that rule with Saturn for a time—Saturn himself originally no more than a powerful man—but later he governed Latium alone. Because people considered the reign of Janus a golden age, they declared him a god upon his death. Though his cult never spread far beyond Italy, it claimed great antiquity there; some said it had been introduced to Rome by Romulus himself. A number of legends strengthened his claims, the most important of which had him, in character as a god, saving Rome from a throng of Sabine men after Romulus and his companions had carried off their women. When the Sabines, bent on revenge, scaled the heights of the Capitol, a crucial gate failed to hold. But all was not lost: "A great stream of water came gushing in a torrent through [the gate] from the temple of Janus, and large numbers of the enemy perished, either scalded by the boiling heat of the water or overwhelmed by its force and depth. It was therefore resolved to keep the doors of the temple of Janus open in time of war, as though to indicate that the god had gone forth to help the city."[16] I quote from Macrobius's influential account, written in the first third of the fifth century A.D. The temple here referred to, constructed in the Forum as a double arch (*jani*) facing east and west, was known as *Janus geminus*, and enclosed a statue whose two faces observed all entries and departures. Because it was part of no wall, it offered no practical defense of the city; yet it symbolically guarded all the doors and gates of Rome.[17] Granted the character and history of that city, those temple doors, closed only in times of peace, were not closed often. Thus, in classical art Janus is typically represented with a key (*clavis*) as "the keeper of all doors" and with a rod (*virga*) as "a guide on every road."[18] A brief treatise written near the end of Chaucer's life, the *Libellus de deorum imaginibus*, describing how Janus should be "pictured," whether in the mind's eye, or in a verbal description, or as a work of art, confirms the continuity of this tradition:

> Janus, to whom they attributed the beginning and end of everything, was accepted into the number of their gods. He was depicted in the following ways. He was a king, a man sitting on a throne that shone with rays all about it. He had two faces, one of which looked before him and the other of which looked behind him. There was a temple next to him as well, and in his right hand he held a key with which he showed how to open the temple. In his left hand, he held a staff with which he was seen to strike a stone and produce water from it.[19]

That sums up the Roman Janus nicely, and in expressly visual terms: he was a wise ruler, a protector of the city, and a sponsor of its military might. But the Middle Ages emphasized aspects of divinity quite other than these. Isidore of Seville, for instance, an encyclopedist writing in the seventh century, tells us the month was named after him because January is "the threshold [*limes*] and doorway [*ianua*] of the year";[20] and so the god stands between two doors, one opening on to a year at its beginning, the other closing a year that has come to its end. Chaucer's pilgrims would have met him figured so in the colored-stone pavement surrounding the original shrine of St. Thomas on their visit to Canterbury Cathedral. In its cycle of the occupations of the months and the signs of the zodiac (dating from the first quarter of the thirteenth century), January with two faces stands between two doors, opening one and closing the other.[21]

For this reason, January's key (*clavis*) remained an important symbolic attribute for a long time.[22] It features prominently, for instance, in the Winchester Psalter, a masterpiece of English Romanesque illumination made circa 1150–61 (Figure IV.4, and Figure IV.4a, an enlarged detail), whose January with two heads (*Janus biceps*, a not infrequent variant) stands between two doors, holding the knocker of one in his right hand and carrying an imposing key in the other, held over his left shoulder. But the Roman god of gates has here been transformed into a monastic porter, or doorkeeper, tending the liminal space between the old year and the new, with only a double head to remind us of his pagan origins.[23]

Chaucer's January will become a key keeper as well, not to a New Year but to a new way of living (marriage) and to an enclosed garden corresponding to the "paradise" he expects to find in his union with young May—a prelapsarian garden where sexual play is guiltless and without remorse. (Should his lovemaking falter elsewhere, he expects to succeed in it there.) This key, jealously guarded, is meant to grant him sole access to the pleasures of that place—and as a silver "clyket" designed to open a "smale wyket" (a small wicket gate), its sexual symbolism is as insistent as its rhyme (IV 2045–46, repeated 2151–52). Because it is a real key controlling entry to a real garden, May has only to "countrefete" it secretly, so that Damian (on the appointed day) can open the wicket with *his* clicket (IV 2153) and rush right in. "And in he stirte," Chaucer says, describing Damian's precipitous entry into the garden, preparing the language he will later use for Damian's entry into May herself: "and in he throng."

That Chaucer knew Janus as the "god of gates," and that this sexual innuendo was fully intended, can be readily shown: when Pandarus sets out for Criseyde's house, having agreed to woo her on Troilus's behalf, the narrator dispatches him with a blessing that is also a double entendre: "Now Janus, god of entree, thow hym gyde" (*Troilus and Crisyede*, II 77). But in *The Merchant's Tale* Chaucer does something much more original, transforming the traditional keeper of gates into an icon of the troubled conscience: a January who looks back less on an old year and forward to a new than onto a disreputable past and toward a future unknown, in fear of hell and with little hope of heaven. Should heaven exceed his means, we learn, he'll settle for a "paradise" here and now. By naming him January, Chaucer imagines his aged lover on a threshold between past and future, where prospect and retrospect, equally alarming, lead him to an uncharacteristic bout of introspection. Rich and wellborn he may be, but he is old as well, and unmarried, and without an heir: "sixty yeer a wyflees man was hee." What he fears

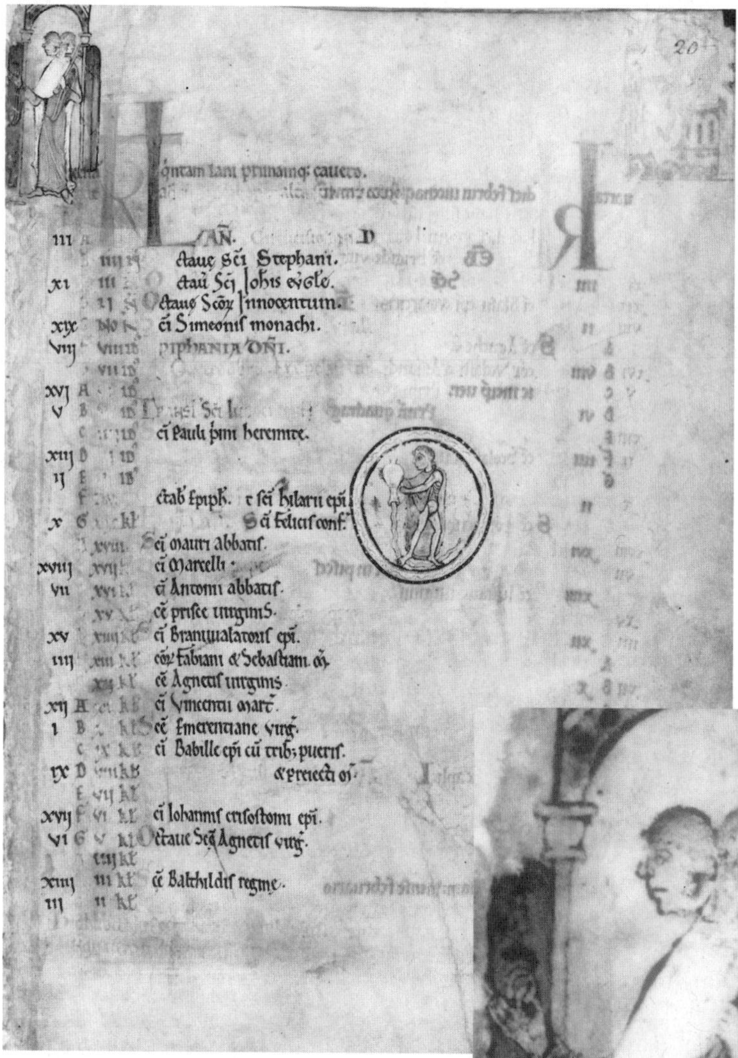

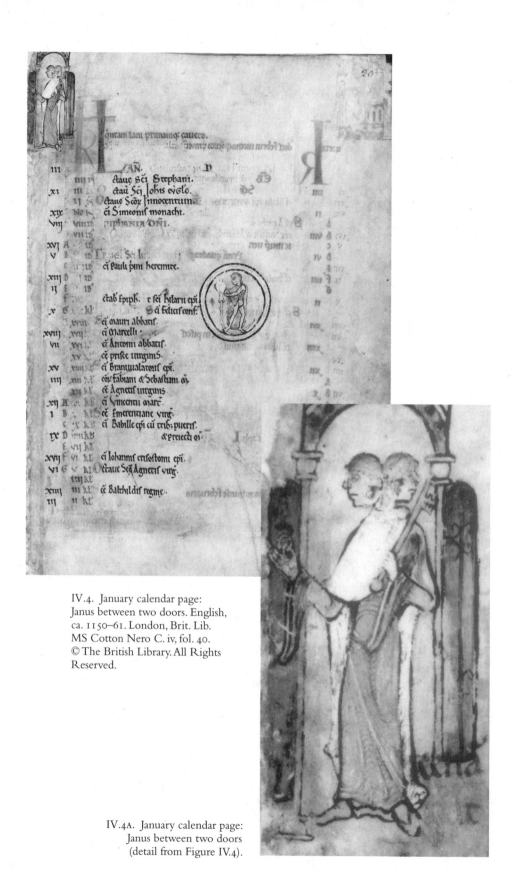

IV.4. January calendar page: Janus between two doors. English, ca. 1150–61. London, Brit. Lib. MS Cotton Nero C. iv, fol. 40.

IV.4A. January calendar page: Janus between two doors (detail from Figure IV.4).

must lie ahead—loneliness, impotent desire, helpless old age—causes only worry, and what lies behind, set against the prospect of eternity, is more troubling still: a life-long history of fornication, casually seeking "his bodily delyt / On wommen, ther as was his appetyt" (IV 1249).

For obvious reasons, moral issues such as these are never broached in the pages of a medieval calendar. Though the twelve-month cycle of the year was sometimes correlated with "the ages of man," the latter cycle, even when divided into a less ambitious "four ages," was quite distinct from what medieval theology termed the "four last things": death and judgment, heaven or hell. The Bedford Book of Hours, however—made in France, circa 1423, but with a noble English provenance—offers an interesting exception. Its January page shows its namesake once again as a feaster (Figure IV.5), here with three faces (this also a commonplace): the middle face, looking directly at us, represents present time. Aquarius is once again correctly shown as a water pourer, but this time figured as a female nude. The page's greatest novelty, however, is revealed in the small roundel on the right (Figure IV.5a, an enlarged detail), which shows January a second time, now dressed as a porter, with faces looking both left and right. Reprising an older iconography, he leans on a long staff and inserts a key into a gate. But behind him, against a blue sky dark with clouds, are written these words: "J'ai veu l'an passe" at left (I have seen the year that is past), and at right, "Je regarde l'an qui commence" (I look to the year that begins). This, on its own, is unusually specific: the gates examined so far require symbolic interpretation but do not literally spell out their psychological meaning. More unexpected still is the monk seated on the ground, holding a double tablet inscribed with a few mordant words (hard to read in a black-and-white reproduction): "Je epleurs les pechez de l'an" (I weep for the sins of the year).[24]

Chaucer's January has a good deal in common with this second Janus, the porter who remembers the past even as he opens a gate to the future (though January's key unlocks only a garden built for private lovemaking). But he shares little beyond a paroxysm of conscience with the monk in the roundel, whose life (we may assume) is devoted to penance and obedience to a rule. Chaucer puts forward instead a willful old man foolishly bent on marriage.

The case January makes for marriage is plausible, if you grant him his assumptions. Bachelors like himself, he says, for all their "libertee" and lack of constraint, live forever on "brittle" ground. Not so the man who chooses the "security" of marriage: "For thanne his lyf is set in sikernesse" (IV 1355). Summoning a council of friends to remedy this situation, he confesses to them his age and moral condition:

> With face sad his tale he hath hem toold. (IV 1399)
> He seyde, "Freendes, I am hoor and oold,
> And almoost, God woot, on my pittes brynke;
> Upon my soule somwhat moste I thynke.
> I have my body folily despended."

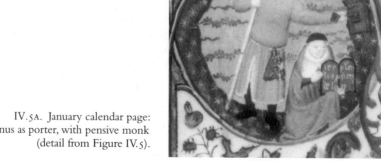

IV.5. January calendar page: Janus feasting; Aquarius; the Old Year and the New. Bedford Book of Hours. French, ca. 1423. London, Brit. Lib. MS Add. 18850, fol. 1. © The British Library. All Rights Reserved.

IV.5A. January calendar page: Janus as porter, with pensive monk (detail from Figure IV.5).

A page from the Luttrell Psalter can help us visualize the subtext of his concern (Figure IV.6). Made in the diocese of Lincoln sometime between 1325 and 1335,[25] it shows a man wholly naked looking down fearfully into a Hell-Mouth gaping below. He holds one wrist with his other hand (a conventional gesture signifying despair). Beneath that complex image, but viewed disjunctively, as if from overhead, one sees a corpse in a winding sheet, laid out in a coffin whose lid is ajar. In the bottom margin, something obscure but unspeakably awful is taking place: water torture perhaps, or some other kind of mundane punishment (probably not relevant to the other images on the page). In Michael Camille's reading of that other iconography, the marble coffin with its elaborate decoration suggests the pomp and privilege of someone very rich—someone, perhaps, like Sir Geoffrey Luttrell himself, the patron for whom the psalter was made—even as the corpse displayed there presents "an image of unspeakable anonymity: the shrouded empty face of death with only a cross marked on its breast." The naked homunculus at the top perhaps invites self-recognition as well, reminding Sir Geoffrey of his physical insignificance, his mortality, and the eternal consequence of his sins.[26]

The brilliant, vertigo-inducing arrangement of these signs is in fact an artist's response to the biblical text that fills the rest of the page (Ps. 87:5–8), in which the psalmist cries out in despair:

> I am counted among them that go down to the pit: I am become as a man without help, free among the dead./ Like the slain sleeping in the sepulchres, whom thou rememberest no more: and they are cast off from thy hand./They have laid me in the lower pit: in the dark places, and in the shadow of death./Thy wrath is strong over me: and all thy waves thou hast brought in upon me.

The psalm, like its illustration, expresses the anguish of a soul in trouble—belated in self-knowledge, sobered by what lies ahead. And that, at least for a time, is the posture of Chaucer's January too. Standing "almoost" on his own "pittes brynke," he looks back on a past given over to lechery and toward a future filled with bleak questions: Who will care for him in old age? Who will fan the flames of his enfeebled desire? Who will furnish him an heir?

This last is no minor concern, especially for a rich man in a feudal culture. To die without an heir, leaving his lands and wealth to a stranger, would be a terrible thing, worse (as January himself says) than being eaten alive by hounds:

> Yet were me levere houndes had me eten (IV 1438)
> Than that myn heritage sholde falle
> In straunge hand, and this I telle yow alle.

Marriage is therefore the obvious answer, obedient to the Church teaching that holds that if a man cannot live chaste, he should take a wife for the

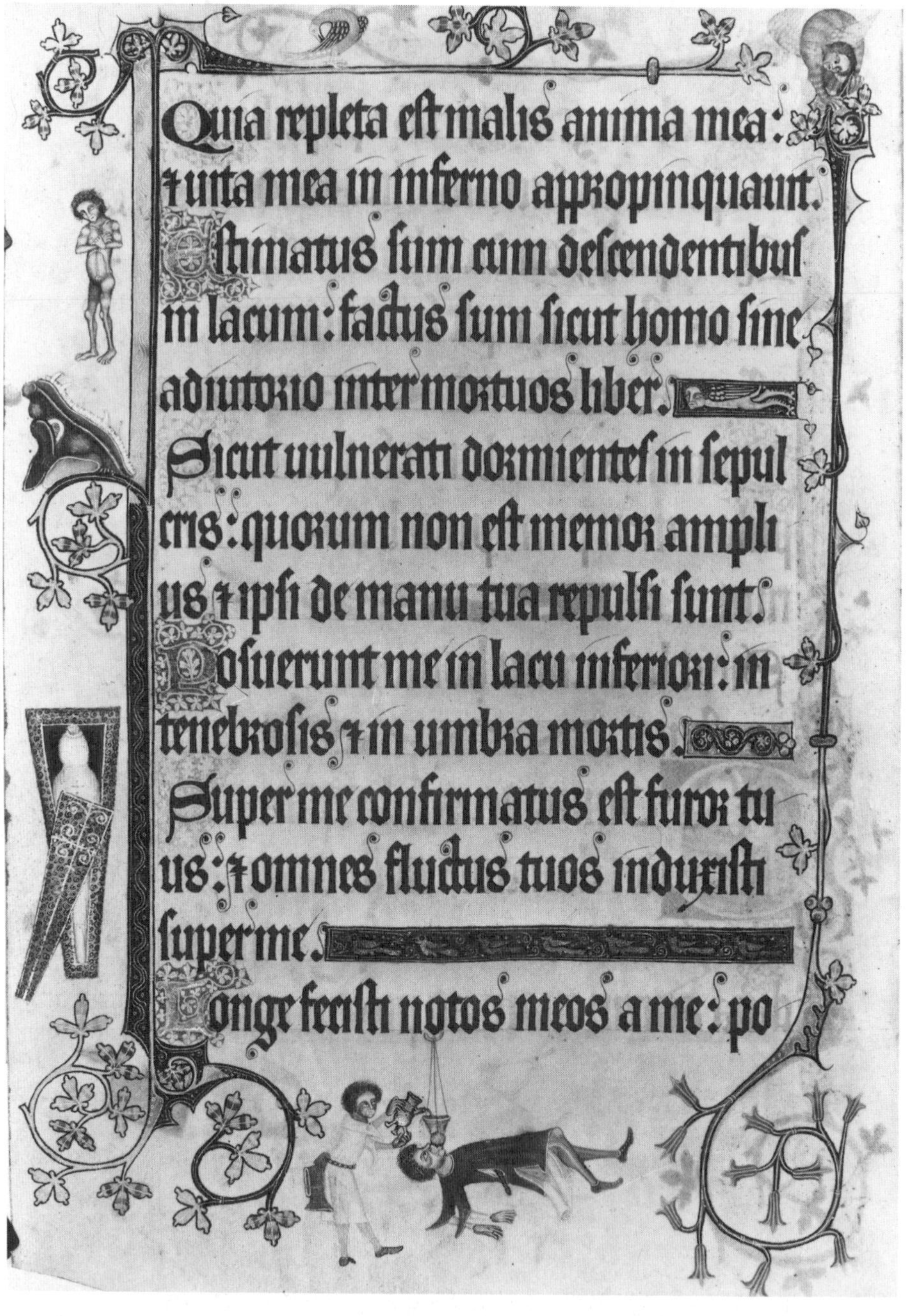

Quia repleta est malis anima mea:
et uita mea in inferno appropinquauit.
Estimatus sum cum descendentibus
in lacum: factus sum sicut homo sine
adiutorio inter mortuos liber.
Sicut uulnerati dormientes in sepul
cris: quorum non est memor ampli
us et ipsi de manu tua repulsi sunt.
Posuerunt me in lacu inferiori: in
tenebrosis et in umbra mortis.
Super me confirmatus est furor tu
us: et omnes fluctus tuos induxisti
super me.
Longe fecisti notos meos a me: po

IV.6. A sinner looking into Hell-Mouth and thinking on his death. English, between 1325 and 1335. London, British Library MS Add. 42130, fol. 157v.

sake of procreation: "leveful procreacioun / Of children to th'onour of God above" (IV 1448). And so old January will finally acquiesce:

> I have my body folily despended; (IV 1403)
> Blessed be God that it shal been amended!
> For I wol be, certeyn, a wedded man,
> And that anoon in al the haste I kan.

He has just one scruple. It is obvious to him that an "oold wyf" will never rouse his lust, nor lead to his begetting children upon her. Only a marriage to a much younger woman will do.

To the formulation of this new intent, calendar art again adds a subtext of unexpected detail. Having transformed Janus with the double face into an old man troubled by past and future, Chaucer now turns him into a special kind of feaster, putting to witty new use a tradition depicted on countless January calendar pages. The calendar origins of this invention are (coincidentally) confirmed just two tales later, in the Franklin's striking evocation of the Christmas season—December 24 to January 6—when frost and sleet have destroyed "the grene" in every yard:

> Janus sit by the fyr, with double berd, (V 1252)
> And drynketh of his bugle horn the wyn;
> Biforn hym stant brawen of the tusked swyn,
> And "Nowel" crieth every lusty man.

Apart from the "double berd," attesting to Chaucer's knowledge of the *Janus bifrons* tradition, every other detail portrays a medieval nobleman at rest, warming himself at a great fireplace, quaffing wine from a drinking horn and feasting on the brawn of a wild boar, all at a time of year when "lusty" men—vigorous men with an appetite for life—salute the season and each other with cries of "Noël!" This descriptive, insistently "visual" verbal icon, imbedded in *The Franklin's Tale* like a roundel on a calendar page, serves there only to specify the season of the year. But for us it can help explain why feasting became so early on the calendar "occupation" for the month of January: the twelve days of Christmas were in many ways the highest, most holy, and certainly most celebratory feast days of the liturgical year. Because the "twelve days" bridge December and January, feasting sometimes appears as the occupation for December.

But there were economic explanations for this prominence as well. Feasting was thought of as an "occupation" of the month, rather than as a "labor," because January, like late December and most of February, falls in the dead time of the agricultural year, when nature rests and little work can be done in the fields. Even the peasant who actually did the work of the other months had little to do except live out the winter as best he could. Yet even for him and his family, it might count as a time of temporary abundance. Pigs every year, having been fattened on acorns in November and butchered in December (the characteristic "labors" of those months),[27] produced in January a surfeit of meat needing to be preserved or promptly eaten. Hence the smoked hams, sausages, and slabs of bacon sometimes shown hanging from the rafters in a humble cottage or a noble kitchen interior. Such images remind us that January, though otherwise marked by cold and scarcity and shortfall, could also be a passing time of plenty.[28] Calendar pages, as many before me have noted, never show the labors of the year in terms of deprivation, exhaustion, or human suffering; they present instead a semi-idealized world, wholly benevolent in its annual rhythm.

Because a season of rest from otherwise hard yet essential labor played an important part in that benevolence, "resting" too became a common "occupation" of the month, usually in the form of a man sitting idle before a fire, warming his feet and drying his shoes. Though this period of repose was not restricted (iconographically) to the elderly, Chaucer's January, we are told, has just turned sixty, in medieval terms the beginning of old age and its many afflictions. Pope Innocent III's treatise *De miseria condicionis humane* (*On the Misery of Human Life*), which Chaucer translated (though his translation does not survive), describes it this way: "Few now reach forty years, very few sixty. If, however, one does reach old age, his heart weakens straightaway and his head shakes, his spirit fails and his breath stinks, his face wrinkles and his back bends, his eyes dim and his joints falter," and so on, one unsavory detail after another.[29] Far outdoing his calendar cohorts in this regard, Chaucer's aged knight seeks sleep and rest with amusing, if disconcerting, frequency.

For instance, after the strenuous exertions of his wedding night have kept him awake until dawn, January suddenly says to May, his young bride:

> "My reste wol I take; (IV 1855)
> Now day is come, I may no lenger wake."
> And doun he leyde his heed and sleep til pryme.

Four days later, when May makes her first appearance again in hall, he sends her off to comfort Damian, said to be ill, promising he will do the same in a little while:

> Have I no thing but rested me a lite; (IV 1926)
> And spede yow faste, for I wole abyde
> Til that ye slepe faste by my side.

When she returns to his bedside, "He taketh hire, and kisseth hire ful ofte," just as he had promised, and then (in the line immediately following) "leyde hym doun to slepe, and that anon" (IV 1949). She accepts this bit of time off gratefully, using it to plan an assignation with her husband's trusted squire:

> Who studieth now but faire fresshe May? (IV 1955)
> Adoun by olde Januarie she lay,
> That sleep til that the coughe hath hym awaked.

When his coughing finally wakes him, once again he doesn't rise, but keeps her in bed with him all day, all naked—"wheither hire thoughte it paradys or helle"—until the bell for evensong is rung (IV 1964).

Calendar tradition, having no interest in the lechery of old men, marks the annual month of rest quite differently. It shows no one sleeping and no one making love; staying warm before a fire is enough. Figure IV.7, from a psalter calendar made in Liège, circa 1280,[30] goes a bit further, granting leisure and abundance to a man at his ease, warming his feet before a fire and

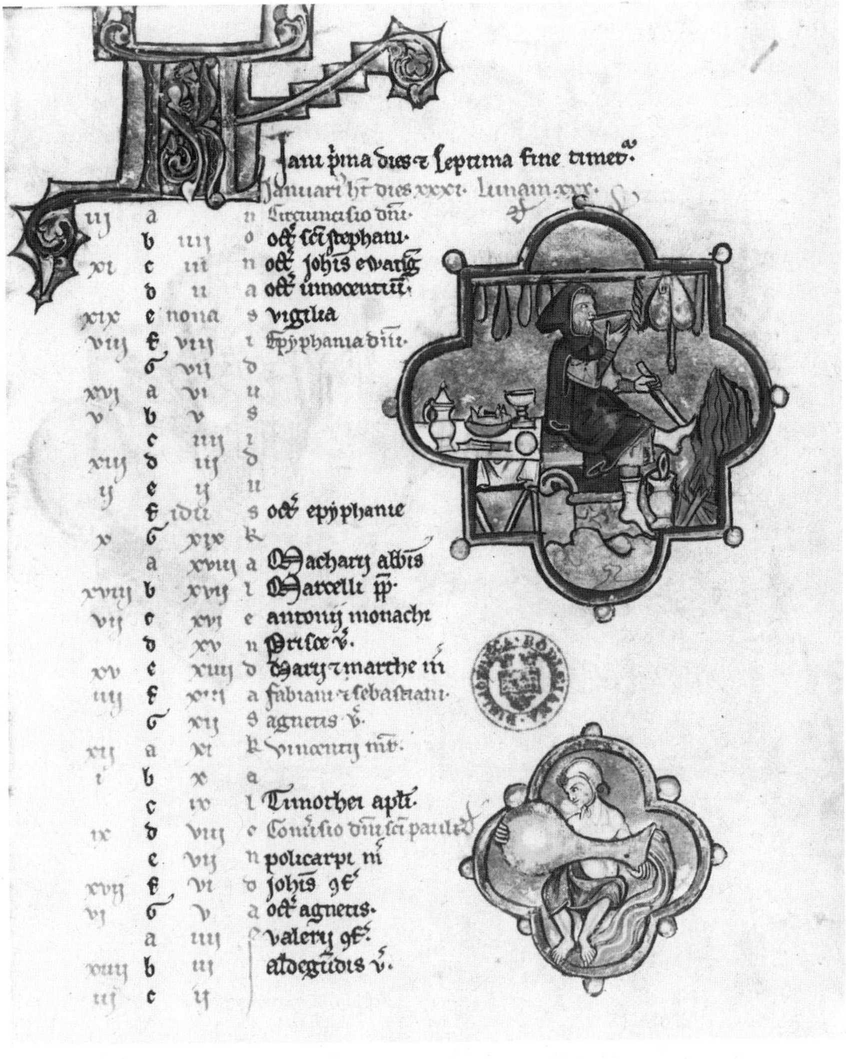

IV. 7. January calendar page: winter provisions, feasting before the fire. Liège, ca. 1280. Oxford, Bodley MS Add. A. 46, fol. 1.

drinking wine from a bowl. The pitcher, goblet, and salt cellar on his table suggest a certain degree of prosperity, while the sausages and cured meats and long-necked goose hanging from the pole above reference a time of abundance. (He is probably a small landholder.) The larger message is certainly clear: take your rest now and let this store of plenty see you through the hardest part of the year.

Social inclusiveness, even to that limited degree, is rare. As in Roman times when Janus was to be named first in any address to the gods, so in medieval art the first of the months was almost always represented by someone of high social standing—usually a king or nobleman at table (very seldom, as above, in the kitchen), feasting alone or attended by servants. (On the highest social level, feasting implies status as well as abundance.) We met such a figure on the first calendar page examined in this chapter—Figure IV.2, from the Peterborough Psalter—and may usefully revisit him now (Figure IV.8, an enlarged detail), vigorous and crowned and seated at a well-dressed table. In Figure IV.5 as well, from the Bedford Book of Hours, we found him dining in a loggia alone, with stately dignity. Only his multiple faces (here three) carry a symbolic meaning, signifying the time of year when past and future and present meet. The more traditional two faces, as we have seen, replace or complement the double gates.[31]

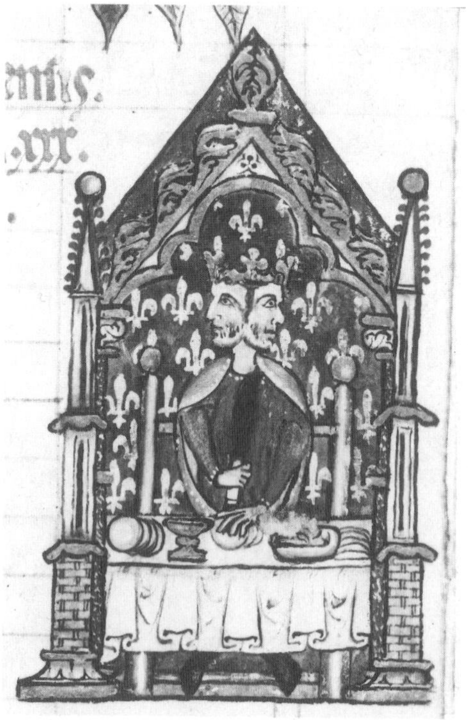

IV.8. January feasting. From the Peterborough Psalter, English, before 1318, Brussels, Bibl. Royale MS 9961–62 (detail of Figure IV.2). Photo © Royal Library of Belgium.

Figure IV.9, from a Book of Hours made in Paris between 1230 and 1239, offers a rare transitional image, in that it shows January feasting between two doors, one of which he opens, the other he closes. This combination of feasting with the traditional doors is unusual in its own right,[32] but even more unexpected (in a picture so early) is January's single face or head. That innovation will have an important future, as *Janus bifrons*, sometimes feasting, sometimes not, is succeeded by a rich man manifesting his wealth and power at table—a portrait, in some cases, of the man who commissioned the book, painted from life. Figure IV.10, the justly famous January page from the Duc de Berry's *Très riches heures*, circa 1411–16, is of this kind. It shows the duke (clearly recognizable from other portraits) seated at table before a magnificent fireplace. Protected from its blaze by an enormous gold-wicker fire screen he is surrounded by a great company of courtiers ceremonially engaged in a New Year's gift exchange. Roast chickens (or game birds) are being carved before him, while two small dogs, roaming freely about the table, lick at dishes nearby. A chamberlain alongside, no doubt under instruction, encourages the gift givers, crying out, "Aproche aproche," in words written in gold.[33]

To bring this tradition into proximity with Chaucer's January, however, we need figures less insistently symbolic than a feaster with two or three faces, and of persons less royal than the Peterborough Psalter's crowned "king" or the (living) Duc de Berry receiving gifts on New Year's Day. We need lesser lords, with single human heads, commanding food and wine from their servants. And these too calendar tradition provides. Though such figures became especially fashionable toward the end of the fifteenth century, they were not unknown before that. Figure IV.11, from a Book of Hours

IV.9. January calendar page (detail): feasting between a closed and an open door. Paris, between 1230 and 1239. New York, Pierpont Morgan Library MS M. 92, fol. 15.

IV.10. January calendar page: the Duc de Berry receives New Year's gifts. French, ca. 1411–16. Limbourg Brothers, *Très riches heures du Duc de Berry*. Chantilly, Musée Condé MS 65, fol. 1v. Photo: Réunion des Musées Nationaux / Art Resource, NY.

made in Paris circa 1400, the year of Chaucer's death, imagines January as a nobleman in his hall, warming his feet at a great fireplace. A table with roast chicken, a loaf of bread, and a jug of wine is laid ready behind him, and, at right, a disembodied arm (Aquarius) pours water from the sky, as a servant might pour wine at a feast.[34] But Figure IV.12, from a Book of Hours made circa 1500 (use of Bourges), because it has a courtier and servant bringing January food, offers a more perfect fit.[35] In this picture, as in Chaucer's *Merchant's Tale*, an iconic figure is to be discovered under a screen of realistic detail. Chaucer will eventually seat his January at an actual feast—his wedding feast—though the aged husband can barely endure it, so impatient is he

IV.11. January calendar page (detail): after a meal, warming himself at the fireplace. Paris, ca. 1400. Oxford, Bodley MS Douce 62, fol. IV.

IV.12. January calendar page: feasting, attended by servants. Bourges? ca. 1500. Oxford, Bodley MS Canon. Liturg. 99, fol. 5.

to take his young bride to bed. But in advance of that, Chaucer had already put the calendar feaster to unexpected use, in witty depiction of yet another aspect of old January's character.

To remedy both his future and his dissolute past, January hopes to find in the licensed sexuality of marriage a paradise here and now (a second "paradys terrestre") that will not lose him the paradise to come. But he quickly abandons this idealized rhetoric when it comes to specifying what he has in mind. Being the sort of lord who "In honest wyse, as longeth to a knyght,/ Shoop hym to lyve ful deliciously" (IV 2024–25), he orders up a wife as if he were ordering up a meal:

> "But o thyng warne I yow, my freendes deere, (IV 1415)
> I wol noon oold wyf han in no manere.
> She shal nat passe twenty yeer, certayn;
> Oold fissh and yong flessh wolde I have fayn.
> Bet is," quod he, "a pyk than a pykerel,
> And bet than old boef is the tender veel.
> I wol no womman thritty yeer of age;
> It is but bene-straw and greet forage."

In *The Wife of Bath*'s Prologue, where the so-called "marriage debate" began, sex and money had assumed a coidentity—an exchange, quid pro quo, at once metaphoric and real. Here sex and food replace that symbiotic relationship. Underwritten by calendar images for January, the tale makes witty poetry out of the idea that Gluttony (excessive or overrefined indulgence in food and drink) leads to Lechery, as surely as an apple in Eden led Adam and Eve to discover their nakedness, lust, and shame. Chaucer's *Parson's Tale* anatomizes Lechery in just such terms: "After Glotonye thanne comth Lecherie, for thise two synnes been so ny cosyns [near cousins] that ofte tyme they wol nat departe" (X 836). Though such a claim was the tired staple of many a medieval sermon, Chaucer refreshes it in *The Merchant's Tale* by combining an old man's sexual fantasy with a rich man's gourmandise, making of them one grandly self-indulgent "feast." Just as January prefers big fish to small ones (more edible flesh on fewer bones) and calves' meat to that of old cows (veal more delicate and tender), so this sixty-year old man will have no woman over twenty (seven MSS specify no one "over sixteen"!).[36]

An "oold wyf," he warns, could never please him sexually—he'd become an adulterer again "and go streight to the devel whan I dye" (IV 1432–36). And a woman of thirty would feed his sexual appetite no better than "bene-straw" (winter fodder for animals). Having "folwed ay his bodily delyt / On women, ther as was his appetyt" (IV 1249), he has developed a taste for finer things. Dreaming up a more sumptuous sexual meal, he calls for a woman as young as May, and lies in bed at night feeding his fantasies, imagining "in his herte and in his thoght"

> Hir fresshe beautee and hir age tendre, (IV 1601)
> Hir myddel smal, hire armes longe and sklendre,

Hir wise governaunce, hir gentillesse,
Hir wommanly berynge, and hire sadnesse.[37]

Though his friends arrange the marriage as hastily as ever they can, the wedding banquet serves chiefly to defer the meal he really desires. Gulping down spiced wines "t'encreessen his corage," and topping them off with a medical aphrodisiac or two, he leaps into bed to do whatever a man of his age can still do (IV 1805 ff.).

There's just one problem with all this. Young May turns out to be a bit of a feaster too, intent upon feeding her own appetite as efficiently as she can. The pears that come to symbolize the object of her real desire have a long history in both art and in literature, not only because the shape of that fruit bears some resemblance to the male genitalia, but because *pirum* (in Latin) and *poire* (in French), one derived from the other, are both ambiguous, meaning either "pear" or "rod."[38] Hungry for young pears ("smale peres grene"), May climbs a tree she has prudently stocked with the same.

Female sexual desire was not always accorded such delicate euphemism. Medieval iconography includes highly literal "penis-trees" as well, most famously in a manuscript of the *Roman de la Rose*, made circa 1330, whose margins (confirming the teachings of La Vieille, the Old Bawd) depict members of religious orders blithely breaking their vows of celibacy. Figure IV.13, one of many, shows a nun plucking penises from a tree to put in her basket; just opposite, she boldly embraces a monk. This border and others like it—briefly described in an endnote below—make May's stated hunger for "small green pears" seem almost ladylike and refined.[39] Though her witty stratagem further proves that sex and appetite can coincide in many ways, it was her husband—January as traditional feaster, ordering up a wife as one might order up a meal—that showed the way.

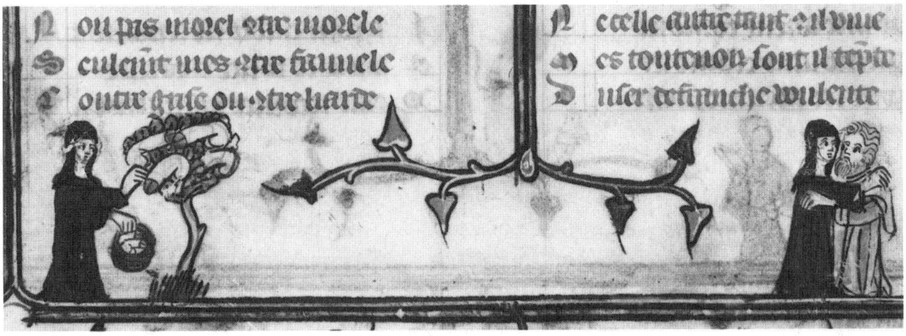

IV.13. *Roman de la Rose*: a nun gathers fruit from a penis-tree, and embraces a monk (border detail). French, ca. 1330. Paris, Bibl. Natl. MS fr. 25526, fol. 106v.

MAY

Calendar occupations for the month of May will seem, at first, to offer less that is relevant to *The Merchant's Tale*. The most frequent choice shows a noble young man on a horse, with a hunting bird at his wrist. Hawking and falconry were sports especially agreeable in good weather, and John Trevisa's *On the Properties of Things* (ca. 1399), translating a Latin encyclopedia by Bartholomew the Englishman (ca. 1230), parsed this iconography as simply as it deserves: "For May is a tyme of solas and of likinge, therefore he is ipeynt a yonglyng [painted as though a youth], ridinge and beringe a fowle on his honde."[40] The relevant page from the Winchester Psalter, circa 1170 (not reproduced here) provides an early English example, and the *Belles heures* of Jean de Berry an elegant later parallel from France (ca. 1408–9), with a vast number of such images surviving from the years in between.[41] But since neither hawking nor falconry figures in our tale, images focused on that pastime alone will not concern us here. (Examples can be seen, however, in pictures I reproduce for another purpose). More relevant is a variant tradition, in which a young man rides out with hawk or falcon between green and blossoming trees, or yet another, in which he carries in his other hand a green or blossoming branch. Figure IV.14, of the former kind, shows him youthful and crowned, riding out between two trees in exuberant bud and bloom. Even the covering of his horse shows a formal pattern of leaves.[42] Figure IV.15, from Jean Pucelle's exquisite Hours of Jeanne d'Evreux—made circa 1325 at the time of Jeanne's marriage to Charles IV of France—is of the second kind, though it parcels out the essentials of this variant tradition in an unexpected way: behind the youthful rider with falcon, a serving man trudges along, carrying on his shoulders two stripling trees.[43]

Many images of this sort, however, dispense with the hawking or falconry altogether. Showing a man on horse or on foot, carrying a flowering branch or tree, they record a folk custom that celebrated the coming of spring on May 1, or on the night before, by "getting some green" from the woods and carrying it back to town. It was called "bringing in the May."[44] This ancient observance, documented in one form or another across most of Europe, has been traced back at least as far as the Roman Floralia, described by Ovid in his *Fasti*, and the Celtic Beltane, a festival on the first of May celebrating the beginning of summer and the open pasturing of cattle in Ireland and Scotland. No doubt it was older still, and took many ceremonial forms.[45] Even the timing proved flexible: in the late medieval and early modern period, it was celebrated in some places at Pentecost (Whitsuntide), a summer festival whose date varies from mid-May to early June; in calendar art it sometimes appears (though rarely) as the occupation for April.[46] Spring, these variants remind us, is a season—not a single month, much less a single day. Yet the custom of "bringing in the green" was especially associated with the beginning of May. The earliest English account of what it once entailed, and what its social logic might have been, comes from Phillip Stubbes's 1583

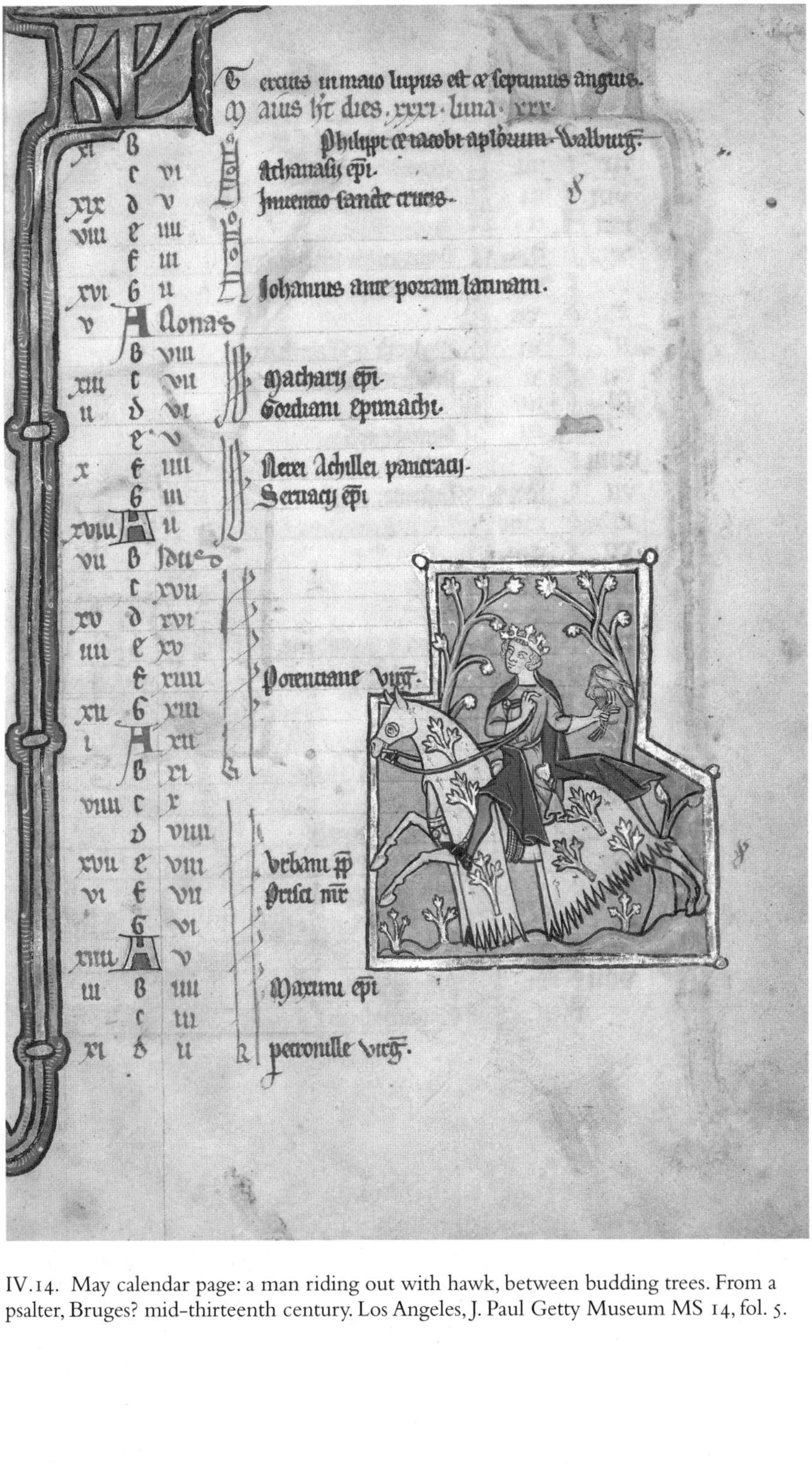

IV.14. May calendar page: a man riding out with hawk, between budding trees. From a psalter, Bruges? mid-thirteenth century. Los Angeles, J. Paul Getty Museum MS 14, fol. 5.

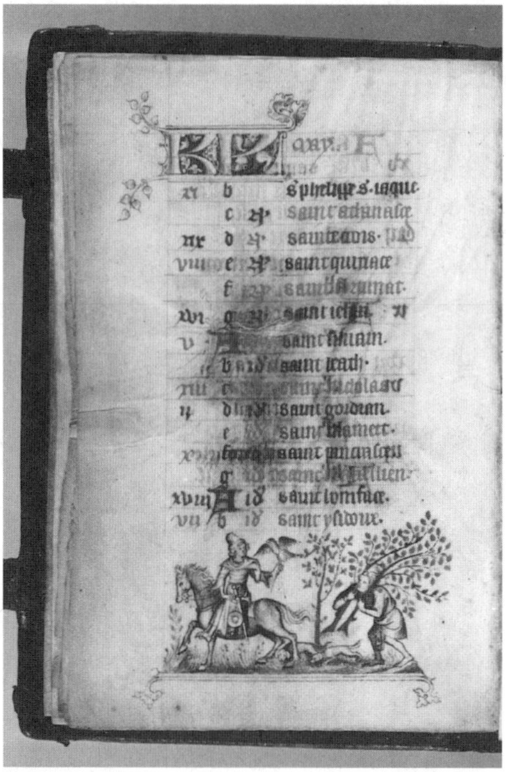

IV.15. May calendar page (detail): a falconer with servant, bringing home the green. Jean Pucelle, the Hours of Jeanne d'Evreux. Paris, ca. 1325. New York, The Metropolitan Museum of Art, Cloisters Collection, 1954 (54.1.2, fol. 5v). Image © The Metropolitan Museum of Art.

description of its observance. A Puritan document, written in stiff-necked disapproval, it is exaggerated in tone and only partially relevant here. But it offers a place to begin:

> Against *May*, *Whitsunday*, or other time, all the yung men and maides, old men and wives, run gadding over night to the woods, groves, hils, & mountains, where they spend all the night in pleasant pastimes; & in the morning they return, bringing with them birch & branches of trees, to deck their assemblies withall. and [*sic*] no mervaile, for there is a great Lord present amongst them, as superintendent and Lord over their pastimes and sports, namely, Sathan, prince of hel. . . . I have heard it credibly reported (and that *viva voce*) by men of great gravitie and reputation, that of fortie, threescore, or a hundred maides going to the wood over night, there have scarcely the third part of them returned home again undefiled.[47]

In Stubbes's time, customs of this sort occasioned political as well as religious controversy, causing both James I and Charles I to defend them as expressing the ancient character of the English people. And by that time, of course, the customs themselves would have undergone change, making Stubbes's account an uncertain guide to their medieval antecedents. But we need not join him in discovering Satan at the center of these ceremonies, or in imagining a wholesale deflowering of virgins in the woods, to sense something social, symbolic, and potentially erotic at the core not only of these customs but of the medieval calendar pictures that record them. As early as 1445–50, Peter Idley, in a book of *Instructions to His Son*, warned him against taverns, dicing, "gestis and fables," and setting out early in the morning "to fette hom fresshe maijs / that maketh maidens stomble and falle in the breris" (to fetch home fresh "Mays" [hawthorn flowers or branches] that make maidens stumble and fall in the briars).[48] Even then, quite clearly, the custom (like its possible consequence) was not new. In marking the regreening of the world by the "getting of some green" or by "fetching in the May" (most often the white hawthorn flower), those ceremonies, like the pictures that record them, celebrate the life force itself, the annual plant- and tree-rhythm that makes visible the perpetual triumph of new life over death.

Chaucer's *Knight's Tale*, at the beginning of the Canterbury tale telling, includes two May Day observances of interest in this regard. In the first, the queen's young sister Emelye, described as fairer to look upon

> Than is the lylie upon his stalke grene, (I 1036)
> And fressher than the May with floures newe,

rises before the dawn "to doon honour to May":

> For May wole have no slogardie anyght. (I 1042)
> The sesoun priketh every gentil herte,
> And maketh it out of his slep to sterte,
> And seith "Arys, and do thyn observaunce."

And so Emelye, rising with the sun, walks up and down the palace garden paths, singing sweetly to herself and picking flowers to braid a garland for her hair. (Girls of the royal household did not welcome May by spending a night in the woods.) For someone like her, to rise with the sun, make a garland of flowers, sing, and feel happy—perhaps even hopeful in some vaguely romantic sort of way—was enough to "do honour" to May. Palamon and Arcite, looking at her from on high in a prison tower, fall instantly in love with what they see. The competition that will turn these two sworn "brothers" into enemies begins at that very moment.

The second "Maying" takes place a year or more later, after Arcite, disfigured by grief, has broken his exile to serve unrecognized in Theseus's court, still in love with Emelye. Moved to do his own "observaunce to May,"[49] he rides off to a wooded grove, where he too makes a garland of May flowers, and sings a song "ayeyn the sonne shene," a song that includes (in its final line) a clear statement of his intent, however obscure to our modern understanding:

> May, with alle thy floures and thy grene, (I 1510)
> Welcome be thou, faire, fresshe May,
> In hope that I som grene gete may.

He does not know that Palamon, newly escaped from prison, is hiding in that same wood, and that their deadly quarrel (over who loved Emelye first or who now loves her more) is about to be renewed.

What exactly Arcite "hopes" for, or expects to obtain, in "getting some green" may have been clearer once than it is now. He intends "to get some greenery," of course—a branch or branches, in leaf or blossom, to take back to the court. That much is confirmed by calendar art, and accomplishing it will be easy. But the words "in hope that I som grene gete may" hint at something less predictable, some happy omen perhaps, or something to refresh and renew his long-frustrated love. He hopes for, or expects, the beginning of something good.[50] Meanwhile, a third ceremony, concurrent with Arcite's "observaunce," is underway: Theseus has decided to go hart hunting in honor of the May, accompanied by Hippolyta his queen and Emelye, "clothed al in grene" (I 1673–87). In the course of their hunt they come upon the young knights, fighting in the grove.

What Arcite really wants from the first of May is better glossed, no doubt, by another variant in the calendar tradition—one increasingly popular in the fourteenth and fifteenth centuries—in which the young man carrying a branch of green doesn't ride alone but has a girlfriend along.[51]

That spring can inspire romantic love needs no learned demonstration. As the Wife of Bath is quick to remind us, some things can be known from experience. But it will do no harm to hear that rapturous truth expressed once more, here by John Trevisa in his fourteenth-century *On the Properties of Things*, translating a thirteenth-century Latin encyclopedia written by yet another Englishman: "In May woodis wexith grene, medis [meadows] springith and florischith and wel nyye alle thingis that beth alive beth imeved [moved] to joye and to love."[52]

If the calendar "Janus" of *The Franklin's Tale*—resting by the fire, drinking wine and feasting on wild boar—represents an aristocratic defense against "the bittre frostes, with the sleet and reyn" that have destroyed "the grene in every yerd" (V 1250), then the calendar's "Mayus," with its several ways of celebrating spring's new growth, enshrines a remedy free of class privilege, available to all. The annual coming of spring, described in medieval French poetry as a *reverdie*—a literal "regreening"—releases nature from winter at last.

January's young bride-to-be, interestingly enough, enters the tale not as May but as "Mayus"—"this mayden which that Mayus highte" (IV 1693)—even though *Mayus* (the Latin name for the month) is masculine in gender. She will be called that three more times before the tale is finished.[53] In the consensus scholarly view, this is no more than a concession to meter: in each of those lines the extra syllable comes in handy. But Chaucer was remarkably deft in verse, and might have circumvented a metrical shortfall in any number of ways, had he not been interested in deepening her thematic association with the month. After so much emphasis on those aspects of January's character that reflect the calendar tradition—his double address to time past and time future, his interest in feasting (both real and metaphoric), his recurring need for rest—this oblique way of naming the young bride suggests that the calendar tradition may have something to tell us about her too. It is as Mayus, not May, that she enters the pleasure garden on the day January will be cuckolded:

> This Januarie, as blynd as is a stoon, (IV 2156)
> With Mayus in his hand, and no wight mo,
> Into his fresshe gardyn is ago.

By calling her so often by the Latin name of the month, Chaucer projects her marriage to January against the annual twelve-month cycle, structuring their union in ways thematically richer than would be the case if it were just another ill-conceived marriage of age to youth, though that stereotype supports it and is certainly not excluded. "Whan tendre youthe hath wedded stoupyng age,/Ther is swich myrthe that it may nat be writen" (IV 1738–39).

In French *fabliaux* and Italian *novelle* alike, marriages of this kind are typically punished by a rough sort of justice, rousing our laughter and inviting our assent. Chaucer's *Miller's Tale* offers a highly relevant example.[54] But the marriage between youth and old age in *The Merchant's Tale* is not punished in that way: no one ends up seriously "corrected" or even unhappy; there is no public exposure of the adulterous couple; January is not forced to face the truth (even privately) for long. In the wedding of Mayus to January, two improbable personal names activate each other, inviting us to think of both in terms of those months—an invitation gracefully supported by verses that see in May her month's true likeness, its emanation:

> But this muche of hire beautee telle I may, (IV 1747)
> That she was lyk the brighte morwe of May,
> Fulfild of alle beautee and plesaunce.

What in the analogues amounts to no more than a blind husband's jealousy—a staple of the fabliau genre—is here given deeper cause and viewed against a different ethical horizon. Because January's sudden blindness makes him more conscious than ever of the discrepancy between her beauty and "the unlikely elde of me" (IV 2180), he seeks to keep her always (quite literally) under hand, in a jealousy so "outrageous" (Chaucer's word),

> That neither in halle, n'yn in noon oother hous, (IV 2088)
> Ne in noon oother place, neverthemo,
> He nolde suffre hire for to ryde or go,
> But if that he had hond on hire alway.

Indeed, she can scarcely signal Damian to climb up the tree because January "hadde an hand upon hire everemo" (IV 2103).

This can, of course, be read in fabliau terms as nothing more than a blind man's ineffectual defense against cuckoldry. But read in terms of the calendar tradition, it gestures toward something more untenable and unworthy, the cold hand of winter clinging to—and holding back—the urgent and essential energies of spring.[55]

In the chapter that follows, there will be more to say about May as a bride, and about *Mayus* as the fifth month of the year. But to get to that I must introduce a third calendar tradition—the sun in Gemini—that Chaucer specifically referenced as a way of thinking about both.

V. Of Calendars and Cuckoldry (2)

The Sun in Gemini and *The Merchant's Tale*

NOTHING in the calendar representations of May—at least nothing examined so far—prepares us for the rude coupling that will resolve what is wrong in the January-May marriage. Though "bringing in the green" records a folk custom or customs having something to do with generation and regeneration, those customs, as pictured, are everywhere graceful, decorous, and socially sanctioned; they have little in common with the graceless bonking in a tree that brings *The Merchant's Tale* to its end. Here is how the Merchant describes that climactic event:

> Ladyes, I prey yow that ye be nat wrooth; (IV 2350)
> I kan nat glose, I am a rude man—
> And sodeynly anon this Damyan
> Gan pullen up the smok, and in he throng.

In modern English, he "pulled up her dress and stuck [it] in." Once January's sight is restored, he speaks in language equally direct: "'Strugle?' quod he, 'Ye, algate in it wente!'" Unlike the lovemaking in the Caxton woodcut, discretely masked by leaves, the coupling of Damian and May elicits neither equivocation nor euphemism. For something in this tonal range we shall have to look elsewhere on the May calendar page.[1]

And so we turn from occupations of the months to the signs of the zodiac, tracking cosmic time on these same calendar pages. There had been no need to include them in our thinking about January: Aquarius has nothing to tell us about *The Merchant's Tale*. But the zodiac sign on the calendar page for May exerts a significant astrological "influence" on the poem, and will, in time, complete the deeper logic of its narrative. Once Damian has climbed the tree "charged" with fruit, and January and May have been set "romynge" merrily below, this ecstatic bit of verse dates the action that must ensue:

> Bright was the day, and blew the firmament; (IV 2219)
> Phebus hath of gold his stremes doun ysent
> To gladen every flour with his warmnesse.

He was that tyme in Geminis, as I gesse,
But litel fro his declynacion
Of Cancer, Jovis exaltacion.[2]

With the sun in Gemini, all that follows will be played out "under" the power of that sign.

CASTOR AND POLLUX

The standard calendar image for the Gemini (standard, in the sense of being textually authorized) shows two young men "figured," in John Gower's words, as naked twins: "lich to tuo twinnes of mankinde,/That naked stonde."[3] Mythographers identified them with Castor and Pollux (Greek: Polydeuces), twins born to Leda after Zeus visited her in the form of a swan. As always in mythological matters, accounts vary, but most have Leda producing two sets of twins: Pollux and Helen from an egg fertilized by Zeus, and Castor and Clytemnestra from an egg fertilized by her husband Tyndareus, whom she had slept with earlier that night. Pollux, by virtue of his paternity, was born immortal, but Castor not. Both were honored in their native Sparta as models for military youth—Pollux as a celebrated boxer, his twin as a great horseman—and they took part in several major expeditions, including the quest of Jason and the Argonauts for the Golden Fleece. On that journey, during a terrible storm, Zeus sent twin flames to hover over them as he calmed the waters, thus establishing them as protectors of those in peril at sea. ("St. Elmo's fire," a discharge caused by the ionization of air after lightning is thought to explain this interesting belief. Sailors believe it signals the end of a storm.) As important as their legendary strength and valor, however, was the love they had for each other—a mythological sign registering the profound empathy that often exists between twins. When Castor was killed in a fight, Pollux swiftly avenged his death, and then, unable to endure the loss of his brother, begged Zeus for permission to die with him. Moved by the depth of their love, Zeus allowed them to share mortality and immortality, spending their days on Olympus among the gods and their nights in the underworld among the dead.[4] Because of these favors they were known as the Dioscuri (*dios kouroi*), "young sons of Zeus" or "youths especially dear to Zeus." Tradition has it their cult was introduced to Rome after the battle of Lake Regillus (499 or 496 B.C.), where their spirits had been seen on white horses, first leading the Roman cavalry to victory, and then later in the Forum, where they watered their horses, and delivered the news. In 486 B.C., a temple was built in the Forum commemorating the event.

In another version, Zeus, at their death, installed them in the constellation Gemini, and named its brightest stars Castor and Pollux in their honor. Early astronomers claimed to see there the stick-outline of two figures, one leaning toward the other in a posture vaguely suggestive of fraternal love.[5] Figure V.1, from an English astronomical treatise made in the mid-twelfth century,[6] shows how the constellation's major stars (indicated by

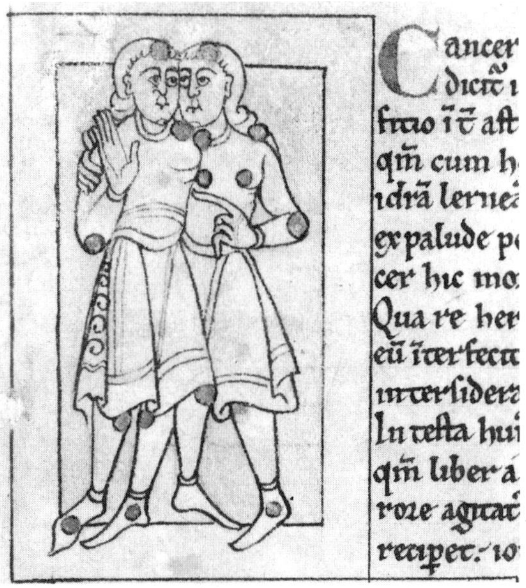

V.1. A star chart of the constellation Gemini (the Twins). English, mid-twelfth century. Oxford, Bodley MS 614, fol. 19.

large red dots at the top of their heads, shoulders, elbows, and feet) might be connected to create such an image. Trevisa's *On the Properties of Things*, citing Isidore of Seville, testifies to the twins' origin and strength ("tweyne brethiren ibore at one birthon, and . . . ful strong men") as well as their astrological influence. When the sun passes through their sign, Trevisa writes, its power is doubled (i.e., twinned) so that the world can grow fruitful and productive again: "for whanne the sonne is in that partie of hevene, the vertu [is] idoubled to make the nethir worlde plentevous." He will later celebrate the month of May as a time when "myrthe and likynge [affection] is idowbled among men."[7]

The standard image for the Gemini emerges quite naturally from this myth. It shows the Twins as wrestlers in the classical manner, naked and idealized. In a stone zodiac on the tympanum of the cathedral at Vézelay, for instance, carved between 1120 and 1132, they struggle shoulder to shoulder in a friendly fashion,[8] as they do on the calendar page for May in the Oscott Psalter, made in England (possibly Oxford) circa 1265–70 (Figure V.2),[9] where, with legs strategically opposed, one or the other seems about to take a fall. Shown below is the occupation of the month: a young man riding out, with hawk and a green branch. Figure V.3, from a Book of Hours made in Paris, 1407, can fairly represent the later tradition, when the design had become formulaic and the elegance of the Twins' wrestling pose predictable and commonplace.[10] The horizon is low, the sky a glorious blue, and the twins perfectly mirror each other, their limbs symmetrically disposed. The contest of strength and skill they are about to undertake is visually echoed in

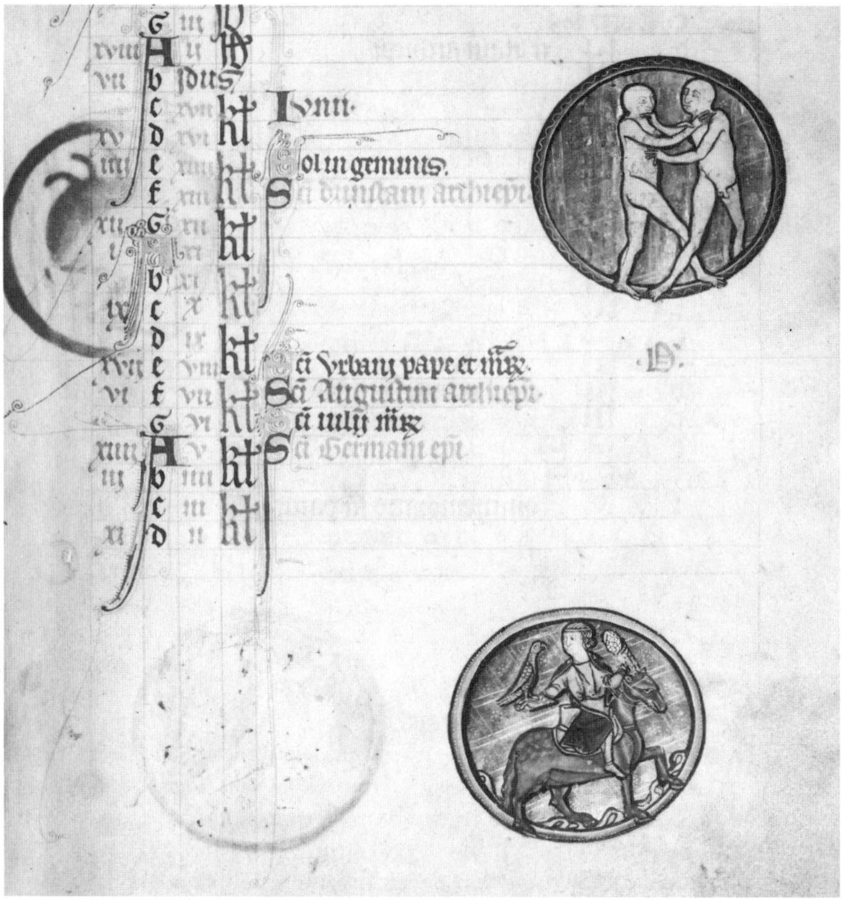

V.2. May calendar page: the Gemini as wrestlers; a falconer with flowering branch. English, ca. 1265–70. London, Brit. Lib. MS 50,000, fol. 3. © The British Library. All Rights Reserved.

V.2A. May calendar page (detail of Figure V.2): the Gemini as wrestlers.

the struggle of two playful young dragons (not shown here) in the decorated margin just to their right. Figure V.4, from a Book of Hours illuminated in France for the English market, circa 1440–50, confirms that impression, and removes their contest even further from any hint of animosity or violence; they seem almost about to embrace or dance. But knowledge of the myth tells us they are "wrestling"—at play in a radiant world, with green trees on either side and a brook running through the green field below. A falconer rides across the companion space, engaged in one of the occupations proper to May. Though this page was illuminated well after Chaucer's death, there is nothing surprising about it; he would have understood it at once.

In this picture, one notes, the Twins are not entirely naked. Their brief undergarments ensure a degree of modesty, even as they call attention to

V.3. May calendar page (detail): a falconer on horse; the Gemini as wrestlers. Paris, 1407. Oxford, Bodley MS Douce 144, fol. 10.

V.4. May calendar page (detail): a falconer on horse; the Gemini as wrestlers. French, ca. 1440–50. Illuminated by the Fastolf Master. Oxford, Bodley MS Auct. D. inf 2. 11, fol. 5.

what they conceal. This highlights a problem intrinsic to almost every depiction of the Gemini: nakedness, in real life as well as in the visual arts, remained a troublesome concept throughout the Middle Ages. Medieval art, it is true, often showed pagan idols as nude (a sign to be read pejoratively), usually without genital specification. But nudity as a positive sign, or as an aesthetic ideal, proved more challenging, with male genital nudity almost wholly beyond the pale.[11] Christ's body, hung naked on the cross in public display, spoke of abjection and humiliation, in contrast to the glorified body (naked beneath a graceful mantle) in which he would rise from the grave on Easter morning. But even on the cross, in medieval art, he was never wholly nude. According to legend, his mother, or a disciple, obtained a loin cloth (the *perizonium*) to cover his sex—a tradition that artists consistently honored.[12] Even St. Sebastian, whose youthful, androgynous body was traditionally shown pierced with arrows, could count on the same. Though this almost naked image was much favored by certain popes and aristocratic patrons, I know of no medieval example in which his genitals are shown.

But representations of a bolder sort could be justified with respect to the Gemini, not only because their origins were pagan and mythological, but because their legend required that they be young, strong, and heroic, and that they express the love they feel for each other *as twins*—a relationship more private and more mysterious than other forms of homosocial affection. This of course entailed risks all its own, for even when they are shown as wrestlers (as in Figures V.2, V.3, and V.4), the formal, stylized way they lay hands on each other's shoulders suggests a potentially homoerotic embrace.

Figure V.5, from an Old Testament picture book made in Paris, circa 1250,[13] will make clear what I mean. It shows David, clothed in mail, embracing Jonathan, the son of King Saul, who had sworn fealty to him "because he loved him: for he loved him as his own soul" (1 Kings 20:17). Having warned David earlier that Saul intends his death, Jonathan now urges him to flee, and in the scene depicted here they take their farewell: "kissing one another they wept together, but David more" (20:41). When Saul learns of Jonathan's complicity in David's escape, he falls into a homophobic rage: "Thou son of a woman that is the ravisher of a man, do I not know that thou lovest the son of Isai to thy own confusion and to the confusion of thy shameless mother?" (20:30). In the end, Saul and Jonathan die together at the hands of the Philistines, leaving David to lament them both, but especially the death of his friend: "I grieve for thee, my brother Jonathan: exceedingly beautiful, and amiable to me above the love of women. As the mother loveth her only son, so did I love thee. / How are the valiant fallen, and the weapons of war perished?" (2 Kings: 1:26–27). The King James translation of this passage is stronger still: "thy love to me was wonderful, passing the love of women."[14] In the picture before us, they embrace fully clothed, in much the same way the Gemini Twins, clothed or naked, take hold of each other to wrestle.[15] From earliest times, Castor and Pollux's mutual love had been as important as their valor in combat.

V.5. Old Testament illustration (detail): David takes leave of Jonathan. Paris, ca. 1250. New York, Pierpont Morgan Library MS M. 638, fol. 32.

All of which leads to an important first conclusion: erotic love—initially, no more than an understated, potential homoeroticism—has functioned as a sort of free radical in the sign of Gemini from the beginning. It can be seen in a French Gospel book from the late tenth century (where the naked Twins, atop a Canon Table, move toward each other with ambiguous intent) as unmistakably as in a zodiacal arch from a thirteenth-century church in the Val di Susa, Italy (where they come to each other fully clothed).[16] In either case, as in many other representations of the Gemini, soon to be brought forward, one cannot tell whether they are wrestling or embracing. But that is my point precisely—an ambiguity that will return us soon to Chaucer's *Merchant's Tale*.

The intrinsic artistic problem then—or the covert opportunity, as it may have seemed to some—had to do with the Twins' nakedness. And that could be dealt with in a number of ways. The simplest was to show them frontally but without genital specification, as in the May page of the Ingebord Psalter,[17] or in acute profile, as in Figure V.3, turning one toward the other just enough to finesse the problem altogether. Or they could cover their sex with their hands, as in a late fourteenth-century manuscript of the *Divine Comedy*, when Dante and Beatrice look up at them in awe in *Paradiso*, Canto XXII. (Dante, born under the sign of Gemini, one of the houses of Mercury, attributed his genius to their influence.)[18] Or the Twins could be shown as sexless children, kissing in innocent play.[19] Figure V.6, from a Book of Hours, Paris, circa 1400, depicts a young man

V.6. May page (detail): a falconer rests his horse; the Gemini as infants (putti), playing in the sun. Paris, ca. 1400. Oxford, Bodley MS Douce 62, fol. 7.

resting his horse in a green meadow as his falcon returns with a bird in its claws. Two naked putti embrace alongside, with the sun (thus in Gemini) blazing away behind.[20] This last tradition was especially unthreatening, since it did not hint at adult sexuality of any kind.

It was, I think, out of a similar concern that Thomas Walsingham, a monk of St. Albans Abbey, in his *De archana deorum* (written in the early fifteenth century) described how the Gemini should be depicted in art. They are to be shown, he wrote, with their arms raised, embracing each other as though they had just reached puberty (*quasi primo pubescentes*), for that relates them to "the time of year when seeds—after their roots have extended downward and are entwined—embrace the earth, and up above mature into plants."[21] Beneath this somewhat strained description a certain anxiety is writ plain. Though Walsingham does not describe the Twins as naked, he seems to have imagined them so, in a pose too intimate to be comfortably affirmed. And so he makes them "innocent" by virtue of their age—on the brink of puberty—and allegorizes their embrace in terms of the natural world's germination and new growth.

The most common solution to this problem, however, was to show the Gemini with arms around each other's shoulders, naked behind a shield that hides their sex—a forthright image projecting their identity as athletic, warlike youths while avoiding sexual display.[22] That choice could guarantee a safe reading, up to a point:[23] any viewer familiar with the Castor and Pollux story would read their embrace as signifying fraternal love. But then, as now, that knowledge could not be generally assumed, and for anyone unfamiliar with it, the modesty shield would have served chiefly to call attention to the nakedness of two men together, in an affectionate embrace untroubled by clothes.[24] A French psalter, for instance, made circa 1260–70, shows the Twins turned halfway toward each other naked (Figure V.7). But in a manner either sweetly innocent or oddly knowing, the one on the left,

V.7. May page (detail): falconer on horse; the Gemini embrace behind a shield. French, perhaps from Beauvais, ca. 1260–70. New York, Pierpont Morgan Library MS 101, fol. 6.

with downcast eyes, seems to be peering at the other's private parts, deftly shielded (pun fully intended) from our view.[25] Figure V.8, from a French Book of Hours in the Pierpont Morgan Library, made circa 1400, is fully as enigmatic. The Morgan's own description of the image reaches no further than this: "Two nude men embrace and cover themselves with a large leaf." Though it is not very helpful, one sympathizes with the author of that entry. What can one possibly make of such an image if one does not know the story of Castor and Pollux? And even if one does, is anything about them really called to mind or served in this way? Though the green leaf they hold between them is not from a fig tree, it serves the same purpose two such leaves once served Adam and Eve, and risks summoning the shame

V.8. May page (detail): falconer; the Gemini embrace between trees, covered by a leaf. French, ca. 1400. New York, Pierpont Morgan Library MS M. 264, fol. 5.

of that other story to mind. Even as wrestlers, the Twins virtually never appear as men competing earnestly and at least partially clothed, the way that sport is depicted elsewhere in medieval art.[26] (One need only think of Chaucer's Miller, big of brawn and bones, who, at wrestling, "always won the ram.") The Twins instead are preferentially youthful, slim, and elegant. They lay hands on each other's shoulders without hostility or aggression, at ease in their physical intimacy and graceful in their play. My halfway point is this: Castor and Pollux, pictured *as the Gemini,* constitute an overlooked vein of homoerotic imagery in medieval art, once valued by some as a covert representation of same-sex desire, even as it troubled others for that very reason.

So far as I know, the tradition has not been studied in this way before, though I do not think doing so is a gratuitous act, imposing a matter of current interest upon an innocent or oblivious iconographic past. The Duc de Berry, for instance, the most important patron of French manuscript illumination in the early years of the fifteenth century, though twice married (the second time, for reasons of state, to the twelve-year-old Jeanne de Boulogne), is known to have been, and was vilified for being, sexually interested in working-class men, first with a hosiery-weaver, later with a road paver, each of whom he maintained as an intimate, at considerable public expense. His heavily taxed subjects strenuously complained. Michael Camille, in a nuanced and well-documented essay, draws upon Jean Froissart's eyewitness accounts of the French court in this period, to suggest, not that the duke was homosexual exactly (gender boundaries were much more fluid then), but that he had more than a connoisseur's interest in representations of human nudity, male as well as female, and that certain images in the books the duke commissioned, particularly in the liberated space of their margins, were designed to appeal to a homoerotic taste. Evidence can even be found in the January "portrait" page from the duke's *Très riches heures* (our Figure IV.10). In the foreground two young men sport purses with golden clasps unmistakably phallic in shape—as well as improbably large and oddly "erect." The purse of the young man at left, moreover, wittily covers his groin. He is serving the duke as wine steward (an allusion, perhaps, to Ganymede), while the other carves before him at table. Though it records a New Year's Day celebration, which might be expected to involve his whole court, the portrait is notably homosocial: there are no women in it.[27]

Several texts too, whether through comment on this issue, or through adroit evasion of it, prove this focus on the Gemini neither gratuitous nor anachronistic. Alain de Lille, for example, in his long allegorical poem *De planctu naturae* (the *Complaint of Nature*; ca. 1160–65), a work Chaucer refers to in his *Parlement of Fowles* (ll. 316–18), imagines "Nature," God's vice-regent on earth, lamenting the degeneration of man and decrying the prevalence of homosexuality in Alain's own time and clerkly milieu. "Venus betrayed" becomes Alain's major theme, though sins other than sodomy will be censured too. In this allegory, Nature, personified as a woman of surpassing beauty, wears a crown of stars in constant motion—the twelve constellations, brighter than all the rest, with the seven planets shining below. Among these stars (seen as "precious stones" in her crown) are the Gemini, who (it becomes clear) must be dissociated from the homosexuality rampant in the world below. To avoid any misunderstanding, Alain describes them chastely as "the shades of Leda's children, showing goodwill in a mutual embrace" (*umbratilis Ledea proles, sibi mutuo amplexu congratulans, incedebat*)![28]

In the *Anticlaudianus*, Alain's other great allegorical poem, Nature the vice-regent sets out to make a perfect man, but since she has no ability to make a soul she must send Prudence to heaven to request one from God. Prudence's journey to that place allows Alain to hymn once again the wonders of the universe, including the glittering zodiac, where, he tells us (in a context no longer focused on sodomy, and therefore less anxiety provoking), "Leda's offspring gleam and do not abandon among the stars the token of love they formerly shared on earth."[29]

The best reason, however, for introducing this topic is that a good number of images of the Gemini carry an unmistakably homoerotic charge. Figure V.9, for instance, from a set of star drawings made in Bayeux, circa 1268–74, shows the pair handsomely clothed, with one twin embracing the other as though in hope of persuading him of something; his lyre lends (or at least intends) a spiritual note.[30] An even earlier star page (mid-twelfth century), now in Vienna, goes further still: there the Twins, also fully clothed, gaze into each other's eyes as one strokes the other's chin—a gesture normally reserved for scenes of heterosexual courtship.[31] A German

V.9. The Gemini (star chart, detail). Bayeux, ca. 1268–74. Oxford, Bodley MS Laud. Misc. 644, fol. 8v.

psalter, from Silesia, Breslau, circa 1260, with Italianate decoration, likewise shows them as long-haired youths, clothed, in tender embrace.[32]

Such images might be said (perhaps were said even then) to reflect the classical ideal of *amicitia*—high-minded, nonsexual friendship between men, transformed in the Middle Ages into a monastic ideal of "spiritual friendship," most eloquently expressed in the writings of Aelred of Rievaulx. But these boys are clearly not young monks in training, nor can one doubt that such ideals did sometimes serve, consciously or unconsciously, as a cover for sexualized emotion. In any case, many such images, early and late, are too fondly sentimental to serve either a classical or a Christian ideal well. The Gemini roundel reproduced as Figure V.10, for instance, offers another example. From the Shaftesbury Psalter, English, circa 1130–40, it shows two young men floating naked in a boat, their heads touching, their arms about each other's shoulders, looking deep into each other's eyes.[33] It is unlikely they are about to wrestle.

The *Grandes heures* of Anne of Brittany, illuminated by Jean Bourdichon in Paris or Tours, circa 1500–1508, comes late in this tradition, but is too interesting to be ignored. Its May page presents the Twins twice (Figure V.11),[34] once as a naked heterosexual couple, painted in dark blue *grisaille*, reclining side by side just below the top border; and then again, on the lower part of the page, as two youths returning from the woods on a May morning, green branches over their shoulders, with one of them leading the other tenderly by the hand. The second "twin" (their features are identical) allows himself to be pulled along, his eyes cast down but simpering with pleasure. A large May pole fills the margin alongside. Whatever else one may think of these boys, they too are in the Castor and Pollux tradition. But instead of suggesting the valor of that myth, they have been absorbed into a traditional occupation of the month, the (potentially erotic) getting of some green.

V.10. The Gemini embrace in a boat (detail). From the Shaftesbury Psalter, English, ca. 1130–40. London, Brit. Lib. MS Lansdowne 383, fol. 5.

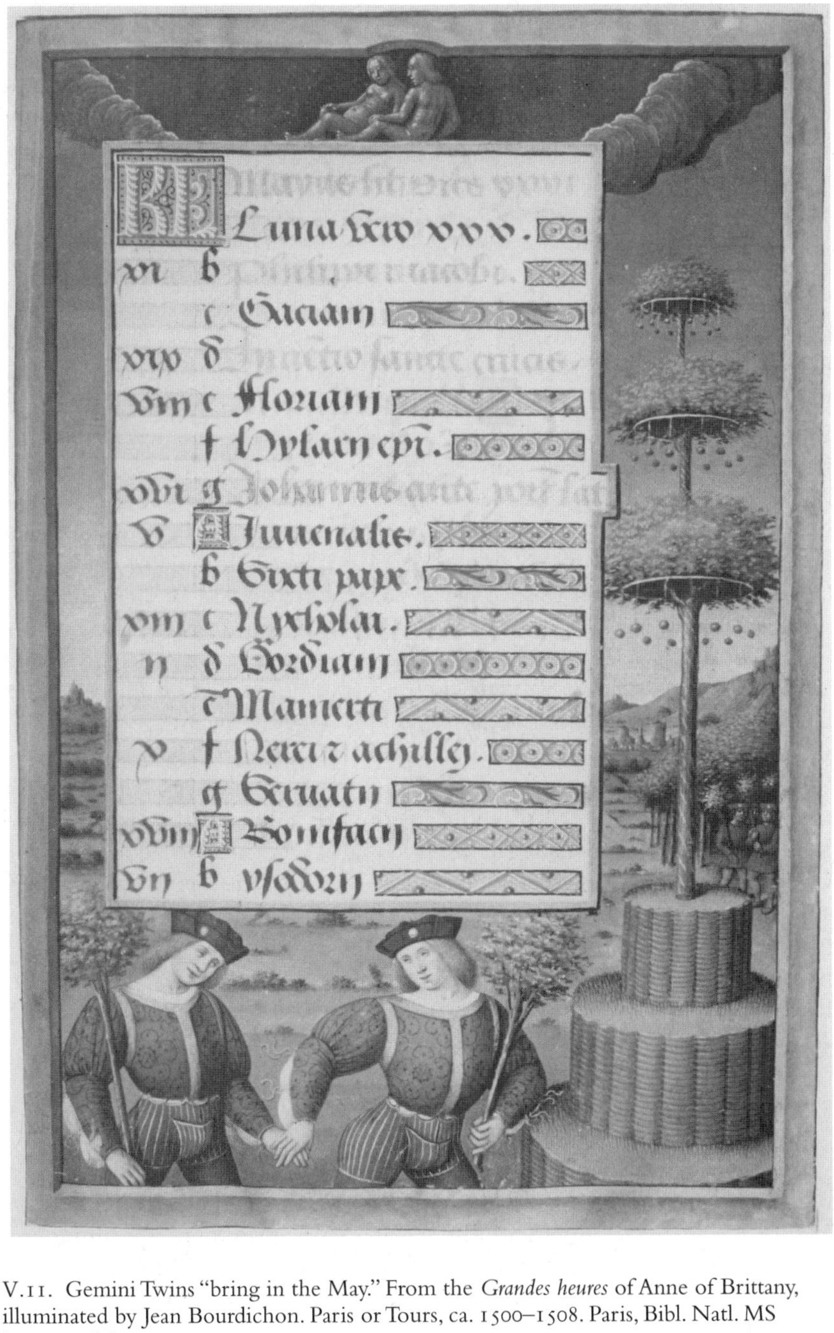

V.11. Gemini Twins "bring in the May." From the *Grandes heures* of Anne of Brittany, illuminated by Jean Bourdichon. Paris or Tours, ca. 1500–1508. Paris, Bibl. Natl. MS lat. 9474, fol. 8.

If the male Gemini (clothed) present at best a sentimental or idealized version of male *amicitia*, the male Gemini (naked), whether in a wrestlers' hold or an embrace behind a modesty shield, imply an intimacy that is physical as well. Medieval art (with examples still to come) offered these versions of the sign almost from the beginning. Though my survey of this tradition will ultimately take us to a very different place, one of its functions from the beginning was to acknowledge, and covertly celebrate, homoerotic love. It continued to do so into the English Renaissance and beyond. In Michael Drayton's ambitious historical poem *Piers Gaveston, Earl of Cornwall: His Life, Death, and Fortune*, written in 1593, Edward II and the upstart courtier Gaveston profess their love in just such terms throughout. Gaveston, for instance, thinking back on his youthful beauty and charm, declares fondly, "With this fayre bayte I fishd for Edwards love," and in mythological mode, not only salutes the king as Jove and names himself as Ganymede, but compares the "imbraces when our sporte begins" to those of "Ledas lovely Twins." Even at the king's nuptials to Isabel of France, the poem sees "These Swan-begotten twins" as "presaging joy" in their embrace of each other; though Isabel may be queen, thinks Gaveston, "yet I alone [am] his love."[35] The murder of the king was caused in part by the scandal of their affair.

Chaucer may have intended a decorous variation on this theme at the beginning of *The Knight's Tale*, when his heroic young knights, Palamon and Arcite, are found nearly dead among a heap of bodies left by Theseus after his assault on Thebes: "Two yonge knyghtes liggynge by and by, / Bothe in oon armes, wroght ful richely" (I 1011–12).

Recognized by heralds as being of the "blood roial / Of Thebes, and of sustren two yborn," the cousins are not only so alike as to be almost indistinguishable, they have made themselves sworn "brothers," pledged to serve each other's interests until they die (I 1129–51). Like the Gemini Twins, they are defined by a homosocial relationship which they value as their highest good—until the moment they see Emily from their prison tower and are instantly disunited, "twins" no longer.[36] Desire for a woman, seen performing the rites of May, marks the beginning of their sexual maturation, with all the suffering and violence that will bring in its train.[37]

THE GEMINI AS MALE AND FEMALE

All very interesting, no doubt. But what, even my most patient reader might ask, has any of this to do with *The Merchant's Tale*? In no way do January and Damian present themselves as "twins," and there is nothing homoerotic in the tale's action or ethos. The short answer is this: the Gemini Twins that *will* prove relevant developed out of the tradition we have been examining, and cannot be fully understood without it. The cultural anxiety we have found there—a discomfort with images combining male nudity with male-to-male affection—could be resolved in a much more decisive way. The Twins could be made heterosexual.

This solution, broader in its scope than any discussed so far, was happily free of any possible homoerotic subtext. Figure V.12, from the Psalter and Prayer Book of Bonne of Luxembourg, painted by Jean Pucelle, before 1349, showing a man and woman embracing naked behind a shield, can fairly introduce this other tradition and return us to Chaucer's tale.[38]

This other major way of imagining the Gemini was enabled, if not necessarily caused, by the gendered ambiguity with which medieval artists often represented the naked body. On a good number of calendar pages

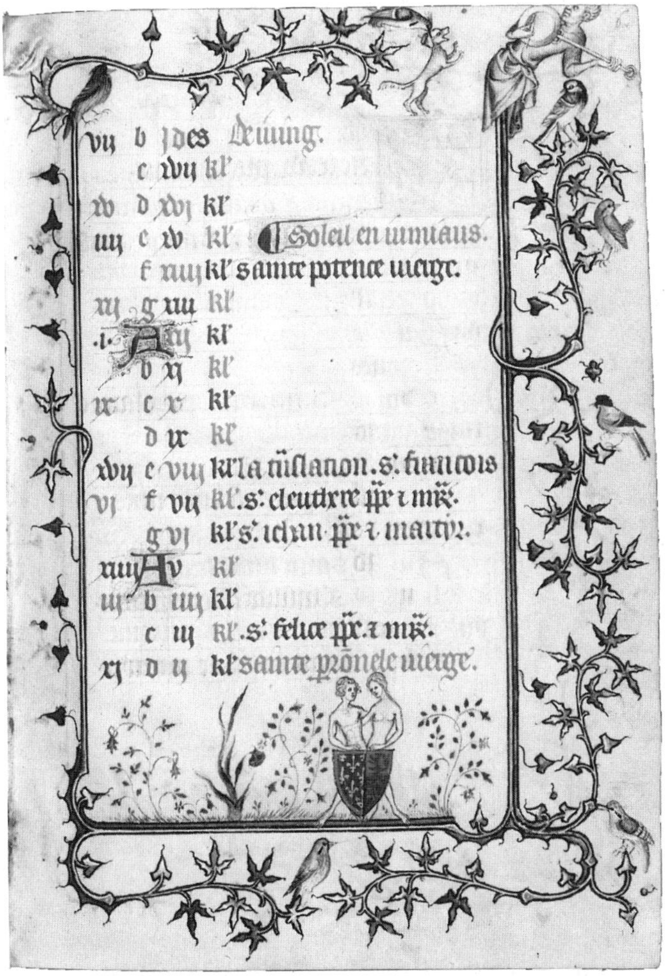

V.12. The Gemini as lovers, man and woman, between flowering trees, behind a shield. The Psalter and Hours of Bonne of Luxembourg, Paris, before 1349. New York, The Metropolitan Museum of Art, Cloisters Collection, 1969 (69.86), fol. 6.

(especially the earlier ones) the sex of the Twins is difficult to ascertain, even when they are shown naked from the waist up. With the woman's breasts little emphasized or wholly ignored, and with bodies otherwise identical, hairstyle alone marks the difference: the woman will usually have longer hair. I suggested earlier that not every medieval viewer (nor, indeed, every medieval artist) would have known that the Gemini had originally been male. To this I can now add: even among those familiar with the myth of the Dioscuri, not everyone would have thought it important they be depicted so. Other purposes might be served—purposes that will figure significantly in the rest of this chapter.

The sexual identity of the Twins pictured in Figure V.13, from a psalter made in Liège, circa 1280, is finally not ambiguous, but the picture will serve to make my larger point. The Twins' hairstyles are the same (so no help there); their bodies are equally strong; their over-the-shoulder embrace is forthright and "fraternal"; they stand behind a heraldic shield. We ultimately read them as male-and-female because their heads are turned to kiss, and because breasts can be discovered on the twin on the right. Yet the power of this image, so stylized and heroic, remains curiously asexual; it's as though the sign's origins in male-on-male affection still guided the artist's hand. Half a century later, reflecting a more finely nuanced interest in emotion, the May page of the Hours of Jeanne d'Evreux, Queen of France, illuminated by Jean Pucelle, circa 1325 (not reproduced here), imagined the Gemini as a handsome young man and woman, naked, looking at each other with a tender regard—their gender unmistakable despite a shield that covers them from their loins down.[39] In that, they are like the couple behind a shield already examined (Figure V.12), also by Jean Pucelle, and like those in another French manuscript, the Wharncliffe Hours, painted in Paris by Maître François, circa 1475–80.[40] In such pictures the high breasts and gently swelling belly of the woman declare her sex unmistakably. Countless Gemini couples are painted in this tradition.

The heterosexual Twins in the Hours of Jeanne d'Evreux, described above, are stationed opposite the page depicting falconry and "bringing home the green" examined in my previous chapter (Figure IV.15)—a juxtaposition of zodiac sign and occupation commonplace in the calendar tradition. The only further innovation needed to create a tradition ultimately resonant with *The Merchant's Tale* was to combine the two into a single picture celebrating the fertility and fecundity of May.[41] The greenery that figures so prominently in many versions of the "occupation of the month" could be carried over—"over the shoulder," even—into the world of the zodiac sign. A calendar page from the Hours of Isabella Stuart (probably from Angers, circa 1431), though it preserves the Twins as male wrestlers, shows how easy and natural such an invention might be (Figure V.14). The man "bringing home the green" in the picture above could as easily (artistically speaking) bring it into the sign of the naked Gemini below.[42] Change the gender of the Twins, and a new pictorial tradition is born.

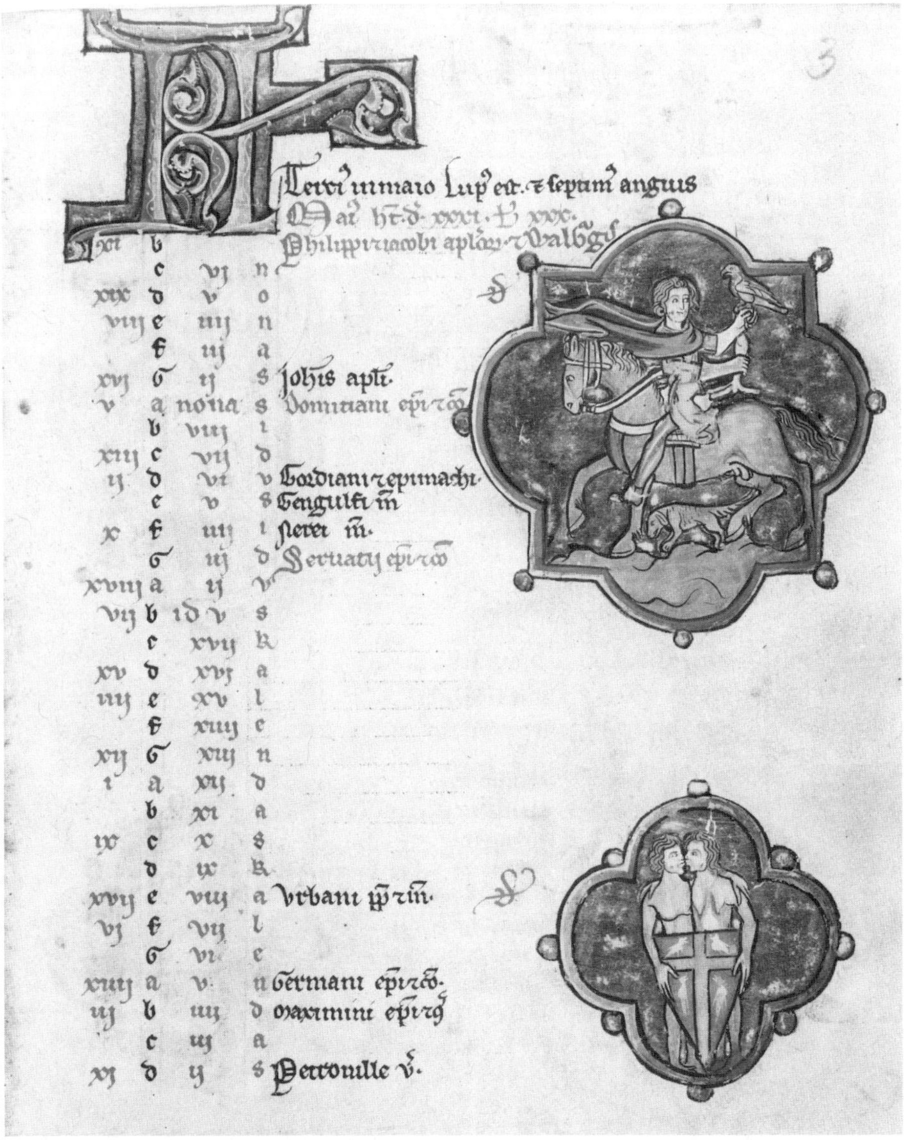

V.13. May page (detail): the Twins as lovers behind a shield. Liège, ca. 1280. Oxford, Bodley MS Add. 46, fol. 3.

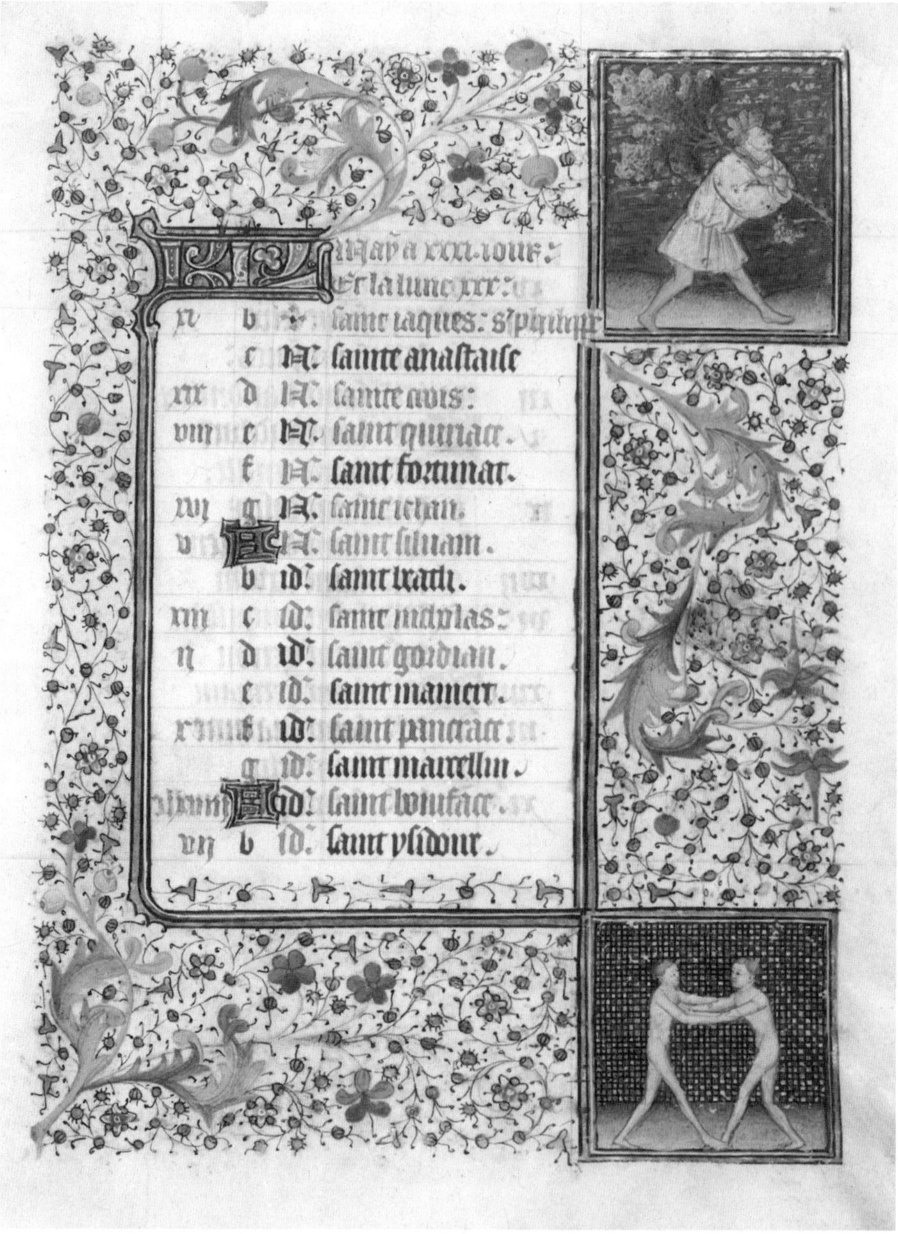

V.14. May page: bringing home the green; the Twins as wrestlers. Hours of Isabella Stuart, from the studio of the Rohan Masters, Angers? ca. 1431. Cambridge, Fitzwilliam Museum MS 62, fol. 5a.

Images of this sort occupy a place certifiably rare within medieval art—an exception, so to speak, to "Panofsky's rule," meaning they owe almost nothing to written texts. Bringing the heroic nakedness of Castor and Pollux into conjunction with the regreening and replenishing of the world at springtime is the invention of artists and their directors working within traditions unique to the visual arts. They found in this combination a new rationale for the nakedness of the Twins and support for a change in their gender, allowing them to serve a theme less marginalized than the fraternal, homosocial love in which the sign had its beginning. Preserving from the Castor and Pollux tradition a welcome pretext for something rare and undeniably provocative (idealized images of beautiful young people, same-sex or heterosexual), it redirected the power of those pictures toward something more safely normative—heterosexual coupling—and used that "adjusted" image, what is more, to express certain cultural meanings and private emotions widely associated with the month of May. This new tradition, first appearing in the early to mid-thirteenth century, gained wide currency in fourteenth-century calendar illumination, and, as we shall see, became especially frank and daring at the far end of the Middle Ages.

Like the homoerotic anxiety it circumvented, the heterosexual tradition has an early history of its own—with examples admittedly few, but interacting with the other here and there. A psalter from Augsburg, Germany, for example, made sometime between 1235 and 1250 and adopted to Cistercian use for a convent of nuns in Constance, shows the Gemini as a couple handsomely dressed (she in a long gown), embracing in a formal sort of way.[43] In this chaste image, acceptable to a house of pious nuns, the Twins seem fully mature and possibly even married. A number of images of this sort span the medieval centuries.

But there can be no doubt: younger people suit the mood and meaning of the season better, and (daring though it be) naked young people suit it best of all. Works like the zodiac cycle carved in stone on the west facade of Amiens cathedral (1225–35) honor the first, at the highest level of early Gothic art, by showing the lovers between trees, tenderly holding hands and gazing into each other's eyes, with only a longer gown identifying one of them as a woman.[44]

But the heterosexual Twins would not stay clothed for long. Naked bodies possessed a greater interest and a broader range of signification—if an artist could find an excuse to use them. Whether a naked version of the heterosexual Gemini would have come into being without Castor and Pollux as naked wrestlers showing the way will forever remain a moot question. Certainly, the "occupation" of the month could authorize images of courtship and marriage on its own, but for heterosexual nakedness and coition—images still to come—one needs, I suspect, the Gemini wrestlers nude. Iconographically speaking, the Dioscuri offered nakedness, love, and physical intimacy, even before the gender change.

And so it comes as no surprise that the heterosexual Twins shed their clothes too, and as the centuries go by, enter more deeply into the surrounding woods, or draw the fresh greenery of that world into their own iconographic space, sometimes to screen from view their private parts, but often with no concern for that at all. Why should they be concerned? From earliest times the constellation Gemini, governing the month of May, had been seen as a site of cosmic regeneration and renewal—a site powered, in Dylan Thomas's lovely phrase, by "the force that through the green fuse drives the flower." Human belief in the influence of the stars is far more ancient than even the myth of Castor and Pollux, to say nothing of their heterosexual cousins in medieval calendar art.

Two early examples will serve to make this point. A Gradual commissioned (and possibly painted) by Henry the Sacristan of Weingarten Abbey around 1225–50 represents the occupation of the month (not shown here) as a young man holding up stylized flowers (more often a sign for April), while the Twins below (Figure V.15), against a background of burnished silver, tenderly embrace between two stylized green trees. They come together naked, without shame or inhibition, at one with the natural world. Though their bodies are not differentiated, the male has shorter hair and lays his hand on his partner's cheek. In this early style, that alone will suffice. Figure V.16, from a French psalter made circa 1260, in England since the late thirteenth century,[45] shows the Twins embracing between two extremely stylized green trees—forms so rude and abstract as to convey the principle of growth itself. An equally primitive green tree shares space with the falconer depicted above (not reproduced here). Though these Twins too differ chiefly in the length of their hair, their nakedness is important to the mean-

V.15. May page (detail): the Twins as lovers between trees. German, ca. 1225–50. New York, Pierpont Morgan Library MS M. 711, fol. 4.

V.16. May page (detail): the Twins as lovers between trees. French, ca. 1260. Cambridge, Trinity College MS B. 11.5, fol. 8. By kind permission of the Master and Fellows.

ing of the picture, situating them in a natural world engaged in renewal and regeneration. I call attention to the symbolic power of these simplified thirteenth-century forms because, in the fourteenth and fifteenth centuries (especially the early sixteenth century), the heterosexual Gemini move into a world far more realistic and verisimilar, but which nevertheless grows out of this one, its thematic and iconographic predecessor.

In Queen Mary's Psalter, a richly illustrated manuscript from early fourteenth-century England (Figure V.17), a naked man and woman (he bearded, and not notably young) stand between two green trees and join hands behind a modesty shield. A third tree, whose green branches shelter them from above, rises from the place where their arms meet. The outer trees are inhabited by two finely observed birds (the male spreading his wings in a courtship display) paired with a lion and a lioness dormant on the ground below (the male looking intently at the female as she looks demurely away).[46] The world celebrated in this picture is not only green and good, it is obviously energized by desire and sustained by generation.

The migration of the Gemini into a world more lushly regreened was not in fact contingent upon (or restricted to) the Twins' becoming heterosexual. A same-sex example from a Paris Breviary, circa 1350, illuminated in the style of Jean Pucelle (Figure V.18), hides the sex of the Twins behind a green-leafed bush or tree. Identical haircuts identify them both as men. In this image, one of several such from the same workshop, a small tree or shrub has replaced the modesty shield as a screen. But one sees in it already, awaiting only a gender change, the potential for something more.[47] Figure V.19, from Normandy in the early sixteenth century, makes good on

V.17. May page (detail): the Gemini behind a shield, with trees and courting birds and courting lions. English, *Queen Mary's Psalter*, early fourteenth century. London, Brit. Lib. MS Royal 2 B. vii, fol. 76. © The British Library. All Rights Reserved.

V.18. May page (detail): a falconer; male Gemini, naked behind a tree. Paris, from a Breviary illuminated in the style of Jean Pucelle, ca. 1350. New York, Pierpont Morgan Library MS M. 75, fol. 3.

V.19. May page (detail): a couple ride out; the Gemini naked in trees. Normandy, early sixteenth century. Oxford, Bodley MS Douce 72, fol. 3.

that promise, showing the heterosexual twins, genitally specific, embracing in the midst of trees. Other versions, such as Figure V.20, a little less bold, show the Twins turned toward each other naked and half hidden among green leaves. Here, heterosexual coupling is to be presumed, though no breasts are shown and the hairstyles are identical. (The somewhat mysterious figure below, crowned and carrying a staff, is either a ceremonial "King of the May," or a symbolic figure reflecting the fact May was sometimes called the "king of the months.")[48] Still other pictures, like Figure V.21, also from about 1500–1510, show the Gemini naked among trees in a tender, full-bodied embrace.

V.20. May page: a King of the May (?); the Gemini in trees. French, early sixteenth century. Cambridge, Fitzwilliam Museum MS. 128, fol. 3.

V.21. May page (detail): a falconer; the Gemini in trees. French, ca. 1500–1510. Cambridge, Fitzwilliam Museum MS 132, p. 5.

In all three of these pictures, and on other calendar pages too,[49] greenery from the occupation of the month has crossed over into the zodiac space, encompassing the Twins, contextualizing their desire, and (sometimes) conferring a degree of modesty upon their sexual embrace. All of them, we should note, even those most genitally explicit, intimate an unusual tenderness between the two lovers, along with an absence of self-consciousness or shame. Their nakedness, these pictures tell us, like their desire for each other, needs no excuse; it is in harmony with the month, the stars, and all that is bursting forth fresh and green around them.

Sometimes this late tradition calls to mind Castor and Pollux, where the Gemini's nakedness began, even as it embraces their change in gender. Look again, please, at images of the male Gemini in wrestling pose reproduced earlier in this chapter (Figures V.2, V.3, V.4, V.14) and compare them with Figure V.22, from a Book of Hours made in Paris between 1430 and 1435,[50] which repeats the pose but makes one of the wrestlers a woman. Here, however, they prepare for a sexual encounter—she somewhat shyly—on a green field furnished with three flourishing green trees, set against an abstract background of patterned red and gold. These trees do not stand-in for a painterly "landscape"; they are an essential part of the sign.

The tenderness with which these Twins customarily couple (I could adduce many, many more examples) is the more striking because (in one final, rather unexpected development of the tradition) they surpass even our youthful male wrestlers in urgency and determination. Figure V.23, from a French Book of Hours, use of Rome, circa 1510, offers a powerful image of mutual desire, with partners well matched in strength and equally eager to engage. French verses at the bottom of the page observe that in May "tout est en vigeur" and man is "en valeur," with everything manifesting "sa force and beaulte de nature." Figure V.24 likewise shows the Twins as erotic combatants—a man and a woman coming to grips in a wooded green landscape they share with the occupation of the month (the young man and woman on a horse pictured alongside).[51]

Some pages ago, concerning certain images of Castor and Pollux, I put the question: are they wrestlers or lovers? In the heterosexual tradition the answer is never in doubt. But in fact these latter-day Twins are stronger, more athletic, and more determined than their classical ancestors, outdoing Castor and Pollux in the energy and vigor of the wrestling pose that they unmistakably reprise. In this late (and rather surprising) development, the athletic strength and fraternal love of the Spartan twins—homosocial at least, and latently homoerotic—has infiltrated a more broadly based iconography of male-female desire and coition, all as a way of expressing the power of the sun in Gemini.

Unlike the tenderness shown each other by the heterosexual couples previously encountered, there is something almost compulsive and nonvolitional about the way these latest heterosexual couples mate amid trees. Whereas the medieval "getting of some green" gave birth to graceful scenes of ritualized courtship—the influence of the stars translated into polite pastimes and occupations—these erotic Gemini rush toward each other ready and eager, untrammeled by sexual modesty or decorum. They have necessary work to do. Such imagery boldly deconstructs two (logically incompatible)

V.22. May page (detail): the Gemini as erotic wrestlers. Paris, illuminated by the Bedford Master and his workshop, between 1430 and 1435. New York, Pierpont Morgan Library MS M. 359, fol. 5v.

V.23. May page: the Gemini as erotic wrestlers. Paris (use of Rome), ca. 1510. Cambridge, Fitzwilliam Museum MS 123, fol. 3.

V.24. May page: a couple ride out; erotic wrestling; music and courtship in the green wood. French (use of Rome), second quarter of the sixteenth century. Oxford, Bodley MS Douce 135, fol. 4.

medieval assumptions about women: that they are by nature modest and submissive to men; and its misogynist contrary, that they are emotionally aggressive and sexually insatiable. In these early sixteenth-century pictures the two sexes, like the male wrestlers they replace, approach each other equal in strength, dignity, and determination. Though Castor and Pollux derive their character from a classical myth, in medieval terms they exercise their influence (their real power) as stars—leaving the heterosexual Twins who replace them in calendar art to *enact* that influence as it manifests itself in the world below, making its means visible, even as other purposes, not all of them high-minded, are acknowledged and served.

In *The Merchant's Tale*, for these reasons and more, May's desire for Damian proves as compulsive, urgent, and without moral scruple as his desire for her. No "courtly" romance is needed: a furtive note and a squeeze of the hand will begin it; a time, a place, and an ingenious strategem will see it through. For Chaucer, as for many a manuscript painter from the thirteenth century on, the sun in Gemini enabled certain kinds of events. It was thought of as a sexually empowering, procreative sign.

It is in this calendar tradition then, which first showed the Twins *between* trees and later surrounded or masked by them, that Chaucer sends his two young people up a tree to make love. With the sun "in Geminis, as I gesse," Damian sits merrily on high "among the fresshe leves grene" (IV 2327), to await the coming of May. And it is in that place that January first sees them making love. After Pluto, the King of Fayerye, has restored his sight, the old man casts " his eyen two" up the tree

And saugh that Damyan his wyf had dressed (IV 2361)
In swich manere it may nat been expressed,
But if I wolde speke uncurteisly;
And up he yaf a roryng and a cry.

. . .

"O stronge lady stoore, what dostow?"

As the Caxton-related woodcut in Chapter IV bore witness (Figure IV.1), this is the primary, indelible image of the poem—the image most likely to remain in the mind of any reader. But Queen Proserpina, not to be outmatched in a marital squabble, has given May (and for her sake, all women after) the ability to justify and get away with anything they choose to do: "For lak of answere noon of hem shal dyen" (IV 2271). Thus enabled, May offers January this account of what he has seen:

And she answerde, "Sire, what eyleth yow? (IV 2368)
Have pacience and resoun in youre mynde.
I have yow holpe on bothe youre eyen blynde.
Up peril of my soule, I shal nat lyen,
As me was taught, to heele with youre eyen,
Was no thing bet, to make yow to see,
Than strugle with a man upon a tree.

God woot, I dide it in ful good entente."
"Strugle?" quod he, 'Ye, algate in it wente!
God yeve yow bothe on shames deth to dyen!
He swyved thee; I saugh it with myne yen,
And elles be I hanged by the hals!"

To restore his sight, she tells him, she was told to "strugle" with a man in a tree—a word that makes good sense in modern English as it stands. But in the fourteenth century it also meant "to wrestle" (Chaucer uses it in this sense elsewhere),[52] a pun made particularly welcome here because it brings to mind images of the Twins as wrestlers, same-sex or heterosexual, featured on calendar pages for May.[53]

In summary then: though the calendar pages that show erotic couples naked *in trees* were made long after Chaucer's death (at the end of the fifteenth century and the beginning of the sixteenth), they do little more than bring together, in a more fully realistic, late-medieval style, a set of iconographic details already ascribed to the Dioscuri (and through them, the Gemini) in the thirteenth century (Figures V.2, V.15, V.16), details that would become even more familiar in the century that followed. I am thinking of nakedness, for one; wrestling for another; a seasonal interest in green branches and trees for a third; and (most important of all) a gender change that could turn the Twins' traditional masculine embrace into something not only erotic but often explicitly sexual. Chaucer and his first audiences could have known these traditions together or in various combinations, so commonplace were Books of Hours among the privileged classes of his time. Like a late-medieval painter admitting explicitly erotic imagery into a traditional calendar page for May, Chaucer found a way of turning the fabliau trick furnished him by his source into a grandly telling narrative image, responsive to both the month and the zodiac sign, and ending quite logically with cuckoldry in a tree. By setting his version of the pear-tree tale "under the sign of Gemini," he made wit and something like natural philosophy out of a denouement too indecent, his Merchant-teller proclaims, for a man as courteous as himself to describe plainly (IV 2362–63). But of course he has already done that, mincing no words: "Strugle?" January cries out in disbelief: "Ye, algate in it wente!" "He swyved thee!" (IV 2376 and 2378). Only when January consents to see the coupling as therapeutic wrestling, undertaken for his own good, can he reclaim in his marriage the fool's paradise he so carefully created—and even, perhaps, gain something more.

JANUARY'S EMBRACE OF THE TREE

In Caxton's version of the fable, entitled "of a blynd man and of his wyf," the wife's explanation reaches no further than this: the goddess Venus, she says, told her "that yf I wold doo somme playsyr [give some pleasure] to the sayd yonge man / she shold restore to the thy syght." As in every other analogue to Chaucer's tale, the wife is not named May, the husband is not named January, and no ingenious pun on wrestling explains the coupling in a tree. But let us revisit the woodcut Caxton had copied for this fable (Figure IV.1 in the preceding chapter) for the attention it pays to yet another subject that Caxton and Chaucer share: the husband, old and blind, clinging tightly to a tree. Nothing surveyed so far has prepared us for such a figure.

Since tree hugging is necessary if May is to get up the tree, perhaps nothing more needs to be said. To reach what she wants, she has to climb up January's back. But Caxton's woodcut shows the trunk of the tree growing, as it were, from the old man's loins—and as a graphic artist's interpretation of the pear-tree tale's conclusion, that is surely of interest. I see in that prolonged and peculiar embrace a reflection of certain May Day customs whose origins are unknown but are certainly ancient. The upper border of the May page from the Getty Museum's Spinola Hours (Figure V.25, and V.25a, a detail), made in Flanders (possibly in Ghent) circa 1510–20, some thirty years after Caxton's book, offers a late but suggestive visual parallel. Painted *en camaïeu* in a rich brown highlighted in gold, it shows a procession of men and women, young and old, "bringing in the green" to a man who sits on the ground holding a large branch or tree upright between his legs. The men in the procession bear branches on their shoulders, as if to do him honor, and he is backed by a court of village dignitaries who look solemnly on. At the center of the procession a crowned queen moves toward him, attended by a young girl who holds up the train of her gown. Though the man himself is not crowned, this ceremony clearly has something in common with ancient folk customs honoring a King and Queen of the May.[54] And, however hard it may be to document now, the tree or branch between his legs just as surely has something to do with nature's renewed fertility in spring, ending the dearth of winter. The manuscript is very late—Flemish, circa 1515—but I think Chaucer would have understood the figure of a man with a tree rising between his legs in something like the way I have suggested here—and not just because it can gloss so entertainingly the ending to his *Merchant's Tale*. (The Breviary of Eleanor of Portugal, made in Bruges, circa 1500–1510, now in the Pierpont Morgan Library, shows a virtually identical scene at the top of a virtually identical page.)

A further reason is this. From the mid-twelfth century the Church chose to visualize the genealogy of Christ in the form of a great tree rising from the loins of an aged man, with the kings of Judah and the prophets of Christ dispersed among its branches, and with the Virgin and Christ child at its top. This image was based on the chief biblical verse used to establish the kingship of Christ: "And there shall come forth a rod [*virga*] out of the root of Jesse: and a flower shall rise up out of his root" (*et egredietur virga de radice Iesse et flos de radice eius ascendet*) (Isa. 11:1). Though Jesse was an Old Testament elder of some standing, he is chiefly remembered as the father of David, first king of the royal house into which Christ would be born. Hence his place in the genealogy that opens the Gospel of Matthew: "And Jesse begot David the king" (Matt. 1:6). And hence the importance of the kings and

V.25. May page: a May Day procession, bringing in the green. Spinola Book of Hours, Flanders, ca. 1510–20. Los Angeles, J. Paul Getty Museum MS Ludwig IX 18, fol. 3v.

V.25A. May page (detail of Figure v.25): a May Day procession, bringing in the green.

prophets, representing Christ's dual lineage, shown seated on the branches of the tree. The best seats—those attached to the trunk itself—were reserved for David, then for Mary with her child, and sometimes, higher still, for the mature figure of Christ. Jesse himself is customarily shown asleep at the bottom of the great tree—a tree whose trunk, in the earliest representations, grows directly from his groin.[55] A magnificent stained glass window, thought to be the first to express this prophecy in visual terms, was made for the cathedral church at St.-Denis in 1144, probably under the direction of Abbot Suger himself. Its design, which would persist for several centuries, was copied at Chartres shortly after its making, and can be seen there still, perfectly preserved. (The window at St.-Denis was damaged during the French Revolution.)[56]

Soon Jesse's tree could be seen in glass in other great churches—York Cathedral, for example—and in the greatest Bibles and psalters of the day, most often in the initial *B* (*Beatus vir*) that begins the psalms of David. Figure V.26, from the Winchester Psalter, made sometime before 1161, offers an early English example, originally placed not in the Old Testament cycle of illustrations where it is presently bound, but at the beginning of the New Testament, where it properly belongs, summing up the ancestry of Christ. Though the bottom of this particular page has darkened over the years, a close look will reveal the "tree" rising majestically from Jesse's loins.[57]

Figure V.27, graceful and leafy in the Gothic manner, comes from the Tickill Psalter, a manuscript written in Nottinghamshire, circa 1303–14, but illuminated elsewhere, possibly by a court artist at York. In this design the stout trunk of Jesse's tree, rising up between his legs, is colored a vivid green.[58] (It is green as well in a French Bible from the last quarter of the twelfth century, referenced below,[59] and no doubt in many other manuscript versions, most of them known to me only in black-and-white.) Though the kings and prophets in the outer branches of the tree often vary, or more often still, defy exact identification, the major persons born of Jesse's loins are unmistakable: in the Tickill example one sees King David lowest on the tree's trunk, playing his harp; the Virgin with child directly above; and Christ in majesty reigning over all, with the Holy Ghost as a dove at his head.

In the Christian understanding of Isaiah's prophecy, the Virgin Mary is the *virga* (rod or branch) that will grow from Jesse's root and will bear the Christ child as flower. (Latin *radix* does not yield "tree" directly.) This rests on a Latin pun: *virga* (meaning branch) and *virgo* (meaning virgin).[60] But those who invented the new iconography knew that *virga* could also mean "rod" in the sense of *membrum virile*, and welcomed this other meaning into their art. Since Jesse's prophecy concerned patrimony and generation, they located his "tree" (or "root," or "rod")exactly where it belonged: somewhere in the region of his loins. "With childlike candor," wrote Emile Mâle a long time ago, "they interpreted the prophet's words literally." That candor was warmly and widely received. According to Mâle, "Of all the prophecies, there is really only one of any lasting inspiration to art, and that is Isaiah's prophecy of

V.26. The tree of Jesse. English, from the Winchester Psalter, before 1161. London, Brit. Lib. MS Cotton Nero C. iv, fol. 9. © The British Library. All Rights Reserved.

V.27. The tree of Jesse. The Tickill Psalter, English, ca. 1303–14. New York, New York Public Library, Spencer Collection MS 26, fol. 5v.

the Tree of Jesse."[61] Because it shares several persons and prophecies with the Prophets' Plays of medieval drama, in both Latin and the vernaculars, it may have played an early role in the history of religious drama as well.[62]

The Church, it comes as no surprise, would ultimately prefer a version of Christ's ancestry less sexually insistent. Though the early tradition remained visible throughout the Middle Ages to any parishioner in these great stained glass windows, and to many clergy at least in illustrations to early liturgical books, a version less starkly rooted in the patriarchal loins became increasingly popular. A tree growing *just behind* Jesse's recumbent form could display Christ's human lineage equally well without calling undue attention to the physical source of its generation.[63] The Hours of Catherine of Cleves (Utrecht, ca. 1440) offered yet another solution (not reproduced here): its Jesse, asleep on a straw pallet, has a large and leafy tree growing from his breast, whose trunk he supports with his hand. Scattered among its branches are portrait busts of kings and prophets, looking very much like prosperous contemporary burghers, and at its top sits the Virgin Mary, robed in white and blue, with a book open in her lap and a gold halo about her head.[64] David plays his harp alongside and gazes on her with prophetic devotion. Because this picture introduces the Saturday Hours of the Virgin, Jesse's tree flowers sufficiently in her. Christ is not shown, neither as child nor as man.

Chaucer's January, of course, does not lie recumbent at the foot of a tree, nor does he experience his startling "vision" asleep. But he does enter the scene as a blind man, and whether one imagines him remaining on his knees after May has climbed his back, holding fast to the tree so that no one can follow her, a detail specified by Chaucer, or on his haunches with the tree between his legs, as in the Caxton woodcut, the narrative image—an old man embracing a tree, with a young couple making love in its branches—manages to imply both futility and fertility, pathos and possible procreation. May, speaking as though she were pregnant ("a woman in my condition has strange appetites") begs her aged husband, "for Goddes sake," to take the pear tree "inwith youre armes" (IV 2330–42), and he, thinking fondly on a possible heir, never questions her sudden but "strange" desire for green fruit. We, of course, have no way of knowing whether May is with child or not. Certainly January has labored mightily in bed to make it happen. But we do hear her warn him that he is likely to see this sort of thing again from time to time—until his sight is perfectly restored. Whatever May's "condition" before she mounts the tree, the likelihood she will one day produce an heir grows ever greater.

So January exits the story a happy man—"this Januarie, who is glad but he?" (IV 2412)—consenting to disavow what he did in fact see, trusting again in his wife's fidelity, and (as his final, husbandly gesture suggests) confident of a baby in her belly:

> He kisseth hire and clippeth hire ful ofte, (IV 2413)
> And on hire wombe he stroketh hire ful softe,
> And to his palays hoom he hath hire lad.

THE GEMINI AS HEALERS

But what of young Damian, cast (by this analysis) in the role of an earthly (certainly, not heavenly) Twin? Whereas May comes to that role by virtue of her zodiacal sign, Damian remains an interloper in the seasonal myth, unless his name provides a clue to something not yet examined. In a tale featuring January and May, Placebo and Justinus, Pluto and Proserpina, his name alone lacks symbolic resonance, possibly because it is the only one (apart from May, originally the name of a month) remotely plausible in real life. But first, some observations regarding his class and station.

The narrator will ultimately denounce Damian as being no better than a "servant traytour, false hoomly hewe" (IV 1785)—harsh, demeaning words, though only Damian's illicit desire for May supports that description. But he is not in fact some lowly servant, as these words might suggest. He is instead a squire—a position of honor and trust—whose duties include serving January at table (IV 1775). Chaucer's Canterbury pilgrim Squire, himself "as fressh as is the month of May," "carves" for the Knight his father in similar fashion (*CT*, I 92).[65] On learning that Damian is sick, January with real concern sends off his new bride to comfort him—"Dooth hym disport—he is a gentil man" (IV 1924)—and promises to visit Damian himself, after he has rested a little. May, in contrast, is of "small degree" (IV 1625), a maiden significantly lower in station than Damian, remembered to January as "Thyn owene squier and thy borne man" (IV 1790).

But Damian's role in the subtext of the tale grows clear only when Chaucer, in an unexpected move, asks us to think of him as a "healer" as well. That transformation hints at the true origin of his name, unique to Chaucer's telling.

The first step toward this revision of Damian's role gives little away. Ancient Pluto, "kyng of Fayerye," making common cause with January, first complains, "By cause, allas, that he is blynd and old, / His owene man shal make hym cokewold!" (IV 2255–56), and then, pointing to Damian, contemptuously declares, "Lo, where he sit, the lechour, in the tree!" (IV 2257).

Lechour in the sense that Pluto uses it here—naming someone given over to lust or inordinate sexual desire—entered Middle English from Old French, and was normally spelled in the French way (as it is above). But as others have noted before me,[66] Middle English *lecher*, a word sounding much alike but meaning "healer," is almost certainly implicated too. It comes, in contrast, from an Old English verb (*lacnian*: to heal), and was supported by the parallel folk etymology that gave us "leechcraft" for the early practice of medicine, when leeches were commonly used to let blood. Chaucer had used the word in this way in his translation of Boethius, where God is praised as a "leche" who knows the health or illness of our souls; God is therefore seen to be the "governour and lechere of thoughtes," preserving the good and driving away the evil (bk. IV, pr. 6: 209–15). This obviously is not the kind of "lechour" Pluto describes as waiting in the tree, but it *is* one of the meanings Chaucer will play with in this tale. (Langland makes a similar pun near the end of *Piers Plowman*.)[67]

This second sense comes into play when May tells her husband that what he saw in the tree was meant to "heal" his blindness:

> As me was taught, to heele with youre eyen, (IV 2372)
> Was no thyng bet, to make yow to see,
> Than strugle with a man upon a tree.

When January names the deed as lechery—"he swyved thee; I saugh it with myne yen"—she insists on a leech-craft interpretation: "'Thanne is,' quod she, 'my medicyne fals / Ye han som glymsyng, and no parfit sighte'" (IV 2380). But her "medicine" has in fact worked very well. May and Damian, the earthly Twins influenced by their heavenly counterparts, have accomplished a good deal of "healing." Damian, sick with desire, has been made well; May's need for "small, green pears" has been satisfied; and January has been cured—not only of his literal blindness, thanks to Pluto, but of his fleeting glimpse of the truth—the truth about his marriage—thanks to Proserpina and May. His urgent need for an heir may have been remedied too. The only cost is to January himself, who finally doesn't much care. He exits the tale agreeing to see whatever May tells him he sees.

Chaucer's witty equation of lechery with leech-craft manifests itself in yet another way. As Philip Griffith noted long ago,[68] Damian is named after one of the patron saints of physicians, himself (significantly) a twin. In *The Golden Legend*, the standard medieval collection of saint's lives, SS. Cosmas and Damian were twins "born of a pious [Christian] mother, Theodoche by name, in the city of Egea." There they "learned the art of medicine, and received such grace from the Holy Spirit that they cured the illnesses not only of men and women but of animals, not taking any payment for their services." This refusal to accept money for their healing gained them a reputation for sanctity and good works, and converted many to the Christian faith.[69] Miraculous cures attributed to them spread their cult far afield, for in an age when physicians could do little for the seriously ill, miracles offered medicine of the only efficacious kind. In the century following their martyrdom in Syria, circa 287, major churches were dedicated to them in Jerusalem, Egypt, and Mesopotamia. The city of Cyrus was restored in their honor; the Emperor Justinian, crediting a personal cure to their intercession, built them a church in Constantinople; and Pope Felix IV (r. 526–30) converted the Library of Peace in Vespasian's Forum into a Roman basilica in their name. It is famous still for an important sixth-century mosaic depicting the saints. Figure V.28, from the Menology of Basileios II, made at the turn of the eleventh century, presents the twins as mirror images of each other,[70] receiving their physician's case from the hand of God. Their names are invoked in the Canon of the Mass as well as in the Litany of Saints, and their feast day in the West, recorded in every medieval calendar, is celebrated on September 27. The Greek Church, in contrast, originally awarded them

V.28. SS. Cosmas and Damian receive a physician's case. Greek, from the Menology of Basileios II, beginning of the eleventh century. Vatican City, Bibl. Apostolica Vaticana MS gr. 1613, fol. 152. Photo © Biblioteca Apostolica Vaticana.

no less than three feast days—July 1, October 17, and November 1—for reasons shortly to be explained. "Cosimo," or "Cosmo," as a personal name became especially popular in Italy, gaining maximum prestige when the Medici chose the twins as their family's patron saints. Damian, his twin, is recorded as an English name as early as 1205,[71] though Leslie Matthews, after an extensive search, remarked on the small number of churches dedicated to them in England compared to the widespread popularity of their cult abroad.[72] The London Guild of Barber-Surgeons, however, with records going back to 1308, honored them as their patron saints, since barbers then performed surgery upon minor wounds, as well as blood letting, leeching, and even the extraction of teeth. The Barber-Surgeons of York did the same. The York guildbook includes beautifully drawn portraits of their four patron saints, with John the Baptist and John the Evangelist above, Cosmas and Damian (with urine flask and medicine box) below.[73] It is quite possible Chaucer had heard of them in their guild-patron role. But he could also have known of them first hand in Kent, since two of the five English churches consecrated to them are found in the area where Chaucer spent most of the

1390s, writing *The Canterbury Tales*.[74] The church at Blean, in the Blean Forest, built about 1233, stands just two and a half miles from Canterbury, and Harbledown, where the Manciple tells his tale (IX 1–3), is only two miles away. A second church, also dating from the thirteenth century, is found at Challock, in the King's Woods, some nine miles from Canterbury in another direction.[75] Though only three other English churches are dedicated to the physician saints—in Sussex, Wiltshire, and Herefordshire—there are relics associated with them preserved in Canterbury Cathedral, Salisbury Cathedral, and lesser churches elsewhere. (Matthews provides exact information on each.) A late fourteenth-century poem, "On the Feast of Corpus Christi," surviving in three manuscripts, offers relevant evidence all on its own, employing the very word on which Chaucer bases his pun: "Cosma and Damianus,/ thei weore leches, I-writen is thus."[76]

It seems likely, therefore, that Chaucer's Damian—the "lecher" in the tree—was named with a physician-saint in mind. And Chaucer's May clearly casts herself as Damian's twin, his counterpart in healing:

> As me was taught, to heele with youre eyen, (IV 2372)
> Was no thyng bet, to make yow to see,
> Than strugle with a man upon a tree.
> God woot, I dide it in ful good entente.

Indeed, the month itself seems to have been thought of as a time of healing. Emerson Brown discovered in an early printed Sarum Breviary a Latin verse connecting the (masculine) name of the month to doctors and their remedies—"Mayus amat medicos et balnea scindere venas" (May loves physicians and baths for opening up veins)—which he linked to Chaucer's tale in this suggestive way: "May does indeed love a '*medicus*,' in the person of Damyan, namesake of a physician and patron saint of healers."[77]

But who exactly were these saints Cosmas and Damian? Apart from their received "legend" (the written life of a saint, or saints), an account problematic in many ways, there is no historical record whatsoever of their existence. Of interest to us is the intriguing possibility, suggested by several scholars learned in the period, that they may have been invented—or memories of real healers co-opted—to replace the ancient cult of Castor and Pollux within the new Christian faith. Consider, if you will, the fact that the Greek Orthodox Church to this day recognizes no less than three pairs of saints by these names—"those from Arabia who were beheaded under Diocletian, those from Rome who were stoned under Carinus, and the sons of Theodote [Theodoche] who died in peace"[78]—and for that reason commemorates them on three separate days (the three feast days mentioned earlier), one for each set of twins. In the Western Church, only the sons of Theodoche, those here said to have "died in peace," were acknowledged and worshiped. Their legend in the West nevertheless claims its own many details that in the East belong to the two other pairs, including the horrific tortures they endure (with their three brothers) after refusing to worship idols. These begin with torture to their hands and feet (a pain they make light of), followed by an attempt to drown them at sea (they are rescued by an angel). Thrown into a huge fire that burns many bystanders (but not the saints), they are then stretched on a rack (which does them no harm). Even when stoned by a crowd, "the stones turned back upon the throwers and injured a great number," causing the judge, beside himself with rage, to order them crucified. But even this does not work: the arrows that are shot at them leave them untouched, returning instead to strike the archers. Beheading them finally does the trick, but it is (ironically) not instrumental. Unknown to the judge, a guardian angel has protected them until the time appointed for their death.[79]

In the Greek legendary this drum roll of tortures is (perhaps) more plausibly inflicted on three sets of saints. But even that distribution is made dubious by the fact all three are called by the same names. The tortures assigned them are depressingly familiar, heroically endured by dozens of saints *not* named Cosmas and Damian. And even the healing miracles assigned to them are highly conventional—with one colorful exception, involving a Moor's amputated leg. Heinz Skrobucha, a careful scholar, suggests that "errors in the editions of martyr accounts and *Synaxaria* have no doubt contributed to the fact that one pair became three." But even concerning that hypothetical first pair—it seems to me equally likely three became one—he concludes "'their origin and true history cannot stand rigid investigation.'"[80] He is sympathetic to the idea these saints may have something to do with the venerable cult of Castor and Pollux.

The Church, understandably, is disinclined to think of them in this way. It does not readily abandon, or call into question, time-honored names in the Canon of the Mass and the Litany of Saints. *The Oxford Dictionary of the Christian Church*, for instance, in a brief entry admitting that "their Passion, which exists in several forms and languages, is late and historically valueless," concludes sourly: "Nothing precise as to their lives seems discoverable, though it is unnecessary to suppose that their legend has a mythological basis founded on that of the 'Dioscuri.'"[81] Perhaps. But even if twin physicians by those names once really existed—Christian in belief and renowned for charitable healing—the veneration accorded their memory may well have been channeled to replace or reorient a pagan cult. The early Church as a matter of policy often reconsecrated temples formerly pagan, as it even adjusted its liturgical calendar to incorporate certain pagan holidays, redefining their purpose in the name of the new faith. Christmas and Easter, for instance, replaced ancient festivals dear to the people, since practical churchmen realized early on that a strategic adaptation of cherished parts of the old religion could make easier an acceptance of the new.

In Heinz Skrobucha's view, "the fact that the Christian twins were particularly apt to replace the pagan cult cannot be disregarded," though he acknowledges scholarly disagreement on this matter. Two documents in particular support his view. In the first, Pope Gelasius I, at the end of the fifth century, refers to the Dioscuri as a cult still vital and attractive to the people: "your Castors whose adoration you do not want to forego." In the second (an early Greek miracle-story), a pagan in the sanctuary of the Dioscuri prays to the original Twins for their help at a time of illness, but is answered instead by the physician-saints, Cosmas and Damian: "'Why do you come to us?' they ask, 'for we are not Castor and Pollux but we are the servants of Christ, the King immortal.'" Having made their identities and allegiance clear, they convert the pagan and cure him.[82] In Constantinople, the pilgrimage place associated with the physician-saints seems to have been a close neighbor to, or identical with, the cult place of the Dioscuri; and "incubation"—the custom of sleeping overnight in a sacred place in hope of a vision or a medical cure—is thought to have furnished the necessary link between them. Though it was a pagan custom, Christianity promoted incubation as a means of transferring the powers attributed to Asclepius, the Greek god of medicine and healing, at sacred places such as Epidaurus, to certain Christian saints at certain traditional shrines. Prominent among the latter was the church of SS. Cosmas and Damian in Constantinople.[83]

Because Chaucer could so readily have known of St. Damian as a healing "twin"—as patron saints of the Barbers-Guild of London; from their story in *The Golden Legend*, which furnished him a major source for his *Second Nun's Tale*; and from two churches near Canterbury dedicated to the physician-saints—we can be reasonably sure the name he gave to Damian, punning on the idea of a healer ("the lechour in the tree"), is deliberate as well. But the possibility that the Dioscuri, under whose sign Damian climbs that tree, might be distantly related to the physician-saints is a different matter. Though Chaucer knew of Castor and Pollux as twins, and SS. Cosmas and Damian as twins (they are never worshiped separately), he could not have guessed that the one pair might be a cultural adaptation of the other. Thinking on that possibility is a pleasure reserved for modern readers alone. But all the rest is in place. We have, in the heavens, the Gemini as male wrestlers, whose love for each other doubles the power of the sun in their sign, inducing new growth and healing the world of winter. And we have, on earth, the Gemini as a male-and-female couple, expressing through their sexual need for each other the same vital force that in springtime renews the world. The tale's denouement leads first to Damian, sitting on high "among the fresshe leves grene," and then to May, climbing up old January's back, to "wrestle" with him in that tree—a tree hung with green fruit, embraced by an old man in urgent need of an heir.

CALENDAR REALISM VERSUS THE FALL OF MAN

I began these chapters on *The Merchant's Tale* with a warning and an apology: that they would do scant justice to those aspects of the tale that evoke the garden of Eden and the Fall of Man. Let me remedy that now. I think the importance of Eden *before the Fall* can scarcely be overstated.[84]

A naive image of Adam and Eve in the prelapsarian garden looms large in the marriage debate that opens the poem, underwriting January's fantasy of marriage as a relationship at once tenderly caring, abundantly sexual, and utterly free of guilt—a paradise lost he thinks marriage to a very young woman might still restore. This is finely detailed in lines 1323–36, as part of a free-floating, unattributed encomium on marriage. But the walled pleasure-garden January constructs for this purpose bears only a fantasy relation to Eden before the Fall (that innocence is lost forever), nor can it be transmuted into the "enclosed garden" of the Song of Songs (symbolizing a wife's sexual fidelity) though he entertains that fantasy as well. This use of a walled garden, both as setting *and as theme,* is unique to Chaucer's version of the pear-tree story. No analogue, early or late, so much as hints at it.

But the Fall of Man seems to matter less, though the ending of the tale does reprise a part of its essential action. Many readers have noted the several narrative elements they share: a husband and wife in an idyllic garden; a tempter in a tree; the wife's desire for forbidden fruit; and the opening of the husband's eyes for one brief moment at least, to a knowledge of good and evil. Others have pointed out that January's compliance with May's wish to climb that tree enacts a commonplace allegorical interpretation of the Fall, in which sensuality (thought of as feminine) overcomes reason (thought of as male), just as women in real life (in the misogynist view) constantly succeed in dominating men. When January stoops low so that May can climb up his back, Chaucer adds a new and truly memorable image to an already venerable tradition, that of "woman on top."

These parallels with the Genesis account of Eden are part of *The Merchant's Tale*'s richness and wit, a "way of seeing" not to be denied or devalued. But I do not think the Fall of man is what the tale (on the deepest level) is finally about. As Kenneth Bleeth noted long ago, these parallels can be discovered in every source and analogue to the tale, even the most unsophisticated, because they are intrinsic to its narrative shape—"a mere sequence of events" in "the plot of a popular folk narrative"—whose likeness to the Fall is latent in every version, whether its author did anything to draw it out or not.[85] Chaucer would certainly have been aware of the similarities, and may indeed have been attracted to the story partly because of the witty perspective they allowed. They may even have suggested to him the role ideas of the prelapsarian garden might play in January's fantasy view of marriage. But in the tale's last eighty lines (where these parallels to the Fall alone are to be found) Chaucer did little to capitalize upon the opportunities they presented. For Chaucer too these parallels in the plot seem to have "come with the story"—a bonus, so to speak, but not what he had first in mind. Never once does he mention the Fall, nor does he make any verbal allusion to it.[86]

And so, just possibly, the differences matter more. In the *Jeu d'Adam*, a twelfth-century Anglo-Norman play, the devil describes Adam and Eve as the first badly matched couple in human history: "Mal cuple em fist li

Criator," he says to Eve, "Tu es trop tendre, e il, trop dur" (The Creator has made an ill-matched pair:/You are too tender, and he too hard).[87] But that is a diabolic strategy intended to disunite them, and the difference the devil exploits is not the same. Adam and Eve are not "ill-matched" in terms of age, the key element in Chaucer's plot. And though medieval art often shows the serpent's face in the lower branches of the Tree of Knowledge, allowing him to speak to Eve directly, the face shown is almost always that of a young woman—a disguise chosen by the devil so as not to frighten her. (A good deal of theological commentary authorizes that disguise.)[88] Nor does Eve climb the forbidden tree to taste its fruit; she eats the delicious apple standing on the ground. But most important of all is the way Chaucer's story ends in accommodation and continuance, without punishment or exile from "the garden," simulacrum though it is. Aged folly and youthful adultery alike go uncorrected; things will continue, with more freedom than before; husband, wife, and lover all entertain happy expectations for the future. The Fall was said to have brought death into the world, and knowledge of sin, and the fear of hell—each of them a factor in January's decision to marry. But Chaucer's fabliau version of an old man's folly brought into a head-on collision with the sexual desires of two young people never insists on original sin as its most relevant cause.

I do not mean that the medieval understanding of original sin, and thus of any deadly sin committed in its wake, is not one of the tale's "ways of seeing." Kenneth Bleeth, in "The Image of Paradise," reads the tale with both wit and considerable learning as a sophisticated scriptural parody. And Eric Jager, in a long chapter on the tale—the triumphant conclusion to an impressive book—provides a thoughtful case study in "the ambiguity of the sign, the instability of oral tradition, the pleasure of the text, and the many rhetorical guises of the tempter's voice,"[89] each of them problems afflicting language "after the Fall." But the evidence I have presented leads me to doubt that a reprise of the Fall itself is what Chaucer had chiefly in mind. By using calendar names and moving the action through certain calendar images, he declared an overriding interest in the ways a mismatched marriage can offend against the cosmic order, and in the power of that order, all on its own, to adjust and correct whatever has gone wrong. His choice of Pluto and Proserpina as the gods who intervene further supports this view, since they too are a famously mismatched couple, she the young and beautiful daughter of Ceres (goddess of growing plants), while he, aged and willful, rules over Hades, the underworld kingdom of the dead. The structural disorder implicit in their marriage, beginning with an infamous "rape" in which he carried Proserpina off by force, was itself resolved in terms of a seasonal myth. Proserpina spends half of each year as queen of the underworld and half in the world above. Her annual return marks the beginning of spring.[90]

Despite the cynicism of its judgments and the satiric nature of its characterizations, *The Merchant's Tale* thus emerges, on some deeper level, as oddly affirmative. Behind a verisimilar screen of fabliau detail, and a series of actions devoted to the most selfish kinds of sexual desire, it invokes the sun in its progress across the country of the stars, tracing a seasonal order essential to the perpetuation of life, and setting right a transgression against that order with little concern for the scandal of its means. As I suggested much earlier, the truth function of literature is less about things than about ways of seeing things—a distinction that opens the door to rhetorical playfulness, incompatible assumptions, variant explanations and nondoctrinal endings. Its special gift, in short, is its openness to the many kinds of "truth" that play out in real life, some of them endorsable only in fiction.

In *The Wife of Bath's Prologue*, just a few tales earlier, Chaucer had explored the comedy and pathos of *five* badly sorted couples, as recollected by a lusty old woman named Alison, party to them all. After four husbands in a row, taken when she was young—three of them old and rich, and another a "revelour"—none of whom she honors with a name, she finally marries one younger and poorer than she, Jankyn (or "Johnny"), the only one she ever loved. Their turbulent but joyous adventures in marriage bring her prologue to an end. The badly sorted couple of *The Merchant's Tale*, in strong contrast, comes before us not only with resonant names drawn from the calendar tradition—"January" and "May," and sometimes even "Mayus" for "May"—but with roles to play that seem iconographically almost predetermined, reaching an almost inevitable conclusion under the sun in Gemini. Let me briefly summarize what I mean.

January, like Janus with two faces, enacts the logic of his sign, looking to both past and future, regretting the one and anxious about the other. Trusting marriage will prove the answer to both concerns, he orders up a wife as though she were a meal to be consumed, whenever and wherever he wants, before giving himself over to sleep and rest. Since feasting and resting are the chief calendar occupations of his month, in these matters otherwise inessential to the plot, January does what January must do.

May, only moderately inconvenienced by marriage to an old man, senses herself similarly empowered. Under the sign of Gemini, and in accord with the occupation of her namesake month, she briskly sets out to get herself "some green," climbing up a pear tree hung with unripe fruit. Since life in this world is always, in the end, on the side of the young, in that moment even the marriage ideals, so beautifully if ironically stated earlier in the tale, drop out and fade away. The sun and the stars, we come to realize, do not care whether we think of Damian and May as healers or lechers, lovers or sinners. As avatars of the Gemini Twins, encoding a seasonal force and a cyclical necessity, they signify something the sun must pass through if life is to renew itself. In choosing a wife so young and unsuitable, January entered into a contest with time itself, careless of the fact that in such a contest May must always triumph, just as spring must win out over winter, the new year over the old, and youthful energy over life soon to reach its term. For January to cling to May, as he does with increased urgency once he becomes blind, is to deny life its right to blossom, its need to set and bear fruit. January likes to think of himself as a blossoming tree, white haired but green in heart and limb:

For—God be thanked!—I dar make avaunt (IV 1457)
I feele my lymes stark and suffisaunt
To do al that a man bilongeth to;
I woot myselven best what I may do.
Though I be hoor, I fare as dooth a tree
That blosmeth er that fruyt ywoxen bee;
And blosmy tree nys neither drye ne deed.
I feele me nowhere hoor but on myn heed;
Myn herte and alle my lymes been as grene
As laurer thurgh the yeer is for to sene.

But wishing and boasting will not make it so. His wealth and power can purchase him such a marriage (by "scrit and bond" he enfeoffs May with all his land), just as the Church, looking to its own institutional interests, can be persuaded to bless it. And old men, it is true, do sometimes sire children upon young wives. But Nature, in general, is not pleased "whan tendre youthe hath wedded stoupyng age" (IV 1738).

Chaucer's friend John Gower notably agreed. In his "lover's confession" (the *Confessio Amantis*), a book-length English poem begun at about the same time Chaucer began *The Canterbury Tales*, he inserted a Latin epigram (here in a prose translation): "Whoever desires what he is unable to have, wastes his time; where there is no possibility of fulfillment, even wishing is unhealthy. The work of summer is not for grey hair; when the heat is gone, winter takes over. Nature does not give May's gifts to December. Mud cannot consort with flowers, nor can the decrepit pleasures of old men blossom into—what Venus herself seeks—a young man's compliance."[91]

Venus herself now enters the poem, to ask the anonymous author/"lover" his name—John Gower, he says ruefully—and then to dismiss him from her service, in language both scornful and amused. Though you seek my love, she tells him, you shouldn't imagine that I take bedroom-pleasure in gray-haired men like you: "For loves lust and lockes hore / In chambre acorden neveremore." And though you fancy yourself still capable in the act of love, it takes more than a wish to drive that plow. She advises instead a strategic withdrawal ("Betre is to make a beau retret"), shows him (for his instruction) his deeply lined face in a mirror, and gives him a necklace resembling a rosary, whose larger beads are inscribed in gold: "Por reposer" (For the sake of rest).[92]

This brilliantly imagined confrontation between old age and sexual desire brings Gower's greatest poem to an end.[93] Like *The Merchant's Tale*, it is both tough-minded and compassionate in acknowledging the way sexual desire tends to persist beyond its useful term. But it is of interest too because it imagines the conflict between youth and age, not as a generalized strife between spring and winter, but in terms of specific months of the year:

"Nature does not give May's gifts to December" (*Sicut habet Mayus non dat natura Decembri*). Such specificity is rare.

Indeed, the only other poem from this period to state something similar is a ballade by Eustache Deschamps, Chaucer's great French contemporary (died ca. 1406), who wrote two brief poems in praise of Chaucer as a rhetorician, and whose mighty *Miroir de mariage* furnished our poet a major source for the marriage debate that dominates the opening half of *The Merchant's Tale*. The ballade begins with a rhetorical question, "What would you say of the cold month of January, if it wished to marry April?" (*Que diriez vous du froit mois de Janvier / S'il se vouloit marier a Avril?*), and ends each of its three stanzas with this repeated refrain: "Is he wise who marries in this way?" (*Est il saiges qui ainsi se marie?*). But that is the case, Deschamps suggests, when a man of sixty marries a girl of fifteen; he brings the rain and sleet of winter into the green world of spring (*Et mettre ainsi le vert o le gresil*).[94]

So far as I can discover, these are the only poems contemporary with Chaucer to think about ill-matched marriages in terms of months rather than seasons. Both are by poets whose work Chaucer knew well, yet neither yields an exact match. Where Gower chose "December and May," Deschamps "January and April," Chaucer opted for a third pair of months, and, if I am not seriously in error, the calendar tradition can tell us why. He chose January over December for the sake of two-faced Janus, looking behind and before, and for the complementary figure of January as feaster, preoccupied with food, warmth, and rest against the season's cold. A few calendars, it is true, show feasting as the occupation for December, and some others move it to February;[95] but neither month could in addition underwrite the crisis of conscience, the thinking on past and future, that first motivates Chaucer's January (Janus) in this tale. In like fashion, I think, Chaucer chose "May" rather than April because the occupation of the month and its astrological sign, taken together, could provide him green trees and branches, nakedness and wrestling, and (not least) a heterosexual version of the Twins, all offering a powerful way of grounding and enriching the ending provided by his source. Though calendar pages for April often show a young girl gathering or holding fresh flowers, they do not "bring in" green trees or branches, nor can they display the sun in Gemini, with all the sexual energy that sign brings in its wake. (April's sun is in Taurus, the Bull.) So far as we know, Chaucer was the first to name an ill-sorted couple January and May.

The ending to *The Merchant's Tale* thus provides all the satisfactions traditional to fabliau: January gets what January deserves (the Merchant, with contempt, will call it "happiness"), just as May and Damian get the sexual relief they need, without benefit of courtship or any real acquaintance. (Damian speaks just two lines in the entire tale, a whispered entreaty begging her not to tell: "For I am deed if that this thyng be kyd" [IV 1943].) Rhetorically, the tale has no sympathy for any of the three. But it also imagines the coupling in a tree in terms of what I shall call "calendar realism": an event in harmony with a larger natural order, restoring the balance in something gone wrong. Because free will is central to Christian theology, sin is deemed volitional, and we are held morally responsible for the choices we make. But the progress of the sun through the regions of the zodiac was an annual, unchanging given, and the power of those stars to influence human life, which no one then seriously doubted, could border on determinism—an "almost necessary" conclusion that Chaucer sometimes played with in his poetry,[96] though he never granted it full credence in his prose. Here is C. S. Lewis's account of medieval thought on this matter, using Aquinas as a guide:

> On the physical side the influence of the spheres [was] unquestioned. Celestial bodies affect terrestrial bodies, including those of men. And by affecting our bodies they can, but need not, affect our reason and our will. They can, because our higher faculties certainly receive something (*accipiunt*) from our lower. They need not, because any alteration of our imaginative power produced in this way generates, not a necessity, but only a propensity, to act thus or thus. The propensity can be resisted; hence the wise man will over-rule the stars. But more often it will not be resisted, for most men are not wise; hence, like actuarial predictions, astrological predictions about the behaviour of large masses of men will often be verified.[97]

In the full medieval understanding, that is to say, a wise person can and should resist the influence of the stars. In *The Merchant's Tale*, no one resists anything for long.

But set against this is another truth. Seen from a sufficient distance, the business of life is to perpetuate life, whatever its means or the moral character of its agents. It is the interplay between these two competing registrations—the individually volitional and the cosmically imperative—that prevents our judging the cuckoldry that concludes *The Merchant's Tale* in any narrowly conventional way. The seasonal cycle can be affirmed as orderly and necessary, even indeed as beautiful, though all its parts are not. Gower, in the *Confessio Amantis*, puts it this way:

> [Gemini's] proper Month wel I wel
> Assigned is the lusti Maii,
> Whanne every brid upon his lay
> Among his griene leves singeth,
> And love of his pointure stingeth
> *After the lawes of nature*
> The youthe of every creature.[98] (italics mine)

The "laws of nature" in Gower's poem are not subjected to theological scrutiny—though of course they could be. They function instead as a counterpoint to theological free will, not claiming philosophical determinism exactly, but standing their own ground.

Bridget Henisch, in her brilliant study *The Medieval Calendar Year*, observed that in calendar labors-of-the-months "no religious touches of any kind are to be found. There is never a hint of divine intervention, never a turning for help or consolation to the Virgin Mary or to some local saint," no offering of harvest tithes, no Rogation-tide blessing of the fields by the parish priest. "Work goes on quite outside the framework of religious belief, doctrine, or discipline."[99] The same may be said for months characterized by "occupations" rather than "labors," and for the signs of the zodiac. The symbolic identities of January and May and the sexual / affectional energies of the Twins emerge from a cosmic natural world, driven by forces deeper and more profound than fabliau but culturally less definitive than doctrinal truth.

The tale, in fact, cares little about old January's relation to truth—it leaves him "happy" in his marriage—and nothing at all about the eternal destiny of his soul. Nor does it invite much respect for Damian and May, whom it distances and degrades from their first flirtation on. But whether we like it or not—even the Merchant doesn't like it much—the momentum of the tale is on their side. May's ingenious version of "getting some green," like the naked Gemini regendered male and female, serve goals larger and more important than the exposure of an old man's folly, or the forwarding of youthful lust. These calendar traditions bring in their train ideas of fertility, fecundity, and renewed generation that bypass conventional moral judgment. In none of the analogues is the husband concerned about his posterity: an old man's folly marital jealousy, and misogynist assumptions about woman's sexual nature are enough to move the story.[100] But Chaucer uses January's need for an heir to further destabilize the cuckoldry, increasing the number of ways in which it may be viewed.[101] If, at tale's end, it seems likely that May will bear January a child, however obscure its parentage, it is partly because sexual couplings in that month reflect the power and purpose of the sun in Gemini. In "calendar realism"—governed by Nature, overshadowed by time and death, and sustained by generation—sexual desire and procreation make no apology for their initiatives or their means.

In the boldest of the images we have looked at here, extending from the thirteenth century to the early sixteenth century, the woman is as strong and forthright in her needs as the man, and as fully engaged in the struggle they undertake to wrestle new life into being. Such figures have nothing to do with the Christian iconography of sin, nor do they emerge from a Christian iconography of marriage. The heterosexual Gemini move toward each other naked and unashamed, "influenced" and empowered by the stars. Though "ill-sorted" marriages will always be with us (some of them even turn out well), in nature's original plan—the default position to which nature endlessly returns—the young seek out each other for life to continue.

The ending of the tale, in the shape of its action and in some of its consequences, unmistakably recalls, at least for a time, the Fall of Man.[102] But if, despite all that, we find ourselves able to assent to this ending—to countenance a bit of adultery up in a tree—the sun in Gemini (*Sol in geminis*, in medieval calendar art) will have done its witty but substantial work.

VI. Rocky Shores and Pleasure Gardens

Poetry Versus Magic in *The Franklin's Tale*

In taking as my subject the rocks and gardens of *The Franklin's Tale*, I promised the convenors of the symposium that led to this chapter—no doubt to their great relief—that I would say almost nothing about love or marriage. Though no one would deny the interest or importance of the tale's exploration of those themes, the "marriage debate" which Kittredge discovered in *The Canterbury Tales*—a debate he declared opened by *The Wife of Bath's Prologue* and concluded by *The Franklin's Tale*—was so endlessly replicated in the pages of twentieth-century criticism that there is little more needing to be said. Scholars have argued so long about Chaucer's view of the Franklin's "conclusion" that it is only in the classroom, or in books addressing the general reader, that we dare broach the question again without embarrassment. All likely positions having been expressed, what remains is largely a matter of casting one's vote—and I am content to give my proxy to two members of the symposium, Jill Mann and Helen Cooper, both of whom have written persuasively about Chaucer's view of love and marriage in *The Franklin's Tale*.[1]

I want to focus instead on the tale's other great subject—that of magic and illusion making—and on the clerk of Orléans, its master practitioner. If we study him carefully, he may lead us to another subject still—more hidden, but no less urgent—a meditation (in those terms) on the poetic art itself, and on the ethical responsibilities of fiction. I have long thought that the best guide to medieval poetic is the practice of poets, closely read and sympathetically imagined—not the handbooks of poetic or rhetorical art, nor the theological defenses of certain preferred kinds of poetry, nor the *accessus* (or "approaches") to classical texts read in the schools, interesting and useful as all those ancillary texts may be. In *The Franklin's Tale* I think one can see Chaucer carefully mapping out his own best sense of what a poet *is* and *does* against a world of alternative possibilities. Because I have an ongoing interest in the relation of literature to the visual arts in the later Middle Ages, I shall use a number of pictures to illustrate (perhaps even illuminate) the moral and aesthetic issues Chaucer raises in this tale.

The novelty of my reading might be said to depend upon a single phrase—"in his studie, ther as his bookes be" (V 1207, repeated with only slight variation at 1214)—a phrase, so far as I can discover, that has not been closely thought about before. It indicates the place where the clerk demonstrates his magic at Orléans, and thus establishes one of the three major locations in this story—the rocks, the garden, the clerk's study—through which the narrative moves and upon which its meaning depends. If each of these loci carry iconographic meaning, as I shall attempt to show, their dialectical relationship may also matter. Not for the first time in Chaucer's work, but here in an especially brilliant fashion, poetic practice becomes a form of theory.

Among these three "places," it is only the clerk's study that has failed to attract sustained critical attention. But its importance depends upon the two others, and so it is with them—with the rocky coast of Brittany and the pleasure garden sited on its banks—that I must begin.

Erwin Panofsky, in his pioneering studies of iconography in the visual arts, long ago excluded most landscape painting (landscapes painted for their own sake, "independent" landscapes) from his purview. Such painting, he said, like the depiction of food and wine and flowers in still life (*nature morte*), represents a late development in the history of art, and is notable for its freedom from cultic, textual, conventional, or symbolic meaning.[2] Landscapes, in particular, do not become an independent subject until the sixteenth century and remain rare for a century thereafter.[3] In poetry, however, the matter is far different. Medieval romancers long before had found ways of using a detailed representation of landscape to mirror (and thus explore) the inner psychological experience of their characters.[4] They moved outward to move inward, describing or invoking a landscape simply because it could stand for something larger. Almost never (apart from school exercises imitating set pieces from classical poetry) was landscape description valued as an end in itself.[5]

It was in this vein that Charles Owen, Jr., some years ago, taught us to recognize the way the rocks along the Breton coast take on symbolic meaning within the Franklin's story.[6] Their significance, he suggested, is largely psychological. When Dorigen's husband, Arveragus, is away in England on a two-year campaign, the rocks (which threaten the safe passage and harbouring of shipmen and seafarers) come to represent in her mind all "the menace of natural forces to her husband's life." Her marital happiness gets caught upon a question: how shall he ever return to her safely, with those rocks so threatening there? Grieving and despairing, she invests the rocks with meaning far beyond any specific or intrinsic danger:

> Eterne God, that thurgh thy purveiaunce (V 865)
> Ledest the world by certein governaunce,
> In ydel, as men seyn, ye no thyng make.
> But, Lord, thise grisly feendly rokkes blake,
> That semen rather a foul confusion

Of werk than any fair creacion
Of swich a parfit wys God and a stable,
Why han ye wroght this werk unresonable?
For by this werk, south, north, ne west, ne eest,
Ther nys yfostred man, ne bryd, ne beest;
It dooth no good, to my wit, but anoyeth.
Se ye nat, Lord, how mankynde it destroyeth?
An hundred thousand bodyes of mankynde
Han rokkes slayn, al be they nat in mynde,
Which mankynde is so fair part of thy werk
That thou it madest lyk to thyn owene merk.
Thanne semed it ye hadde a greet chiertee
Toward mankynde; but how thanne may it bee
That ye swiche meenes make it to destroyen,
Whiche meenes do no good, but evere anoyen?

. . .

Thise rokkes sleen myn herte for the feere.

This meditation on a landscape—characterized by Chaucer in line 844 as Dorigen's "derke *fantasye*"—is a kind of truncated theodicy, one that questions the ways of God to man, but cannot get beyond a formulation of the question itself. In Dorigen's mind, the rocks come to stand for everything in the world that seems counter to human values, threatening to human enterprises, and inimical to the happiness of two lovers—a man and woman who (in a very modern way) have invented their own ceremony and covenant of marriage.

In fact, the rocks are not quite adequate to the heavy significance Dorigen would lay upon them—as the story itself will ultimately make clear. So would a visit to the coastal shore on which Chaucer sets his story: Pedmark—modern Penmarc'h—on Finistère in Brittany. Since few Chaucerians seem ever to have journeyed to the site, I reproduce a photograph of it here (Figure VI.1): a beach covered by black rocks, low enough (perhaps) to be covered by a very high tide. Some greater rocks can be seen farther out from the coast (*les roches de Penmarc'h*). But Chaucer's "Pedmark," it will soon be clear, in most major details does not correspond at all.[7] We are dealing with an invented landscape whose meaning remains to be determined.

Chaucer takes care to show us the larger scene first, partly through Dorigen's eyes:

Now stood hire castel faste by the see, (V 847)
And often with hire freendes walketh shee
Hire to disporte upon the bank an heigh,
Where as she many a ship and barge seigh
Seillynge hir cours, where as hem liste go.

These many ships and barges sail apparently without impediment, moving freely "wherever it pleases them to go." No rocks are mentioned.

VI.1. The rocky coast of Pedmark (Penmarc'h) in Brittany. Photo: Ellin M. Kelly.

And the whole is seen from a bank *high above*, a walk-with-a-view where she and her friends promenade for pleasure's sake ("hire to desporte"). It is the absence of a certain ship, not danger to *all* ships, that comes to obsess her—and with that narrowing of emotional focus comes the first notice of the "grisly feendly rokkes blake" (in the meditation quoted above). Their meaning is more attributed than intrinsic—as other details will soon make clear.

For just as there had been no mention of the rocks when Arveragus left for England, so there is no mention of them when he returns safely home—though his homecoming precedes by some considerable time (perhaps two years) Aurelius's visit to the clerk of Orléans and the rocks' subsequent "removal." Arveragus's return is narrated in just half a line—he "is comen hoom" (V 1089)—and marital happiness is renewed. The rocks, in short, pose little *real* danger in the poem: they are absent from our first view of the seacoast; they are absent in the notation of Arveragus's return; and they are "apparently" absent for a week or two, when Aurelius claims his reward. Their importance is iconographic rather than literal: they are made to stand for something larger (and other) than themselves.[8] Chaucer allows Dorigen to create her own "iconography of the rocks," and then (by means of the narrative) discover how little wisdom and truth she derives from that image. Her first conclusion is despair.

And so her friends lead her to the poem's second major "place"—a garden "ther bisyde . . . ful of leves and of floures," where

> . . . craft of mannes hand so curiously (V 909)
> Arrayed hadde this gardyn, trewely,
> That nevere was ther gardyn of swich prys
> But if it were the verray paradys.
> The odour of floures and the fresshe sighte
> Wolde han maked any herte lighte
> That evere was born, but if to greet siknesse
> Or to greet sorwe helde it in distresse,
> So ful it was of beautee with plesaunce.

Unlike the world outside its walls—which has come to be symbolized by the rocks—the garden contains nothing *not* delightful. It is a human artifact, made by "craft of mannes hand," from which all that is harsh, threatening, and ugly has been excluded.[9] Medieval pleasure gardens were intentionally modeled upon the garden of Eden—"the verray paradys," with its trees, birds, animals, and four rivers. And they were modeled as well upon the enclosed garden and fountain of the Song of Songs—a garden at once the symbol and the habitation of Christ's beloved.[10] Because of these textual models, medieval gardens could readily carry iconographic meaning. But as Panofsky would have been the first to recognize, such gardens communicate a symbolic significance only dimly potential in natural landscape itself. The garden, we may say, welcomes and expresses all that is young and beautiful and happy; to other conditions it offers consolation and cure. Figure VI.2, from an English manuscript of Marco Polo's *Li livres du Graunt Caam*, made circa 1400, shows the "garden paradise" of the Old Man of the Mountain, illustrating a text that brings together this whole complex of ideas—some of them no doubt based on travelers' accounts of real gardens seen in Persia, India, and the exotic East. It illustrates Book I, chap. 22 of the work, which describes a luxurious garden, "stored with every delicious fruit and every fragrant shrub that could be procured," maintained by a Persian chieftain who worships "Mahomet." The description is worth quoting at some length:

> Palaces of various sizes and forms were erected in different parts of the grounds, ornamented with works in gold, with paintings, and with furniture of rich silks. By means of small conduits contrived in these buildings, streams of wine, milk, honey, and some of pure water, were seen to flow in every direction. The inhabitants of these palaces were elegant and beautiful damsels, accomplished in the arts of singing, playing upon all sorts of musical instruments, dancing, and [displaying other skills] especially those of dalliance and amorous allurement. Clothed in rich dresses they were seen continually sporting and amusing themselves in the garden and pavilions, their female guardians being confined within doors and never suffered to appear.[11]

The garden seems infinitely desirable, until we learn that the Old Man of the Mountain has created it for political reasons. It is his custom to tell

VI.2. The garden paradise of the Old Man of the Mountain. From an English manuscript of Marco Polo's *Li livres du Graunt Caam*, English, ca. 1400. Oxford, Bodley MS 264, fol. 226.

the young men of his kingdom that, if they are brave and utterly obedient in his service, he can admit them to paradise. He makes good on his word by drugging them, bringing them into this garden where sensual and erotic pleasures overwhelm them for four or five days, and then drugging them again before returning them to ordinary life. From that time on they are his to command, for the experience has ravished them. They do not recognize the garden as a false paradise.

The standard medieval pleasure garden—the garden of romance literature and courtly relaxation—shares many of these charms, and is potentially (if not necessarily) as dangerous. It is characteristically a place of *artificial* beauty, set apart from the real world by garden walls, entered by a narrow gate, and ruled by geometry—however natural the trees and grasses and flowers in formal beds within those walls. Little is untouched, untrained, or untutored in this world. Here love-talk and witty conversation replace earnest discourse, music and song frequently replace speech, and dance makes a social art of motion. The God of Love's "carole" being danced in a late fourteenth-century *Roman de la Rose* (Figure VI.3) offers a kinetic image of those values. Social and highly patterned, it expresses life and love in idealized terms, protected and free from care.[12] Here, as in the garden of *The Franklin's Tale*, the governing mood—and mode—is *play*.[13]

Two of the three signifying locations in *The Franklin's Tale* are thus set in binary opposition to each other: what one includes the other excludes, and vice versa—a juxtaposition of settings whose conflicting claims as registrations of truth will be tested by the action played out between them. In fourth-century Egypt, the desert father Abraham defended his monastic vocation in terms of a similar dialectic, likewise expressed in terms of landscape. "We are not ignorant," he wrote, "that in our land there are fair and secret places, where there be fruit trees in plenty and the graciousness of gardens. . . . But we have despised all these and with them all the luxurious pleasure of the world: we have joy in this desolation, and to all delight do we prefer the dread vastness of this solitude."[14]

Within the bounds of *The Franklin's Tale*—a highly specific fiction—Chaucer had no reason to put his elegant, courtly young people to such a choice. But as the maker of many fictions—not all of them (like this one) set "in pagan times," not all of them courtly romances—Chaucer knew that *for a poet* every fiction implies some decision of this kind. The implications of this antithesis (whether garden/desert or garden/rocks) go deep. Artistic and ethical choice will overshadow each other, in ways that become clear only when we have left the rocks and the garden for the tale's other major setting: the magician's study in Orléans.

But first we must pause to notice (again with Charles Owen, and affirmed by many after him) a narrative reversal that greatly complicates the meaning of these two opposed settings in *The Franklin's Tale*. Once

VI.3. The God of Love's carol dance in the *Roman de la Rose*. French, late fourteenth century. Oxford, Bodley MS Douce 332, fol. 8v.

Dorigen has made her rash promise, linking her destiny to Aurelius for the first time, the iconic values of the harsher location—the *locus non amoenus*—change. From this point forward, the happiness of Dorigen's marriage *depends* upon the rocks remaining in place; they have become foundational to it, the essential guarantee of her fidelity in love and marriage. The garden, as an image for the joy that is possible in this world, is now *secured* by the rocks' continuance.[15] It is their disappearance that would be terrible.

Upon Arveragus's return, however, the rocks shrink once again to their proper size in the larger landscape of the poem—little more problematic (we may guess) than the juxtaposition of harbor, cliff, and pleasure garden shown in Figure VI.4, a detail from a fifteenth-century Netherlandish painting now in Liège.[16] But Dorigen's rash promise to Aurelius gives new meaning to the rocks' danger as an iconographic presence within the tale.

Aurelius, believing with Dorigen that removal of those rocks is an "inpossible" (V 1009), falls into a lovesickness near to death. He lingers so for two years and more, until his brother proposes a remedy—and brings the action

VI.4. A harbor with rocky cliffs. Detail from a panel painting, "Madonna and child with an anonymous benefactress and St. Mary Magdalen." Netherlandish, ca. 1470. Liège, Musée Diocésain.

of the poem to its third significant setting. Thinking back on his days at the university at Orléans—where "yonge clerkes" were famously "lykerous / To reden artes that been curious" (V 1119)[17]—Aurelius's brother remembers seeing a book of "natural" magic on the desk of a fellow student. Through such magic (it occurs to him), Aurelius might accomplish his impossible task and lay claim to the intimacy Dorigen had so foolishly vowed.

Natural magic ("magyk natureel")—the key term here—was a large and inclusive "art." Though in *The Franklin's Tale* it probably means little more than astrology, predictive or manipulative in kind, we can be certain only that it excludes magic dependent on diabolic powers, the sort shown in a mid-fourteenth-century English illustration of a clerk observing the heavens, one hand on a book, the other gesturing toward a demon just below (Figure VI.5).[18] Whatever the "magyk natureel" Aurelius thinks he is buying—and whatever exact variety the clerk of Orléans will use to make the rocks seem to go away—it is not of this demonic sort.

But "magic" *is* Chaucer's word for it, a choice further complicated by the speech that follows, in which Aurelius's brother recalls still other

VI.5. Black magic: a clerk studies the heavens with demonic assistance. English, from an encyclopedia, *Omne bonum*, mid-fourteenth century. London, Brit. Lib. MS Royal 6 E. vi, fol. 396v. © The British Library. All Rights Reserved.

evidence for thinking that some such solution might suffice. Aurelius's brother muses thus:

> My brother shal be warisshed hastily; (V 1138)
> For I am siker that ther be sciences
> By whiche men make diverse apparences,
> Swich as thise subtile tregetoures pleye.
> For ofte at feestes have I wel herd seye
> That tregetours withinne an halle large
> Have maad come in a water and a barge,
> And in the halle rowen up and doun.
> Somtyme hath semed come a grym leoun;
> And somtyme floures sprynge as in a mede;
> Somtyme a vyne, and grapes white and rede;
> Somtyme a castel, al of lym and stoon;
> And whan hem lyked, voyded it anon.
> Thus semed it to every mannes sighte.

Aurelius's brother recites this catalog of illusions ("apparences") with excitement and wonder—and Chaucer surely meant his first audiences to wonder at them too, though perhaps in a specially qualified way. For, as Laura Hibbard Loomis demonstrated long ago, at least some of these marvels recapitulate an actual event, a great feast given in 1378 by the French king Charles V in honour of his uncle, the Emperor Charles IV of Luxembourg. The visit is recorded in a deluxe manuscript of the *Grandes chroniques de France*—in unusually detailed prose, as well as in the miniature reproduced here (Figure VI.6).[19] It shows three royal personages standing together under canopies ornamented with fleur-de-lys, the bearded emperor on the left, the king of France in the middle, and the emperor's son and heir, Wencelas, on the right. A short play, the siege and conquest of Jerusalem by Godefroy de Bouillon, is being enacted before them as an *entremès*, an entertainment between courses at a banquet. On the right a castle is being scaled and defended by soldiers, with one of them already hurled down from the fortifications. From the left a small ship sails toward them, its wheels hidden by painted waves.[20] Only Peter the Hermit, a monk who preached the First Crusade, remains on board, all others being already engaged in the assault. Though the picture records something indeed worth wondering at—a feast so famous there is every likelihood Chaucer knew of it—that "something" worthy of wonder has nothing to do with magic as we normally define it.[21] It represents instead a triumph of the mimetic, scenic, and mechanical arts, joined together to create an "apparence." The "subtile tregetours" to which Aurelius's brother attributes this spectacle were in fact "actors, craftsmen, artisans mecaniques, who, in effective unison, produced spectacular results."[22] Yet it is also clear he thinks of this spectacle as a kind of magic, bringing to mind a clerk's book "of magyk natureel." Something rather subtle—or very muddled—is going on.

The picture before us documents perfectly well the "water and a barge" in the brother's recital, as well as a castle made to seem "al of lym and stoon."

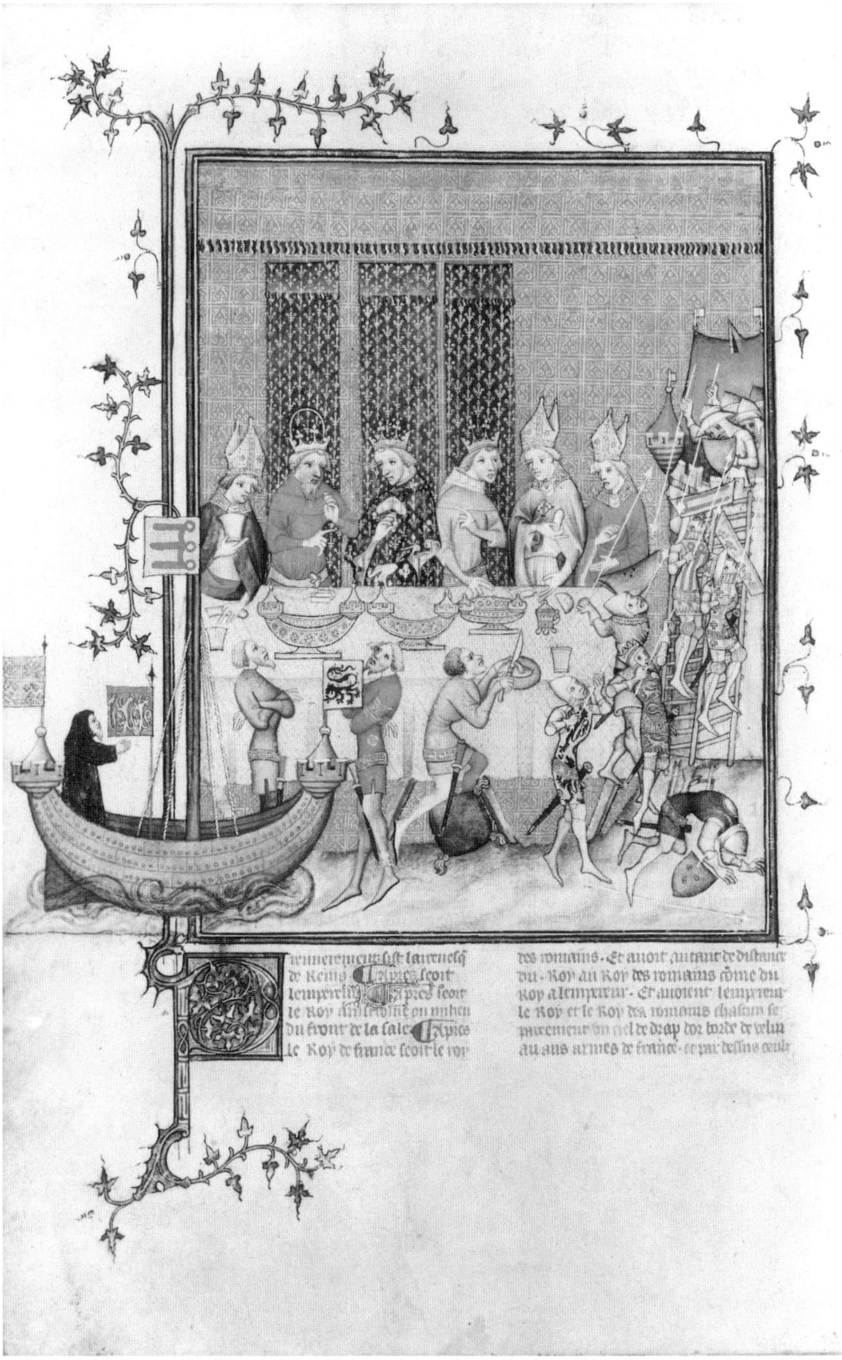

VI.6. Entertainment at a royal feast, Paris, 1378. From Charles V's *Grandes chroniques de France*. Paris, Bibl. Natl. MS fr. 2813, fol. 473v.

The boat and waves could be easily "voided"—pulled out of sight—when the eating and drinking resume, and so too perhaps the castle itself, though its position to the side may indicate it was built to remain in place throughout the feast. The other "wonders" here cataloged have historical precedent as well: actors dressed in lion costumes, mechanical flowers that close and unclose, lifelike models of grapes and vines, can all be paralleled in medieval accounts of courtly entertainments, state pageantry, and royal entries.[23] Medieval romances describe other "wonders" still, many of them well within the range of such art: mechanical giants, for example, and magic storms; bronze singing birds, and a golden stag operated by means of a bellows.[24] The sketchbook of Villard de Honnecourt, dating from the second quarter of the thirteenth century, shows a wheel-and-pulley mechanism labeled, "How to make an angel keep pointing his finger toward the sun," and (bottom left) another device, for the inside of an eagle lectern, labeled, "How to make the eagle face the Deacon while the Gospel is being read" (Figure VI.7).[25]

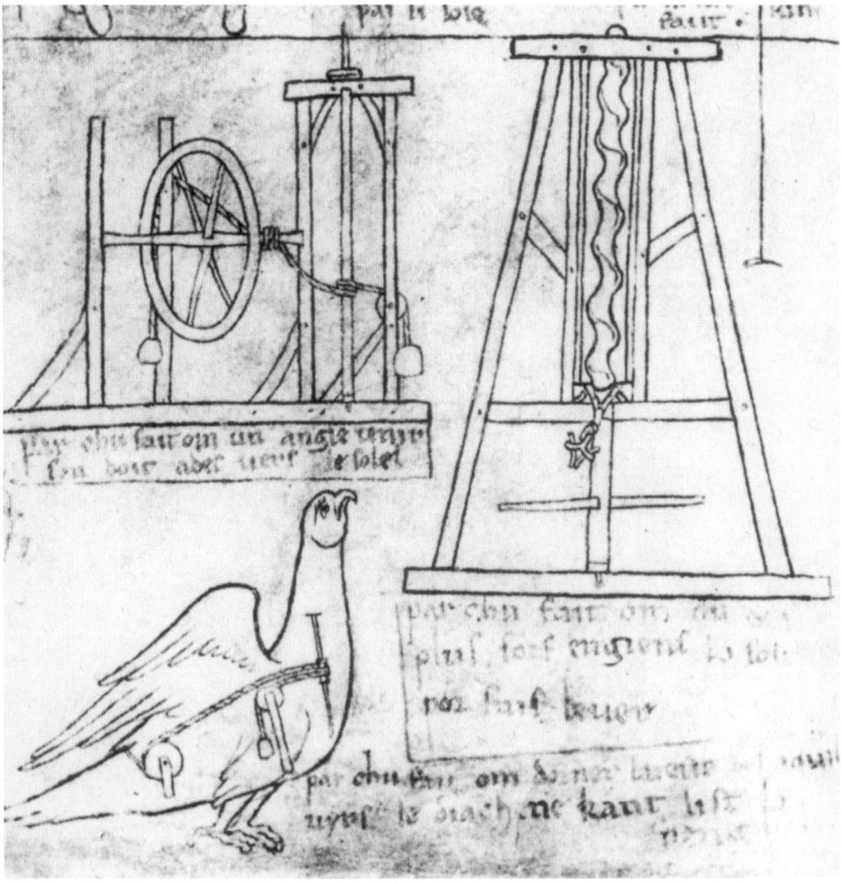

VI.7. Automata from the sketchbook of Villard de Honnecourt. French, ca. 1225–50. Paris, Bibl. Natl. MS fr. 19093, fol. 22v (detail).

Automata of this kind were often confused in the popular mind with magic and the occult, not just in the Arab world where they seem to have originated,[26] but in western Europe as well. Though their real nature would have been clear to Chaucer and to many in his courtly audiences—as the brother's reference to "tregetours" and noble "feestes" makes clear—we should respect the fact that Chaucer makes no mention of machines. The rhetorical emphasis of the passage is instead, overwhelmingly, on mystery and illusion: "Thus *semed it* to every mannes sighte."

That is the first of the "magic shows" in the tale—a retrospective report, based on memory and hearsay:

> For ofte at feestes *have I wel herd seye* (V 1142)
> That tregetours withinne an halle large
> Have maad come in a water and a barge,
> And in the halle rowen up and doun.

The second show, however, takes place in the tale's real time, in Orléans at the house of the clerk, and is in several ways grander and more mysterious. Again, the passage needs to be read in its full detail:

> He shewed hym, er he wente to sopeer, (V 1189)
> Forestes, parkes ful of wilde deer;
> Ther saugh he hertes with hir hornes hye,
> The gretteste that evere were seyn with ye.
> He saugh of hem an hondred slayn with houndes,
> And somme with arwes blede of bittre woundes.
> He saugh, whan voyded were thise wilde deer,
> Thise fauconers upon a fair ryver,
> That with hir haukes han the heron slayn.
> Tho saugh he knyghtes justyng in a playn;
> And after this he dide hym swich plesaunce
> That he hym shewed his lady on a daunce,
> On which hymself he daunced, as hym thoughte.
> And whan this maister that this magyk wroughte
> Saugh it was tyme, he clapte his handes two,
> And farewel! Al oure revel was ago.
> And yet remoeved they nevere out of the hous.

Chaucer's rhetoric serves to *link* the two "magic shows," describing each as a random list of wonders, and emphasizing their common evanescence: both can be "voided" in an instant, at their presenters' will (1150, 1195). For a long time, critics took their cue from that rhetorical parallelism, treating the two shows as one, seeking a single explanation for all their singular detail, and accepting both (despite the Loomis essay) at face value, as "magic" capaciously defined. Such wonders, after all, are to be expected in romances; "tregetoures" tricks merely make more credible the show. But two recent essays—inspired by Loomis, while going well beyond her—seek to deny the "magic" of these shows altogether, reducing them to entertainments of an entirely conventional, nonmysterious kind.

Anthony Luengo sees both shows as "stage magic"—a "theatre of illusion" made to seem mysterious by astrological jargon alone.[27] The clerk of Orléans is a "tregetoure" whose magic show depends on "skillfully constructed and lavishly decorated mobile pageant wagons upon which actors and mechanical figures [play] out a simple scenario." "One can reasonably assume," he goes on, "that the members of Chaucer's audience would have recognized the 'automates' for what they were," "a common part of both indoor and outdoor dramatic entertainments in England and on the Continent." Highly mobile contrivances wheeled and drawn or pushed from within, they gave three-dimensional form to stock motifs such as a castle, a forest, or a ship at sea. For Luengo, that presumed recognition on the part of Chaucer's courtly audience becomes a key to reading the poem: because neither the Franklin nor the characters in his fiction are "of the court," they do not understand what they are talking about or witnessing within the tale. "In confusing scientific astrology with black magic, [the Franklin] betrays his ignorance of contemporary thought. In failing to recognize a theatrical presentation, he betrays his ignorance of courtly entertainment." In Luengo's reading, this failure "to separate appearance from reality' is the real subject of the tale, an ironic exposure of the pretensions and limitations of its teller.[28]

Mary Flowers Braswell puts her emphasis less on actors and pageant wagons than on automata: ingenious machines meant to amuse the rich and noble, machines whose history as an art form is not well known.[29] "A bastard genre," she calls it, "not completely espoused either by art historians or by technologists."[30] Braswell reminds us that Chaucer was (among other things) a scientific writer, responsible for a treatise on the astrolabe and more than likely the author of another on the equatorie of the planets. His responsibilities as clerk of the King's Works in 1389, and as commissioner of walls and ditches along the Thames from Greenwich to Woolwich in 1390, would have necessitated some knowledge of mechanics and machines. And his role as courtier and court poet would have given him access to many elaborate rituals and entertainments—among them (in Braswell's well-chosen example) the experience of watching a mechanical golden angel bend down to offer Richard II his crown at his coronation.[31] Such things, she says rightly, were

> an integral part of late medieval culture. On the simplest level, a manor lord could entertain his dinner guests by means of a magic trick: red wine turning white, a cooked chicken dancing in a pan, or four and twenty blackbirds emerging live from a pie and flying into the room. In church, Eucharistic doves with moveable wings, such as that in the Cloisters Museum in New York, might have given new impetus to the Mass. Pageant wagons, ferocious dragons with moveable tongues, propelled by wheels, like that from the *Luttrell Psalter*, probably sent audiences scurrying. . . . But magic frequently required much more enterprise than this. When the mechanical clock was invented in the fourteenth century, for example, its mechanism was often used to make inanimate objects seem alive.

At the very highest levels of medieval culture, she argues, "*artists created magic* by designing automata" (my italics).[32]

This sort of thing alone, according to Braswell, constituted "the magic of the late Middle Ages."[33] For her—as for Luengo—the magic of *The Franklin's Tale* is something to be *seen through*, a series of marvels requiring of us nothing more than accurate recognition and classification.

I shall argue against that view, but before I do, let me join Braswell in bringing into this discourse the most attractive evidence for believing that contemporary automata *might* explain it all: the artful amusements of the noble park at Hesdin in Artois. Built by Count Robert II in the late thirteenth century, and extensively renovated by Philip the Bold around 1390—more or less at the time Chaucer was writing *The Franklin's Tale*—Hesdin had been for generations the favorite castle of the dukes of Burgundy. Amid its extensive grounds and gardens (including a garden called *li petit paradis*) there was located a pavilion—a kind of royal funhouse—renowned for automata and "magic" devices. A sixteenth-century copy of an earlier tapestry or painting, thought to show a wedding held at Hesdin in 1431, proudly displays the pavilion in the middle distance (Figure VI.8).[34] Records tell us that this structure, built upon marshy land with a river running beneath it, was filled with contraptions—including (to quote from Braswell's lively summary)

> stuffed monkeys covered with hair, which were chained to a dais, though they contained some mechanism which allowed them to descend from the platform and frighten the guests. At the vestibule was an automated lion. The walls sported large mirrors which distorted the images of the guests, and hidden under the floor were jets of water which sprayed the hapless visitors from below [ladies were special targets]. Trick windows spurted water when opened and mechanical birds in a cage spit on those who came too close.[35]

Anne van Buren, who is editing the Hesdin archives, notes with wry amusement that "whatever the Duke's hapless guests may have thought of them," in the records these devices "are regularly called *ouvraiges ingenieux et de joyeuseté et plaisance*."[36] Hesdin castle, standing elsewhere in the park, contained a room famous for wall paintings depicting Jason and the Golden Fleece, as well as mechanisms capable of still other astonishing effects: lightening, thunder, snow, and rain. The English printer William Caxton, proud of having personally visited the castle, described the room that held these paintings so:

> Well wote I that the noble Duc Philippe firste foundeur of this sayd ordre [of the Golden Fleece] / dyd doo maken a chambre in the Castell of Hesdyn / where in was craftyly and curiously depeynted the conqueste of the golden flese by the sayd Iason / in which chambre I haue ben and seen the sayde historie so depeynted. & in remembraunce of Medea & of her connyng & science he had do make in the sayde chambre by subtil engyn that whan he wolde it shuld seme that it lightend & then thondre / snowe & rayne. And all within the sayde chambre as ofte tymes & whan it shuld please him. which was al made for his singuler pleasir.[37]

VI.8. The pavilion at Hesdin, with festive courtiers (possibly a 1431 wedding) in the foreground. Sixteenth-century copy of a lost original. Versailles, Musée des Beaux-Arts du Château. Photo: Réunions des Musées Nationaux / Art Resource, NY.

It's doubtful that *real* snow falling through the ceiling at Hesdin castle would have charmed anyone, but a room with imitation snowstorms (machines strewing flour) was enough to make it famous throughout Europe. Medea *as magician and sorceress* is said to be the link between the room's "magic" machines and the story of Jason painted on its walls: those machines were made in remembrance of her "cunning" and her "science."

Most of the devices at Hesdin, van Buren has shown, date from the late thirteenth century, not from the late fourteenth-century renovation—and thus predate Chaucer's tale by almost a hundred years. Among aristocratic audiences, at least, they were widely known, and Chaucer might have heard of them from many sources. He had, at the very least, read about the charms and attractions of the park in Machaut's *Remède de Fortune* (ca. 1340), a poem he drew upon in writing his own *Book of the Duchess*, *Anelida and Arcite*, and *Troilus and Criseyde*. In Machaut's poem the despairing lover retreats into the park of Hesdin, which he describes so (783–822):

> I went along thus for a while, ever lost in my thoughts, until I saw a very beautiful garden called the Park of Hesdin. . . . And when I'd succeeded in entering and found myself all alone, I bolted the lock on the wicket. I walked along among the plantings, which were more beautiful than any I'd ever seen, nor will I ever see any so beautiful, so fair, so agreeable, so pleasing, or so delightful. And I could never describe the marvels, the delights, the artifices, the automata, the watercourses, the entertainments, the wondrous things that were enclosed within.[38]

Chaucer knew at least this much of the Hesdin wonders; he may well have known more.

Instructed by all this beguiling evidence from Paris feasts, English royal entries, and Hesdin funhouses, we might well conclude that the magic shows of *The Franklin's Tale* have been sufficiently described, both "seen" and seen through. But I think there are good reasons not to do so, the first of which is simple indeed: it makes both the Middle Ages and the tale itself entirely too neat and tidy.

We must remember that the medieval centuries, for all their high intellectual and theological ambition, were also centuries marked by superstition, imperfect knowledge, and widespread credulity. The Church, after all, claimed several kinds of "white magic" all its own—including the transformation of substance (wine into blood) at the heart of the Mass, the demonic struggle implicit in the rituals of exorcism, and the demonstration of power over natural law in the miracles of the saints.[39] The distinction between natural magic and black magic, dear to scholars then as now, was, moreover, variously drawn. Richard Kieckhefer's distinguished study *Magic in the Middle Ages* summarizes the possibilities so:

> At the popular level the tendency was to conceive magic as natural, while among the intellectuals there were three competing lines of thought: an assumption, developed in the early centuries of Christianity, that all magic involved at least an implicit reliance on demons; a grudging recognition, fostered especially by the influx

of Arabic learning in the twelfth century, that much magic was in fact natural; and a fear, stimulated in the later Middle Ages by the very real exercise of necromancy, that magic involved an all too explicit invocation of demons even when it pretended to be innocent.[40]

If you add to this account a widespread tendency to attribute to occult or magical powers any operation or mechanism not well or widely understood, even automata and the machinery of theatrical illusion become magical.[41] And while I believe (along with most previous writers on the subject) that Chaucer was skeptical of most of what was called magic—as he clearly was of practical alchemy, to name another semimagical "science"—I suspect he did not dismiss it as confidently as we dismiss it in our modern lives. Chaucer leaves too much of the tale's magic mysterious—perhaps even the apparent removal of the rocks—for the mystery not to signify.

Concerning *that* event, certainly, Chaucer shows himself reluctant to pay magic any real respect: he is contemptuous of both the profession and its practice (1131–34, 1261–96). But he never explains it all away: "thurgh his magik"—the magic of the clerk—"for a wyke or tweye, / It semed that alle the rokkes were aweye" (V 1295). Something *seems* to have happened—or, to put it another way, a *real* illusion has been created. For historical reasons, if for no other, we should not sweep the magician's study too clean.

But there is a better reason still for thinking the tale's magic something more than the product of automata, pageant wagons, and human actors. It derives from the fact (ignored in most critical writing on the tale) that the two magic shows are not similar in kind. Their ontological status—the ground of their being—is different, and that difference matters greatly.

The first "show" (to recapitulate briefly) seems to me perfectly well glossed by the material I have been presenting. It invokes entertainment of a kind sometimes presented at great feasts or other noble occasions, invented by "tregetoures" whose skill lay in bringing together human actors, automata, and "mansions" or pageant wagons of a kind familiar from the medieval stage. There is nothing mysterious about any of this *in mode*, however ingenious its machines or metaphorically "magical" their effects. Artful entertainments of this kind were valued precisely because they were not the real thing—because they were *other* than the effect they imitated. Such shows are part of the history of pageantry, mime, and masque; they do not invoke forbidden powers or exercise forbidden arts. Their intention is to surprise and delight; they "deceive" mechanically, not ontologically.

The tale's second show is different. Whereas the first is simply a poetic catalog, some hearsay remembered by Aurelius's brother ("ofte at feestes have I wel herd seye"), the second happens within the *real time* of the narrative, and in a particular place. But it is not set in a grand royal hall (like the Palais de la Cité in Paris, where the 1378 feast was held, attended by some eight hundred knights),[42] nor in a rich and costly pavilion such as that at Hesdin (with its automated rooms and corridors and galleries). Chaucer locates it instead in a house in Orléans—a "wel arrayed" house, no less no more, where a single squire serves the supper. The clerk seems prosperous enough, as clerks go, but there is no suggestion that he commands great wealth or great space; indeed, the setting is domestic and homely. But the show that takes place there is truly fabulous, exceeding in sweep and scope anything credibly reported from distant banqueting halls.

The clerk first shows them "Forestes, parkes ful of wilde deer" (V 1190), where they witness the death of a hundred harts, their antlers the greatest ever seen, some slain by hounds and others by arrows, bleeding from deadly wounds. That vision "voyded," he shows them falconers "upon a fair ryver," hunting heron with their hawks, and following that, a company of knights jousting upon a plain. It is only after these visions—these three demonstrations of the power of illusion—that he directly addresses Aurelius's desire, showing him "his lady on a daunce, / On which hymself he daunced, as hym thoughte." The vision is described paratactically, revealing its subject in successive stages, the second more intimate and erotic than the first: it is as though Aurelius first sees his lady (Dorigen) dancing with others, as in Figure VI.9—illustrating Machaut's *Remède de Fortune*—and only then *himself* dancing with her in that dance.[43] As soon as that final voluptuous illusion

VI.9. A courtly dance in the park at Hesdin. An illustration from Machaut's *Remède de Fortune*, French, ca. 1350. Paris, Bibl. Natl. MS fr. 1586, fol. 51.

is complete, it too is voided: the clerk of Orléans claps his hands and: "Al oure revel was ago." "And yet," the story continues (in several crucial lines, which, following Chaucer's lead, I have held back until this moment),

> And yet remoeved they nevere out of the hous, (V 1205)
> Whil they saugh al this sighte merveillous,
> *But in his studie, ther as his bookes be,*
> They seten stille, *and no wight but they thre.* (italics mine)

To underscore the importance of where this all takes place, Chaucer has the clerk himself repeat it just seven lines later, in a complaint that is really a concealed boast, intended to remind his Breton guests how much he has managed to show them in a very short while:

> To hym this maister called his squier, (V 1209)
> And seyde hym thus: "Is redy oure soper?
> *Almoost an houre* it is, I undertake,
> Sith I yow bad oure soper for to make,
> Whan that thise worthy men wenten with me
> *Into my studie, ther as my bookes be.*" (italics mine)

Unlike the privileged guests at Hesdin, Aurelius and his brother (and we, in the act of imagining the tale) have not been touring a noble pavilion or castle. We are in an intimate space—a scholar's study with books—and the ontological nature of what happens there is far from clear. If Aurelius "sees" the things he is said to be shown, then *magic of some kind* is being worked in that place, not dependent on complicated machines, hidden mechanisms, or concealed attendants working levers and bellows, winches and weights below.

Braswell (to my mind) pays insufficient attention to both the setting and Aurelius's response to the magic in her explanation of this second show. "This continuous change of scene," she writes, "could easily have been accomplished by a fourteenth-century device employing the principle of a mill wheel. Such a tool could make a globe spin or a stage turn, thus creating continuous changes in scene. . . . [Or] perhaps the deer, the falconers, the knights and the dancer were all parts of a medieval pageant that has not survived."[44] Such a show might indeed have been mounted, in the fashion of the Paris *entremès*, and it might indeed have evoked wonder. But not, I think, in a clerk's study, and not with any hope of deceiving Aurelius *in the way he is deceived*—a deception in the mind.

Aurelius is not shopping for ingenious machines, automata, or traveling players. He wants *real magic*—nothing less will remove the rocks—and he is *convinced* by this demonstration that the clerk has that power. For "real" magic (if there is such a thing) a room of any size will do. And the books are a key to its meaning. The magician must be a figure of power, authority and mystery, a man *capable* of creating convincing illusion.

As I see it, the subtext of the tale requires no less, for Chaucer means to define himself against this figure, to set himself in contest with him. We are asked to imagine the clerk among his books, creating illusions of a courtly, chivalric kind, because it can bring to our minds another image, similar in many ways: the image, so deeply familiar from Chaucer's early works, of the poet himself "in his studie, ther as his bookes be," afflicted with insomnia, dulled by his work at the counting house, grieving over his own unhappiness in love, but "dreaming" poems that grow out of those books—dreams that likewise violate the logic and laws of the waking world with their magical flights, astonishing visions, and golden eagles that speak. I think that Chaucer invented this magic in Orléans—so very different from that which he found in Boccaccio's *Filocolo*, his most proximate source—as a means of assessing the mystery and grandeur of his own craft, the making of fictional poems.[45] Behind the figure of a magician in his study one sees the figure of a poet among his books, a comparison that is for poetry as troubling as it is exalting.

By unleashing this magic in such a setting, and by describing (in even less than the clerk's "space of an hour") its four spectacular illusionary events, Chaucer makes *us as audience* see them too—in our mind's eye, the eye with which we imagine fictions—just as surely (and just as mysteriously) as Aurelius is said to do. Chaucer's "bookish art" allows both himself and his audience to imagine the real and the unreal, the natural and the naturally impossible, and to do so (what is more) with a facility greater than anything automata and stagecraft have ever aspired to. Chaucer's personal investment in the Orléans magic show can be read very clearly in its voiding movement, when he writes of the clerk, "He clapte his handes two, / And farewel! Al oure revel was ago." The possessive pronoun "oure" (intentionally or accidentally) marks the fact that the creator of what we have just "seen" does not stand outside the charmed circle at this moment of maximum power. And the force of this most unexpected pronoun reminds us that we too stand within it. It is "oure revel"—a cooperative enterprise—that has vanished, that is now "ago." Like Aurelius and his brother, we "see" what the artist would have us see without moving from the room where we read or listen, the room—perhaps—where our own "bookes be," and where our own role in the creation of literary illusion is most unequivocally acknowledged.[46]

I rest that claim not only upon evidence from the tale itself,[47] but upon a long Western tradition connecting magic and poetry—a tradition whose earliest expression (in Greek, Roman, Celtic, and Germanic culture) must, for want of space, be passed over here.[48] Let us look instead at its later (metaphorical) expression in a text Chaucer knew, the *Poetria nova* of Geoffrey de Vinsauf, written circa 1210. Near the beginning of that treatise, Geoffrey carefully notes the limitations of "natural order" in a narrative, restricted as it is to a single way of organizing a story, moving from its temporal beginning to its temporal end. The high art of poetry, in contrast, offers no less than eight ways of ordering such material: "Art can draw a pleasant beginning out of either [the end or the middle of a work]. *It plays about almost like a magician*, and brings it about that the last becomes the first, the future the present, the oblique direct, the remote near; thus rustic matters become polished, old becomes new, public private, black white, and vile precious."[49] In Geoffrey's concluding examples, values and identities are invoked as well as temporal sequence, because the magic of poetry is capable of transforming them all.

Geoffrey de Vinsauf addresses us from the high road of high art, where poetry is related to magic only metaphorically. Its reorderings and transformations are praised as acts of imaginative power without specific social or moral consequence, ideational rather than "real." But Chaucer in his last great work is unwilling to celebrate for long the illusion making at Orléans as though it were morally neutral, as if it offered entertaining spectacle only. The clerk's final illusion—offering Aurelius a vision of himself and Dorigen together in a dance—marks the end of Chaucer's sympathy, a rupture in his imaginative identification with an allied art. Things swiftly take a sinister turn as the magician-clerk transforms himself into a shrewd business man, demanding a ruinous price for making the rocks (seem to) disappear, and later embarks on something worse, a set of calculations and operations designed (and apparently competent for a time) to alter something foundational in the created world.

Chaucer makes only a half-hearted attempt to imagine what the magician actually does, dismissing it *as false poetry*, a confusing techno-babble that reduces to one of two possibilities—"apparence or jogelrye"—whose details and language are of little interest to him: "I ne kan no termes of astrologye" (V 1265–66). This third magic show, the apparent real-life removal of the rocks, borders on blasphemy and presumption, and is castigated by the poet as nothing more than "japes," "wrecchednesse," "supersticious cursednesse," "illusiouns and swich meschaunces / As hethen folk used in thilke dayes." Though this catalog of scorn takes proper measure of the event—the most this magician (or any author) can do is make the world *seem briefly* other than what it is—we quickly discover that even in these reduced terms there is implicit a world of moral danger. In what follows, Chaucer defines his own art by its difference, proving himself no trafficker in appearances-for-their-own-sake, no vendor of easy fantasies, no lousy juggler, no clerk of Orléans.

The art of poetic illusion originates in, and addresses itself to, the *phantasy*—in medieval faculty psychology that power of the mind (generally located in the brain's second "cell") that is able to process sensory images stored in the imagination (located in the first cell) and combine them into images of things never seen—a human torso on the body of a fish, let us say, or (to use a prophetic example from Roger Bacon's treatise on magic) a machine with wings that can fly (Figure VI.10).[50] But *phantasia* is also a name for the *deceptive* power of the mind: our power to imagine, and sometimes to trick ourselves into believing, that something we particularly desire or fear is real. As the culmination of his magic show, the clerk creates an illusion so pleasant and so convincing—Dorigen in a dance—that Aurelius thinks himself *included* within it. But the magician's art is as remarkable

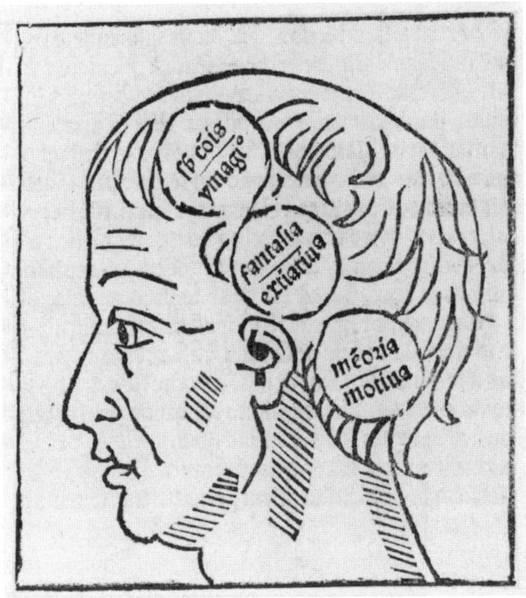

VI.10. A three-cell diagram of the brain (*phantasia* in the middle cell), from Triumphus Augustinus de Anchona, *Opusculum perutile de cognitione animae*, rev. Achillini, Bologna, 1503, sig. f. (viii). London: Brit. Lib. © The British Library. All Rights Reserved.

for what it is has excluded: Dorigen's husband and her love for him, the rocks, all care for society, all thought of a future. He offers the young knight the most dangerous of illusions—desire fulfilled, in a world without moral consequence.

Once the bargain has been made, the clerk-magician must go further, using his art to conform the coast of Pedmark to the landscape of a lover's fantasy (first Dorigen's, now Aurelius's). The narrative outcome of that third magic show—the testing of a marriage, the triumph of courtesy—is so well known it need not be rehearsed here. I shall focus instead on Chaucer's resolution of the more hidden issues it raises: the power and peril of illusion making within poetic fiction.

The clerk of Orléans, in presenting us with an alternative ending to the present fiction—Dorigen and Aurelius together, carefree, in a dance—removes one of the iconographic centers of the tale: the rocks in the sea, and all the hard meanings that Dorigen has laid upon them, however short-lived her reasons for doing so. By creating the "appearance" of their removal, the clerk in effect rewrites *The Franklin's Tale* from within—presenting the world all as "garden." In bringing the poem back to a more truthful relation to reality, Chaucer profoundly distinguishes his "art poetical" from the "art magical" of Orléans.

For central to the aesthetic of this tale is the conviction that both rocks and garden symbolize something essential in human life. Either of them alone, as a moral landscape of the soul, has its dangers. Address yourself too exclusively to the rocks—Dorigen's initial error—and you risk blasphemy and despair: life will lose its savor and suicide can seem an appropriate response. Dorigen falls into despair over Arveragus's long absence (817–36), just as she turns to thoughts of suicide (1346–1458) when Aurelius tells her it is time to keep her promise, the rocks having been removed. On this latter occasion, she becomes (allegorically speaking) Sorrow itself, tearing out her hair (Figure VI.11), as that emotion was understood in the *Roman de la Rose*.[51] Too much sadness (Tristesse), we learn near the poem's beginning, excludes one from Love's grand adventure, and for that reason it is depicted (together with other sins against erotic love) in wall-paintings on the *outside* of the love garden. In Figure VI.12, her portrait decorates the wall to the right of the entry gate (here in a translation that may be Chaucer's own):[52]

Sorowe was peynted next Envie (*R of R*, 301–48)
Upon that wall of masonrye.

. . .

Her roughte lytel of playing
Or of clypping or kissyng;
For whoso sorouful is in herte,

VI.11. A portrait of Sorrow (Tristesse) tearing her hair. From a *Roman de la Rose*, French, ca. 1330. London, Brit. Lib. MS Add. 31840, fol. 5.

VI.12. The Lover admitted into the Garden of the Rose by Lady Idleness, porteress of the gate. From a *Roman de la Rose*, French, beginning of the fifteenth century. On the wall, from far left, we see three other sins that exclude one from the garden: Covetousness, Avarice, and Envy. London, Brit. Lib. MS Egerton 1069, fol. 1.© The British Library. All Rights Reserved.

Him luste not to play ne sterte,
Ne for to dauncen, ne to synge,
Ne may his herte in temper bringe
To make joye on even or morowe,
For joy is contrarie unto sorowe.

Though Dorigen cannot quite bring herself to suicide, she spends a day or two thinking luxuriously upon it: it is, one might say, her only joy.

To that troubled vision—that "derke fantasye"—the garden offers an authentic and valuable antidote. It is a place of beauty, comfort, and joy, where psychological health and moral equilibrium can be restored. But if you focus too exclusively on the garden—as Aurelius does in his love fantasy, as the friends of Dorigen do who would comfort her, and as Dorigen herself does, at a crucial moment—you may fall into other kinds of danger: carelessness, folly, infidelity, adultery, each more perilous than the other.

The rocks, in short, genuinely matter to the moral economy of the tale.[53] Though they do not literally injure anyone or anything, the poem would be something very different without them. For just as Chaucer seems to have had only a limited interest in the emotional histrionics of young lovers, so the poetry proper to pleasure gardens or gardens of love engaged him very little.

Nor does he seem to have cared much more for poetry focused exclusively upon a harsher moral landscape—the poetry of rocks and barren ground, of suffering and death. Like the painter of a fifteenth-century diptych from the upper Rhine (Figure VI.13), Chaucer sought in this tale to express a dialectical truth, setting the two side by side, in appropriate scale and balance. The left wing of this diptych shows a dead man laid out on a wintry bank, with grass that is dead, and with trees that are bare and broken; the river and sea are frozen over, and one sees in the far distance ruined houses and towers, high rocks and cliffs; the only road up the mountain apparently ends in a man-made cave. The right wing shows, instead, an elegant young man and woman in courtly conversation, seated in sunshine on green grass and soft herbs, with children (or *putti*, symbolizing childlike innocence) playing below. Behind them one sees green trees and fields, prosperous houses and castles, and the other side of the mountain, here made accessible by a road winding upward through broad meadows.[54] The diptych's frame separates the two halves of the painting, isolating the mood and season of each, but we slowly realize that they share the same landscape, constitute the same rocky mountain, even (at different seasons) experience the same seasonal change. What initially seems divided and antithetical is in fact a complex unity: the beautiful and the ugly, the comfortable and the austere, the courtier and the corpse are part of the same world. In *The Franklin's Tale* Chaucer does not allow his young people to escape into a garden without paying a certain price—some growth in wisdom and experience not native to that privileged and protected place. But neither does he demand of them (in the manner of the desert father Abraham, quoted earlier) that they renounce all garden values once harsher truths are known. When Arveragus returns from England, and Dorigen's first grief is at an end, the courtly life quite *fittingly* resumes: he "daunceth, justeth, maketh hire good cheere;/And thus in joye and blisse I lete hem dwelle" (1098).

The *real* magic in *The Franklin's Tale*, as many have said before me, is that which (at the end of the tale) transforms selfishness into generosity, debt into forgiveness, and courtly loving into courteous living. And that "magic" has been made morally attractive—and psychologically credible—by the poet, not the magician. Any poet can make rocks disappear in a poem. But it is only in literature that such magic happens.

In his dream-vision visit to *The Hous of Fame* (1193 ff.), Chaucer describes at length a motley company installed on and about the castle's outer walls, a company of his own kind—

> alle maner of mynstralles
> And gestiours that tellen tales
> Both of wepinge and of game,
> Of al that longeth unto Fame,

as well as harpers and musicians of every sort. Among them he discovers a company even more diverse, "jugelours,/Magiciens, and tregetours,"

VI.13. An allegory of human life. Panel painting from the upper Rhine, ca. 1480. Germanisches Nationalmuseum, Nurnberg.

"charmeresses," "sorceresses," "And clerkes eke, which konne wel / Al this magik naturel," including Medea, Circes, Simon Magus, and even a specific English magician, "Colle tregetour," able by sleight of hand to produce miniature windmills from under walnut shells. It is a wild and turbulent group—uncomfortable company for an ambitious poet still planning his career—but we should not think it a private nightmare unrelated to social categories. Every person in this company offers some artful form of illusion and "apparence," and John Southworth's recent study of *The English Medieval Minstrel* amply confirms the bond that joins them. Medieval English *minstrel*, he tells us, like the Latin *mimus*, *histrio*, and *joculator* it translated, was used indiscriminately to name "musicians—composers, instrumentalists and singers—oral poets and tellers of tales (often to a musical accompaniment), fools, jugglers, acrobats and dancers; actors, mimes and mimics; conjurors, puppeteers and exhibitors of performing animals—bears, horses, dogs, even snakes." This terminological confusion, he continues, "undoubtedly reflects a large degree of versatility and flexibility of role on the part of the performers, but is also an indication of the low esteem in which they were generally held—especially by clerics."[55]

As in *The Hous of Fame*, so in *The Franklin's Tale*. Through a memorial recital of the entertainments at a recent Paris feast, and by setting the Orléans magic show in a clerk's study "there as his bokes be," Chaucer acknowledges his own intimate relation to practitioners of those other arts, locating his own craft somewhat ruefully among them—an act of humility (we may believe), qualified by a certain pride. Though the tale has much to say about love and marriage, it explores a poetics of illusion as well, distinguishing the truth-telling potential of poetic fiction from other forms of "magic" and "apparence," despite all that those arts might seem to have in common.

VII. *The Second Nun's Tale* and the Iconography of St. Cecilia

CHAUCER'S first audiences, whether noble, religious, or common, brought to the experience of his text essentially four things: their own experience of life, a certain store of religious and moral doctrine they had been taught, a rich memory of other stories they had heard, and a shared vocabulary of *signs*—of signifying visual images, conventional in nature, addressed to literate and illiterate alike. Some six centuries later we recover knowledge of such imagery most confidently through the visual arts: through a study of the pictures, carvings, and stained glass that expressed it in material form. As I argue elsewhere,[1] however, our sense of such imagery must include as well the *mental images* that medieval literature invited its readers and hearers to frame in their minds' eye as they read or listened to narrative. Ideas concerning the mental image played an important part in medieval theories of how a poet invents his material, how an audience remembers it afterward, and how an audience is affected by that experience. I share the view that Chaucer was not a "painterly" poet:[2] he seldom sought to imitate, in the tradition of *ut pictura poesis*, descriptive effects more native to painting than to literature; he did not often seek to discover how much like a painting a poem could be. But he was, in common with most other serious writers of the time, an iconographic poet: one who drew upon a language of sign and symbol in shaping the images his poems make in the mind. In this chapter I shall examine a number of medieval images illustrating the life of St. Cecilia, hoping to suggest thereby some of the ways the visual arts can help us read better a medieval narrative poem.

For reasons not difficult to understand, *The Second Nun's Tale* has not occasioned any major critical controversies or attracted very much critical attention.[3] It was written, the poet himself tells us, "after the legende, in translacioun" (l. 25), and nothing about it suggests substantial invention or innovation on his part. In the first half he translates the *Legenda aurea* version of the saint's legend with scrupulous care;[4] in the second he follows an expanded *Passio* of her martyrdom, the precise exemplar of which has not yet been discovered, but whose every significant detail can be paralleled in the tradition at large.[5] The tale is, moreover, early work, written before *The Legend of Good Women* (where it is mentioned in the Prologue, F 426 or G 416), itself written before *The Canterbury Tales* was begun. Although Chaucer ultimately included the tale in his pilgrimage collection, its importance there is chiefly thematic and structural: its teller is given no portrait in *The General Prologue*, nor is her voice significantly individuated in the tale she tells. Whatever its novelty as the only canonical saint's life we have from Chaucer's pen, and for all its distinction as the finest work in that genre to survive in Middle English verse, its range is precisely and deliberately limited: a saint's life "Englished," no more, no less.

The body of criticism that has grown up around the tale is, as a result, comparatively small, but it does not lack distinction. Although I shall take issue in some of what follows with certain published opinions, I do so with respect: they are expressed in essays from which I have learned much. But I have chosen my present subject—St. Cecilia in a fiery bath—not only because I hope to read that passage more fully and accurately than it has been read before, but because it will allow me to dissent as well from an assumption that underlies two of the most useful and engaged of these essays: Joseph E. Grennen's "St. Cecilia's Chemical Wedding: The Unity of the *Canterbury Tales*, Fragment VIII," and Bruce A. Rosenberg's "Contrary Tales of the Second Nun and the Canon's Yeoman."[6] Both critics deny *The Second Nun's Tale* any substantial literary interest on its own, valuing it only as a prefatory occasion for something better, *The Canon's Yeoman's Tale* of alchemists and their craft. Grennen concludes his analysis with the claim that we may not "any longer think of the two tales as separable poetic facts," while Rosenberg begins with comparable assurance: "In order to appreciate Chaucer's artistry we must go beyond the lines of *The Second Nun's Tale* to its fragment-mate, for only when this life of St. Cecile is read in conjunction with and in light of the *Canon's Yeoman's Tale* will the Nun's story gain literary stature."[7]

Let us think about these matters one at a time, beginning with the story of St. Cecilia read on its own, reserving the question of its relationship to *The Canon's Yeoman's Tale* for after. And let us look at the saint's story as it was depicted in the visual arts, for I think visual evidence can help us assess both claims the better. For reasons less perverse than they may at first seem, I begin with an elegant though (for our purposes) nearly useless example.

The follower of Jean Pucelle whose drawings ornament a magnificent Franciscan missal from the mid-fourteenth century chose to illustrate the legend with images of martyrdom only. Figure VII.1 represents accurately enough the deaths of Valerian and Tiburce, Cecilia's husband and brother-in-law, but Figure VII.2, which places the saint and her executioner between Almachius holding the staff of secular authority and the hand of Christ blessing her sacrifice from above, gets one essential event in the legend wrong. The attempt to behead Cecilia should not take place upon the ground.[8] For all the beauty of its line, the drawing is conventional and unspecific; it could serve as well the life of any decapitated (or almost decapitated) saint.

VII.1. The deaths of Valerian and Tiburce, Cecilia's husband and brother-in-law. French, mid-fourteenth century. Oxford, Bodley MS Douce 313, fol. 268.

VII.2. Christ blessing the sacrifice of St. Cecilia. Oxford, Bodley MS Douce 313, fol. 332v.

I bring it forward as a reminder that most medieval imagery is formulaic in its language, and that on occasion it uses a formula that does not really apply. Sometimes, we must admit, evidence from the visual arts illuminates nothing specific at all.

If, however, we turn to manuscript illuminations that address St. Cecilia's history with greater precision—as the vast majority do—other curiosities remain. The visual tradition that honors her as patron saint of church music, dominant in the Renaissance and after, was in the earlier period largely unknown. Figure VII.3, a historiated initial from an Italian manuscript of the fifteenth century, is rare among medieval versions in that it shows, as one of its major subjects, music being made.[9] The scene illustrates that moment in her marriage which Chaucer translated so:

> And whil the organs maden melodie, (VIII 134)
> To God allone in herte thus sang she:
> "O Lord, my soule and eek my body gye
> Unwemmed, lest that I confounded be."

VII.3. Cecilia as the patron saint of church music. Historiated initial from an Italian manuscript, late fourteenth or early fifteenth century. Cambridge, Fitzwilliam Museum MS McLean 201, fol. 26v.

Yet nothing in Cecilia's legend identifies her literally as musician. Her song is silent: the "new song" of the spiritual man or woman that is sung within the heart. That inward song earned Cecilia her role as patroness of the technical art, but it is not what her history is most centrally about, nor does it significantly account for her importance in the Middle Ages.

More common by far are pictures which show an angel presenting two crowns to the married couple, one of lilies, symbolic of virginity, the other of roses, symbolic of martyrdom. Figure VII.4, from the early fifteenth century, invites us to think about these crowns in relation to the marriage bed shown behind the kneeling couple, for the eternal crowns and the richly canopied nuptial bed represent entirely different spiritual vocations and destinies.[10] It is a dialectical difference that Chaucer will explore by other means.

VII.4. Angel presenting crowns of lilies and of roses to the married couple. From a French Breviary, ca. 1413–19. London, Brit. Lib. MS Harley 2897, fol. 440v.

Figure VII.5, from a late fifteenth-century *Légende dorée*, offers a visual epitome of the larger action, including not only the bestowal of the crowns but also the mysterious old man with a book who figures in Valerian's baptism (the text in banderole reads *Unus deus una fides una baptisma*), along with Pope Urban kneeling within a tomb, in token of the fact that he lives in the catacombs ("among the seintes buryeles lotynge"). The figure at the right must be Tiburce, astonished by the ravishing odor of incorruptible flowers that he cannot yet see. (The "invisible" flowers in Valerian's crown are red, for martyrdom, and in Cecilia's crown, white for chastity.)

VII.5. Scenes from the life of St. Cecilia. From a late fifteenth-century *Légende dorée*. The flowers in Valerian's crown are red; those in Cecilia's crown are white. Paris, Bibl. Natl. MS fr. 245, fol. 179v.

For the most part, however, representations of St. Cecilia focus upon her martyrdom, and that is the scene I propose to examine in some detail. They most often show her naked in a cauldron bath, with a fire blazing below and an executioner alongside ready to strike at her neck with a sword.

Let us take this up first in Chaucer's version, at the point where she has defeated Almachius in argument, deriding both the power of his office and his religious idols made of stone:

Thise wordes and swiche othere seyde she, (VIII 512)
And he weex wroth, and bad men sholde hir lede
Hom til hir hous, and "In hire hous," quod he,
"Brenne hire right in a bath of flambes rede."
And as he bad, right so was doon the dede;
For in a bath they gonne hire faste shetten,
And nyght and day greet fyr they under betten.

The longe nyght, and eek a day also,
For al the fyr, and eek the bathes heete,
She sat al coold, and feelede no wo.
It made hire nat a drope for to sweete.
But in that bath hir lyf she moste lete,
For he Almachius, with ful wikke entente,
To sleen hire in the bath his sonde sente.

Thre strokes in the nekke he smoot hire tho,
The tormentour, but for no maner chaunce
He myghte noght smyte al hir nekke atwo;
And for ther was that tyme an ordinaunce
That no man sholde doon man swich penaunce
The ferthe strook to smyten, softe or soore,
This tormentour ne dorste do namoore,

But half deed, with hir nekke ycorven there,
He lefte hir lye, and on his wey is went.

In his 1977 edition of Chaucer, John Fisher became the first to gloss the word *bath* in this passage in a historically accurate way, suggesting it means "bath in the Roman sense: a hypocaust, a room with a space under the floor where the heat from the furnace accumulated to heat it."[11] Well-born Romans condemned to death for political reasons were sometimes executed in this fashion, the heat and vapor of a bath permitting them the relative dignity of death by suffocation. The Church of St. Cecilia in Trastevere, in Rome, which the saint's legend claims is built upon the house in which she was martyred, contains just such a room, its heating conduits still well preserved.[12] But the characteristic medieval representation of her martyrdom makes no attempt at an archaeologically exact setting. Figure VII.6, for instance, errs in showing St. Cecilia wholly decapitated (the painter has succeeded where the historical executioner failed), but we cannot explain as inadvertence or error his failure to locate the event in a room in an Italian

VII.6. St. Cecilia's martyrdom. From a French Book of Hours, early fifteenth century. Cambridge, Trinity College MS B. 11. 31/32, fol. 216. By kind permission of the Master and Fellows.

villa: the painter, working from within an equally coherent medieval tradition, shows instead a tub in which the saint is naked.

The details of Cecilia's martyrdom linger long in the memory and invite meditation. Its importance relative to other events in her life can be gauged in Figure VII.7, a very large, early fourteenth-century Tuscan altar piece whose central panel displays an image of the saint in majesty. At its sides we see depicted (in an Italian mode) a sequence of narrative images, all but the first of which Chaucer's poetry invites us to imagine in our turn. (Robert Pratt suggests that Chaucer may well have seen this very painting during his visit to Florence in 1373).[13] At the upper left is shown the wedding banquet and, alongside, the scene in the bridal chamber, where Cecilia tells her husband she has an angel who will not allow her body to be touched in any carnal way. The crowning of Valerian by an angel is depicted below, along with Cecilia converting Tiburce as her husband listens. At the upper right is shown the baptism of Tiburce by Pope Urban and, alongside, Cecilia teaching at the house of Maximus. Below, Cecilia stands before Almachius, engaged in a battle of wits and theology, while in the final picture (see also Figure VII.8) Cecilia, naked in a bath heated by a fierce fire, prays to God as her executioner prepares to strike.

This last image is heroic in both style and substance, but in respect to Cecilia's nakedness it is erotic too—and in that emphasis it does not stand alone. Figure VII.6, already examined, is notably sensual in its depiction of the beauty of the saint's body, as are portraits of her in manuscripts commissioned by Jean, Duke of Berry. In Figure VII.9, for instance, an illumination from the *Belles heures* made for him circa 1408–9, the beautiful young woman who sits in a boiling bath offers much to reward the eye, not all of it devotional:[14] the saint's nakedness is emphasized, as it will be in Figure VII.10, a picture made some hundred years later. These images invoke a sense of the pathetic and vulnerable, to be sure, but of the voluptuous and desirable as well.

There is nothing in the legend of St. Cecilia to invite so compromised a gaze. Chaucer properly locates the saint's martyrdom within her own house ("in a bath they gonne hire faste shetten") and without specification of her nakedness. But, following the *Passio S. Caeciliae*, his source for the second half of the poem, he does ask us to imagine—to see in our mind's eye—St. Cecilia in "a bath of flambes rede," and for many, or all, in his first audiences, as for these painters contemporary with them, what would have come to mind is not a hypocaust in a Roman villa, which few persons then could have imagined, and which the poet does not detail. Instead they would have visualized the baths they knew, whether public or private: the small domestic tubs seen in some of these illuminations, or those to be found in public bathhouses—a familiar part of everyday life in the cities, frequently denounced in episcopal decrees and occasionally depicted in the art of the time.[15] Figure VII.11, for instance, from the margins of a deluxe manuscript of *The Romance of Alexander*, shows an invitation to the bath, followed by

VII.7. The saint in majesty. From an early fourteenth-century Tuscan altar piece, originally in the Church of St. Cecilia in Florence, now in the Uffizi Gallery. Courtesy of the Ministero per i Beni e le Attività Culturali, Firenze. Photo: © Gabinetto Fotografico, S.S.P.M.F., Firenze.

VII.8. St. Cecilia in a bath, heated by flames (detail of Figure VII.7).

VII.9. Portrait of St. Cecilia. From the *Belles heures* of Jean, Duc de Berry, French, ca. 1408–09. New York, The Metropolitan Museum of Art, Cloisters Collection, 1954 (54.1.1.), fol. 180. Image © The Metropolitan Museum of Art.

VII.10. St. Cecilia in a boiling bath. Ca. 1500–1510. Cambridge, Fitzwilliam Museum MS 118, fol. 198v.

the possible pleasures of such an occasion with a man and woman embracing there (Figure VII.12).[16] Such bathing is one of the occupations of the "children of Venus" in the Children of the Planets tradition: the relevant page in the famous German *Hausbuch* shows in its lower-left corner a bath in an arbor, with an aged female attendant ready to offer food and wine to the amorous couple taking their pleasure naked there. Venus rides high in the sky above.[17] The Bible, of course, offered its own cautionary tales concerning the nakedness of the bath and the fueling of sexual desire: in Figure VII.13 (upper register) we see David looking upon Bathsheba in her bath and lusting after her;[18] in Figure VII.14, Susanna, spied upon by the elders while bathing, arouses in them such lust they charge her with fornication when she refuses them her body.[19]

The medieval iconography of the bath, however, reflects above all the ordinary experience of town and city life, for public bathhouses throughout the Middle Ages were often charged with sexual licentiousness. In many of them men and women bathed together, naked or scantily clothed; food and drink were available, adding fuel to the metaphoric fire (in the words of Chaucer's Pardoner, as in many another medieval sermon, "The fyr of lecherye . . . is annexed unto glotonye" [VI 481–82]); and private rooms could be rented, ostensibly for resting. In Figure VII.15 we are shown a full range of the services that might be expected in elegant late fifteenth-century establishments of this kind, for public baths often served as brothels in the later Middle Ages,[20] their ostensible function furnishing a respectable cover. Indeed, the Old French word for a bathing place, *estuve*—literally, a small heated room with a fireplace into which a tub might be brought—provided fourteenth-century England with its preferred name for brothels: "the stews."[21] Chaucer used the word casually in both its French and its English

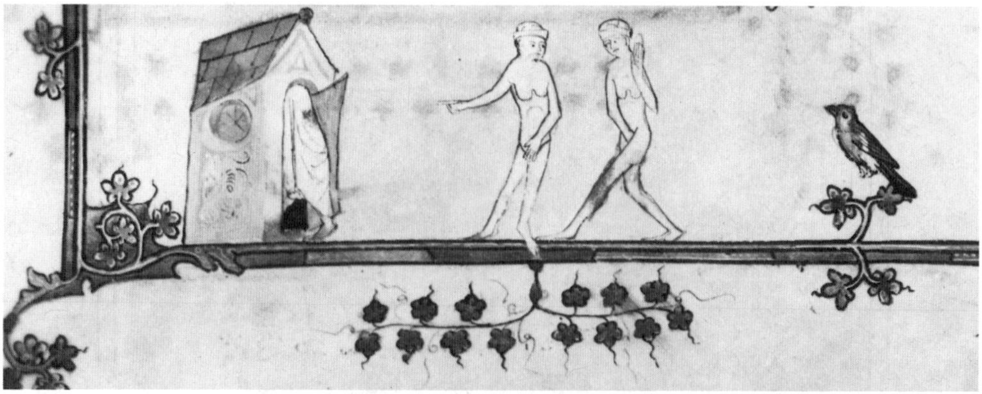

VII.11. Invitation to a bath. From the margins of *The Romance of Alexander*. Flemish, between 1339 and 1344. Oxford, Bodley MS 264, fol. 75.

forms: "So been the wommen of the *styves* / . . . y-put out of oure cure!" says the Summoner (III 1332–33), in speaking of limitations on his power, while the Pardoner focuses his tale upon young folk who "haunteden folye, / As riot, hasard, *stywes*, and tavernes" (VI 464). But Chaucer used the idea of the bath in its full ambiguity most subtly in *Troilus and Criseyde*, where it functions in moral counterpoint to the rhetorical celebration of Troilus and Criseyde's sexual union that dominates Book III. So far as I am aware, this usage has not been commented upon before; let me briefly examine its detail.

When Pandarus brings Criseyde to his house so that Troilus, in hiding, may ultimately bed her, the eager Troilus watches their arrival from a place characterized far more precisely than the action requires, and for which there is no cue in Chaucer's source, Boccaccio's *Il Filostrato*: "Troilus . . . stood and myght it se / Thorughout a litel wyndow in a stewe" (*TC*, III 600–601). Which is to say, he watches their arrival from a bathing room in Pandarus's house—on the face of things, a perfectly neutral domestic space. But in specifying it so, Chaucer allows other associations of the word *stewe* to complicate, ever so slightly, our larger identification with the lovers and the declared idealism of their love. For the *Troilus*, as any careful reader knows, contains within itself a variety of attitudes toward its central action, ranging from the closest emotional empathy to the most austere and distant philosophical rejection. Many details, even in the early books, prepare us for the palinode's revision and rejection of the love affair, and among them is this treatment of the room in which Troilus awaits Criseyde. In Boccaccio's *Il Filostrato*, in contrast, Criseida does not have to be tricked, and Troilus is hidden "in a certain dark and remote spot" for nothing more than propriety's sake, until she can secretly come to him.[22] Chaucer makes the room a "stewe" in order to link it to Pandarus's worries that his help in arranging the seduction of his niece might seem a kind of "bauderye" (III 249ff., 397)—or a kind of

VII.13. David looking upon Bathsheba in her bath. Paris, ca. 1250. New York, Pierpont Morgan MS M. 638, fol. 41v.

VII.12. Pleasures of the bath (from the same margin as Figure vii.11).

VII.14. Susanna spied upon by the elders as she bathes. From a German book of prayers to the saints, fifteenth century. London, Brit. Lib. MS Egerton 859, fol. 31. © The British Library. All Rights Reserved.

pandering, as we might say, to use a word his role in Chaucer's poem has added to our language. Troilus reassures him that there are distinctions to be made (III 400 ff.), but the question survives its ostensible answer, to be raised again when the lovers are finally brought together in bed. Chaucer describes that final act of conveyance as follows:

> But Pandarus, that wel koude eche a deel (*TC*, III 694)
> The olde daunce, and every point therinne,
> Whan that he sey that alle thynge was wel,
> He thoughte he wolde upon his werk bigynne,
> *And gan the stuwe doore al softe unpynne*;
> And stille as stoon, withouten lenger lette,
> By Troilus adown right he hym sette. (italics mine)

The rhetoric of the poem has been dominated to this point by ideas of love's idealism and its noble suffering, of love as heaven's bliss discoverable within the beloved's arms. These ideas dominate much of Book IV as well. But the claims of that language will be undercut—by external events, and by the falseness of Criseyde—just as they are, more subtly, by our troubled sense of what Pandarus is doing in this moment, admitting Troilus to the possession of Criseyde's body through a "stuwe doore." Although their ensuing union will be celebrated in a hymn to love of the greatest profundity and moving power, second only perhaps to the hymn to Christ's love reserved for the palinode, the poet has made us aware, in a fashion very different from irony, that there may be less here than meets the eye and feeds the heart—or, if not less, at least something other as well, which bears a different relationship to society and to the moral universe, and which bears within it the seeds of shame, of disillusion and loss, of tragedy and death.

In *The Second Nun's Tale*, Chaucer invokes something of this same background, though to a different end and without having to invent the essential detail: the martyrdom in a bath is given him by his sources. All versions known to me imply the symbolic identity of lechery with heat and fire, in

VII.15. Late fifteenth-century bathhouse. An illustration from Valerius Maximus, *Des faits et des paroles memorables*. Paris, Bibl. de l'Arsenal MS 5196, fol. 372.

saying of St. Cecilia that she remained in that bath as if in a cold place—"que quasi loco frigido mansit."[23] But Chaucer takes this one step further, to internalize the cold. In saying that she "sat al coold and feelede no wo," he focuses not on the *place* as it seemed to her but on what she felt within herself.

In making that subtle change, Chaucer does little more than emphasize the contrast between heat and cold already present in his sources. At its deepest level, the scene concerns neither torture—though that is what Cecilia's enemies intend—nor purification and testing—though that has been suggested by some critics. Except for its symbolic equation of fire and lechery, this scene has little in common with, say, the episode in Dante's *Purgatorio*, Cantos XXV and XXVI, where Dante, Virgil, and Statius regard the lustful being purged of their fleshy sin on a terrace of fire (Figure VII.16).[24] Our poem concerns instead the power of chastity to safeguard those who serve it absolutely. The coolness of Cecilia's chastity protects her from the fiery bath as surely as it protected her from Valerian's demands on the night of their wedding. Her martyrdom in the bath is simply a demonstration and celebration of that power. Through an act of grace, a metaphor (the coldness of chastity) is made literal; her survival is never in doubt.

This scene, considered on its own, evokes awe and wonder, emotions proper to miracle and to saints' legends. But it does not much invite pity, and it excludes any ordinary sort of human identification. Though virgin saints are common in the literature of hagiography, celibate marriages are not (and for obvious reasons seldom were) unequivocally advocated by the Church:[25] devotion to virginity does not normally express itself in marriage. As the Parson reminds us, the "entente of engendrure of children to the ser-

VII.16. Dante, Virgil, and Statius in purgatory. From a late fourteenth-century manuscript of the *Divine Comedy*. Venice, Bibl. Marciana MS it. 9. 276, fol. 45v.

vice of God . . . is the cause final of matrimoyne" (X 938), and to the great relief of the Wife of Bath (for one) that "entente"—the command that we be fruitful and multiply—remains valid under the New Law, however much other scriptural texts may imply different conclusions and higher goals. The Wife of Bath is troubled by those other texts, and in her Prologue offers inimitable comment upon them; for all her difficulties with the Christian "counsel to perfection," it is an integral part of her discourse. But in *The Second Nun's Tale* the situation is exactly the opposite: St. Cecilia enacts the counsel to perfection with such chastity of will that ordinary human life seems untouched by her example. Valerian is allowed to express doubt in response to her extraordinary claims and to have his doubt put to rest. But how is the Wife—or her surrogate in the minds of Chaucer's audiences—to be answered? Where indeed *are* future virgins to come from, if the "actes" and "fruyt of mariage" be denied? (I quote from *The Wife of Bath's Prologue*, III 71 ff., 114.) Where are we to find the woman in Cecile?

The poem deals with these questions on a level that transcends mere perpetuation of the race. God's command to Noah that we be fruitful and multiply is obeyed by Cecilia in spiritual ways—through spiritual procreation, spiritual fecundity. When Pope Urban thanks God for her conversion of Valerian, he refers to her husband as "the fruyt of thilke seed of chastitee / That thou has sowe in Cecile" (VIII 193). Which is to say, because God impregnated Cecilia with the seed of chastity she has born him a spiritual son: a husband moved to become Christian by her example. Conversion, from earliest times, has been thought of as an act of rebirth: "except ye be born again . . . "[26] Later portions of the poem will adopt a different rhetoric—the language of military alliance and victory, then of juridical debate[27]—but its overall action has to do with multiplication and the growth of a family, intimately related to this first event and deriving its inner meaning from it. In *Purgatorio*, XXII 76–78, Statius uses a similar metaphor to describe the world when Christianity was new and when he himself (in Dante's invention) was moved, by Virgil's fourth *Eclogue* and the teaching of the new preachers, to become a Christian: "Already the whole world was big [*quanto pregno*] with the true faith, sown [*seminata*] by the messengers of the eternal realm."[28]

In *The Second Nun's Tale*, Valerian and Cecilia then convert Tiburce; Valerian and Tiburce convert Maximus and his household; Maximus, in testifying to the deaths of Valerian and Tiburce, converts still others; Cecilia converts the ministers sent to bring her to Almachius; and for three days after her throat has been cut she preaches to those who survive her, strengthening them in the faith, recommending their souls to Urban, and leaving to them her house as a church in which they may worship. In such "generation" there is growth and increase, uncompromised by carnal heat. The chaste virgin proves herself fruitful: she becomes spiritually a mother.

Cecilia's marriage thus remains central to the entire poem, conferring upon her martyrdom in the fiery bath a meaning more subtle and interesting than comparable episodes in the lives of other saints. For while certain others, like St. Agatha, St. Agnes, or St. Margaret, are often also shown naked and beautiful in their martyrdoms,[29] St. Cecilia in a bath offers something more particular than yet another miraculous deliverance from torment, or of erotic beauty covered metaphorically, if not literally, by a cloak of sanctity. The image in Chaucer's poem—by which I mean the picture we make in our mind, colored by all that he has to say about it—presents not only Cecilia's saintly ordeal but a moral demonstration of her chastity. Like the children in the fiery furnace, whose virginity was understood to have preserved them from the fire (Dan. 3:91–94);[30] like God's appearance to Moses in a burning bush that was not consumed by the flame (Exod. 3:2), prefiguring Mary's virginity preserved during the conception of Christ;[31] and like the legend of St. John the Evangelist being thrown into a cauldron of boiling oil, which causes him no harm;[32] St. Cecilia in a bath "al coold" represents a condition beyond the reach of carnal heat or physical fire. It is a chastity both militant and maternal, and it is symbolized by another kind of flame:

> And right so as thise philosophres write (VIII 113)
> That hevene is swift and round and eek brennynge,
> Right so was faire Cecilie the white
> Ful swift and bisy evere in good werkynge,
> And round and hool in good perseverynge,
> And *brennynge evere in charite ful brighte*. (italics mine)

An English artist of the late fourteenth century may have had this other kind of fire in mind when he painted the saint in the pages of a Carmelite missal (Figure VII.17).[33] By depicting her standing serene and fully clothed amid flames, her halo radiating beams of light, he *may* have intended to suggest the fire of her martyrdom. But in the absence of a literal bath, or of an executioner swinging a sword alongside the flames,[34] I suspect that we are meant to discover here instead an image of the saint burning with this holier sort of love, "brennynge evere in charite ful brighte." St. Paul had expressed the supremacy of that other virtue unequivocally: "And though I give my body to be burned, and have not charity, it profiteth me nothing" (1 Cor. 13:3).[35] It seems likely that the artist of the Carmelite missal is at one with the author of the *Legenda aurea* and with Chaucer's Second Nun in visualizing this greater virtue as itself a kind of flame.

There is, then, beauty and complexity in *The Second Nun's Tale* that the visual arts of the time can help us recover. We have had time to examine only one part of that achievement here. But if Grennen and Rosenberg have too readily dismissed the Cecilia legend as negligible on its own, they may also, in their enthusiasm for it as a preface to *The Canon's Yeoman's Tale*, have overstated that relation in one respect closely associated with the present theme: the alchemical gloss they provide for the wedding of Valerian and St. Cecilia.

The mystifying manuals that claim to instruct in the "great work" of alchemy do often speak, it is true, as though its crucial procedures seek to

VII.17. St. Cecilia amid flames. In a Carmelite missal illuminated near the end of the fourteenth century. London, Brit. Lib. MS Add. 29704–5, fol. 160v (fragment 4/79). © The British Library. All Rights Reserved.

achieve a perfect union of male and female (a union of opposites, of contraries), from which some other, higher thing will be born. So described, the marriage of Valerian and Cecilia might seem indeed, in the words of Grennen's title, a "chemical wedding." If, however, one turns to the visual arts associated with alchemy, one is struck by how unequivocally sexual they are in depicting the several "marriages" that must occur in the course of the great work.[36] In this respect the pictures directly translate the language of the treatises they illustrate. In Figure VII.18, for instance, from the fifteenth century, the Red King (sulfur) and the White Queen (mercury) meet in full nakedness, as a sign that they have been freed from impurity. That condition is necessary to their chemical union, depicted as coition in the lower register of Figure VII.19, which symbolizes the dissolving of the two materials into one liquid state. Figure VII.20 represents a later stage in the work; because the materials have become volatile, the couple has grown wings. Though this picture dates from the sixteenth century, it illustrates the famous alchemical treatise by Arnaldus de Villanova from which Chaucer claims to quote at the end of *The Canon's Yeoman's Tale*: "Lo, thus seith Arnold of the Newe Toun, / As his Rosarie maketh mencioun" (VIII 1428).[37]

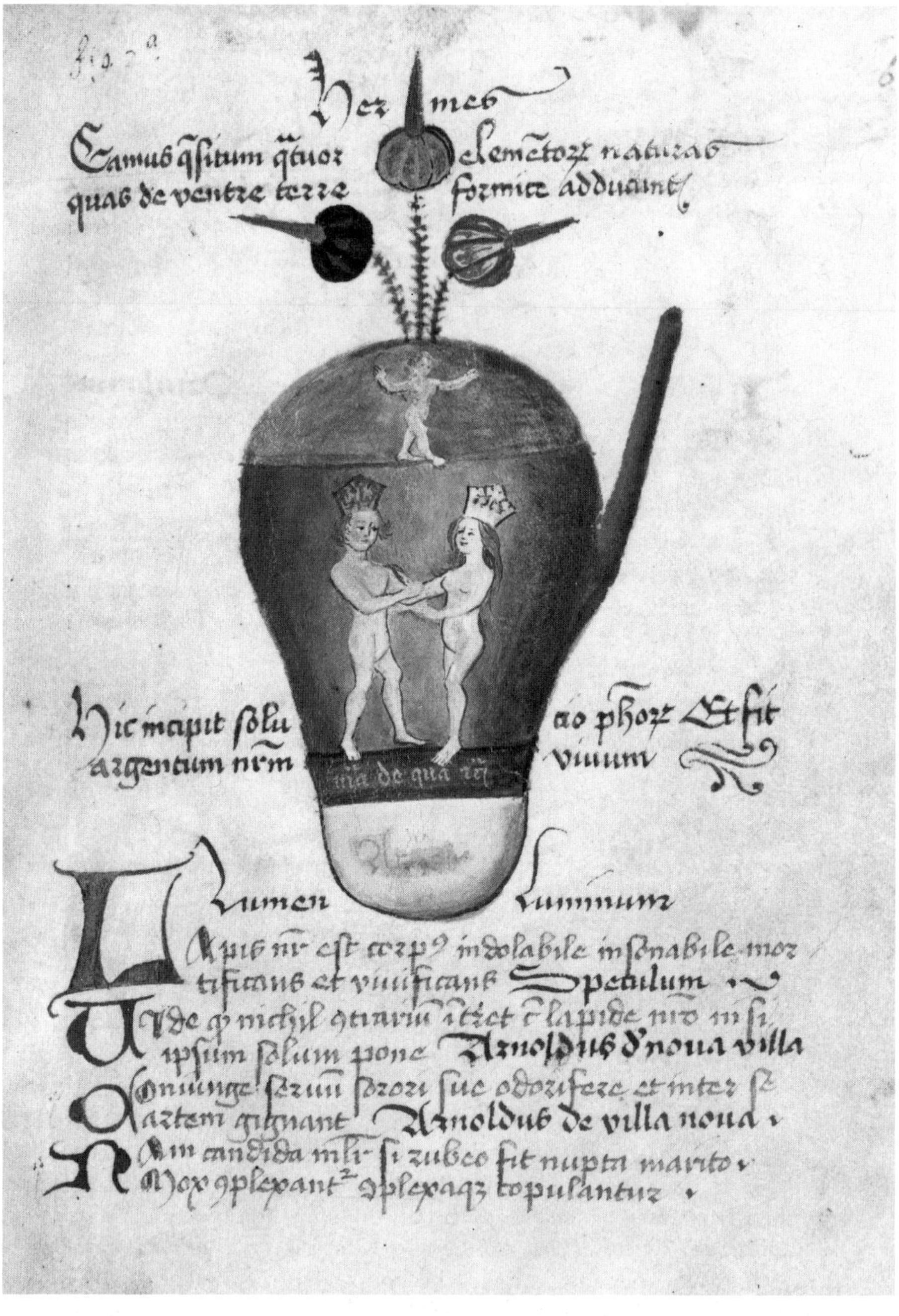

VII.18. The Red King (sulfur) and the White Queen (mercury), freed from impurity. From a fifteenth-century alchemical treatise by Johannes Andreae. London, British Library MS Sloane 2560, fol. 6. © The British Library. All Rights Reserved.

VII.19. The chemical union of the Red King and the White Queen. London, Brit. Lib. MS Sloane 2560, fol. 7.

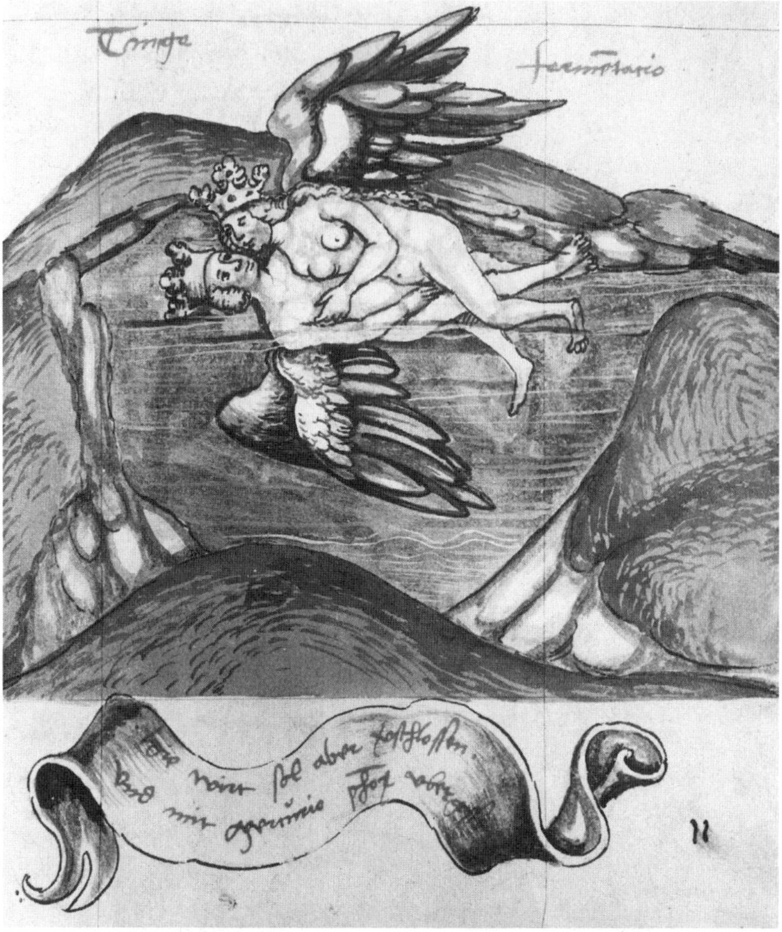

VII.20. The Red King and the White Queen with wings, illustrating Arnold of Villanova's earlier *Rosarium philosophorum*, in a sixteenth-century alchemical manuscript. St. Gall, Kantonsbibliothek St. Gallen, Vad. Sig., MS 394a, fol. 64.

The eroticism of these pictures is as explicit as it is inevitable. In seeking to *redeem* matter—to make matter more nearly perfect—alchemy was necessarily rooted in the physical world, and its symbolic language accurately reflects that fact. Grennen knew this, of course; he began his essay by characterizing the obscure and elusive science as "a perversion of orthodox religious ideals such as zeal and perseverance, . . . a profane parody of the divine work of Creation and an unwittingly sacrilegious distortion of the central mystery of the Christian faith."[38] But just as it was his proper business to focus upon possible relationships, it is mine in this essay to emphasize what is particular in the Cecilia legend. And so I must formally doubt that such a union is meant to be in our minds as we read of the marriage of St. Cecilia—however unusual that marriage may be. Her marriage *does not* take place in the flames (read by Grennen as analogous to the fire under the alchemists' crucible)[39]—indeed, her husband has been killed *before* she is subjected to the fire—and the higher thing that is born of their union, the increase of a Christian community, neither waits upon her martyrdom in the bath nor is it completed there. In the words of the Prologue, the "busynesse" of the saint (a very important aspect of her character) continues in heaven.

As I stated at the beginning of this chapter, there can be no question that *The Second Nun's Tale* illuminates *The Canon's Yeoman's Tale*, in word, theme, and image, in ways Grennen and Rosenberg have shown us more richly than anyone else. But I do not think that illumination significantly reciprocal or retrospective. Second only to *The Parson's Tale*, which manages without story of any kind, *The Second Nun's Tale* is the most absolute of the Canterbury narratives—uncompromised by irony, unmediated by larger context, and uncolored by the idiosyncrasies of a personal narrative voice. I think that Chaucer chose it to begin the concluding movement of *The Canterbury Tales* precisely because it is *about* clarity, light, brightness, fire. It exemplifies the *claritas* of truth, as it was then understood, as well as the *claritas* of medieval aesthetic theory. The light this tale casts upon the darker corners of what is to come—the darkness of the alchemists' world, or the Manciple's calculated praise of prudent silence—is like a searchlight moving outward from its source, not a candle whose flame is made brighter by reflection within a hall of mirrors. The legend of St. Cecilia might more accurately be said to imply a Christian answer to the alchemists' failure—the possibility of spiritual conversion and of moral change—than a Christian parallel to their vision of success. I think it a mistake, however, to read the tale in terms of that relationship only. The legend itself is powerful and complex, in ways that can be lost to us if we focus our attention too exclusively on what lies ahead.

So let me end this chapter where it began, with the tale itself taken at its thematic and iconographic center: with St. Cecilia "al coold" in a "bath of flambes rede." The paradox of that penultimate scene recapitulates the shock of her nuptial address to Valerian: I have an angel who loves me, who will kill you if you touch my body in any carnal way. But it does so within an altered context, made significantly less austere by ideas of spiritual fecundity. Leaving behind the rhetoric that has dominated the middle of the tale—the language of a "warfaring" Christianity, in which battles are won by a patient submission to death—the poet speaks once again in the language that earlier declared Valerian to be the "fruyt" of the seed of chastity sown by God in Cecile. At her fervent request the King of Heaven allows her to live on for three days, half dead "with hir nekke ycorven there," so that she can continue to teach and preach to those "that she hadde fostred" (VIII 533, 538).

In a last will and testament she leaves to them her household furnishings ("hir moebles and hir thyng") and asks Pope Urban to make of her house a church where they can worship. The domestic scale of that literal legacy is as important as the modesty—and tenderness—of the verb *fostred*: the concluding rhetoric of the poem is warmed once again by the idea of a family and its nurture, of maternal love and care. The coldness of Cecilia's chastity is circumscribed by the fire of her charity; and in that, according to the medieval Church, she will forever continue to burn "ful brighte."

VIII. God-Denying Fools

Tristan, Troilus, and the Medieval Religion of Love

At the 1994 congress of the New Chaucer Society, hosted by Trinity College, Dublin, Jill Mann delivered her Presidential Address under the provocative title "Chaucer and Atheism"—the atheism in question being, of course, not Chaucer's but her own. "I am uncomfortable," she said, "with the implicit notion that we in the twentieth century can somehow free ourselves from our own historic moment and read texts in their own terms in a way that earlier centuries could not manage." Marxism, Lacanian psychology, deconstructionism, feminism, all engage critically—and at a distance—with the medieval text and the culture that produced it. But in matters concerning religious faith, historicism reigns. Medieval Christianity is a given, to be thought about only from within, and those of us who do not share its beliefs—whether atheist or agnostic, Asian, Muslim, or Jew—mostly suppress that fact. "It is as if religion, unlike feminism, is not an issue"—as if, on a global scale, religious faith had no continuing relevance, no (often appalling) political consequence. We settle for the pleasure of thinking in terms other than our own—a real pleasure, not to be disdained—only occasionally wondering at just what it is we are doing. "Sometimes," Jill Mann said, "I frighten myself with the power of my Christian apologetics."[1]

I suspect many scholars and teachers might confess the same, sharing Mann's concern that we discuss religion in this way as an act of secular bad faith, potentially misleading to our students and troubling to ourselves. Casting a skeptical eye on our habit of thinking chiefly "from within" the religious assumptions of the original culture, Jill Mann offered some striking examples of how a nonbeliever openly in dialogue with a Christian text might enrich its historical as well as contemporary significance.

Charles Muscatine, himself a former president of the New Chaucer Society, just two years earlier in an essay entitled "Chaucer's Religion and the Chaucer Religion," offered an equally pointed critique of "the religious, almost puritanical Chaucer who emerges powerfully and suddenly at mid-century and is with us still," an idea of Chaucer that seems to him essentially new in the Chaucer tradition. Like Jill Mann, he finds this religious Chaucer "peculiarly difficult to connect to late twentieth-century sensibility"—by which I take him to mean, hard to relate to the way we actually live, the things we actually believe in.[2]

Whether or not a "religious" Chaucer emerges legitimately from the Chaucer texts is too large a question to pursue here. (I feel both honored and chagrined to be named among its chief proponents.) But along with Professors Muscatine and Mann (and perhaps no small number of others) I sometimes wonder at the fact that so much of my professional life, in the classroom, the library, and at the personal computer, should be spent attempting to recover the intellectual and emotional force of religious beliefs I do not share. In this chapter, I want to take this "emerging topic of presidential discourse" a step or two further, not only to correct an imbalance in my own critical practice, but to introduce a figure generally assumed never to have existed at all—the medieval nonbeliever—and to say a few words on his behalf. I cannot, it is true, produce an atheist who would have been recognizable to the age of Enlightenment—an age when the universe became entirely rational and God an unnecessary hypothesis. But I can bring forward someone at least as interesting, if only because he was so difficult for medieval culture to conceive: the fool of Psalms 13 and 52,[3] who says in his heart, There is no God. (*Dixit insipiens in corde suo: non est Deus.*)

Medieval ideas of nonbelief can be found, to some degree, in patristic commentary on these psalms, but more telling by far in illustrations to the second of them—Psalm 52—in psalters dating from the thirteenth through the early fifteenth centuries. Because that psalm was illustrated, for liturgical convenience, in virtually every deluxe psalter—the most important class of book produced in the thirteenth century, central to monastic and lay devotion alike—there are many pictures to show us what a God-denying fool looked like in the medieval imagination.

The commentators, we should note, do their best to avoid any confrontation with what we would call the atheistic sense of his claim. In the words of St. Hilary of Poitiers, commenting upon Psalm 52 in the fourth century, such words are said *in the heart* by those who don't want to be known as fools: "Who can look at the world and not perceive there is a God?"[4] St. Augustine, commenting upon Psalm 13, affirmed the same: "Not even those philosophers whose impiety and false and perverse theories concerning the Godhead are to be detested have dared to say: 'There is no God.' This assertion is therefore made merely *in his heart*; even if he dare to think such a thing, he dares not proclaim it [aloud]."[5] Eusebius, writing in Greek in the fourth century, and already using the word *átheos* for such a person, had explained why such persons must be rare indeed: a "knowledge of God is instilled in all of us by nature."[6] Not until the seventeenth century was it possible to respond to "There is no God" as a credible proposition, for which a rational case might be made.[7]

Before then the idea could be stated in only in the most minimal terms—

seldom more than a repetition of the formula *non est deus*—and only within the safety of a text that worked its way to a statement of faith or put forward logical counterproof. The psalm itself offers reassurance in its closing verses: "When God shall bring back the captivity of his people, Jacob shall rejoice, and Israel shall be glad" (52:7). And philosophic texts demonstrating the opposing truth were provided across the medieval centuries, most notably by St. Augustine in his treatise on free will, *De libero arbitrio voluntatis*, completed around 395; by St. Anselm in his *Proslogion*, in 1077–78; and by St. Thomas Aquinas in his *Summa theologiae*, ca. 1265–68, where the second question—"whether there is a God"—is answered by five magisterial proofs of His existence. All three of these texts—each of them enormously influential—address their argument explicitly to the psalter fool. But in each he is brought forward as a straw man, a striking way to launch the proof, nothing more.[8] The Middle Ages otherwise preferred to see *non est deus* as an irrational statement, useful at best in teaching the nature of false logic in the schools. A collection of six *impossibilia* composed by Siger of Brabant between 1266 and 1276—witty explorations of propositions self-evidently untrue—is careful to begin with: "Primum impossibile fuit deum non esse" (The first impossibility [is] that God does not exist).[9] The generic absurdity of such an idea can be deduced from another example explored by Siger, "The Trojan War is still in progress," or from other propositions in similar collections, such as "Things infinite are finite" and "A man's foot is greater than the world." Like these, the notion that God might not exist seemed preposterous, worth thinking on only as a way of developing logical skill. In Siger's examples, it goes without saying, the refutations form the major part of the text.[10]

The Middle Ages, in short, could make no sense of the proposition *non est deus*, and we should not imagine that anyone then really wished to do so. To believe that the order and beauty of the universe did not imply a Creator, Governor, and Supreme Being would have involved a paradigm shift as profound as imagining that the earth was not the center of the universe, with psychological consequences even more unsettling. For us, of course, it is different. Christianity is but one religion among many, and there is—in the West at least—no social or moral obligation to choose any at all. We decide for ourselves. But, as Lucien Febvre concluded in a landmark book, *The Problem of Unbelief in the Sixteenth Century*, even in that period Christianity "happened somehow automatically, inevitably, independently of any express wish to be a believer, to be a Catholic, to accept one's religion or to practice it. . . . One found oneself immersed from birth in a bath of Christianity from which one did not emerge even at death," for the Church not only baptized one before one had any say in the matter, but buried one when one's say was gone. It provided "rituals that no one could escape"—no matter what the mood of one's participation, not even if one sometimes mocked and scoffed. Between birth and death every aspect of human life—educational, marital, economic, political—was stamped by religion, so much so that "even the most intelligent of men, the most learned, and the most daring, were truly incapable of finding any support either in philosophy or science against a religion whose domination was universal."[11] If a coherent case for atheism could not be made even in the sixteenth century, as Febvre decisively demonstrates—and he focuses upon the bold and brilliant circle of Rabelais—how slight the chance of it during those earlier centuries oversimply but not inappropriately styled an Age of Faith?

Small chance indeed. Medieval commentators on these psalms chiefly make *non est deus* mean *something other* than "there is no God" and modern scholars, one way or another, have mostly followed their lead. But for a long time now, as other duties and projects have permitted, I have been doubting that proposition, and for the simplest of all possible reasons. Many years ago, in the pages of a medieval psalter, I came upon the image of a "nonbeliever" (Figure VIII.1)—or so it seemed to me—and like those zealous folk among us who claim to have seen UFOs, I found myself unwilling to abandon that possibility, at least not without further testing. Soon I came upon another such; eventually upon dozens; by now, I would guess, somewhere near two hundred. And there were parallel sightings, equally difficult to explain. I started encountering these enigmatic figures elsewhere, carrying with them (it struck me as possible) the proposition *non est deus* into other pictorial sites and other iconographic traditions—most especially those concerned with the Passion of Christ and the persecution of saints. I started finding fools there, sometimes in the role of a tempter or tormentor, sometimes simply as a spectator, as a face in the crowd looking on. I started thinking seriously about what all these pictures might mean.

But let us examine more closely the first such image I ever encountered—Figure VIII.1, from the Psalter of Jean, Duc de Berry, painted by Jacquemart de Hesdin circa 1386, after a model by Jean Pucelle.[12] What struck me about it, above all, was its almost shocking modernity: its pitiless rendering of human suffering, alienation, emptiness, and despair. I had never before encountered a medieval painting so austere, so unrooted in any meaning external to, or larger than, itself. I saw in it the image of a secular man—or as much as the age could imagine of such a person—half-naked, frail, inhabiting an emptied universe. Like Job in his afflictions, he wears little more than torn undergarments, with a hospital cloth or winding sheet about his back and head. No God looks down on him. Though his figure is not without grace, the draperies not without beauty, the club shapely and of some potential menace, it is a tragic picture for all that—for those details count for nothing when set against the misery of the face (Figure VIII.2), the death in the eyes, the gnawing at something that seems unlikely to yield nourishment of any kind. What the fool is shown eating, I discovered, invites a variety of interpretations. Art historians mostly take it to be a cake, a cheese, a loaf. But my first guess was that it is a stone—an intuition I can now verify as authentically medieval. The picture spoke of an abject and insatiable hunger, and I saw in it a likeness—how shall I say?—embarrassingly personal. I made some notes on it, not because it reminded me of anything in Chaucer—the

VIII.1. Psalm 52: Dixit insipiens: "The Fool hath said in his heart: 'There is no God.'" Duc de Berry Psalter, Paris, painted by Jacquemart de Hesdin, ca. 1386, after a model by Jean Pucelle. Paris, Bibl. Natl. MS fr. 13091, fol. 106.

VIII.2. Psalm 52 (detail from Figure VIII.1). Madness, hunger, and alienation.

research I was in fact beginning—nor as a seed for the major research project it would become—it was years before I recognized that—but because I did not want to lose the details of this image. I wanted to know what the fool was eating. I wanted to know what *his* denial of God's existence entailed.

The book I continue writing on this subject, greatly expanding a series of four lectures already given as the Alexander Lectures at the University of Toronto and the Clark Lectures at Trinity College, Cambridge, will reproduce a great many fool-pictures of this kind, and introduce them with appropriate care.[13] Here a few must stand in for the many—in all their strangeness, without much explanation—to establish a minimum visual matrix for this chapter. But I have carefully chosen them to represent the dominant tradition in the thirteenth and early fourteenth centuries. As we will see, it virtually never depicts the fool as someone capable of rationality. He is shown instead as feeble-minded or insane (Figure VIII.3).

There was no textually inevitable reason for that choice. As the text itself in its third and fourth verses makes clear, the psalmist had a much broader human reference in mind: "God looked down from heaven on the children of men: to see if there were any that did understand or did seek God./All have gone aside, they are become unprofitable together: there is *none* that doth good, *no not one*" (italics mine).

St. Augustine's commentary on the Psalms, the most influential ever written, openly acknowledges the need to transform the unthinkable text into some more general kind of folly, lest the psalm seem to pertain to "very few." "A difficult thing it is to meet with a man who says in his heart, 'There is no God.'"[14]

VIII.3. Psalm 52: David prays to the Lord; the God-denying fool runs mad. Isabella Psalter, Paris, ca. 1255–65. Cambridge, Fitzwilliam Museum MS 300, fol. 57.

Augustine too found one sort of larger relevance by noting that the fool's denial is not spoken aloud; it is said in the heart, secretly. Surely, he wrote, this concerns that multitude of folk who live in sin shamelessly, as a matter of daily habit. Because God has not punished them, they carry on as though he condoned their way of living—as though, indeed, he were pleased by it. But, continues Augustine, in a voice of thunder, "he who thinks to please God with evil deeds, thinks God not to be God. For *if* God *is*, He is just; if He is just, injustice displeases Him, iniquity displeases Him. When you think, God does not care about my sins, you say nothing else but 'There is no God.'"[15] Augustine's explanation is both ethical and abstract: to deny God's justice is to deny God's existence, inconceivable without that quality. And to live as though something were true is to say it in your heart. (We should note that the African psalter, so called, used by Augustine, translated *nabal*—the Hebrew word for fool in these psalms—as *imprudens*, not *insipiens*.)

But one virtually never sees persons of this kind—capable of reason, however imprudent or unwise—illustrating this psalm. Instead, in a cycle of eight psalter illustrations invented in Paris circa 1205–30 and soon standard across Europe,[16] he is shown as a madman or congenital idiot (Figure VIII.4)—even though in Christian theology reason must consent to sin before sin becomes

VIII.4. Psalm 52: the God-denying fool, tonsured and anguished, with fool's food and jester's "marotte." *Bible historiale*, Paris, 1357. London, Brit. Lib. MS Royal 17 E. vii, fol. 241. © The British Library. All Rights Reserved.

deadly. This severely marginalizing choice is striking, of course, and was suggested by the semantic valence of several words used (in psalter Latin and its vernacular translations) for "fool." But its relation to the text makes less and less sense the longer one looks. Where the text speaks simply of human folly, these images present a radical dysfunction or deficiency of mind.

These versions of the God denyer are therefore of interest not just as a medieval freak show, enticing to the voyeur in us all (Figure VIII.5), but because they so obviously swerve from, and seek to evade, the text's most culturally destructive meaning, the possibility of *no God*. (This is true, with a difference, even for those court fools and jesters who in the mid-fourteenth century begin to replace the feebleminded and the insane.)[17] For to answer the question, "Who among us does not believe in the existence of God?" by pointing to a moron, an idiot, a madman (Figure VIII.6), is on the face of it absurd. Such persons are as credulous as any—if, indeed they are able to form any such idea at all—and as little likely to deny the existence of God.[18] Nor will such creatures serve to answer the question, "Who among us is an enemy of God's people?" (the psalm's own internal gloss on the fool). Socially outcast, confused in mind, peculiar in behavior, such men pose no threat to kingly

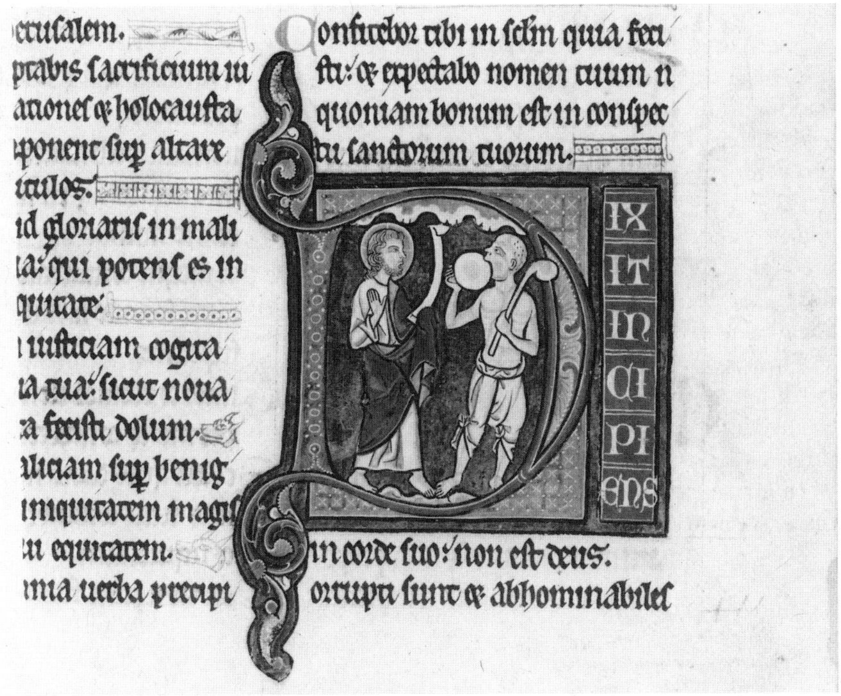

VIII.5. Psalm 52: the God-denying fool encounters Christ, with fool's food and club. Guines Psalter, Paris, after 1228 (ca. 1240?). London, Brit. Lib. MS Add. 30045, fol. 28. © The British Library. All Rights Reserved.

VIII.6. Psalm 52: the God-denying fool cavorts before David, naked and mad. Breviary, East Anglia, 1322–25. London, Brit. Lib. MS Stowe 12, fol. 180. © The British Library. All Rights Reserved.

rule, or to things as they are, or to anyone's religious faith. They lack cultural standing. The moron's bauble is no more than a soft toy—a bladder filled with air, or stuffed with hair or feathers—incapable of causing harm. Even the madman's club (Figure VIII.7), though it could be swung in anger or self-defense,[19] most often simply rests on his shoulder. In the most anguished and ineffectual of these images, he uses it to threaten God in the sky (Figure VIII.8). What the psalmist has to say of "the children of men"—"there is none that doth good, no, not one"—has been shrunk and narrowed, to implicate only the most marginal of creatures: madmen who have lost their wits and morons who never had any to begin with. Images of lunacy and mental frenzy uncouple the devastating text (*non est deus*) not only from any possible connection with truth but from any connection with mental processes at all (Figure VIII.9). It cannot even be contemplated as error.

In a rare example that shows both a fool and a proper man wagging his finger at God (Figure VIII.10), we may be meant to read the fool symboli-

VIII.7. Psalm 52: the God-denying fool in contention with some person (or persons) unseen, his body turned against itself. Psalter, Milan, beginning of the fifteenth century. Oxford, Bodley MS. Canon. Liturg. 378, fol. 59v.

VIII.8. Psalm 52: the God-denying fool eating at fool's food and threatening with his club; Christ looks down from above. *Bible historiale*, by Jean de Papeleu, presented to Charles V. Paris, 1317. Paris, MS Arsenal 5059, fol. 237v.

cally, as standing for the hidden nature of the other.[20] But pictures of a fool alone, or looked on only by God, or rebuked by a king frustrate a symbolic transfer to others more mentally competent (Figure VIII.11). Their signification is stubbornly literal, their hidden logic unacknowledged anxiety and fear. At their most powerful, I suggest, they tell us that the Middle Ages was *in fact* able to imagine something like atheism—if by that we are willing to mean what it would be like to live in a world without God, or within a mind unable to conceive the idea of God. If medieval man could not think such an idea through, he could at least give it body and gesture. The opening initial to Psalm 52 thus became a site of existential danger, hospitable only to the radically other. Within its ornamented frame religious nonbelief was made identical with the suffering and alienation experienced—for wholly unrelated reasons—by the medieval madman/moron/fool (Figure VIII.12).

VIII.9. Psalm 52: the God-denying fool, with "marotte," makes music by biting the tail of a dog; Christ looks down at him in sorrow. *Bible historiale*, by Jean de Vaudetar, presented to Charles V. Paris, 1372. The Hague, Museum Meermanno-Westreenianum MS 10B23, fol. 293.

VIII.10. Psalm 52: two God-denying fools, one simple-minded, the other ostensibly sane, but wagging his finger in contention with Christ above. Huth Psalter, Lincoln, ca. 1280. London, British Library MS Add. 38116, fol. 60v.

VIII.11. Psalm 52: the God-denying fool rebuked by David, eating at fool's food and carrying a soft bladder on a stick. Psalter, East Anglia, ca. 1310–20. Oxford, All Souls MS lat. 7, fol. 49v. By kind permission of the Warden and Fellows.

VIII.12. Psalm 52: a "natural" fool, hairless and naked beneath his mantle, prepares to eat fool's food while brandishing his club against Christ. Psalter, Artois, end of the thirteenth century. Oxford, Bodley MS Douce 118, fol. 60v.

So it was not in fact the portrait of a nonbeliever I met so long ago in the pages of the Duc de Berry's psalter—that has been just a way of talking—but rather an apotropaic image of one, an image meant to do ideological work. Just as gargoyles on the cathedrals were designed to ward off evil spirits from without, so these psalter fools were meant to ward off the unbeliever—that part of us capable of existential doubt—always potential within.

Yet the text they illustrate had, paradoxically, a performative dimension. Because the Divine Office of the Church required that the Book of Psalms be recited in its entirety every week of the liturgical year, monastic communities *in their own voices* chanted aloud the words of the fool—twice weekly, reciting Psalms 13 and 52 across the medieval centuries. The text denying divinity—*non est deus*—was not (and could not) in itself be denied or suppressed. But it could be made safe by attributing it visually solely to the senseless or insane (Figure VIII.13). Scarecrows of the mind, these fools return us to ground zero: to the terror, confusion, and vulnerability out of which religious belief is born,[21] and to the fear by which, in moments of greatest stress or doubt, it is sustained. They illustrate the anxiety induced by the text rather than the text itself.

There is about this whole tradition, in fact, a startling incoherence, a telling pile-up of cultural and religious self-contradiction that can take us deeper into the otherwise largely unrecorded history of medieval nonbelief. As we know from many sources, medieval madmen and idiots were treated harshly in real life. Europe was still an agrarian, sparsely populated society in which few traveled far from their birthplace; local inbreeding was inevitable; and born fools were not uncommon, though never perfectly assimilated or understood. They could be mocked, knocked about, driven from town to town, stoned by children, and set upon by dogs (Figure VIII.14), all in thoughtless affirmation of the normal, the healthy, the whole. It must have seemed appropriate in its way. Even now, mental illness remains the most puzzling of human conditions, and in those days was understood largely in biblical terms, as a punishment from God for sin.[22] Feeblemindedness too offered fair game, for if reason represents God's image within us, the fool's natural deficiency reveals him less than fully human, in ways mordantly embodied in the manikin or homunculus psalter fool (Figure VIII.15). To treat such creatures roughly must have seemed to reflect in some careless, almost carnival way the mystery of God's inscrutable justice—though even the Middle Ages sometimes judged that justice harsh indeed.[23]

For there is another part to this story. In more thoughtful contexts and by more thoughtful minds, the mad and simple-minded were elsewhere judged to be in need of protection, deserving of pity and compassion. Canon and

VIII.13. Psalm 52: the God-denying fool, with no God in the sky, but with fool's food and "marotte." Breviary, near Ghent, early fourteenth century. London, Brit. Lib. MS Add. 29253, fol. 41v. © The British Library. All Rights Reserved.

VIII.14. Psalm 52: the God-denying fool eating at fool's food (compare the orb held by Christ), beset by dogs. Prayer book of Queen Joanna, Naples, third quarter of the fourteenth century. Vienna, Österreichische Nationalbibliothek MS 1921, fol. 65.

VIII.15. Psalm 52: the God-denying fool before King David, naked and mad. Aurifaber Bible, Paris, end of the thirteenth century. Paris, Bibliothèque Sainte-Geneviève MS 1181, fol. 184v. Photo © Bibliothèque Sainte-Geneviève, Paris.

VIII.16. Psalm 52: the God-denying fool as Jew, drinking from a chalice and tormented by a Christian. The Psalter and Hours of Bonne of Luxembourg, Paris, before 1349. New York, The Metropolitan Museum of Art, Cloisters Collection, 1969 (69.86, fol. 83v). Image © The Metropolitan Museum of Art.

secular law alike recognized that such persons could not be held responsible for their actions, for the vagaries of what they might do or say.[24] Common sense dictated as much, as did the example of Christ, who cast out devils to cure the tortured in mind, and who is recorded as loving the simple and the afflicted with special care. The history of his Passion complicated the matter even more, for in other medieval commentary on these psalms, excluded here, the Jews bring Christ to trial explicitly as a God denyer—a carpenter's son who by claiming God as his Father denies the divinity that distinguishes God from man. In a notable exchange vividly staged in plays of the Passion, Herod, enraged by Christ's silence, deems him an idiot-mute and sends him back to Pilate in the white coat of a natural fool.[25]

The dressing of Christ as a fool goes far beyond insult, though Herod in the Gospels intends nothing more. In terms of medieval iconography, it made visible a deeper truth, first expressed by St. Paul when he described the crucifixion (including his preaching on it) as "foolishness"—a startling vision of the Passion at once resistant to theological system and diminished by comforting exegesis. Whereas the Jews seek a sign, he wrote, and the Greeks wisdom, "we preach Christ crucified; unto the Jews indeed a stumbling-block and unto the Gentiles foolishness." Since God has "made foolish the wisdom of this world" (1 Cor. 1:18–25), those who follow Christ must imitate his example in this respect also, just as he, Paul, and the apostles have done: "We are made a spectacle to the world and to angels and to men. / We are fools for Christ's sake, but you are wise in Christ. . . . / Even unto this hour we both hunger and thirst and are naked and are buffeted and have no fixed abode" (1 Cor. 4:9–10). In a prayer full of paradox he pleads, "Take me as one foolish that I also may glory a little" (2 Cor. 11:16–23).[26] For this reason too, images of Christ as the Man of Sorrows sometimes bring to mind the psalter fool, for those images, meant to stir our compassion, employ a similar language of nakedness, abjection, humiliation, and abandonment.[27] The most terrible moment on the cross, after all, occurs when Jesus "with a loud voice" cries out at the ninth hour, "My God, My God, Why hast thou forsaken me?" (Mark 15:34). For Christ too, shortly before his death, there was no certain God. In this respect, the lolling head and dead eyes of the Duc de Berry fool might almost have been copied from a painting of Christ crucified (Figure VIII.2): absent the Resurrection, Christ's Passion would read like the fool's. Augustine embraced the paradox in its full power: "We were trapped by the wisdom of the serpent; we are freed by the foolishness of God."[28]

But illustrations to Psalm 52, such as that from the Psalter of Bonne of Luxembourg forbid compassion and admit no complexity (Figure VIII.16).[29] Instead, the mysterious place of madness and simple-mindedness in God's provision for our race is brought to bear upon a text too destructive to be confronted directly, leaving both as unintelligible as before. The madman/idiot/fool is a bearer of surplus, inchoate meaning, testifying to an anxiety otherwise unacknowledgeable within the *imperium* of the medieval Church.

I used to think the point of historical research was to reconstruct the logic and coherence of the past, especially in the case of cultures unlike our own. I still believe that to be the first among our professional tasks, the one that teaches us most and best keeps us human. But cultural apologetics—reading "from within"—can take us only so far. I have traced a few of the contradictions latent in medieval attitudes toward the mentally impaired, along with others arising from the illuminators' translation of psalter fool into halfwit or madman, in order to account for the power of such an image. (Clarity is not the only source of what stirs us most deeply.) But I have done so as well to free myself from complicity in its purpose, coerced by a creed and ideology I do not share.

I want now to go further, to suggest a *resistant* reading—a reading "against the grain"—that might speak on behalf of such imagery, according it a dignity and importance wholly unintended by those who first imagined mental deficiency or madness as a suitable illustration to this text. We have reached an aporia, a breakdown in common sense and logic normally sufficient to signal the end of a discourse. Let us see if it can also begin one, now in the character of that rarest of all psalter fools (Figure VIII.17)—a philosophical man, downcast but clearly rational, capable of *thinking* the thought that denies God.[30]

VIII.17. Psalm 52: the God-denying fool as a troubled but thoughtful man. Bible, probably Paris, beginning of the thirteenth century. Florence, Bibl. Medicea Laurenziana MS Plut.15.11, fol. 286v. Courtesy of the Ministero per i Beni e le Attività Culturali, Firenze. Photo ©: Biblioteca Medicea Laurenziana. All Rights Reserved.

A resistant reading might run something like this. For those of us agnostic by temperament and intellectual conviction, there must always be an honored place for that which refuses assimilation or incorporation, for those eruptions and fissures that belie otherwise totalizing claims to cultural authority and explanatory truth. The medieval churchmen who first commissioned these images of madman/simpleton/fool testify, almost against their will, to the fool's relevance: to the urgency of our human need for significance beyond ourselves, and to the terror with which we experience the possibility of its absence. And so one may claim for the psalter fool this dignity at least: he presents us with an image instead of an answer to the deepest of all human questions, the question of what life means, and whence such meaning derives. If, in truth, there is no transcendental answer, or if it must include *without transcendence* all that is most abject and unaccommodated in our nature, then we had best learn to acknowledge without flinching—as we have learned to do in the case of *King Lear* or the works of Samuel Beckett—our kinship with this figure, the product of a medieval system otherwise not particularly prescient in imagining *us*, we who look upon such pictures now. The psalter fool is a nightmare, intentionally so, but he is also a relevant nightmare. Better than any other image during the medieval centuries, he kept the possibility of nonmeaning open, the questions too confidently answered by religious faith alive.

Commentary on Psalms 13 and 52 has remarkably little to do with the madman-moron tradition. The latter, born of existential fear and cultural scapegoating, found its natural expression in the visual arts, where logical, defensible explanation is not necessary. The commentators instead sought to avoid the atheistic sense of *non est deus* altogether, swerving from it in a number of ways. Across the medieval centuries, they discovered the fool in ordinary sinners who behave as though God were not offended by their sin (the Augustinian reading referred to above). They found him too in those who love earthly things, branding them in a generalized way as followers of Antichrist. Or they found him, more confidently still, in the Jew of history—whom they charged with the death of Christ—and in contemporary Jews, whom they saw as perversely denying Christ's divinity still. (The fool as Jew, and the historical consequence of that identification, will furnish me the other major subject of my forthcoming book; it will not be noticed further in this chapter.)[31] Certain other groups are stigmatized as well: pagans, heretics, and idolators are all sometimes named, usually without elaboration, as versions of the psalter fool.

A motley, ill-sorted crew, linked together (it is important to note) by this single remarkable fact: none of them can reasonably be said to doubt the existence of God. They may from the Christian point of view worship the wrong God, or hold false opinions about His nature, or live less than well. But they do not imagine themselves living in a universe unanchored in divine intelligence and purpose. We might well call them God forgetters (those who live complacently in sin), or God supplanters (those who prefer a false or inappropriate God), or God mistakers (those who hold heretical beliefs). But not God denyers. These weaker versions of the fool of Psalms 13 and 52 are culturally less revealing than the psalter madmen and idiots we have been examining. But they nevertheless underwrite one further move, his unexpected migration into medieval literary "courts of love." That move will be my further topic in this chapter. In two great medieval poems, the *Folie de Tristan*, and Chaucer's *Troilus and Criseyde*—one from early thirteenth-century France, the other from late fourteenth-century England—themes and images related to the psalter *insipiens* once again break open a topic that Christian orthodoxy preferred to think of as settled and closed. In a song from *Stop the World! I Want to Get Off*, Anthony Newley used to ask of love, "What kind of fool am I?"—a question I once intended to ask on behalf of Tristan and Troilus in the title of this chapter. But the question I have in mind might be better put so: what did the fool of Psalm 52 bring to "love *paramours*," the medieval "courtly" "religion of love"?

The larger story of Tristan and Yseult's adulterous love, fueled by a love potion they drink unaware, is well known to modern readers, but possibly less well the *Folie de Tristan* version in its most relevant detail. Let me retell it briefly, from the version preserved in Berne, using a French ivory casket (Figure VIII.18), made circa 1325, to illustrate its iconographic potential.[32] The first panel, far left, is irrelevant to my present topic: it illustrates an earlier episode in which King Mark, uncle to Tristan and husband to Yseult, hides in a tree to spy upon the lovers, who see him reflected in the water of a spring. But the other three panels illustrate the story of Tristan's "folly," an episode common to French, German, and English versions from the twelfth

VIII.18. Tristan plays the fool (panels 2, 3, 4). The Hermitage Tristan Casket II, Paris, ca. 1325. St. Petersburg, State Hermitage Museum.

through the fifteenth centuries, but never more powerfully told than in the Norman poem I shall summarize here.[33]

As the poem begins, Tristan, long exiled from King Mark's court, decides he must return to Tintagel, no matter how great the danger, to see again the woman he loves. "Alas," he laments,

> what shall I do if I cannot see her? . . . I am in great agitation at every moment of the night and day. When I do not see her I nearly go out of my mind. Alas, what shall I do? . . . She might think me a coward if threats were enough to stop me; for I could always go to her in secret or dressed like some pitiable madman. For her sake I am willing to be shaven and shorn if I cannot disguise myself any other way.[34]

He sets out at once for the distant sea, carrying no armor, and suffering so greatly that the poet describes him as being already a madman. To prevent anyone thinking him sane, on reaching Cornwall "he tore his clothes and scratched his face. He struck any man who crossed his path. He had his fair hair shorn off. Nobody on the seashore thought he was anything but mad, for they did not know what was in his mind."[35] Walking like this for days, among people who shout at him and throw stones at his head, he nevertheless thinks all this suffering good, because he would soon achieve his desire: "he would make himself appear to be a fool, for he wanted to speak to Yseult."[36]

Because, the poem tells us, no door is closed to a fool, Tristan enters the court and immediately draws the attention of the king, who sees in him some possible entertainment. "Fool," the king says, "what is your name?" "My name is Picous." "Who was your father?" "A walrus." "By whom did he have you?" "A whale. I have a sister I will bring to you. The girl is called Bruneheut: you shall have her and I will have Yseult."[37] But soon this fool's patter, so aggressively rude and sexual, gives way to something imaginatively finer: "Listen to this!" said Tristan. "Between the clouds and the sky, where there is no frost, I shall build a house of flowers and roses and there she and I will enjoy ourselves."[38] Yseult listens to all this with ever mounting alarm, thinking Tristan dead and their secrets somehow made known to this ugly fool, who recounts the story of their love in riddling ways. His narration begins with reference to the love potion—"she and I drank it—ask her!"[39]—and reaches its climax as he raves on: "I have leaped and thrown reeds and balanced sharpened twigs, I have lived on roots in a wood and I have held a queen in my arms. I shall say more if I have a mind to."[40]

The king, suddenly uncomfortable, tries to end the *récit*: "Rest yourself now, Picolet. I am sorry you have done so many things. Leave your jesting for today."[41] But Tristan, ever more daring, presses on, reminding the king that he once found the lovers asleep in the forest with a naked sword between them—an adventure that only the king and Yseult and Tristan (and somehow this fool) could know. Mark looks to the queen, who has bowed her head and covered her face with her cloak, and hears her say: "Fool, a curse on the sailors who brought you across the sea and did not throw you into the water."[42] But Tristan deflects that insult onto one he thinks a greater fool, her cuckolded husband: "My lady," he answers, "a curse on your *cocu*."[43] Brangain later brings him to Yseult's chamber, where the dog Husdant and a certain gold ring finally convince Yseult that the fool is indeed her lover. And so the poem is able to end happily: "Tristan slipped under the sheets without another word and held the queen in his arms."[44]

But even in that happy final embrace their love is inseparable from suffering, offense, alienation, and danger. In disguising himself as a fool, Tristan symbolically enacts the *real* nature of his passion as it would have been understood in the literature of wisdom: a passion sustained in defiance of the king and all feudal obligation, in opposition to God's laws against adultery, and in denial of the true celestial Jerusalem to which all Christian souls must aspire. The only happy place Tristan can imagine—a house of flowers and roses between the clouds and the sky, where there is never frost—is quite literally a fool's paradise, a fantasy born of love that seeks its heaven near earth, in contempt of Christian eternity. In the Oxford version of this poem, Tristan invents an even more fantastic setting for their transfigured love, "a hall which I visit . . . large and beautiful and made of glass, pierced through with sunbeams. It hangs in the clouds high in the air but the wind does not rock nor shake it. Within the hall is a room made of crystal and fine panelling and when the sun rises in the morning it is filled with light."[45]

Medieval medicine thought of erotic love as a sickness—a pathology capable of driving a lover literally mad, whether through excessive desire, overwhelming despair, or grief over some failure to be faithful. Gawain and Lancelot both undergo madness of this kind elsewhere in the Arthurian story. Figure VIII.19, for instance, shows Lancelot, indistinguishable from an idiot, in the company of King Arthur and Queen Guinevere.[46] But Tristan's "folly," in its willful embrace of the signs of madness and its disdain for conventional moral wisdom, draws to itself ideas more complex by far. By moving Tristan into iconographic register with the psalter fool, the poet suggests that anyone who loves in this fashion, making a mortal woman his highest good and seeking his only heaven in her arms, becomes, in Christian terms, a God-denying fool.[47] The real madness of Lancelot and Gawain can be cured. The "feigned" madness of Tristan is of a different pathology altogether.[48]

Elsewhere in the legend, Tristan presents himself to Yseult in other forms of symbolic disguise, most notably as a pilgrim and as a leper. In those instances too he transforms himself into an "image" with iconographic resonance, a disguise both false and true. But his disguise as a fool is the last in the series, subsuming all the rest. In that guise, before the king and queen and court, he tells again the full story of their love—a tale told by an idiot, in fragments and riddles, evading sense, precluding ordinary judgment.[49] And it is in the guise of a madman-fool that Tristan takes Yseult in his arms for the last time.[50] They never meet again alive.

One would expect such imagery—Panofsky called the technique "concealed symbolism"—to clarify the moral intention of the poem. But the

VIII.19. Lancelot plays the fool. Prose Lancelot, Amiens, 1286. Bonn, Universitätsbibliothek MS 526, fol. 404v.

magic potion, and the lovers' struggle to resist its power, prevent the fool disguise from functioning so simply. All that is compelled and unchosen in their relationship prevents any confident dismissal of them. When they call upon God for help against their enemies, as they often do, they generally receive his protection, even in circumstances as equivocal as Yseult's ordeal by fire.[51] And so it is in the *Folie*. The weird illogic that could see in an idiot or madman a God-denying fool is carried over, unresolved and entire, into a narrative of erotic love, leaving us uncertain whether Tristan's madness is feigned or real—and if real, whether it is a precondition or a punishment for this kind of loving. As with the fool in the psalter illustrations, we once again reach an aporia, a breakdown in logic that takes us beyond the certainties of cultural systems and deeper into the mystery of being human. The love of Tristan and Yseult refuses to be reduced to simple madness, or foolishness, or Christian adultery. Grander and more awesome than any of those alone, it is folly of the God-denying kind.

It must be admitted that none of this much looks like, or sounds like, Chaucer's *Troilus and Criseyde*. In the two hundred years (more or less) that separate the Norman and the English poems, the "courtliness" of court literature has greatly increased, and a court fool or jester has begun to replace the madman-idiot in psalter illumination to Psalm 52 (Figure VIII.20). But Chaucer too draws deeply upon the language of religion to give tragic stature to a story of unsanctioned erotic love. At the conceptual center of his poem an identification is made between Criseyde, a young Trojan widow, and a statue of the goddess Pallas Athena—a religious idol called the Palladion—whose continued presence (and worship) in Troy guarantees the safety of the city. (In the course of time, both will be removed, and Troilus/Troy destroyed.) By this means, as D.W. Robertson, Jr., suggested a long time ago, and as John Fleming more recently has shown in careful detail,[52] Judeo-Christian ideas of idolatry interpenetrate the pagan ethos of the poem, in which a beautiful woman is loved and worshiped in ways Christianity deemed appropriate only to God. In its first three books, Troilus is *converted* to the *service* of love; he *worships* the idea (the idol) of Criseyde; he is *initiated* into the mysteries of sexual experience, as into the mysteries of a sacred *rite*; and he finds *heaven* in her arms (the timeworn metaphor renewed in some

VIII.20. Psalm 52: the fool as court jester. Psalter, England, illuminated, third quarter of the fifteenth century. Oxford, Bodley MS. Laud. Lat. 114, fol. 71.

of the most sublime love poetry ever written), a heaven he declares worth even the price of his soul. In Books IV and V he experiences the loss of that love with the shattering intensity of someone losing his religious faith—a loss that ultimately destroys him, though his soul is rewarded after death in certain carefully delimited ways.[53] Ideas of idolatry generate much of the poem's religious language and ritualized devotion, while alerting us also to the possibility of transgression, contamination, and category error.

But idolatry cannot fully account for the ethos of the poem. A discourse of folly is operative as well, varying in force from the ordinary foolishness of lovers, scoffed at by Troilus before he first sees Criseyde, to the God-denying folly—including frenzy and despair—intrinsic to the way he finally loves her. The Tristan legend explores the power of love, symbolized by a magic potion, to set itself up against God and feudal society in ways that refuse all compromise and resolution. Chaucer's *Troilus*, in contrast, explores the power of love to become a religion of its own, founded on illusion and tragically incomplete. This maximum version of love's folly—in which sexual love is asked to express and fulfill our deepest spiritual needs—brings something distinctive to the medieval discourse of love, extending its range from the comic to the tragic, the trivial to the sublime, without ever losing touch with the carnal and obscene.

Patristic commentary, as I have said, made the fool's *non est deus* remarkably inclusive by attributing it, in its weakened form, to pagans, heretics, and idolators as well as sinners who just don't give a damn, and think God doesn't either. None of these turn up often in initials to the psalm, but two exceptions (each supported by a sister manuscript or two) are perhaps worth thinking about in relation to Chaucer's poem. In a late twelfth-century Bible illuminated by Manerius of Canterbury, working as an itinerant painter probably in Troyes (Figure VIII.21), the *insipiens* kneels before an altar worshiping an idol in the form of a goat.[54] The image communicates a sense of transgression and category error very powerful still, and may (just possibly) represent a form of devil worship.[55] But another, probably better, reading might recognize in the goat a commonplace symbol of lechery (both as adultery and fornication),[56] which had been closely linked to idolatry from earliest biblical times. In the Old Testament Yahweh characteristically thinks of Himself as married to Israel, even though she is often unfaithful, "whoring after strange gods."[57]

An alternative iconography for Psalm 52 that not only focuses upon erotic love but stands closer to Chaucer's *Troilus* in both provenance and date provides intriguing visual evidence to support such a claim. I know of just three examples, but their interest is considerable, particularly the one we shall look at first—from a great display Bible made in England that may have been owned and treasured (more on this later) by Henry IV and Henry V. In its *insipiens* initial three kinds of folly are represented (Figure VIII.22).[58] The first shows God mocked by a jester or court fool, wearing a professional costume of long pointed hood, dagged tunic, and bells. He points to his mouth to indicate speech, and wags his index finger

VIII.21. Psalm 52: the fool as idolator, here worshiping a goat. Manerius of Canterbury Bible, illuminated by Manerius of Canterbury, possibly in Troyes, late twelfth century. Paris, Bibliothèque Sainte-Geneviève MS 9, fol. 209.

against God, signifying argument, contention, or presumption. A second kind can be seen in the frivolity and carelessness of the courtly group on the left—a casual, complacent forgetfulness of God, as though justice were no part of his nature. This company gazes at, points to, and smiles upon an elegant young couple (the third kind) who stand in their midst in passionate embrace—a love that in English moral writing of the time was called "fol-delit," just as prostitutes were called "fol-wommen," and sexual love outside marriage the doing of "folye."[59] Looking down from the heavens, God sees no one doing well. We see in this picture a subtle iconographic shift. In the *Folie de Tristan*, Yseult's task was to recognize her lover beneath the appearance of a God-denying fool. In *Troilus*, the task is reversed. We are asked to recognize a God-denying fool in the form of a courtly lover.

This image from an English "show" Bible is capacious in the manner of the commentaries, ready to include almost anyone except a *credible* nonbeliever, someone actually engaged in thinking "there is no God." But it is serious in its own highly *mondaine* way. A courtly milieu of this sort, marked

VIII.22. Psalm 52: the fool as jester in the company of courtiers and courtly lovers, God the Father looking down from above. Bible, England, ca. 1405–15. London, Brit. Lib. MS Royal I E. ix, fol. 148. Photo © The British Museum. All Rights Reserved.

by ease, urbanity, and sexual sophistication, correlates very well not with only the ethos of *Troilus and Criseyde* but, more strictly speaking, the Augustinian interpretation of *non est deus* noted earlier: to cease to fear God's Justice is effectively to deny His existence.[60] The embracing couple makes another point as well, emphasizing the carnal basis of this love, however otherwise "courtly" its manner. Despite the public nature of the occasion, the lover manages to press his leg forward, ever so delicately, between his lady's thighs. In a closely related English psalter now in Turin (Figure VIII.23),[61] the company is (if anything) more courtly still in dress and behavior, and the parallel gesture even more shocking: the lover has his hand up his lady's dress. In this picture, either the model for, or a copy of, the picture we have been examining, someone I take to be a "natural" fool—the bald head, vacant manner, and simple shoes suggest as much—stands next to the couple, smiling vacuously at God as though nothing here were to be taken seriously. A court fool mocks God with speech as well. And Figure VIII.24, from a French *Bible moralisée*, continues the tradition into the late fifteenth century.

VIII.23. Psalm 52: two God-denying fools (a "natural" and a jester) mock God in the company of courtiers and courtly lovers, the latter in an erotic embrace. Psalter, England, ca. 1405–15. Turin, Bibl. Naz., Universitaria di Torino MS I. 1. 9, fol. 16. Courtesy of the Ministero per i Beni e le Attività Culturali, Torino. Photo © Biblioteca Nazionale, Torino. All Rights Reserved.

VIII.24. Psalm 52: the fool at a woman's spindle, above; two fools make love to women below. *Bible moralisé*, commissioned by Philippe le Hardi of Burgundy, Paris, ca. 1470–80. Paris, Bibl. Natl. MS fr. 166, fol. 120.

This manuscript, commissioned by Philippe le Hardi of Burgundy, illustrates an abbreviated text of Psalm 52 (in both French and Latin) with a twofold image, as is customary in moralized Bibles. This one shows a court fool spinning with distaff and spindle—reversing traditional male and female roles—beneath the words "Sans nombre," a comment wittily relevant to fools, but also the motto of the royal house of Anjou. The picture below shows two erotic couples in a landscape, one in a standing embrace, the other seated. The standing man is a monk, the other, youthful and sporting a rich fur hat, holds his lady on his lap, her skirt pushed high with his hand between her legs. The text tells us that this psalm is spoken against worldly persons (*les mundains*) and sinners who give themselves up to sin as though there were no God (*si ne fust point de dieu*).[62]

An early connection of the English Bible with the English court is a real possibility—that same court for which, some two decades before, Chaucer's *Troilus* had been written, a court indeed in which that poem remained well known. The Bible came to the British Library as part of the Royal collection of manuscripts and was thought by earlier scholars to have belonged to Richard II. They saw in it stylistic affinities with the school of Bohemian illumination introduced to England at the time of Richard's marriage to Anne of Bohemia. Art historians these days date it more conservatively, to the reign of Henry IV, circa 1405–15, and are cautious about even the royal association, since the manuscript lacks marks of ownership of any kind. But Jenny Stratford has recently reopened the question, suggesting that this manuscript—so huge one person can scarcely lift it—may well be the "Great Bible" mentioned by Henry V in his last will and its codicils (1421–22). Henry there bequeathed to the nuns of Syon Abbey (which he had founded) all the books he had lent them, except for the *magna Biblia*, described as having belonged to his father, Henry IV, which he left as a legacy to his unborn son.[63] The size and grandeur of MS Royal I. E. ix make it a plausible candidate for the Bible that Henry V treasured so. His father, we know, was briefly Chaucer's patron, in the year before Chaucer's death, and the son himself clearly admired the poet's work, acquiring one of the earliest and best copies of Chaucer's *Troilus* (now Pierpont Morgan MS M. 817) sometime during the same years in which scholars would now date the huge Bible, between 1403 and the year he became king, 1413; the Morgan copy bears Henry's coat of arms as prince on the first leaf.[64] (If this Bible in fact belonged to Henry IV, and was passed on to Henry V, I am possibly not the first to think about this image of God-denying courtiers and Chaucer's *Troilus and Crisyede* together.)[65]

But my argument is thematic, not circumstantial. I call attention to the blatantly sexual gestures in these pictures because Chaucer's *Troilus* explores the sacralization of erotic love with a comparable double vision. It plays Troilus's idealized view of Criseyde against all that Pandarus more cynically claims to know of her and of her sex; it conducts the love affair through a number of awkward and embarrassing events; and it explores the most sublime moments of this love—both happy and tragic—in sexually allusive language so bold as to leave many readers resistant still to its implications. When Pandarus, for instance, in a brief moment of conscience, needs reassurance that he is doing nothing dishonorable, Troilus offers to procure in exchange any of his sisters that Pandarus might desire. Similarly destructive of love's idealized self-image is the way Criseyde is brought to Pandarus's house, not knowing Pandarus intends to deliver her there to Troilus's desire. To recapitulate briefly some evidence used in the last chapter apropos of St. Cecilia's "fiery bath": Troilus, in hiding, watches Criseyde's arrival through the window of a "stewe"—a word that in a private house (like Pandarus's) means simply a "bath," a room for bathing, but elsewhere and more commonly means "public brothel." Pandarus indeed unlocks "the stuwe door" to usher Troilus into his first experience of "heaven": "Make thee redy right anon, / For thow shalt into hevene blisse wende" (III 703). But to reach that room where he will make love to Criseyde for the first time, Troilus must creep through a gutter, a "privy wente," that sounds as if it were part of the palace's sanitation system, or an opening in the female anatomy (III 787). And after her departure from Troy, he and Pandarus will visit her empty house, comparing it not only to a reliquary robbed of its holy relic—its "seynt"—but to a lantern whose light has been quenched (extinguished). Here too the language chosen has a double meaning: "queynte [i.e., cunt] is the lyghte" (V 553, 543). This pun on *queynt* is not locker-room humor, however uncomfortable to some, but punning notation of a profoundly serious kind, more subtle and understated than the sexual gestures in the two psalter pictures just examined, and in service of a double truth.[66] Troilus is at once a young man experiencing sexual love for the first time, and an idealist whose capacity for "trouthe" (fidelity in that love) separates him as decisively from Pandarus as from Diomede the Greek, the rival who eventually replaces him in Criseyde's heart. Like a Tuscan tray made circa 1400 depicting a radiant Venus (Figure VIII.25), in which "queynte" is quite literally "the lyghte," puns of this sort remind us that "courtly" ways of thinking about love both dignify and disguise ordinary sexual desire.[67]

Rhetorically speaking, the religious temple of Chaucer's Book I and the "stewe" of Book III are thus alternative versions of the same erotically charged space in which Troilus looks with longing on Criseyde—each revealing a different aspect of that desire. The Tuscan tray, we should note, creates a timeless space whose goddess represents something constant in human experience. Making no distinction between lovers who lived before Christ (Samson, Achilles, Paris, Troilus) and those who lived after (Tristan and Lancelot), the tray spiritualizes carnal love, presenting it as something glorious and ennobling, transcending history. (The fact such trays were commissioned to commemorate a marriage or a birth virtually precludes ironic interpretation.) The erotic illustrations to Psalm 52 we have examined do otherwise: their passionate couples embrace beneath the gaze of an offended God.

VIII.25. Venus, radiant, is worshiped by famous lovers, including Tristan and Troilus (Tristan second from the left, Troilus last on the right): "queynt is the light." Birth tray or salver, Tuscany, ca. 1400. Paris, Musée du Louvre (RF 2089).

But Chaucer has it both ways, in a manner that these images can help us chart more precisely. For it is only with regard to the final thirty-five lines of the *Troilus* (the so-called Palinode to a poem 8,239 lines long) that these psalter illustrations become fully relevant to its complex of feeling and idea. There Chaucer speaks at last in his own unmediated voice, to an audience addressed for the first time as Christian, of a love that will not "falsen" or betray:

> O yonge, fresshe folkes, he or she, (V 1835)
> In which that love up groweth with youre age,
> Repeyreth hom fro worldly vanyte,
> And of youre herte up casteth the visage
> To thilke God that after his ymage

Yow made, and thynketh al nys but a faire,
This world that passeth soone as floures faire.
And loveth hym the which that right for love
Upon a crois, oure soules for to beye,
First starf, and roos, and sit in hevene above;
For he nyl falsen no wight, dar I seye,
That wol his herte al holly on hym leye.
And syn he best to love is, and most meke,
What nedeth feynede loves for to seke?

Chaucer here tells us, in verse of the gravest beauty, that what Troilus sought in loving Criseyde can be found only in the love of Christ. But Chaucer does not imagine, here or anywhere else in the poem, that loving Christ was an option available in Troy.[68]

Until those final stanzas, Chaucer employs the language of worship and idolatry not to judge Troilus as though he were Christian—that would be absurd—but to explore human experience on that far shore where "love celestial" and "love of kind" overlap, blurring their difference, obscuring their true relation. For eros too promises transcendence, creates its own gods, and has the power to destroy even its most faithful servants. This is why "pagan love" remained relevant to medieval Christian audiences, and why it is capable of moving us (and instructing us) still.

But the poem is also about something culturally more specific: the relation of Christian humanism to all that was most noble in the pagan past, to all that aspired to honor and truth before the Incarnation. It was necessary to believe, on Christ's own authority, that except through Him no one comes to God the Father. And so one had to believe as well in the damnation of all who lived before His birth—give or take a few Old Testament Jews—including even those who were honorable and "just" but had no access to His salvation. This response to the problem of the "good pagan," at once totalizing, inhumane, and theologically essential, constituted for the Middle Ages another great aporia—another breakdown in logic and sense—that was troubling to many, including (most famously) Pope Gregory the Great in his prayers for the Emperor Trajan; William Langland in his anguished quest in *Piers Plowman* to understand the terms of salvation; and Julian of Norwich, hinting at a Great Event to come, in which all who ever lived, regardless of their sins, will be saved. To this (admittedly various) list—which could easily be extended—I would add the name of Geoffrey Chaucer.

For *Troilus and Criseyde* seems to me more than a poem about erotic love. It is also, in its highest ambition, a poem about the tragedy of paganism, written out of a humanist sympathy that determines both its tone and its proportions. Until Christ is named in its final lines, the poem's deepest longings are expressed in terms of erotic love, and its wisdom can reach no further than the fact that such love, like all our worldly bliss, will end in woe. The Palinode could not move us so deeply—even those of us who are not Christian—were it not for the pressure generated by all that has gone before.

The exact relation between "love of God" and "love of kind" (*our own kind*) is the great unresolved overlap of the poem. Both are fired by a version of "love's hete" (I 978) and both are explored within a pagan ethos valuable in no small part because it keeps the question open, acknowledging all that Troilus's love for Criseyde has in common with idolatry and with fornication, but refusing to see it only in those terms. Up to a point, St. Augustine himself might have been sympathetic to that refusal, for in his theology he acknowledges the role that desire plays in all human life—amounting to a confession that we have our life *from* God, not from ourselves and for ourselves. Because we are incomplete, there is nothing reprehensible in desire per se. To live as though we possessed our "good" in ourselves, with no need to seek it elsewhere, would be to claim for ourselves something of the divine independence and self-sufficiency.[69] Because desire expresses our true condition as created beings, it can be praiseworthy in the highest degree.

But this, of course, describes only the foundation of Augustine's validation of desire: for him it must lead ultimately to the love of God, rather than to the things, or the creatures, of the created world. But Augustine was writing after the Incarnation, when Christ had redefined the goals and possibilities of such devotion. Yet the first premise remains important all the same. To my mind, Augustine's generalized understanding of desire, as summarized above, resonates more deeply with the confused idealism of Troilus's love than does (say) the full theology of his *City of God*, or those modern readings that would use the Palinode to erase (or declare ironic) everything that has gone before, leaving only a hymn to the love of Christ—the love that will not fail. Chaucer uses religious language before the Palinode, to be sure, but he carefully keeps the Christian God out of the picture: we are not invited to imagine him looking down upon Troilus and Criseyde, as He does upon the lovers in the psalter illustrations just examined. By freeing the poem of that scrutiny until his story has come to an end, Chaucer is able to imagine paganism in its fullest reach while taking an exact measure of its limitations.

Troilus's love for Criseyde is foolish in several senses, not excluding the comically naïve, and it has much in common with psalter folly, especially of the kind shown in these two nearly contemporary English illuminations. But his love is also a quest for transcendence, and in that, it lays claim to tragic stature, enacting a higher form of "trouthe" than anyone else in the poem attempts or achieves. It earns him at the end a certain reward: a soul journey to the eighth sphere, where he hears ravishing music and is granted a moment of total ethical clarity. Looking down on "this litel spot of erthe that with the se / Embraced is," Troilus declares all earthly joy mere "vanite / To respect of the pleyn felicite / That is in hevene above" (V 1815). Learning at last contempt for the world, he laughs at the sorrow of those who weep for his death, and curses "al oure werk that foloweth so / The blynde lust, the which that may nat laste, / And sholden al oure herte on heven caste" (V 1818).

For pagans and Christians alike, heaven is, by definition, eternal and unchanging. But human history is born of time, in a linear progress that the

Middle Ages divided into Seven Ages (the Sixth inaugurated by the birth of Christ) or a sequence of Three Laws (Natural Law, the Written Law of Moses, and the Christian Law of Grace). And so Troilus, loving and dying long before the birth of Christ, can be allowed only a partial glimpse of this heaven, followed by the decent obscurity of a pagan afterlife: "And forth he wente, shortly for to telle,/Ther as Mercurye sorted hym to dwelle"—wherever Mercury determined he should remain (V 1826). If Elysium is implied, it is not named, nor is there any mention of Hell. In that imprecision and obscurity the tragedy of Troilus merges with the general tragedy of the world before Christ: there is no Christian God in that sky, and nothing of what follows death is known. The truth that Troilus's soul sees with such perfect vision from the eighth sphere is a truth about human love, not the redemptive love of Christ.

In this poem, then, the destiny of the honorable pagan dead remains a mystery—an aporia—fully as much as the spiritual value of erotic love. (In the poem's closing lines, the gods Troilus supplants in worshiping Criseyde can be dismissed as nothing more than pagan "rascaille," because his moment in history gives him access to no worthier kind.) Though the Palinode can put the question about paganism, here rendered as a question about love, into new historical perspective, the poem cannot resolve either question from within the boundaries of the narrative proper. In commenting on the verse, "There is none that doth good, no, not one," in Psalm 13, the other *non est deus* psalm, Augustine wrote, "No man has really practiced virtue until the coming of Christ, because unless Christ has first instructed him, no man is able to practice virtue."[70] Chaucer's poem has to separate itself from itself in order to offer more.

For those of us who do not share the Christian belief, Chaucer's carefully nuanced respect for the pagan past offers a valuable model for our own response to his poem—a way of participating even in its concluding truths without denying our own. It comes down to something like this. If, as we believe, "love of kynde" (our love for one another) is the *best* there is, then that is also *what* there is, and we might as well accept it, in all its limitations, without despair. For us, the "correction" proposed so eloquently in the Palinode becomes a way of describing the fragility, instability, and incompleteness of human love, without in fact replacing it with some higher kind that is eternal, unchanging, and ever true. To name something is not to demonstrate its existence; to lack something is not to call it into being. For nonbelievers too the need to posit such a love from within the poem becomes almost unbearably moving, and we acknowledge the simple beauty with which it is announced, when its moment comes, as part of the poem's grandeur of design and nobility of spirit. But from outside the Palinode's system of belief—the place from which the rest of us read the poem—the redemptive love of Christ as an answer to all that limits and denies us here must seem as wishful and tenuous, and every bit as human, as the love of Troilus for Criseyde. For us the Palinode reads differently, but not ignobly. We honor it as yet another "soul journey" into the unknowable unknown.

Jill Mann proposed a kind of "dialogism" as a way of resolving the argument between her own atheism and the Christianity of the poems she teaches and serves. There is much to be said for that sort of conversation, and I try to practice it too. But we need not—nor does she—conceive of it solely as a dialogue spanning the ages. The illustrations to Psalm 52 with which we began were already in dialogue with the great images of theological order that dominate the iconography of the age—images of Doomsday, for instance, that show Christ in the heavens, displaying his wounds as he separates the saved from the damned. We have only to give these psalter fools their full voice to right the balance. We may even, if we wish, reaffirm Christ's kinship with them as "holy fool" to clear once again the threshing floor, to free his memory from all the horror that Church and State have perpetrated in His name.

So let us reclaim, for our own study of the Middle Ages, the dignity and seriousness of God-denying folly—as St. Paul did for Christian folly, in dialogue with Greek ideas of wisdom, and as Erasmus did for Renaissance humanism at large. Even Aquinas granted it a provisional dignity, turning to the psalter fool as evidence for his own ground-zero proposition: "That God exists is therefore not self-evident."[71]

That has surely always been so, though Aquinas, like other medieval thinkers, could admit it only as the preface to a contrary proof, in his case a *Summa theologiae*. For an unmediated image of nonbelief we may look to the madmen, idiots, and jesters of Psalm 52 illustration, as avatars of that which Christian orthodoxy could least explain: the fact of madness and imbecility per se; the unbroken continuity of existential fear even within religious faith; the category-confusions intrinsic to erotic love; the destiny of the virtuous pre-Christian dead; and not least, as it was then understood, the *necessary* role of the Jews in crucifying Christ, mocking him as a fool, so that mankind as a whole might be redeemed. God-denying folly is called upon to explain it all. There is a medieval literature that celebrates the system—Dante and Aquinas are its great masters—and a medieval literature that testifies to our human unease within it, attentive to all that remains excluded and obscure. Out of the real but puzzling existence of idiots and madmen the Middle Ages constructed a symbolic iconography of the fool, using a figure—a condition—it could not adequately explain to stand for many other things it could not explain. Its full history is a horrendous story, with painful human consequence. But this much at least can be said. Wherever God-denying folly is found, the deepest questions remain open, establishing the disturbing relevance of the medieval experience to our own. It is possible to embrace all that is most abject in the psalter fool and reject the stigma he is meant to carry.

Notes

PREFACE

1. V. A. Kolve, *Chaucer and the Imagery of Narrative: The First Five Canterbury Tales* (Stanford, CA: Stanford University Press, 1984).

2. Charles A. Owen, Jr., "The Crucial Passages in Five of the *Canterbury Tales*: A Study in Irony and Symbol," *Journal of English and Germanic Philology* 52 (1953), 294–311, an essay important to me when I first started thinking about Chaucer and the visual arts, though Owen himself makes no reference to the latter. The "crucial passages" of his title, repeated in the body of his text, gives way to "controlling images" when he talks about "the garden, the blindness and the tree" in *The Merchant's Tale*, topics he explores only briefly but with his usual sureness and subtlety. While recognizing their "symbolic and unifying function," he claimed to find only five such "crucial passages" in the whole of the *Tales*, each of which he briefly addresses in his essay.

3. V. A. Kolve, *The Play Called Corpus Christi* (Stanford, CA: Stanford University Press, 1966).

4. V. A. Kolve, "Chaucer and the Visual Arts," in *Geoffrey Chaucer (Writers and Their Background)*, ed. Derek Brewer (Athens: Ohio University Press, 1975), pp. 290–320.

5. Mary J. Carruthers, *The Book of Memory: A Study of Memory in Medieval Culture*, Cambridge Studies in Medieval Literature 10 (Cambridge: Cambridge University Press, 1990); *The Craft of Thought: Meditation, Rhetoric, and the Making of Images, 400–1200*, Cambridge Studies in Medieval Literature 34 (Cambridge: Cambridge University Press, 1998). My readers will find chapter 7 in *The Book of Memory* especially relevant, along with much in *The Craft of Thought*, which focuses on monastic meditation as a way of thinking with and through images. To these volumes Carruthers has since added another, coedited with Jan M. Ziolkowski, *The Medieval Craft of Memory: An Anthology of Texts and Pictures* (Philadelphia: University of Pennsylvania Press, 2002). Her recent essay, "Moving Images in the Mind's Eye," in *The Mind's Eye: Art and Theological Argument in the Middle Ages*, ed. Jeffrey F. Hamburger and Anne-Marie Bouché (Princeton, NJ: Princeton University Press, 2006), pp. 287–305, brilliantly continues these inquiries. Carolyn P. Collette, *Species, Phantasms, and Images: Vision and Medieval Psychology in "The Canterbury Tales"* (Ann Arbor: University of Michigan Press, 2001), focuses on late medieval faculty psychology and medieval optical theory; as does Norman Klassen, *Chaucer on Love, Knowledge and Sight*, Chaucer Studies 21 (Cambridge: D. S. Brewer, 1995). Both are

of value. Susan K. Hagen, *Allegorical Remembrance: A Study of "The Pilgrimage of the Life of Man" as a Medieval Treatise on Seeing and Remembering* (Athens: University of Georgia Press, 1990), based on a dissertation I was privileged to direct, uses Guillaume de Deguileville's popular allegorical poem, along with its traditional program of illustrations, to explore many of these same ideas.

6. Michael Riffaterre, "The Mind's Eye: Memory and Textuality," in *The New Medievalism*, ed. Marina S. Brownlee, Kevin Brownlee, and Stephen G. Nichols (Baltimore: Johns Hopkins University Press, 1991), pp. 29–45 (I quote from pp. 30, 33, 44). For essays influenced by, or sympathetic to, these ideas, see note 13 below.

7. V. A. Kolve, "Religious Language in *Waiting for Godot*," *Centennial Review* 11 (1967): 102–27.

8. V. A. Kolve, "*Everyman* and the Parable of the Talents," in *The Medieval Drama: Papers of the Third Annual Conference of the Center for Medieval and Early Renaissance Studies, State University of New York at Binghamton, 3–4 May, 1969*, ed. Sandro Sticca (Albany: State University of New York Press, 1972), pp. 69–98; reprinted in *Medieval English Drama: Essays Critical and Contextual*, ed. Jerome Taylor and Alan H. Nelson (Chicago: University of Chicago Press, 1972), pp. 316–40; and V. A. Kolve, "Ganymede/*Son of Getron*: Medieval Monasticism and the Drama of Same-Sex Desire," *Speculum* 73 (1998): 1014–67; reprinted in *Medieval Drama: Critical Concepts in Literary and Cultural Studies*, ed. John Coldewey, 4 vols. (London: Routledge, 2007). For a study of visual traditions underwriting a major feminist text, see my essay "The Annunciation to Christine: Authorial Empowerment in *The Book of the City of Ladies*," in *Iconography at the Crossroads: Papers from the Colloquium Sponsored by the Index of Christian Art, Princeton University, March 23–24*, 1990, ed. Brendan Cassidy (Princeton, NJ: Index of Christian Art, 1993), pp. 171–96.

9. D. W. Robertson, Jr., *A Preface to Chaucer: Studies in Medieval Perspectives* (Princeton, NJ: Princeton University Press, 1962). For Robertson's own account of how his thinking developed, see the "Author's Introduction" to his *Essays in Medieval Culture* (Princeton, NJ: Princeton University Press, 1980), pp. xi–xx.

10. We owe to Lee Patterson a powerful account of the Robertsonian challenge and its aftermath in "Historical Criticism and the Development of Chaucer Studies," included in his book *Negotiating the Past: The Historical Understanding of Medieval Literature* (Madison: University of Wisconsin Press, 1987), pp. 3–39. In the introduction to his recent *Temporal Circumstances: Form and History in the Canterbury Tales* (New York: Palgrave Macmillan, 2006), he revisits the question in a more personal way ("Historicism and Postmodernity"), esp. pp. 1–3. "Robertson presented—and still presents—medievalists with an immense challenge, and one that for me at least proved to be immensely creative. The mode of historicism that I worked out in response to Robertson, and to the times in which I was living, was also shared, to various degrees, by many of my cohort" (p. 3). I am among their number.

11. Ernst Robert Curtius, *European Literature and the Latin Middle Ages*, trans. Willard R. Trask, Bollingen Series 36 (New York: Pantheon Books, 1953) (German edition, 1948), focuses on "topics" (topoi) as "the stockroom" of rhetoric and poetry, from Homer to Goethe (p. 79), and surveys, with extraordinary learning, the history and range of a great many of them. See especially his chapter 5, and much of what follows. His book, written under the shadow of Nazism during and just after World War II, is an impassioned humanist defense of the continuity of European culture from classical antiquity to the present.

12. The temple descriptions in Part III of *The Knight's Tale* offer a notable excep-

tion (I 1181–2088), but they too are purposeful and carry meaning in their every detail. For a very different medieval poetic, see Sarah Stanbury's *Seeing the Gawain-Poet: Description and the Act of Perception* (Philadelphia: University of Pennsylvania Press, 1991), which focuses on the use that poet makes of "a textual spectator whose emotions are reflected in the objects or places he perceives," always elaborately described (p. 5). Dorigen's "view" of the rocks on the coast of Brittany, as analyzed in my essay in *The Franklin's Tale*, offers a relatively spare example of this kind, as does Palamon's and Arcite's sense of the prison/garden in *The Knight's Tale*, studied in my earlier volume. But, in general, that is not Chaucer's way, as Stanbury is careful to note, pp. 122–23.

13. Organized by Arlyn Diamond and Nancy Bradbury, it was published in *SAC* 28 (2006), pp. 217–61, with special reference to *Sources and Analogues of the Canterbury Tales*, ed. Robert M. Correale and Mary Hamel, 2 vols. (Cambridge: D. S. Brewer, 2002, 2005).

14. For Bleeth, see *SAC* 28 (2006): 221–24; for Beidler, pp. 225–30; for Goodwin, pp. 231–35; for Bradbury, pp. 237–42; for Collette, pp. 243–48; for Frese, pp. 249–56; for McCormick, pp. 257–61; and for Evans, pp. 263–70.

15. Kolve, *Chaucer and the Imagery of Narrative*, p. 8.

16. I have elsewhere proposed Hugo de Folieto's *De rota verae et falsae religionis*, an example of this kind of composition, as a possible source for the fart-division that ends *The Summoner's Tale*. See "Chaucer's Wheel of False Religion: Theology and Obscenity in The Summoner's Tale," published in *The Centre and Its Compass: Studies in Medieval Literature in Honor of Professor John Leyerle*, Studies in Medieval Culture 33 (Kalamazoo: Western Michigan University, Medieval Institute, 1993), pp. 265–96. That essay too was originally meant for this collection, but to make space for the new chapters on *The Merchant's Tale*, it had to be given up. I regret that, because it still seems to me valuable, and because I remember with undiminished affection and respect my friend John Leyerle, to whom it was dedicated.

CHAPTER I

The primary texts brought together in this chapter have often been mentioned in scholarship on the poem. *The Riverside Chaucer*, for instance, lists several of them in a single note—including the "Dream of Scipio," Bartholomew on the weakness of our human eyes and ears, Bestiary lore on the eagle, and Beatrice's ability to look at the sun. But they are brought together, chiefly by author and title, in a note to *The Hous of Fame* (1015–17), not to *Troilus and Criseyde*. (See *Riverside Chaucer*, p. 985.) John Norton-Smith, *Geoffrey Chaucer*, Medieval Authors (London: Routledge and Kegan Paul, 1974), in a few brief sentences, connects the dream eagle with the sun in Antigone's song (p. 206). But so far as I know (I do not claim to have read everything ever written about the poem) he is the only one to have done so. He takes the idea no further, being chiefly concerned to derive the five-book structure of the poem from the five acts of classical drama, as it was read in the schools: Plautus, Terence, and especially the tragedies of Seneca, along with medieval glosses on those texts.

Brevity is proper to an explanatory note: the Riverside editors did what they should do, at least with respect to the other poem. But notes of this kind leave undone the sort of work I have attempted here: an unpacking of what there seems almost too compact for use, laying it out, taking pleasure in it, and speculating on what it all means, or better still, on what it might once have meant.

The origins of this chapter will not be found in the Riverside note on *The Hous of Fame*, nor in the several that complement it in annotations to the *Troilus* proper. It grows instead out of reading and rereading this poem, and some of these texts, with students almost yearly for nearly forty years—the last fifteen of them at UCLA as a colleague of Andy (H. Ansgar) Kelly. I offer him this chapter in tribute to those years, in friendship and with high regard.

1. V. A. Kolve, *Chaucer and the Imagery of Narrative: The First Five Canterbury Tales* (Stanford, CA: Stanford University Press, 1984. Chapters 1 and 2—"Audience and Image: Some Medieval Hypotheses" and "Chaucerian Aesthetic: The Image in the Poem"—develop at length the theory briefly introduced above.

2. A theologian at Merton College, Oxford, from 1325 to 1335, he became chancellor of St. Paul's, and even for a brief time archbishop of Canterbury, before dying of plague in 1349.

3. See James J. Murphy, *Rhetoric in the Middle Ages: A History of Rhetorical Theory from Saint Augustine to the Renaissance* (Berkeley: University of California Press, 1975); and Martin Camargo, "Rhetoric," in *The Seven Liberal Arts in the Middle Ages*, ed. David L. Wagner (Bloomington: Indiana University Press, 1983), pp. 96–124, on the history and importance of rhetoric in medieval culture.

4. Mary J. Carruthers, *The Book of Memory: A Study of Memory in Medieval Culture*, Cambridge Studies in Medieval Literature 10 (Cambridge: Cambridge University Press, 1990); and the same author's *The Craft of Thought: Meditation, Rhetoric, and the Making of Images, 400–1200*, Cambridge Studies in Medieval Literature 34 (Cambridge: Cambridge University Press, 1998). She builds upon Frances A. Yates's groundbreaking *The Art of Memory* (London: Routledge and Kegan Paul, 1966).

5. Carruthers, *Book of Memory*, p. 133; see pp. 130–37 for her full discussion of the treatise *De memoria artificiali*, which she translates in appendix C, pp. 281–88. Compare the advice given in the *Rhetorica ad Herennium* (III.xxii.37):

> We ought, then, to set up images of a kind that can adhere longest in the memory. And we shall do so if we establish likenesses as striking as possible; if we set up images that are not many or vague, but doing something; if we assign to them exceptional beauty or singular ugliness; if we dress some of them with crowns or purple cloaks, for example, so that the likeness may be more distinct to us; or if we somehow disfigure them, as by introducing one stained with blood or soiled with mud or smeared with red paint, so that its form is more striking, or by assigning certain comic effects to our images. (p. 221)

6. Quoted from Carruthers, *Book of Memory*, pp. 283–84.

7. Ibid., p. 134.

8. Sister Mary Charlotte Borthwick, F.C.S.P., "Antigone's Song as 'Mirour' in Chaucer's *Troilus and Criseyde*," *Modern Language Quarterly* 22 (1961), p. 228, writes about the song "as a reflector of the object both as it is and as it should be." In this sense, she argues, Antigone's song might be called a "mirour" of love, in the tradition of the medieval literary "mirror" or *speculum*. She sees its high idealism as self-correcting and self-critiquing by its very nature—as do I. But I would dissent from her view (p. 234) that the imagery of the eagle-dream presages evil.

9. I write about the symbolism of Figure I.1 at some length in Kolve, *Chaucer and the Imagery of Narrative*, pp. 441–42n76.

10. Michael Camille, *The Medieval Art of Love: Objects and Subjects of Desire* (New York: Harry N. Abrams, 1998), pp. 111–19, with well-chosen color illustrations, some of them parodic. I quote from pp. 112, 114.

11. Here is Albertus Magnus on "intentions," from his extensive treatise on memory in *De bono*, written circa 1245, and newly translated by Carruthers, *Book of Memory*, appendix B, pp. 267–80: "the reactions [*intentiones*] which memory stores do not exist absolutely apart from the images of particulars. . . . And so these reactions are taken in at the same time along with the images, and therefore there is no need to have special [memory] rules for them" (p. 279; see also pp. 59–60). Donald R. Howard, "Experience, Language, and Consciousness: *Troilus and Criseyde*, II, 596–931," in *Medieval Literature and Folklore Studies: Essays in Honor of Francis Lee Utley*, ed. J. Mandel and B. A. Rosenberg (New Brunswick, NJ: Rutgers University Press, 1970), p. 189, writes of this dream: "The eagle is Troilus, but Troilus as he exists in Criseyde's inner thoughts, made white by hope and sentiment, made violent and rapacious by expectation and fear . . . at once predatory and gentle. Perhaps indeed the eagle is love itself, Criseyde's hopeful and fearful image of it." A. C. Spearing, *Criticism and Medieval Poetry*, 2nd ed. (London: Edward Arnold, 1971), p. 145, finds in it "the authentic strangeness of a dream experience," saturated in obscure meaning. He uses medieval dream theory, along with Freud's distinction between manifest and latent dream content, to offer a psychoanalytic reading: the (real) nightingale who sings outside her window becomes the eagle of her dream, betokening what she otherwise cannot yet admit, "a secret wish to give herself to Troilus."

12. I here quote from Albertus Magnus, in Carruthers, *Book of Memory*, pp. 273–74. On these matters he echoes the *Rhetorica ad Herrenium*, which he cites as the work of "Tully" (Marcus Tullius Cicero). Carruthers writes about the treatise on pp. 137–42.

13. See Joyce E. Salisbury, "Bestiality in the Middle Ages," in *Sex in the Middle Ages: A Book of Essays*, ed. Joyce E. Salisbury (New York: Garland Publishing), pp. 173–86, for an account of changing attitudes toward bestiality, ranging from its accepted place in classical myth (gods in the form of animals often seduce humans), through Old Testament prohibitions, early Church penitentials, and so on. For the thirteenth century scholastics, see pp. 180–82.

14. Giovanni Boccaccio, *Il Filostrato*, ed. Vincenzo Pernicone, trans. Robert P. apRoberts and Anna Bruni Seldis, Garland Library of Medieval Literature, series A, vol. 53 (New York: Garland Publishing, 1986), pt. VII, vv. 23–24, pp. 348–49:

> Erasi un di, tutto malinconoso
> per la fallita fede, ito a dormire
> Troiolo, e 'n sogno vide il periglioso
> fallo di quella che 'l facea languire:
> che gli parea, per entro un bosco ombroso,
> un gran fracasso e spiacevol sentire;
> per che, levato il capo, gli sembiava
> un gran cinghiar veder che valicava.
>
> E poi appresso gli parve vedere
> sotto a' suoi pié Criseida, alla quale
> col grifo il cor traeva, ed al parere
> di lui, Criseida di cosí gran male
> non si curava, ma quasi piacere
> prendea di ció che facea l'animale;
> il che a lui sí forte era in dispetto,
> che questo ruppe il sonno deboletto.

15. Ibid., bk. VII, vv. 25, 27, pp. 350–51:

> Questo cinghiar ch'io vidi é Diomede,
> per ció che l'avolo uccise il cinghiaro
> di Calidonia, se si puó dar fede
> a' nostri antichi, e sempre poi portaro
> per sopransegna, si come si vede,
> i discendenti il porco. Oh me, amaro
> e vero sogno! . . .

16. Figure I.3 is reproduced in color by Richard Barber, *Bestiary: Being an English Version of the Bodleian Library, Oxford M.S. [sic] Bodley 764* (Woodbridge, Suffolk, Eng.: Boydell Press, 1993), p. 86. On this manuscript, see Nigel Morgan, *Early Gothic Manuscripts [II], 1250–1285*, A Survey of Manuscripts Illuminated in the British Isles, vol. 4 (in 2 parts) (London and New York: Harvey Miller and Oxford University Press, 1988), cat. 98, pp. 53–55. The text is very full and furnished with pictures unusually elaborate in their iconography; those in London: Brit. Lib. MS Harley 4751 are closely related.

17. Translated by Barber, *Bestiary*, p. 87; the Vulgate Bible numbers the quoted verse 79:14. On Bestiaries, a type of book that will figure significantly in this chapter, see Florence McCulloch, *Mediaeval Latin and French Bestiaries*, University of North Carolina Studies in the Romance Languages and Literatures 33, rev. ed. (Chapel Hill: University of North Carolina Press, 1962); Debra Hassig, *Medieval Bestiaries: Text, Image, Ideology* (Cambridge: Cambridge University Press, 1995); Joyce E. Salisbury, *The Beast Within: Animals in the Middle Ages* (New York: Routledge, 1994); and Jacques Berlioz, Marie Anne Polo de Beaulieu, and Pascal Collomb, *L'animal exemplaire au Moyen Age, Ve–XVe siècles* (Rennes: Press Universitaires de Rennes, 1999). Willene B. Clark and Meradith T. McMunn, eds., *Beasts and Birds of the Middle Ages: The Bestiary and Its Legacy* (Philadelphia: University of Pennsylvania Press, 1980), list all known Western medieval Bestiary manuscripts, and include a bibliography of Bestiary studies since 1962, the year McCulloch's bibliography came to an end. Marie-France Dupuis, Sylvain Louis, et al., *Le bestiaire* (Paris: Philippe Lebaud, 1988), translates yet another English Latin Bestiary—Oxford, Bodley MS Ashmole 15ll—to add to those listed elsewhere in these notes; it has commentaries by Xenia Muratova and Daniel Poirion. Beryl Rowland has an essay on "The Art of Memory and the Bestiary," in Clark and McMunn, *Beasts and Birds of the Middle Ages*; and Carruthers has speculated on its possible mnemonic function: see her *Book of Memory*, pp. 125–29.

18. Beryl Rowland, *Blind Beasts: Chaucer's Animal World* (Kent, Ohio: Kent State University Press, 1971), p. 80, thought to wonder "why Chaucer should transfer to the eagle the active qualities of the boar and make the boar passive, slumbering through the kisses of the faithless lady." Her answer turns on differences between the two suitors, and is helpful, as far as it goes: "The eagle exchanging hearts suggests the sincere wooer, a sleeping boar a gross, indifferent one."

19. *On the Properties of Things: John Trevisa's Translation of "Bartholomaeus Anglicus De Proprietatibus Rerum"; A Critical Text*, 2 vols. (Oxford: Clarendon Press, 1975), bk. XVIII, chap. 87, 2: 1237; the author notes that all swine of the male gender, wild or tame, are commonly called "boars," a usage that may have contributed to the conflation of pig and boar noted above.

20. Ibid., II, bk. 18, chap. 7, pp. 1117–20; I quote from pp. 1118–19. See Rowland, *Blind Beasts*, pp. 74–86, for a learned study of the boar, both wild and do-

mestic, in literature and art, and her *Animals with Human Faces: A Guide to Animal Symbolism* (Knoxville: University of Tennessee Press, 1973), pp. 37–43, for further information.

21. Rowland, *Blind Beasts*, pp. 77–78, explains the symbolic relation to lechery. Marjodoc's dream of Tristan's adulterous love for Isolde in the *Tristan* of Gottfried von Strassburg offers a striking example:

> The Steward saw in his dream as he slept a boar, fearsome and dreadful, that ran out from the forest. Up to the King's court he came, foaming at the mouth and whetting his tusks, and charging everything in his path. And now a great crowd of courtiers ran up. Many knights leapt hither and thither round the boar, yet none of them dared face him. Thus he plunged grunting through the Palace. Arriving at Mark's chamber he broke in through the doors, tossed the King's appointed bed in all directions, and fouled the royal linen with his foam.

Gottfried von Strassburg, *Tristan . . . with surviving Fragments of the Tristan of Thomas*, trans. A. T. Hatto (Harmondsworth, Eng.: Penguin Books, 1960), pp. 219–20.

22. A commonplace, here from the Anglo-Norman *Bestiaire* of Philippe de Thaon, quoted by Albert C. Baugh, ed., *Chaucer's Major Poetry* (New York: Appleton-Century Crofts, 1963), p. 67n331. In *The Parlement of Foules* the "tersel egle . . . the foul royal" (393) is followed in the wooing order by two tersels of slightly lower degree, all seeking a certain "formel egle," the most gentle and virtuous of all Nature's birds, as their mate (393–94, 415, 449–50).

23. Albertus Magnus in his *De animalibus*, composed between 1258 and 1262, subjects the tradition to closer scrutiny: "While the golden eagle is called the king of birds, it earns this title not because of any real governance over other birds, but because of the tyrannical violence of its actions; for it dominates all birds by oppressing and devouring them." Albert the Great, *Man and the Beasts: De Animalibus (Books 22–26)*, trans. James J. Scanlan, Medieval and Renaissance Texts and Studies 47 (Binghamton, NY: State University of New York Press, 1987), p. 195. Rowland, *Birds with Human Souls*, pp. 51–57, provides a wide-ranging guide to eagle lore and symbolism.

24. Albert the Great, *Man and the Beasts*, p. 191.

25. *On the Properties of Things*, bk. XII, chap. 2, 1: 603.

26. Barber, *Bestiary*, p. 119, translating Bodley 764; cf. T. H. White, ed. and trans., *The Book of Beasts: Being a Translation from a Latin Bestiary of the Twelfth Century* (London: Jonathan Cape, 1954), p. 107, translating Cambridge University Library MS 11.4.26.

27. On this MS, see Nigel Morgan, *Early Gothic Manuscripts [I], 1190–1250*, A Survey of Manuscripts Illuminated in the British Isles, vol. 4 (in 2 parts), (London and New York: Harvey Miller and Oxford University Press, 1982), cat. no. 64, p. 111. Other Bestiaries show the test itself, with an eagle and his two true offspring looking directly the sun, as he pushes out of a boat or out of a nest the one who looked away. For examples see Ann Payne, *Medieval Beasts* (New York: New Amsterdam Books, in association with the British Library, 1980), pp. 61, 63. Morgan, *Early Gothic Manuscripts [II]*, fig. 159, publishes a page whose main subject (the baptism of Christ by Christian bishops and clerks, with an angel and a devil pushing Jews out of the scene) is echoed by a smaller picture showing eagles gazing steadfastly at the sun, while another bird (presumably the discredited eagle) stares at the earth beneath its feet. It illustrates Guillaume le Clerc's Anglo-Norman verse bestiary. See cat. no. 129, pp. 110–12.

28. White, ed. and trans., *Book of Beasts*, p. 107 n1.

29. Barber, *Bestiary*, pp. 118–19; cf. White, *Book of Beasts*, p. 105.

30. Book II of the *Hous of Fame* tells us other things Chaucer knew about eagles. In that dream-vision, an eagle, whose gold feathers shine so bright it seems as though the heavens had another sun, descends like a thunderbolt, seizes the dreamer in his claws, and tries to show him at first hand everything he might wish to know about the cosmos, all this on his way to the house of Fame (Book III). The eagle appears as an emissary of Truth, to save the dreamer from fantasy and illusion (492–94). A great deal of scholarly attention has been devoted to this eagle, but not to the eagle of Criseyde's dream. See B. G. Koonce, *Chaucer and the Tradition of Fame: Symbolism in "The House of Fame"* (Princeton, NJ: Princeton University Press, 1966), pp. 126–77, for a deeply learned account of the exegetical tradition, useful whether or not one agrees with his interpretation of that poem; and John M. Steadman, "Chaucer's Eagle: A Contemplative Symbol," *PMLA* 75 (1960): 153–59, for a fundamental study, both philosophical and theological.

31. White, *Book of Beasts*, p. 105; cf. Barber, *Bestiary*, p. 119. Rowland, *Birds with Human Souls*, p. 53, reproduces a two-tiered illustration in which an eagle is first shown flying across the sea with a fish in his claws, and then flying upward toward the sun, while (below) he plunges into a well or fount of water to complete his rejuvenation. White, *Book of Beasts*, p. 107n1, notes that the "mist" on the eyes "probably refers to the nictitating membrane"—"a transparent third eyelid hinged at the inner side or lower lid of the eye of various animals, serving to keep the eye clean and moist" (*Webster's New World Dictionary*, 2nd college ed.).

32. Barber, *Bestiary*, reproduces Figure I.5 in splendid color. Closely related is the illustration from London, Brit. Lib. MS Harley 4751, fol. 35v, reproduced in color by Payne, *Medieval Beasts*, p. 62.

33. White, *Book of Beasts*, adorns his translation with line drawings based on illustrations in his principal manuscript. That shown on p. 106, otherwise arranged like the pictures under discussion here, shows the eagle descending into an abstract design almost certainly meant to represent the fountain, though no water is shown. Brunsdon Yapp, *Birds in Medieval Manuscripts* (London: British Library, 1981; repr., New York: Schocken Books, 1982), color plate 18, pp. 114–15, depicts the events separately, with water for the fish and water for the fountain into which the eagle descends. This picture is very literal in showing the eagle singeing his wings; they are overlapped by the red rays of a burnished gold sun. The iconography of the Bestiary was settled early, displaying a remarkable consistency throughout the thirteenth century, when its greatest manuscripts were made.

34. See James I. Wimsatt, "Medieval and Modern in Chaucer's *Troilus and Criseyde*," in *PMLA* 92 (1977): 207, summarizing his earlier essay, "Guillaume de Machaut and Chaucer's *Troilus and Criseyde*," in *Medium Aevum* 45 (1976): 277–93, whose concluding note, p. 293n32, finds no parallel in Machaut to the verses under examination here (II 862–65).

35. Macrobius, *Commentary on the Dream of Scipio*, trans. William Harris Stahl, II.14–15, Records of Civilization, Sources and Studies 48 (New York: Columbia University Press, 1952), pp. 85–86. "Philosophers" approve the use of fabulous narratives only "when speaking about the Soul, or about spirits having dominion in the lower and upper air, or about gods in general" (p. 85).

36. Chap. V of Cicero's text, printed in Macrobius, *Commentary*, p. 74; for Macrobius's explanation of this, IV. 14, see pp. 199–200.

37. I have written about this aspect of the poem in my presidential address to the New Chaucer Society, "God-Denying Fools and the Medieval Religion of Love," reprinted as Chapter VIII in this volume.

38. The first to have written specifically about "the male gaze" seems to have been Laura Mulvey in 1975; for that reference, and for materials more germane to this essay, see Jenny Jochens, "Before the Male Gaze: The Absence of the Female Body in Old Norse," in *Sex in the Middle Ages*, ed. Salisbury, pp. 3–29, and n1. See also Linda T. Holley, "Medieval Optics and the Framed Narrative in Chaucer's *Troilus and Criseyde*," *ChauR* 21, no. 1 (1986): 26–44, and especially Sarah Stanbury, "The Lover's Gaze in *Troilus and Criseyde*," in *Chaucer's "Troilus and Criseyde": "Subgit to alle Poesye"; Essays in Criticism*, ed. R. A. Shoaf, Medieval and Renaissance Texts and Studies 104, Pegasus Paperbooks 10 (Binghamton: State University of New York, 1991), pp. 224–38, a subtle and rewarding essay, though chiefly concerned with the way the two lovers first see each other. Cynthia Hahn, "*Visio Dei*: Changes in Medieval Visuality," in *Visuality Before and Beyond the Renaissance: Seeing as Others Saw*, ed. Robert S. Nelson (Cambridge: Cambridge University Press, 2000), pp. 169–96; and Michael Camille, "Before the Gaze: The Internal Senses and Late Medieval Practices of Seeing," in the same volume, pp. 197–223, theorize the gaze historically. John M. Bowers, "How Criseyde Falls in Love," in *The Expansion and Transformations of Courtly Literature*, ed. N. B. Smith and J. T. Snow (Athens: University of Georgia Press, 1980), pp. 141–55, reads Criseyde's first sight of Troilus—riding on a horse—iconographically, against an earlier stanza comparing Troilus to blind "Bayard," a frisky horse who forgets he is one. Criseyde, Bowers notes, *first* begins to fall in love by hearing Pandarus's reports of Troilus, rather than by seeing him (*pace* Andreas Capellanus, love can enter through the ear). Hymen (the god of marriage) otherwise counts for little, though as Henry Ansgar Kelly, *Love and Marriage in the Age of Chaucer* (Ithaca, NY: Cornell University Press, 1974), has shown, much of book III reads like a Christian marriage ceremony, and the lovers, having pledged their troth in the presence of a witness, could (in medieval, if not necessarily "Trojan" terms) consider themselves legally bound in a clandestine marriage.

39. Barry Windeatt, *Oxford Guides to Chaucer: Troilus and Criseyde* (Oxford: Clarendon Press, 1992), pp. 339–41, notices in the poem "a marked use of imagery of light and darkness which is not in Chaucer's source," and presents a good deal of evidence, well assessed. His book is an indispensable companion to all aspects of the poem.

40. Boccaccio, *Il Filostrato*, pt. III, stanzas 73–89, pp. 171–79. Chaucer made use of this song in all three hymns noted above, amplifying the Boethian themes already present in it.

41. Boethius, *The Consolation of Philosophy*, IV, m. 1, trans. Richard Green, Library of Liberal Arts (Indianapolis: Bobbs-Merrill, 1962), p. 76, with an interpolated gloss from Chaucer's own translation, *Riverside Chaucer*, p. 441.

42. The translation is by Louis de Beauvau, sénéchal of Anjou. See Avril and Reynaud, *Les manuscrits à peinture*, cat. no. 134, p. 245, for a description of the manuscript. Brewer, *Chaucer: Third Edition, Extensively revised and with additional material* (London: Longman, 1973), pp. 74–91 (3rd edition uniquely), publishes a generous selection of pictures from this manuscript, though not this one. In the *Filostrato*, the brooch is simply "a brooch of gold" ("un fermaglio d'oro") (pp. 398–99).

43. Cicero, "Dream of Scipio," chap. II, in Macrobius, *Commentary*, p. 71: "Scipio, be persuaded of this: all those who have saved, aided, or enlarged the commonwealth

have a definite place marked off in the heavens where they may enjoy a blessed existence forever."

44. Most scholars agree on counting outward, from the earth to the sphere of the fixed stars, rather than from the outermost planet (Saturn) inward, which would place Troilus in the sphere of the moon. See Windeatt, *Oxford Guides to Chaucer: Troilus and Criseyde*, pp. 209–11, for a discussion of the issue.

45. Karla Taylor, *Chaucer Reads "The Divine Comedy"* (Stanford, CA: Stanford University Press, 1989), pp. 189–94, considers this carefully.

46. Barber, *Bestiary*, p. 119. The Greek *Physiologus*, trans. Michael J. Curley (Austin: University of Texas Press, 1979), dating back to the fourth century, had already (pp. 12–13) drawn this allegorical lesson from a number of scriptural texts. The first of them proved especially important: "Your youth will be renewed like the eagle's" (Vulgate Psalm 102:5; 103:5 in later Bibles), and is voiced in the last sentence of the Bestiary passage above.

47. I quote Dante in the translation by Mark Musa, *The Divine Comedy*, vol. 3, *Paradise*, rev. ed. (Harmondsworth, Eng.: Penguin Books, 1986), by permission of the publisher. Because of space limitations, and the ready availability of the Italian text to anyone who might want to consult it, I do not print the original here.

48. Figure I.8 is reproduced in color by John Pope-Hennessy, *Paradiso: The Illuminations to Dante's Divine Comedy by Giovanni di Paolo* (New York: Random House, 1993), p. 103, who describes it so: "The Sun is a wheel of green, white and gold circles, from which golden rays descend over a panorama of hills and castellated farms" (p. 102). On fol. 179, illustrating Canto XXVIII (Pope-Hennessy, p. 165), Dante is shown looking directly at the light of God, a huge bright sphere with a mysterious head at its center, possibly Boreas, more likely Christ. For other illustrations of the heaven of the Sun, see Peter Brieger, Millard Meiss, and Charles S. Singleton, *Illuminated Manuscripts of the Divine Comedy*, Bollingen Series 81, 2 vols. (Princeton, NJ: Princeton University Press, 1969), 2: 454–65, and commentary in 1: 190–92. Charles H. Taylor and Patricia Finley, *Images of the Journey in Dante's Divine Comedy* (New Haven, CT: Yale University Press, 1997), pp. 204–11, 241, argue that the head is that of Christ, and are probably right.

49. From Wycliffe's commentary on the eagle in the canticle of Moses, Deut. 32:10–12, quoted by Koonce, *Chaucer and the Tradition of Fame*, p. 131.

50. *Hous of Fame*, bk. II, in its dream of an eagle (modeled on Dante's dream in *Purgatorio*, IX 19 ff.), makes a similar point. The eagle, in its pedantic eagerness to teach, takes "Geffrey" much too high, giving Chaucer a thrilling view of fields, plains, mountains, and rivers, for a time. But soon they fly so high he can see almost nothing at all. The earth becomes no more than "a prikke," and the stars shine so brightly he fears they will "shenden" (destroy) his sight (1016). "Geffrey's" incapacity and reluctance are a delectable part of the poem's comedy, but they make a serious point: what the eagle shows him in his dream is too much for human eyes. Books, "Geffrey" demurs, do it well enough at home, more safely and more comfortably.

51. Boccaccio, *Il Filostrato*, pt. VIII, stanzas 29–33; and IX, 5, 7, 8, pp. 410–19.

52. John M. Steadman, *Disembodied Laughter: "Troilus" and the Apotheosis Tradition; A Reexamination of Narrative and Thematic Contexts* (Berkeley: University of California Press, 1972), remains an essential study of this part of the poem, including its emphasis on "contempt of the world."

CHAPTER II

1. Boccaccio, in *De claris mulieribus*, worked under a more capacious rubric, as he is careful to point out in his preface:

> Nor do I want the reader to think it out of place if together with Penelope, Lucretia, and Sulpicia, who were very chaste matrons, they find Medea, Flora, and Sempronia, who happened to have very strong but destructive characters. For it is not my intention to give the word "famous" so strict a meaning that it will always seem to signify "virtuous," but rather to give it a wider sense, if the reader will forgive me, and to consider as famous those women whom I know to have become renowned to the world through any sort of deed.

Giovanni Boccaccio, *Concerning Famous Women*, trans. Guido A. Guarino (New Brunswick, NJ: Rutgers University Press, 1963), pp. xxxvii–viii. The work lacks a modern edition; Guarino translates from that of Mathias Apiarius (Berne, 1539).

2. The reasons for this neglect can be briefly stated: though the Prologue is found charming, the legends have not appealed, and it has been customarily assumed (partly because the poem is incomplete, partly because of explicit comments made by its narrator), that they did not appeal to Chaucer either. The best writing on the Prologue, that of Robert O. Payne, *The Key of Remembrance: A Study of Chaucer's Poetics* (New Haven, CT: Yale University Press, 1963), chap. 3, dismisses "the legends themselves, which follow the brilliant Prologue" as "flat, more or less unrelieved failures" (p. 111); his more recent essay, "Making His Own Myth: The Prologue to Chaucer's *Legend of Good Women*," *ChauR* 9 (1975): 197–211, is similar in focus. Insofar as the poem has been considered as a whole, it has customarily been described as a royal commission uncongenial to the poet, or more recently, in a useful book by Robert Worth Frank, Jr., *Chaucer and "The Legend of Good Women"* (Cambridge, MA: Harvard University Press, 1972), as a set of exploratory exercises in the art of short narrative, imperfectly achieved in the *Legend* but mastered in *The Canterbury Tales*. Frank's book considers the legends one at a time, with learning and often with critical acumen, but without any compelling vision of what they were meant to amount to as a whole.

3. Beverly Taylor, "The Medieval Cleopatra: The Classical and Medieval Tradition of Chaucer's *Legend of Cleopatra*," *Journal of Medieval and Renaissance Studies* 7 (1977): 249–69, offers a condensed but very learned survey of the tradition; it should be supplemented by Ilse Becher, *Das Bild der Kleopatra in der griechischen und lateinischen Literatur* (Berlin: Akedemie-Verlag, 1966), which provides an exhaustive study of the classical sources. Pages 151–73 concern Cleopatra's death. On the question of Chaucer's immediate source or sources, see W. K. Wimsatt, Jr., "Vincent of Beauvais and Chaucer's Cleopatra and Croesus," *Speculum* 12 (1937): 375–81; and Pauline Aiken, "Chaucer's *Legend of Cleopatra* and the *Speculum Historiale*," *Speculum* 13 (1938): 232–36.

4. Taylor suggests these changes are meant to invoke the Cleopatra one finds in other books, with Chaucer's omissions and discrepancies establishing a comic, ironic intention for the *Legend* as a whole: "Chaucer depicts subjects who illustrate the most perfidious and destructive—or in some instances, the most ludicrous—aspects of worldly love," and begins with Cleopatra in order to establish this "ironic principle" with particular clarity (p. 250). In my view, Taylor's essay fails to recognize the real materials out of which Chaucer invented Cleopatra's death, and substitutes for the poem he actually wrote a modern scholar's knowledge of the Cleopatra tradition—an enormous compilation of texts few of which could have

been known to Chaucer or to his original audiences, but knowledge of which is essential to her interpretation of the poem.

5. Donald R. Howard, *The Idea of the "Canterbury Tales"* (Berkeley: University of California Press, 1976), chap. 1: "The Idea of an Idea."

6. Note that, in our present poem, *The Legend of Philomela* explicitly describes the experience of literature as a visual event: the story of Tereus infects with venom the eyes of anyone who would "behold" it (2238–43), and Philomela weaves her story in pictures and letters together (2350–65).

7. Florus, *Epitome of Roman History*, ed. and trans. E. S. Forster, Loeb Classical Library (London: W. Heinemann, 1929), p. 327.

8. *De claris mulieribus*, chap. 86 (trans. Guarino, p. 196). Boccaccio continues, "In this sleep the wretched woman put an end to her greed, her concupiscence, and her life." Chaucer's version could not conceivably yield such a moral.

9. Giovanni Boccaccio, *The Fates of Illustrious Men*, trans. Louis Brewer Hall (New York: Ungar, 1965), p. 174 (a partial translation of the Latin text as published by Gourmont and Petit in Paris, 1520). Boccaccio again concludes with a moral: "Her body, softened with the greatest delicacies, used to the most tender embraces, was at last embraced by serpents while she was still sensitive to sight and touch. And the poison nourished the same blood that had been nourished by wines. The beauty she displayed with her feminine vanity, she buried alive. . . . And she who had yearned for great power, finished her life in a mausoleum."

10. Figure II.1: see Adam von Bartsch, *Le Peintre-Graveur*, 21 vols. (Vienna: Degen, 1803–21), 8.88.12. Other impressions date the engraving 1524.

11. Figure II.2: Bartsch, 9.172.5.

12. Figure II.3: Bartsch, 8.147.77. For another engraving by the same artist, likewise set in prison, see Bartsch, 8.146.76; it is dated 1529.

13. Figure II.4: Bartsch, 14.161.198. See also 14.162–64, and 14.199–200.

14. The manuscript from which Figure II.5 is taken is a copy of the second translation (1409) by Laurent de Premierfait, freer than the version he had made in 1400. The third miniature I refer to above (Munich, Bayerische Staatsbibliothek MS gall. 6, made in the workshop of Jean Fouquet) also illustrates the *De casibus*: it allows Cleopatra to meet her death totally naked, with serpents at her breasts. But that is just one event, barely visible in the middle distance, in a picture that also shows Anthony's cavalry victory over Octavius, the sea battle at Actium, and (far more prominent) Anthony stabbing himself in a room filled with tombs and funeral effigies. It has been reproduced by Paul Durrieu, *Le Boccace de Munich* (Munich: Jacques Rosenthal, 1909), pl. 20. On the French tradition of illustrations to the Boccaccio texts, see Carla Bozzolo, *Manuscrits des traductions Françaises d'Oeuvres de Boccace, XV siècle* (Padua: Antenore, 1973); and *Boccace en France: De l'humanisme à l'erotisme*, catalog of an exhibition at the Bibliothèque Nationale (Paris, 1975), compiled by Florence Callu and François Avril, esp. pp. 53–58. Though the *De casibus* text on its own is enough to explain the nakedness and serpents, these two instances may bear some kinship to a twelfth-century French tradition in stone carving, represented at Moissac, Vézelay, and Charlieu, that depicts Lust (*Luxuria*) as a naked woman with two serpents at her breast. On this tradition, see Emile Mâle, *Religious Art in France: The Twelfth Century*, ed. Harry Bober (Princeton, NJ: Princeton University Press, 1978), pp. 373–76, and figs. 17, 264, 265, and further references there. The Boccaccio text can readily support such an interpretation; Chaucer's text does not.

15. Figure II.7 illustrates the French translation made in 1401 (the attribution

to Laurent de Premierfait has been questioned), variously titled *Des femmes nobles et renomées* or *Des cleres et nobles femmes*; the present manuscript was presented to Philippe le Hardi in 1403.

16. Figure II.8 is from a manuscript presented to the Duc de Berry in 1404. Its illuminations bear a family relationship to those of MS fr. 12420 above. For a detailed account, see *Boccace en France*, pp. 53–54, and Millard Meiss, *French Painting in the Time of Jean de Berry: The Limbourgs and Their Contemporaries*, 2 vols. (London: Thames and Hudson, 1974), 1: 287–90. Two other versions of Cleopatra's death are of interest. London, Brit. Lib. MS Royal 16 G. v, fol. 101, shows her royally dressed with two dragons crouching beside her, catching in their mouths the blood that spurts from her arms. This interpretation of the serpents is without textual precedent, though another manuscript (London, Brit. Lib. MS Royal 20 C. v, fol. 131v) copies this picture. The image is otherwise bland and without expressive force, but its rendering of the customary serpents as dragons may be meant to move her death into a context of sin and its affiliations: perhaps her blood feeds dragons to signify that even in her death the devil is served. Compare Boccaccio's text (note 8 above) in its medieval French translation: Cleopatra thus "*print fin de avarice de vie et de plaisance charnele*" (fol. 104). The picture is reproduced by Patricia Gathercole, *Tension in Boccaccio: Boccaccio and the Fine Arts*, Romance Monographs 14 (University of Mississippi Press, 1975), fig. 6, though she does not identify the creatures as dragons—describing them merely as "two strange animals" (p. 60)—and offers no guess as to their meaning. Boccaccio's *Buch von dem fürnembsten Weibern*, ed. Kurt Pfister (Potsdam: G. Kiepenhauer, 1924), a facsimile of a German translation of this work published at Ulm in 1473, reproduces on p. 233 its woodcut illustration of the lovers' death (a serpent at each of Cleopatra's arms), juxtaposed to a scene of the lovers feasting, with a servant attending them at table. The traditional moral association of gluttony with lechery may be the explanation of this double scene.

17. This manuscript was first owned by Jean sans Peur, Duke of Burgundy; its illuminations were published by Henry Martin, *Le Boccace de Jean sans Peur* (Brussels: G. van Oest, 1911). On it see *Boccace en France*, p. 56, and Millard Meiss, *French Painting in the Time of Jean de Berry: The Boucicaut Master* (London: Phaidon, 1968), pp. 35, 47, 50, 54. That the snakes are shown *within* the tomb oddly—though fortuitously—suggests what Chaucer had already made of this event.

18. Figure II.10: likewise illustrating Laurent's *Des cas des nobles hommes et femmes* in its second translation, 6: 15 (the manuscript is not foliated). See Meiss, *Boucicaut Master*, p. 50, for a description of this miniature (which he reproduces in color as figure 392) and pp. 102–4, for a description of the manuscript as a whole.

19. Figure II.11: Millard Meiss, *French Painting in the Time of Jean de Berry: The Late Fourteenth Century and the Patronage of the Duke*, 2 vols. (London: Phaidon, 1967), 1: 93, 318, describes this manuscript; see too his *French Painting . . . The Limbourgs and their Contemporaries*, 1: 259, 261–62, 367, 378. Meiss dates the manuscript ca. 1415, and attributes its illuminations to the Rohan workshop. Callu and Avril, *Boccace en France*, p. 57, date the manuscript ca. 1420.

20. In the early decades of the twentieth century, when the search for sources and analogues dominated Chaucer studies, certain parallels were adduced, among them the fact that serpents are included in the punishments of hell, and that confinement in a serpent pit is a feature of certain medieval romances as well as of certain saint's lives. Griffith suggested that Chaucer may have invented such torture as

a justification for thinking of Cleopatra as a martyr; Tatlock suggested that Chaucer may have known of serpent pits in contemporary Africa, an idea which brings F. N. Robinson's note on the matter (in his 2nd edition of *The Works of Geoffrey Chaucer* [Boston: Houghton Mifflin, 1957] to an end: "This would be," he writes, "one of the most striking cases of [Chaucer's] use of local color." (See his note, or that in *The Riverside Chaucer*, for the relevant bibliography.) All these explanations are deficient in one important respect: they cannot explain what Cleopatra intends by the action. Since she invents her own death, it has to make some sense from within her story—from within the range of hypotheses concerning life and death available to her. Professor Frank judges her legend an artistic failure, and thinks it altogether "an odd choice and what seems on several counts an unfortunate choice" as the opening legend of the poem; he suggests that Anthony's tomb and Cleopatra's death are best seen as "acts of devotion" whose "appeal is their exoticism, their suggestion of opulence and passion" (pp. 37, 44). Taylor believes the death is a case study in immoderation: "Even her manner of committing suicide may be seen as partaking of this excess, for Chaucer's queen is content not with an asp or a few serpents, but with nothing less than a pit filled with 'alle the serpentes that she myghte have,'" (p. 261). One wonders what the appropriate number would be.

21. See the *OED* evidence for *pit*, sense I.3, and, e.g., *English Lyrics of the XIIIth Century*, ed. Carleton Brown (Oxford: Clarendon Press, 1932), no. 13 (6–7); *Religious Lyrics of the XIVth Century*, ed. Carleton Brown, 2nd ed., rev. G.V. Smithers (Oxford: Clarendon Press, 1952), no. 117 (20); and the lyric quoted by Rosemary Woolf, *The English Religious Lyric in the Middle Ages* (Oxford: Oxford University Press, 1968), p. 88 ("thync on me her in thys pet!"). Cf. old January in *The Merchant's Tale* (IV 1400–1401): "Freendes, I am hoor and oold, / And almoost, God woot, on my pittes brynke." See also the *OED* evidence for *worm*, senses I.1, 2, 6, and, e.g., *English Lyrics of the XIIIth Century*, no. 20 (21), no. 29 (31), no. 51 (48); *Religious Lyrics of the XIVth Century*, no. 100 (65), no. 134 (33), no. 135 (7, 15, 31); Woolf, *English Religious Lyric*, p. 88 ("Her sal I dwellen wermes to fede"); *St. Erkenwald*, ed. Ruth Morse (Cambridge: D. S. Brewer, 1975), p. 62; *Ludus Coventriae*, ed. K. S. Block, EETS, e.s. 120 (London: Oxford University Press, 1922), p. 177 (the death of Herod). *English Lyrics of the XIIIth Century*, no. 29 (47) and no. 30 (2, 4) refer to worms and pit together. Woolf, *English Religious Lyric*, chaps. 3 and 9, offers a magisterial study of medieval lyrics on death and their backgrounds. Douglas Gray, *Themes and Images in the Medieval English Religious Lyric* (London: Routledge and Kegan Paul, 1972), chap. 10, is also valuable. For the burial rites accorded several of Chaucer's friends or associates, see Edith Rickert, *Chaucer's World*, ed. Clair C. Olson and Martin M. Crow (New York: Columbia University Press, 1948), pp. 401 ff.

22. *The Bestiary: A Book of Beasts, Being a Translation from a Latin Bestiary of the Twelfth Century*, trans. T. H. White (London: Jonathan Cape, 1954), pp. 190–91. Woolf, *English Religious Lyric*, p. 318, quotes an unedited lyric from the first half of the fifteenth century that preserves this idea, though she does not remark upon it: "In mi riggeboon bredith an addir kene." White's translated Bestiary identifies the hypnale (a species of asp) as the snake that caused Cleopatra's death, p. 174, and describes the dragon as "the biggest of all serpents," p. 165.

23. Figure II.12: von Bartsch, 8.116–17.6; it copies a print made by his brother Barthel Beham. The engraving is fully described in *Images of Love and Death in Late Medieval and Renaissance Art*, a catalog by William R. Levin for an exhibition at the University of Michigan Museum of Art (1975), pp. 71–72, and reproduced

there as pl. 51 (fig. 30). Plates 67 and 68 are also of interest. Oxford, Balliol College MS 238, a *Fontis memorabilium universi* (German, 1445–48), fol. 65, depicts a living woman whose body is filled with snakes, bones, and a skull, as an image of bodily corruption—of what the body will become.

24. The first is quoted from *English Lyrics of the XIIIth Century*, no. 10-B (34), the second from John Lydgate's translation of the *Dance Macabre*, in *The Dance of Death*, ed. Florence Warren, EETS, O.S. 81 (London: Oxford University Press, 1931), p. 74 (640).

25. This is so in fourteen out of the twenty-one medieval wall paintings of this subject still clearly visible in English churches. See Philippa Tristram, *Figures of Life and Death in Medieval English Literature* (London: Elek, 1976), p. 234 (n60); for her general discussion of the theme, see pp. 162–67 and fig. 25. Woolf, *English Religious Lyric*, pp. 344–47; and Kathleen Cohen, *Metamorphosis of a Death Symbol: The Transi Tomb in the Late Middle Ages and the Renaissance* (Berkeley: University of California Press, 1973), pp. 33–38, offer useful discussion and bibliography.

26. I quote the English phrases inscribed above the illumination; the full dialogue (which begins beneath) is in Anglo-Norman verse. The cadavers to some extent mirror the postures of their living counterparts.

27. The verses under Figure II.15 serve as a kind of preface to the debate poem itself, which is formally begun (with a title) on fol. 33. The preface reads:

> Take hede vn to my fygure here abowne
> And se how sumtyme I was fressche and gay
> Now turned to wormes mete and corrupcoun
> Bot fowle erth and stynkyng slyme and clay
> Attende therfore to this disputacion written here
> And writte it wysely in thi herte fre
> At therat sum wisdom thou may lere
> To se what thou art and here aftyr sal be.
> When thou leste wenes. venit mors te superare
> When thi grafe grenes, bonum est mortis meditari.

I quote from the edition by Karl Brunner, "Mittelenglische Todesgedichte," *Archiv für das Studium der neuren Sprachen* 167 (1935): 30–35; the debate poem itself consists of thirty-one seven-line stanzas. For commentary on it, see Woolf, *English Religious Lyric*, pp. 313–14, 328–30; and Cohen, *Metamorphosis*, pp. 29–30. Both term it a picture of a double *transi* tomb, but Ralph E. Giesey, in a review of Cohen's book, in *Speculum* 52 (1977): 537–41, perhaps describes it more accurately: "Clearly the cadaver is not a picture of a sculpted *transi* that a spectator at the tomb could see, but rather a picture of the corpse itself decaying in the coffin. . . . The tomb [is] levitated to reveal the worm-eaten corpse" (p. 639). He regards the poem as a commentary upon (and explanation of) the double tombs already in existence rather than as a literary representation of them.

28. Brunner, "Todesgedichte," p. 31 (v. 5).

29. Ibid., p. 32 (vv. 13, 14). Note the thematic relation of this last catalog to Chaucer's *Legend of Good Women*.

30. Verse 16 offers a comprehensive list of all the "venomos wormes" that eat the corpse; it corroborates the evidence cited in note 21 above. In v. 19 (p. 33) the worms explain to the cadaver that the lice and nits and stomach worms that tormented her (as they do all human beings) all her life long were sent as messengers, to warn her to make ready.

31. The text that goes with Figure II.17 has not been published. Woolf, *English*

Religious Lyric, pp. 312–13, describes several variant versions and their provenance, and Gray reproduces this picture (his pl. 8) and summarizes the plot, pp. 206–7; both reprint the concluding verses. Woolf, appendix H, surveys "The History of the Warning from the Dead"; it is of great antiquity.

32. Cohen, *Metamorphosis*, offers a comprehensive study of the *transi* tomb, exhaustively researched, beautifully written, and richly illustrated, with an appendix that lists all known examples by both country and type. The English examples are listed on pp. 192–94. The style develops late; only five examples date from the fourteenth century, while seventy-five date from the fifteenth. England furnishes more examples than any other country, by a vast proportion (p. 194), but it favored an emaciated *transi*, whereas France provides most of the examples riddled with worms, and Germany and Austria most of the examples of a corpse covered with frogs and snakes (p. 2). Only three *transis* in England are covered with snakes or frogs, and they are relatively late in date (ca. 1510–30)—see p. 78 (n102)—whereas France provides thirteen *transis* with worms, and Germany most of the twenty *transis* that are covered with snakes or other reptiles (p. 195). Cohen is careful to emphasize that the *transi* represents "a specific dead individual and not Death itself"; the word is derived from *transire*, and signifies one who has "gone across," "passed over," "passed away"; the noun is first recorded in a sixteenth-century tomb contract in France ("la portraiture d'un transsy et mort d'environ huit jours"), but the verb *transir* in the sense of "to die" had been common in French from the twelfth century (p. 10). Cohen notes that the first men to commission *transi* tombs—cardinals and archbishops—were churchmen famous for their power, political acumen, and worldliness, and that these tombs, while serving the traditional purpose of expressing hope for the salvation of the deceased (pp. 3–4, 62), also represent an attempt "to alleviate some of the anxiety felt by these men as a result of the conflict between their own pride and the traditional religious demand for humility" (p. 7). Erwin Panofsky, *Tomb Sculpture*, ed. H. W. Janson (New York: Harry N. Abrams, 1964), pp. 63–66 and figs. 256–71, locates the form within a history of tomb sculpture from ancient Egypt to Bernini.

33. Figure II.18: the tomb was constructed in the church of St. Martial, Avignon; this fragment (all that survives) is now in the Musée Calvet of that city. Cohen, *Metamorphosis*, fig. 3, reproduces a seventeenth-century drawing of the full tomb, and writes about it, pp. 12–14; I quote her translation of the Latin epitaph, p. 13. In his will, Lagrange requested that his bones be boiled and buried in Amiens, and that his flesh and entrails be buried under his *transi* in Avignon. The latter city was, of course, the seat of the French papacy. See Arne McGee Morganstern, "The La Grange Tomb and Choir: A Monument of the Great Schism of the West," *Speculum* 48 (1973): 52–69.

34. Figure II.19: Chichele's tomb was built in connection with a chantry chapel, and was in place by 1425; in 1437, he founded All Souls' College, Oxford; in 1443, he died. On this tomb, and for his epitaph, see Cohen, *Metamorphosis*, pp. 15–16.

35. Figure II.20: Fleming was bishop of Lincoln; this tomb, too, is part of a chantry chapel. Cohen describes it, ibid., pp. 17–18, and prints his vivid epitaph, probably composed by Fleming himself. Cf. the tomb of John Fitzalan (died 1435), in Arundel, Sussex, reproduced by Tristram, *Figures of Life and Death*, fig. 32.

36. On this tomb, see Cohen, *Metamorphosis*, pp. 77–83. The chapel that houses it in the village church at La Sarraz was built in 1360, and Herbert Reiners would date the tomb to about that same year. Erwin Panofsky and Ernst Kantorowicz suggest a date nearer to 1370; Raoul Nicolas argues for the late 1390s (see Cohen,

pp. 77–78nn100, 101); Cohen accepts Nicholas's dating). On p. 83, Cohen develops an elaborate interpretation of this effigy, in which the frogs at the mouth represent unclean spirits expelled by the deceased's confession of his sins, the snakes represent his contrition (the gnawing pangs of conscience), and the scallop shells on his pillow and carved into his chest his hope of eternal life. I think the first part of this reading unlikely; on p. 93 Cohen admits later sculptors show no evidence of having understood it so. The Wakefield play of *Lazarus*, as a counterexample, includes Lazarus's firsthand account of all those creatures at work in the grave: see *The Towneley Plays*, ed. George England and Alfred W. Pollard, EETS, e.s. 71 (London: Oxford University Press, 1897; rpt. 1952), pp. 390–91. Like Cohen, I take the scallop shells to be an image of hope and faith, but set in juxtaposition to imagery of the body's corruption.

37. Manuscripts get lost or wear out; they rot, burn, or are eaten by worms; sometimes they are willfully destroyed. On the systematic destruction of religious art and sculpture in England during the Reformation, see John Phillips, *The Reformation of Images: Destruction of Art in England, 1535–1660* (Berkeley: University of California Press, 1973).

38. *De contemptu mundi*, bk. III, ch. 1, quoted by Cohen, *Metamorphosis*, p. 43. Chaucer's translation has been lost, though he tells us he translated the work in the G version of the Prologue to our present poem (414–15).

39. The tomb has been briefly described by T. S. R. Boase, "King Death: Mortality, Judgment and Remembrance," chap. 6 of *The Flowering of the Middle Ages*, ed. Joan Evans (London: Thames and Hudson, 1966), pp. 220 (fig. 34) and 240; it is treated more extensively by Arthur Bolton, *Guide to St. Mary's Church, Ewelme, and to the Almshouse and the School*, rev. by K. St. C. Thomas (Ewelme, Eng.: Printed for the church, 1967), pp. 12–13. Russell Krauss, "Chaucerian Problems: Especially the Petherton Forestership and the Question of Thomas Chaucer," in *Three Chaucer Studies*, ed. Carleton Brown (New York: Oxford University Press, 1932), suggested that the rise of Thomas Chaucer to great riches and power may imply that he was the illegitimate son of John of Gaunt by Chaucer's wife Philippa, born during Chaucer's absence from England in 1372–73. Though this is the purest conjecture, it could also explain the high marriage(s) and elevation to the peerage of Thomas's daughter, Alice, buried in the tomb described above. The idea has been given renewed currency by John H. Fisher, ed., *The Complete Poetry and Prose of Geoffrey Chaucer* (New York: Holt, Rinehart, Winston, 1977), p. 958; as well as by John Gardner, *The Life and Times of Chaucer* (New York: Alfred A. Knopf, 1977), pp. 158–62.

40. Brunner, "Todesgedichte," p. 30 (prefatory verses). Cf. the epitaph from a woman's tomb in Picardy, quoted by Cohen, *Metamorphosis*, p. 74: "Celle qui dit ces vers / Est mangie des vers / Et serez-vous" (She who speaks these verses is eaten by worms: you will be too).

41. *Vox clamantis*, bk. VII, chs. 9–15 ff., in *The Complete Works of John Gower*, ed. G. C. Macaulay, 4 vols. (Oxford: Oxford University Press, 1899–1902), 4: 291–96; *The Major Latin Works of John Gower*, trans. Eric W. Stockton (Seattle: University of Washington Press, 1962), pp. 270–74 ff. Each of the Deadly Sins is shown to corrupt the dead body in its own particular way. I am grateful to Patricia J. Eberle for calling my attention to this passage.

42. See the concluding pages of this chapter, and the passage quoted above in note 1.

43. Because the legend of Hypermnestra is unfinished, it accidentally epitomizes the larger poem as we have it: its last line, which is also the last line of the collection as a whole, begins a new sentence—"This tale is seyd for this conclusion" (2723)—and ends in silence.

44. An illumination in Paris, Bibl. natl. MS 12420, fol. 61v (*Des cleres et nobles femmes*) likewise depicts her death as isolated and distant; it was made between 1401 and 1403.

45. Figure II.27: from the latter MS, fol. 121v. On the iconography of Despair (Desperatio), see Adolf Katzenellenbogen, *Allegories of the Virtues and Vices in Mediaeval Art*, trans. Alan J. P. Crick (1939; rpt., New York: W. W. Norton, 1964), pp. 76–81, figs. 72(b), 76, and pp. 13 (n1), 59 (n3), 83 (n1).

46. Leroy P. Percy, when he was my student, first taught me to read *The Physician's Tale* of Virginius and Virginia in such a way. *The Legend of Lucrece* offers a partial exception to the generalization I make above, for Lucrece is innocent victim, and Augustine (the poet tells us) felt compassion for her (1690); she became "a seynt" among the Romans (1870). Indeed, as noted in my text, Chaucer concludes his praise of her by recalling Christ's statement that He had found no faithfulness greater than He had found in a woman. But Chaucer knew Augustine had also condemned Lucrece for her suicide (Christianity cannot convert such a death into a virtuous act), and he makes it clear that the only consequence of her death was oblique and political: it brought down a corrupt dynasty. Though her history is noble, it is irredeemably tragic.

47. The idea is doubtless borrowed from Boccaccio, *De casibus*, where countless persons who fell from Fortune's favor are imagined as crowding the author's study, hoping to have their stories told; in *The Fates of Illustrious Men*, trans. Hall, see for instance pp. 9, 156, 168, 226, 241. That throng of self-mourners, only some of whom get their histories narrated, is often shown in deluxe manuscripts of the poem: *Boccace en France*, p. 50, reproduces in color the opening illumination of the famous Munich manuscript.

48. Frank writes well on this, *Chaucer and "The Legend of Good Women,"* pp. 148–49.

49. D. W. Robertson, Jr., *A Preface to Chaucer: Studies in Medieval Perspectives* (Princeton, NJ: Princeton University Press, 1963), pp. 378–79; see pp. 141–42 on the Christian assimiliation of the Hercules myth.

50. See Franz Cumont, *Recherches sur le symbolisme funéraire des romains* (Paris: P. Geunthner, 1942), pp. 30 (n4), 499 (add. n4); Hellmut Sichtermann and Guntram Koch, *Griechische Mythen auf römischen Sarkophagen* (Tübingen: E. Wasmuth, 1975), pp. 20–22, pls. 17–19; and Carl Robert, *Die antiken Sarkophag-Reliefs*, 3.1 (Berlin, 1890–1919; rpt., Rome: "L'Erma" di Bretschneider, 1969), pp. 25–38, pl. 6. Marcel Simon, *Hercule et le Christianisme* (Paris: Publications de la Faculté des lettres de l'Université de Strasbourg 2: sér. no. 19, 1955), offers an extensive study of the larger myth that brought Alceste into early Christian art. André Grabar, *Christian Iconography: A Study of Its Origins* (Princeton, NJ: Princeton University Press, 1968), pt. 1, contributes a masterly introduction to this subject. Though the earliest sources of the Alceste tradition are without direct medieval consequence, it is in Euripides' *Alcestis* that she finds her fullest and most memorable life; it was written in 438 B.C. She is praised in Plato's *Symposium* 179B–C as an example of the sacrifice a lover will make for the beloved, and of the reward granted by the gods for such a deed; at 208D it is suggested instead that she died for the sake

of immortal renown. Her story and that of Admetus are narrated with extreme brevity in the *Fabulae* of Hyginus, a Latin work written sometime shortly before the year 207, which John of Salisbury clearly knew and which Chaucer may have known; it has been edited and translated by Mary Grant as *The Myths of Hyginus* (Lawrence: University of Kansas Press, 1960), p. 58 (no. 50, no. 51). Macrobius, *Saturnalia*, 5.19.3–5, briefly quotes and comments on a passage from Euripides' play; it is of no relevance here. Among Chaucer's English contemporaries only Gower tells Alceste's story, probably in imitation of Chaucer. In Book VII of the *Confessio Amantis*—the book that summarizes the education given Alexander by Aristotle—she is included as exemplary proof that women can be "goode and kinde" (ll. 1917–49). Gower briefly narrates her decision to die so that her husband might live, but says nothing of her resurrection. He mentions her again among the company of lovers that he sees in a dream (8.2640–46) when he senses himself growing old and is led to renounce the adventure of love (8.2440 ff.). The lovers include Cleopatra, Dido, Phyllis, Penelope, Lucrece, and many others as well—a group that might have wandered in from the pages of *The Legend of Good Women*. It is very likely a literary debt.

51. The paintings have been published by Antonio Ferrua, *Le pitture della nuova catacomba di via Latina* (Vatican City: Pontifico Istituto de Archeologia Cristiana, 1960); see esp. pls. 75, 76, 79 (our Figure II.28), 80, 81, and (in color) 111, 112; these paintings are described on pp. 77–78; Grabar writes about them, *Christian Iconography*, p. 15, and in his *The Beginnings of Christian Art, 200–398* (London: Thames and Hudson, 1967), pp. 225 ff; on p. 228 he reproduces in color our Figure II.28. In room E of this same catacomb there is a painting of the death of Cleopatra with an asp at her breast and a halo around her head (see Ferrua, pl. 102 and p. 61). Ferrua offers no guess as to the logic of her presence there, nor can I; see Grabar, *Christian Iconography*, p. 9, on the frequency with which early Christian imagery eludes any confident interpretation.

52. *Mythologiae*, 1.22. I quote from the translation of Leslie George Whitbread, *Fulgentius the Mythographer* (Columbus: Ohio State University Press, 1971), p. 63.

53. *Scriptores rerum mythicarum Latini tres Romae nuper reperti*, ed. George Henry Bode, 2 vols. (Celle, 1834; rpt., Hildesheim: G. Olms, 1968), 1: 31, 128–29, 247–48. Fulgentius discovered in the name Admetus the word for "mind" (*mens, mentis*), and the phrase *adire metus* ("as one whom fear could seize upon"). Alcestis he derived from the Greek *alce*, glossed as *praesumptio* by him and by the Vatican mythographers after him. The latter word is difficult to translate confidently in this context (Whitbread's "succour" seems a curious choice): in biblical usage, *praesumptio* means simply "opinion" or "thought" (Alexander Souter, ed., *A Glossary of Later Latin to 600 A.D.* [Oxford: Oxford University Press, 1949; corr. 1957]); in many medieval contexts it retains its original sense of "preconception, supposition, presumption," but the Third Vatican Mythographer glosses it as *animositas* (*Scriptores rerum mythicarum Latini*, p. 247), probably in the sense of "boldness, confidence, or fearlessness of spirit." Only the identification of the yoked beasts with the strengths of mind and body, and of the gods who assist Admetus as standing for wisdom (Apollo) and strength (Hercules) makes the point of the marriage clear, even in the pages of the mythographers. Boccaccio, *Genealogie deorum gentilium libri*, 13.1, ed. Vincenzo Romano, 2 vols. (Bari: G. Laterza, 1951), 2: 642, offers essentially the same reading, and then one other in which Admetus stands for the rational soul, Alcestis for *virtus*, and the winning of her in marriage for a bridling of the irascible and concupiscent

appetites. Such virtue or strength, he continues, can oppose our passionate desires for our soul's sake and, if we fall, can raise us up again.

54. Pierre Bersuire, *Ovidius moralizatus*, ed. F. Ghisalberti, *Studij Romanzi* 23 (1933): 101; I quote Robertson's translation, *Preface to Chaucer*, p. 378. Bersuire's notice concludes: "Hercules igitur i. Christus istas de inferno eripit, et ad gloriam secum ducit. Psalmus: propter te mortificamur tota die."

55. On this text, and on the present manuscript, see Jean Seznec, *The Survival of the Pagan Gods*, trans. Barbara F. Sessions (1953; rpt., New York: Harper, 1961), pp. 170–79. The text above the picture states that reason and strength of mind (*ratio et virtus animi*) vanquish all cupidinous desires and earthly vices, especially the vice of gluttony, whose three heads demand abundance (in terms of quantity), delicacy (in terms of quality), and steady attention (in terms of time): strength (*virtus*) overcomes all of these. And if anything were to be overcome through weakness of mind, that too it draws back (*abstrahit*) from hell. The text is printed by Hans Liebeschütz, *Fulgentius metaforalis* (Leipzig: B. G. Teubner, 1926), p. 125. The picture bears a clear iconographic similarity to late-medieval representations of Orpheus, that other great (though unsuccessful) harrower of hell, as my colleague Hoyt N. Duggan has suggested to me; Orpheus too was read as a Christ figure. See John Block Friedman, *Orpheus in the Middle Ages* (Cambridge, MA: Harvard University Press, 1970), esp. figs. 23 (from this same MS), 27, 29; and Penelope B. R. Doob, *Nebuchadnezzar's Children: Conventions of Madness in Middle English Literature* (New Haven, CT: Yale University Press, 1974), pp. 164–207.

56. The *Fulgentius metaforalis* was written by John Ridevall, an English Franciscan, sometime before 1333; on it see Beryl Smalley, *English Friars and Antiquity in the Early Fourteenth Century* (Oxford: Blackwell, 1960), pp. 110–15. The illustrations to this manuscript, for all their graphic power, are often difficult to interpret; they have even been presented as covert illustrations of alchemical mysteries, by Stanislas Klossowski de Rola, *Alchemy: The Secret Art* (London: Thames and Hudson, 1973), figs. 53–62. Though de Rola's alchemical interpretations wholly ignore the written text, his reproductions from this manuscript are of the highest quality (Cerberus is also shown in figs. 56 and 62). Unfortunately he does not reproduce our figure 30, which I describe above in only a provisional way. One other reading seems possible: the seated figures may be Alcestis and her father, in which case the figure riding the two beasts is probably Admetus, winning her as bride. But it is unlikely the father and daughter would be shown holding hands in that fashion, and the club used to discipline and direct the beasts belongs by iconographical tradition to Hercules (no such club is mentioned in the text). In Hyginus's fable, only Apollo aids Admetus in his assigned task, but in Fulgentius and the Vatican mythographers, Hercules and Apollo together harness the lion and the boar. Since Hercules is the strong man of the pair, he is also more than likely the figure shown here. A Troyes manuscript contains a memorial reduction of the legend: "A rege postulata, regi copulata, precio donata, facie venundata, infernis allata, Hercule salutata" (Liebeschütz, *Fulgentius metaforalis*, p. 116). Coluccio Salutati commented on the myth in *De laboribus Herculis*, written ca. 1378–81, expanded and revised in 1391, 1398, 1400; see the edition by Berthold L. Ullman, 2 vols. (Zurich: Thesaurus mundi, 1951), 1: 612–13, and 2: 486, 526. But as Ullman makes clear, the work was virtually unknown in its own time; see his *The Humanism of Coluccio Salutati* (Padua: Antenore, 1963), esp. pp. 21–26. On Renaissance interpretations of the myth, see Don Cameron Allen, *Mysteriously Meant: The Rediscovery of Pagan*

Symbolism and Allegorical Interpretation in the Renaissance (Baltimore: Johns Hopkins University Press, 1970), pp. 59, 267.

57. Lisa J. Kiser, "In Service of the Flower: Chaucer and the *Legend of Good Women*," a doctoral thesis I codirected at the University of Virginia in 1977, argues that Alceste stands for poetry itself—an art whose "figures" (images, fables, rhetorical devices) mediate between our limited human capacities (Chaucer, the offending poet) and the awesome nature of divine truth (the poem's God of Love). (This became a book, *Telling Classical Tales: Chaucer and the "Legend of Good Women"* [Ithaca, NY: Cornell University Press, 1983].)

58. *Disteyne* can mean simply "stain" (the prefix intensive in force); it does so in *Troilus* 2.840. But Chaucer's example of the sun and the fire makes clear that the prefix is here privative in function. It means "destain," that is, deprive of hue, or (following Skeat, Robinson, Baugh, and Fisher) "bedim," "dull," "outshine," "make pale." There is almost certainly a pun on "disdain" as well—the more expected word and a close homophone—but (as we learn when we discover more about this lady) an action not suited to Alceste's nature. She outshines rather than disdains.

59. F 490–91. This characterization of the poem's narrator is made even more emphatic in the G version of the Prologue, where the God of Love describes Chaucer as one grown too old for love's adventure (G 258), and who slanders love as a result: "thow reneyed hast my lay, / As othere olde foles many a day" (G 314).

60. The manuscript is sixteenth century and probably a copy (at one or more removes) of the so-called Hoccleve portrait of Chaucer; Roger Sherman Loomis, *A Mirror of Chaucer's World* (Princeton, NJ: Princeton University Press, 1965), figs. 2, 3, reproduces both with commentary. In the portrait before us, Chaucer's death is mistakenly dated 1402. The English daisy (*Bellis perennis*) has a yellow crown and white petals tinged with pink: "thise floures white and rede, / Swiche as men callen daysyes in our toun" (F 42–43).

61. John Livingston Lowes, "The Prologue to the *Legend of Good Women* as Related to the French *Marguerite* Poems, and the *Filostrato*," *PMLA* 19 (1904): 593–683, remains an essential study. More recently, James Wimsatt has begun a scrupulous reassessment of Chaucer's debt to the French tradition in his early poetry; see his *Chaucer and the French Love Poets: The Literary Background of the "Book of the Duchess"* (Chapel Hill, NC: University of North Carolina Press, 1968); along with his monograph, *The Marguerite Poetry of Guillaume de Machaut* (Chapel Hill, NC: University of North Carolina Press, 1970); and his essay, "Chaucer and French Poetry," in *Geoffrey Chaucer*, Writers and Their Background, ed. Derek Brewer (Athens: Ohio University Press), pp. 109–36, esp. pp. 127, 134.

62. On this ritualized courtly contest, and for the text of a poem that enshrines it, once attributed to Chaucer but now thought to have been written in the third quarter of the fifteenth century, see *"The Floure and the Leafe" and "The Assembly of Ladies,"* ed. D[erek] A. Pearsall (Edinburgh: Thomas Nelson, 1962), pp. 20–52 (a remarkable introduction) and 85–102.

63. *Concerning Famous Women*, trans. Guarino, pp. xxxiv, xxxviii.

CHAPTER III

This Biennial Chaucer Lecture for 1988 was to have been Donald Howard's—and I wish with all my heart that he had lived to give it, to share with us once more his wit and learning and urbane good sense. He was my friend for many years, and

I want the last words of this lecture to be his. I take them from the conclusion to his essay "The Idea of a Chaucer Course," where he reflects on what he thinks our teaching is for:

> While there can never be agreement on methods [of teaching], there can be agreement on goals, and on this point I will risk being dogmatic.
>
> The goal and idea of teaching *The Canterbury Tales* is to put the student in touch with the mind of Geoffrey Chaucer. Chaucer had a certain frame of mind, a way of looking at the world, which in our time we could use to our own great benefit if we could but grasp it. . . . [For there] are moments when we grasp with special clarity Chaucer's unique sanity—his impatience with cant and hypocrisy and with the posturings of seriousness, his sad tolerance for human orneriness, his humorous view of the world and of himself, his tragic and comic sense of life. This sanity is what we have it in our power to offer students. (Donald R. Howard, "The Idea of a Chaucer Course," in *Approaches to Teaching Chaucer's* Canterbury Tales, ed. Joseph Gibaldi [New York: Modern Language Association, 1980], pp. 61–62)

I like to think that Donald Howard would have joined me in seeing that sanity writ large, even in a hypocritical Friar's tale.

1. I publish this chapter essentially in the form it was delivered, as the Biennial Chaucer Lecture to the New Chaucer Society, convening in Vancouver, August 9–11, 1988.

2. Derek Pearsall, *The Canterbury Tales* (London: Allen and Unwin, 1985), confirms a long critical tradition in writing about the Friar's and Summoner's performance under the chapter heading "Comic Tales and Fables." He notes that these tales are often associated with fabliaux but prefers to distinguish them instead as "satirical anecdotes" (p. 166), "anthologies of abuse traditionally appropriate to the two classes," whose point "is not to demonstrate that the person who is the object of attack is wicked, but rather that he is stupid" (p. 170); see also pp. 217–22. N. R. Havely's introduction to his edition of *The Friar's, Summoner's, and Pardoner's Tales from "The Canterbury Tales"* (New York: Holmes and Meier, 1976) concludes: "The *Friar's Tale* as a whole can be seen as both the Friar's satire on summoners, and as Chaucer's satire on blind and violent greed."

3. H. Marshall Leicester, Jr., "'No Vileyns Word': Social Context and Performance in Chaucer's *Friar's Tale*," *ChauR* 17 (1982): 21–39.

4. Thomas Hahn and Richard W. Kaeuper, "Text and Context: Chaucer's *Friar's Tale*," *SAC* 5 (1983): 67–101.

5. David Aers, *Chaucer*, Harvester New Readings (Atlantic Highlands, NJ: Humanities Press, 1986), p. 38; Stephen Knight, *Geoffrey Chaucer*, Rereading Literature (Oxford: Blackwell, 1986), pp. 104–8. For the larger ecclesiastical subject, and an important reading of *The Summoner's Tale*, see Penn R. Szittya, *The Antifraternal Tradition in Medieval Literature* (Princeton, NJ: Princeton University Press, 1986).

6. R. T. Lenaghan, "The Irony of the *Friar's Tale*," *ChauR* 7 (1973): 281–94; see esp. p. 294, where he offers a summary account of this unusual critical harmony:

> There is character conflict for the old-fashioned critic; there are ironic shifts in point of view for the more or less new critic; and there are interesting social and doctrinal points for the historical critic. More importantly, these features are so prominent that no approach is likely to be exclusive, and the result is a substantial critical consensus.

Leicester, "'No Vileyns Word,'" pp. 21–22, focuses on some disagreements.

7. For example, in Piero Boitani and Jill Mann, eds., *Cambridge Chaucer Companion* (Cambridge: Cambridge University Press, 1986)—a collection of essays that organizes its discussion of *The Canterbury Tales* by genres—*The Friar's Tale* is

convincingly claimed by two contributors. Derek Pearsall examines it under the rubric of "Comedy," linking it with the tales of the Miller, Reeve, Shipman, Merchant, Summoner, and Cook as displaying the "narrative structure and expectations" particular to "comedy as a specific genre." He describes *The Friar's Tale* as a "masterpiece of satirical anecdote," operating according to the basic comic rules of fabliaux. A. C. Spearing, two chapters later, treats the tale with equal conviction under the rubric "Exemplum and Fable"—narratives that "illustrate general truths and make them memorable," exempla generally purporting to be true, while fables present themselves openly as invented fictions. In Spearing's chapter *The Friar's Tale* keeps company with the tales of the Pardoner, the Nun's Priest, and the Manciple.

8. Roger Ellis, *Patterns of Religious Narrative in the "Canterbury Tales"* (Totowa, NJ: Barnes and Noble, 1986), pp. 15, 12. These passages (here only slightly reduced) and three other footnote references (p. 29n43, p. 269n56, p. 270n68) constitute his only references to *The Friar's Tale*. He admits his method is "Procrustean," justifying it as necessary to limit the scope of his book. But, in fact, among the tales he studies at length are several (those of the Monk, the Physician, the Pardoner, and the Nun's Priest) whose "religious" content is made problematic by its own limitations or in relation to the teller.

9. C. David Benson, "Chaucer's Neglected Religious Tales," session C-4.

10. Lenaghan, "Irony of the *Friar's Tale*," p. 293.

11. C. David Benson, *Chaucer's Drama of Style: Poetic Variety and Contrast in the "Canterbury Tales"* (Chapel Hill: University of North Carolina Press, 1986), pp. 16–19. "The Anachronism of the Dramatic Theory," makes this case well; and see the important essay on which he builds, A. I. Doyle and M. B. Parkes, "The Production of Copies of the *Canterbury Tales* and the *Confessio Amantis* in the Early Fifteenth Century," in M. B. Parkes and Andrew G. Watson, eds., *Medieval Scribes, Manuscripts, and Libraries: Essays Presented to N. R. Ker* (London: Scolar Press, 1978), esp. pp. 190–91.

12. Lenaghan, "Irony of the *Friar's Tale*," p. 282.

13. A version in couplet verse by the Austrian poet Der Stricker (fl. ca. 1230). See Archer Taylor, "The *Friar's Tale*," in *Sources and Analogues of Chaucer's "Canterbury Tales,"* ed. W. F. Bryan and Germaine Dempster (1941; repr., London: Routledge and Kegan Paul, 1958), pp. 272–73, for a partial text, and Peter Rickard et al., trans., *Medieval Comic Tales* (Cambridge: D. S. Brewer, 1972), pp. 72–74, for a full translation. That offered by Taylor in "The Devil and the Advocate," *PMLA* 36 (1921): 36–37, is little more than a paraphrase. Taylor's source studies are significantly corrected by Peter Nicholson, "The Analogues of Chaucer's *Friar's Tale*," *English Language Notes* 17 (1979): 93–98, esp. in redating the Cotton MS analogue ca. 1380–1400 and establishing its English provenance (Taylor thought it fifteenth century). Siegfried Wenzel, "Chaucer and the Language of Contemporary Preaching," *Studies in Philology* 73 (1976): 143, notes two further analogues in manuscripts written by Englishmen—one made for preachers in the first half of the fourteenth century, the other a volume of notes and reading excerpts made by a monk at Canterbury in 1448—and concludes: "The evidence seems overwhelming that in Chaucer's England this particular story 'lived' primarily in sermons."

14. The earliest exemplum version, by Caesarius of Heisterbach (d. 1240), can be conveniently read (with translation) in Larry D. Benson and Theodore M. Andersson, eds., *The Literary Context of Chaucer's Fabliaux* (New York: Bobbs-Merrill, 1971), pp. 362–65. It concerns an *advocatus*, usually glossed as "lawyer." By defining

that term more accurately—as a lay official charged with ecclesiastical administrative affairs—the editors argue that this version is closer to Chaucer's tale than has previously been recognized.

15. Peter Nicholson, "The Rypon Analogue of *The Friar's Tale*," *Chaucer Newsletter* 3, no. 1 (1981): 1–2: "*Ista inquam narracio, licet in parte iocosa, tum est a certis malis revocacio*" (p. 1). Nicholson's translation of the full exemplum can be conveniently read in Geoffrey Chaucer, *The Canterbury Tales: Fifteen Tales and the General Prologue*, ed. V. A. Kolve and Glending Olson, *Norton Critical Edition*, 2nd ed. (New York: W. W. Norton, 2005), pp. 397–98.

16. See, for instance, Richard H. Passon, "'Entente' in Chaucer's *Friar's Tale*," *ChauR* 2 (1968): 170–71; Lenaghan, "The Irony of the *Friars Tale*," p. 284; Helen Cooper, *The Structure of "The Canterbury Tales"* (London: Duckworth, 1983), p. 129; Spearing, in *Cambridge Chaucer Companion*, pp. 161 ff. Cooper, in her recent and valuable *Oxford Guides to Chaucer: The Canterbury Tales* (Oxford: Clarendon Press, 1989), pp. 167–68, writes particularly well about the question of genre. The tale is offered as a "game" of a summoner, she tells us, which leads us to expect fabliau—and, like fabliau, it is swift and economical in its narrative style, contemporary in time and localized in place, and at its center concerned with trickery and stupidity. But it is, in fact, she goes on, "an extended exemplum," which on p. 170 she links with "Chaucer's other moral or pseudo-moral tales."

17. On the German version see William Caxton, *The Book of the Knight of the Tower*, ed. M.Y. Offord, EETS, s.s. 2 (London: Oxford University Press, 1971), p. xix (and n3 on the woodcuts). At least twenty-one manuscripts of the French original survive; there was slightly earlier English translation as well, made in the reign of Henry VI. For Caxton's version of this story (chap. 84), see pp. 114–15.

18. See the cooking scenes reproduced in V. A. Kolve, *Chaucer and the Imagery of Narrative: The First Five Canterbury Tales* (Stanford, CA: Stanford University Press, 1984), p. 261 (fig. 122, detail of fol. 207); and the feasting scene in Roger Sherman Loomis, *A Mirror of Chaucer's World* (Princeton, NJ: Princeton University Press, 1965), fig. 107, detail of fol. 208. For a facsimile, see Eric G. Miller, ed., *The Luttrell Psalter* (London: British Museum, 1932).

19. On the implications of such a format, see Meyer Schapiro, "Marginal Images and Drolerie," in his *Late Antique, Early Christian, and Mediaeval Art: Selected Papers* (New York: George Braziller, 1979), pp. 196–98.

20. "Nequaquam mihi ex intimo corde donavit, et ideo eum tollere non possum." "Non enim donavit illum mihi ex corde, sed talis est consuetudo hominibus loqui, cum irascuntur." In Benson and Andersson, eds., *Literary Context of Chaucer's Fabliaux*, pp. 364–65.

21. For the Latin text see Taylor, "The *Friar's Tale*," p. 271; Robert Dudley French, *A Chaucer Handbook*, 2nd ed. (New York: Appleton-Century-Crofts, 1947), pp. 286–87, translates it.

22. For the text, see Taylor, "The *Friar's Tale*," pp. 269–70.

23. A fifteenth-century exemplum in London, Brit. Lib. Cotton Cleopatra D viii, also printed by Taylor, pp. 271–72, and translated by French, *A Chaucer Handbook*, pp. 285–86.

24. Nicholson, "The Rypon Analogue," pp. 1–2.

25. Nicholson, "The Analogues," p. 97, likewise thinks the choice of carter and horses is probably original to Chaucer—though of that invention he says only that it seems "designed to give greater realism and economy to the tale."

26. Quoted fully later in this chapter. See note 51.

27. The painting reproduced here in Figures III.3, III.4, III.5, III.6 is in the Prado, Madrid, but another version is hung in the Escorial. It is uncertain which is the original; see Virginia C. Tuttle, "Bosch's Image of Poverty," *Art Bulletin* 43 (1981): 88–95, esp. p. 88.

28. As Jeffrey Hamburger writes, in "Bosch's *Conjuror*: An Attack on Magic and Sacramental Heresy," *Simiolus* 14 (1984): 4–24: "The study of Hieronymus Bosch's iconography is a quagmire which the historian should enter with trepidation. For the most part, Bosch's paintings present an enigma which . . . seems to have puzzled his contemporaries only slightly less than it confounds us today" (p. 5). Or, as he put it to me in a private letter, "Anyone who publishes on Bosch is soon known as fool, madman or both." Elaborate symbolic, cultic, and hierophantic interpretations are frequently invoked to explain the fantastic detail of Bosch's paintings; I focus here simply on its larger organization, its implied narrative, and on what I take to be its central theme.

29. On this painting see R.-H. Marijnissen et al., *Jheronimus Bosch* (Brussels: Arcade, 1975), pp. 56–63, for a "Compte rendu des interprétations." David L. Jeffrey, "Bosch's *Haywain*: Communion, Community, and the Theatre of the World," *Viator* 4 (1973): 311–33, likewise sums up previous scholarship, p. 311n1. The painting can be examined in detail, in many color and black-and-white plates, in, e.g., Charles de Tolnay, *Hieronymus Bosch* (New York: Morrow, 1966), pp. 116–33; or Walter S. Gibson, *Hieronymus Bosch* (London: Thames and Hudson, 1973), pp. 69–77. See also Gibson's *Hieronymus Bosch: An Annotated Bibliography* (Boston: G. K. Hall, 1983).

30. De Tolnay, *Hieronymus Bosch*, p. 118; though challenged by Jan Grauls as being a modern proverb (Jeffrey, "Bosch's *Haywain*," p. 311 n. 1), its currency has since been demonstrated in Bosch's time (Marijnissen et al., *Jheronimus Bosch*, p. 57).

31. On these proverbs see Jeffrey, "Bosch's *Haywain*," pp. 311–12 and 329. On p. 329, Jeffrey quotes to good effect the opening chapter of Thomas à Kempis's *Imitation of Christ*, written nearby, some forty years before the painting of *The Hay Wain*: "Vanity it is, to wish to live long, and to be careless to live well. Vanity it is to mind only this present life, and not to foresee those things which are to come. Vanity it is to set thy love on that which speedily passeth away, and not to hasten thither where everlasting joy abideth." This is a book Bosch may well have known.

32. De Tolnay, *Hieronymus Bosch*, p. 24, offers an astute but incomplete reading: "With hands raised in sadness [Christ] is the anguished witness of the inescapable consequence of vanity, mankind's descent into hell." Bosch's painting *The Last Judgment* (ibid., pp. 189, 196–97) shows Christ in essentially the same posture—the traditional iconography of Christ as Judge, displaying the wounds that affirm his power to save as well as damn. Cf. the circular *Tabletop of the Seven Deadly Sins* at the Prado, centered on a related image framed by the motto "Cave, cave, Dominus videt" (Beware, beware, God is watching), pp. 58–59.

33. Jeffrey, "Bosch's *Haywain*," believes that the courtly pair with lute and musical score are singing the biblical "new song," expressive of virtuous living and the hope of heaven, in strict contrast to the pair embracing in the bush behind. I doubt this interpretation. The devil, after all, provides the pair with further musical accompaniment; and they, quite as much as the fornicators, are on a wagon heading for hell, as self-engrossed as anyone else in the picture. Their song seems no more directed toward Christ than the carnal coupling in the bushes. Unlike the devil, the

good angel takes no part in their action; he prays to Christ, presumably in concern over *all* the activity before him on the wagon.

34. Gibson, *Hieronymus Bosch* (1973), pp. 100–109, writes sensibly about this picture and reproduces it on p. 103. Bosch's second version of it—made perhaps a decade later and altered in its background details—is a circular painting now in Rotterdam. Tuttle, "Bosch's Image of Poverty," argues against those who would interpret this subject as the Prodigal Son. She thinks it instead an allegory of Poverty, shown in some Italian Franciscan art (and in the tarot deck's "Misero") as "a ragged man with a walking stick, harried by a vicious dog" (p. 92). Tuttle distinguishes between the two versions so: on the exterior of *The Hay Wain* he is to be understood as a Christlike figure who suffers poverty voluntarily; in the Rotterdam tondo he embodies instead the involuntary poverty caused by sin (p. 93). René Graziani, "Bosch's *Wanderer* and a Poverty Commonplace from Juvenal," *Journal of the Warburg and Courtauld Institutes* 45 (1982): 211–16, lends textual support. I prefer (following Gibson) to define the figure more broadly, as wanderer, wayfarer, or pilgrim, leaving his moral condition ambiguous or unknown. He seems to me to parallel, rather than to "answer" or "correct," the vision of life the inner painting will display.

35. Pauline Aiken, "Vincent of Beauvais and the Green Yeoman's Lecture on Demonology," *Studies in Philology* 35 (1938): 1–9, remains valuable; and a good deal of attention has been paid to the theological niceties of cursing.

36. George Kane and E. Talbot Donaldson, eds., *Piers Plowman: The B Version* (University of London: Athlone Press, 1975), pp. 227–28 (Prologue 17–19).

37. One thinks (for example) of the mise-en-scène of a Passion play performed in 1547 at Valenciennes, its Renaissance architecture very different from anything that would have been known in fourteenth-century England, but a setting nevertheless structurally analogous. It was depicted on the frontispiece to Paris, BN MS Rothschild 1.7.3, painted by Hubert Cailleau (who designed the performance) and Jacques de Moëlles. For a reproduction see A. M. Nagler, *The Medieval Religious Stage: Shapes and Phantoms* (New Haven, CT: Yale University Press, 1976), p. 85. A second version, differing only in minor details, is in the same library, MS fr. 12536; it can be seen in Jerome Taylor and Alan H. Nelson, eds., *Medieval English Drama: Essays Critical and Contextual* (Chicago: University of Chicago Press, 1972), p. 123 (and on the dust jacket, nearer its true size). This version is reproduced in color by Jacques Burdick, *Theatre* (New York: Newsweek Books, 1974), p. 35. On the difficulties of using these manuscripts to reconstruct the actual twenty-five days of performance of the text, see Nagler, *Medieval Religious Stage*, pp. 82–88; the arrangement (and choice) of mansions would have changed each day, with only the mansions of heaven and hell retaining their permanent (and metaphysically definitive) location (p. 87). On p. 42, Nagler reproduces a specimen opening showing the events dramatized on the eighteenth day of that cycle. Alan H. Nelson, "Some Configurations of Staging in Medieval English Drama," in *Medieval English Drama*, ed. Taylor and Nelson, pp. 116–47, offers a useful introduction; see also Martin Stevens, "The Theatre of the World: A Study in Medieval Dramatic Form," *ChauR* 7 (1973): 234–49.

38. See Jean Fouquet, *The Hours of Etienne Chevalier*, ed. Charles Sterling and Claude Schaefer (New York: George Braziller, 1971), color pl. 45; it is less easily legible in black and white in, e.g., *Medieval English Drama*, ed. Taylor and Nelson, p. 85. The paintings are dated ca. 1452–56.

39. Mark Eccles, ed., *The Macro Plays*, EETS, o.s. 262 (London: Oxford University Press, 1969), p. 1, transcribes the written instructions that accompany the

diagram. David Bevington, ed., *Medieval Drama* (Boston: Houghton Mifflin, 1975), p. 797, prints a modernized version of the plan. Edgar T. Schell, "On the Imitation of Life's Pilgrimage in *The Castle of Perseverance*," in *Medieval English Drama*, ed. Taylor and Nelson, pp. 279–91, writes well about the larger action. The fact that the yeoman-fiend of *The Friar's Tale* comes from the north country points to stage custom as well as to the biblical text (Isa. 14:12–15) that ultimately underlies both.

40. On this manuscript, a Carthusian compilation of religious and devotional pieces, many of them illustrated—a veritable compendium of late-medieval religious iconography—see Rosemary Woolf, *The English Religious Lyric in the Middle Ages* (Oxford: Clarendon Press, 1968), pp. 185 ff.; Douglas Gray, *Themes and Images in the Medieval English Religious Lyric* (London: Routledge and Kegan Paul, 1972), pp. 51–55; and a comprehensive study that has just appeared, Jessica Brantley, *Reading in the Wilderness: Private Devotion and Public Performance in Late Medieval England* (Chicago: University of Chicago Press, 2007). Alan H. Nelson, "'Of the Seven Ages': An Unknown Analogue of *The Castle of Perseverance*," *Comparative Drama* 8 (1974): 125–38, writes specifically about this poem and publishes its text.

41. For the texts see Bevington, ed., *Medieval Drama*, pp. 196–98 (ll. 441–513) and 207–8 (ll. 57–91); in the latter the stage direction before line 88 ("et amator recedat, et diabolus") makes it clear that the devil has been a counselor-companion to the lover throughout the action; see also Bevington's note to line 63 s.d. The manuscript is dated ca. 1230, but the plays may have been written as early as 1160 (ibid., p. 178).

42. Eccles, ed., *Macro Plays*, p. 12 (ll. 297–310); cf. the Banns's description of this opening situation, p. 3 (ll. 14 ff.), and notice how its summary of the play's entire action makes reference over and over to the two angels, Good and Bad. In lines 1260–72 the Good Angel makes it clear that he has been constantly (and visibly) in attendance: "Ye se wel all sothly in syth / I am abowte bothe day and nyth / To brynge hys sowle into blis bryth, / And hymself wyl it brynge to pyne" (p. 40). The Banns emphasize that it is *God* who has assigned both angels (as in *The Friar's Tale*, everything is part of God's ordinance and under his control) and that he has given man free will ("fre arbritracion") sufficient to save or lose his soul. The Digby play of *Mary Magdalene* also stages a long action involving a Good and Bad Angel (together with the Three Foes and the Seven Deadly Sins) to dramatize the Magdalene's life in sin: see Bevington, ed., *Medieval Drama*, pp. 699–713 (ll. 305–747).

43. London, Brit. Lib. MS Cotton Tiberius B iii, fol. 147v, illustrating a fifteenth-century English "litany" poem, shows a man kneeling before his Good Angel, who wards off his Bad Angel with a spear; reproduced in Douglas Gray, "A Middle English Illustrated Poem," in *Medieval Studies for J. A. W. Bennett*, ed. P. L. Heyworth (Oxford: Clarendon Press, 1981), p. 188 (fig. 1d).

44. F. J. Furnivall, ed., *Hymns to the Virgin and Christ*, EETS, o.s. 24 (London: Trübner, 1867), p. 58.

45. Figure III.10 illustrates the action begun in chapter 2 of the *Pèlerinage*.

46. Figure III.11 can be seen in color in John Plummer, *The Hours of Catherine of Cleves* (New York: George Braziller, 1966), pl. 102. Though Plummer describes the figure on the left as the corpse's guardian angel, its sword and battle dress identify it as St. Michael, God's usual representative and the soul's defender in depictions of human death.

47. See, e.g., fig. 147 in C. M. Kauffmann, *Romanesque Manuscripts, 1066–1190* (London: Harvey Miller, 1975); figs. 163–66 in Millard Meiss, *French Painting in the*

Time of Jean de Berry: The Boucicaut Master (New York: Phaidon, 1968); figs. 528, 846, in Millard Meiss, *French Painting in the Time of Jean de Berry: The Limbourgs and Their Contemporaries* (London: Thames and Hudson, 1974), vol. 2; pl. 34 (pp. 145–47), in A. G. and W. O. Hassall, *Treasures from the Bodleian Library* (New York: Columbia University Press, 1976); pl. 37 (p. 145), in Roger S. Wieck, *Time Sanctified: The Book of Hours in Medieval Art and Life* (New York: George Braziller, 1988). See Carl Horstmann, ed., *The Minor Poems of the Vernon MS [I]*, EETS, o.s. 98 (London: Kegan Paul, Trench, Trübner, 1892), 1: 166–67, for a miracle of the Virgin in which angels and devils dispute the possession of a dead man's soul.

48. See Jon Whitman, *Allegory: The Dynamics of an Ancient and Medieval Technique* (Oxford: Clarendon Press, 1987), pp. 71–77.

49. See John Trevisa's English translation, made in 1398–99, *On the Properties of Things*, 2 vols., ed. M. C. Seymour et al. (Oxford: Clarendon Press, 1975), 1, bk. II, chaps. 18–20, describing "the aungel that is i-ordeyned singulerliche to oure kepinge" who "pricketh vs and waketh vs that we slepe not in sinnes and in vices," pp. 82–84, and his counterpart: "As a good angel is iyeue to men for help and kepinge, so euery man hath an euel angel to assailinge and temptinge" (pp. 84–89). Eight manuscripts of the translation survive; it was printed by Wynkyn de Worde ca. 1495.

50. The thirteenth-century exemplum by Caesarius of Heisterbach, one of the two earliest versions of this story (see note 14) concludes the action by affirming its basis in fact: "The words of the conversation between the gentleman and the devil were revealed and told by the servant of this gentleman"; Benson and Andersson, *Literary Context*, p. 365. The fifteenth-century version by Johannes Herolt, also an exemplum, does the same (see Bryan and Dempster, eds., *Sources and Analogues*, p. 271).

51. Augustine, *De ordine rerum*, bk. II, quoted in Judson Boyce Allen, *The Friar as Critic* (Nashville, TN: Vanderbilt University Press, 1971), p. 23 (summarizing a commentary by John Lathbury on Lam. 1:1).

52. *Time Magazine*, August 8, 1988, pp. 55–57.

53. Hahn and Kaeuper, "Text and Context: Chaucer's *Friar's Tale*," p. 100.

54. The passage, based ultimately on Claudian, is translated from the *Liber Catonianus*, the popular medieval schoolbook that Chaucer called his "Catoun." See Larry D. Benson, ed., *The Riverside Chaucer*, 3rd ed. (Boston: Houghton Mifflin, 1987), p. 996nn99–105).

55. Kane and Donaldson, eds., *Piers Plowman*, p. 278. Cf. the second version (1464) of *The Chronicle of Iohn Hardyng*, ed. Henry Ellis (London: Rivington, 1812), p. 175: "Lechery and aduoutry . . . was common as [the] carte waye." Cited in *MED*, p. 71 (s.v. *cart*, sense 7).

56. See John Lydgate, *The Minor Poems*, ed. Henry Noble MacCracken, 2 vols., EETS, e.s. 107, o.s. 192 (London: Oxford University Press, 1911, 1934), 2: 779, for his "Mesure is Tresour," in which plowmen and carters are named first in the lowest of the Three Estates ("othir laborerys, / Dichers, delverys" follow). In his translation of Guillaume de Deguileville, *The Pilgrimage of the Life of Man*, ed. F. J. Furnivall and Katharine B. Locock, 3 vols., EETS, e.s. 77, 83, 92 (London: Kegan Paul, Trench, Trübner, 1899, 1901, 1904), plowmen and carters are the only representatives of the laboring class; see pp. 310–11 (specifically ll. 11400–401): "Carte & plowh, they ber vp al / The clergye & the cheualrye." John Burrow has reminded me that the second of John Ball's letters written during the Peasants' Revolt of 1381 salutes (in riddling fashion) "John Nameless," "John the Miller," and "John Carter," and bids

them stand together against deception in the state; see Rossell Hope Robbins, ed., *Historical Poems of the XIVth and XVth Centuries* (New York: Columbia University Press, 1959), p. 55 (and p. 274, n. *a*). On these letters, including one purporting to have been written by that same "John Carter," see Rossell Hope Robbins, "Poems Dealing with Contemporary Conditions," in *A Manual of the Writings in Middle English, 1050–1500*, vol. 5 (New Haven: Connecticut Academy of Arts and Sciences, 1975), pt. 13 (1511–12, 1710–11).

57. *Riverside Chaucer*, pp. 462–63 (bk. V, pr. 4, lines 86–98), translating: "Plura etenim dum fiunt subiecta oculis intuemur, ut ea quae in quadrigis moderandis atque flectendis facere spectantur aurigae atque ad hunc modum cetera. Num igitur quidquam illorum ita fieri necessitas ulla compellit?" "Minime. Frustra enim esset artis effectus, si omnia coacta mouerentur" (Boethius, *The Theological Tractates and The Consolation of Philosophy*, ed. H. F. Stewart and E. K. Rand [Cambridge, MA: Loeb Classical Library, 1962], p. 386). Victor E. Watts offers this modern translation: "'We see many things before our eyes as they happen, like the actions we see charioteers performing in order to control and drive their chariots, and other things of this sort. But no necessity forces any of them to happen in this way, does it?' 'No, for if they all happened of necessity the exercise of skill would be futile'" (Harmondsworth, Eng.: Penguin Books, 1969), p. 156. The *quadrigae* of Boethius denotes a team of four horses pulling a chariot, and *carte* in Middle English could mean that as well (cf. Chaucer's *HF* 943–44, 956, where the chariot of the sun driven by Phaeton is called a "carte" and is pulled by "carte-hors," plural). But I do not think Chaucer's translation of *quadrigae* as "cartes or chariottes" chiefly alludes to an ancient prototype, designed for battle or racing. In *The Nun's Priest's Tale* a corpse is hidden in a "carte" that carries dung (ll. 3018 ff.); *The Friar's Tale* itself, with its "cart that charged was with hey" offers further evidence of Chaucer's ordinary usage. The artist responsible for fig. III.12 clearly understood Boethius's meaning so.

58. Another great book from the medieval library, Frère Laurens's *Somme le roi* (1279), translated several times into English, most notably as *The Ayenbite of Inwit* (1340), as *The Book of Vices and Virtues* (ca. 1375?), and by Caxton as the *Royal Book* (ca. 1486), speaks of "discrecion and resoun" as "maister cartere of alle vertues," attributing the figure to St. Bernard; see W. Nelson Francis, ed., *The Book of Vices and Virtues*, EETS, o.s. 217 (London: Oxford University Press, 1942), p. 159. This is part of a discussion of "equite," also called "evenhede," a way of life that requires a true accord between will and reason (p. 152); from it (as from a tree) the seven virtues grow (p. 159). Once again the choice of a carter is no accident: for an image of rational free will, you need a person who guides or directs things.

59. Cooper, *Oxford Guides to Chaucer: The Canterbury Tales*, p. 168, stresses the story's implicit morality as "an exemplary tale about rapacity and intent" and attributes to the Friar's blindness the "extra moral at the end, distinctly at odds with the plot, where the audience is invited to consider how the devil lies in wait to entrap the *innocent*—scarcely the point of this story." Spearing, *Cambridge Chaucer Companion*, ed. Boitani and Mann, p. 162, likewise finds the moral "odd, for the summoner who is the devil's victim is plainly *not* innocent." Pearsall, *The Canterbury Tales*, dismisses the ending as "some solemn-sounding warnings about hell, and a pious prayer that even the summoners may repent"—the Friar's way of "getting a last jab in at the Summoner" (p. 222). Mary J. Carruthers, "Letter and Gloss in the Friar's and Summoner's Tales," *Journal of Narrative Technique* 2 (1972): 208–14, likewise thinks it proves that

> the Friar himself cannot properly understand his own tale. He tacks on a lengthy moral, which cautions his audience to withstand the fiend, and reminds them that he may not tempt them beyond their might. But the devil in his tale is not a tempter . . . and the story suggests strongly that instead of withstanding the fiend one would do better to listen to him, especially if one is as immoral . . . as the summoner.

This "attempt to elevate his tale into a general exemplum for the company" backfires on the Friar, by dissipating the strength of his attack on the Summoner (p. 210). See also Leicester, "'No Vileyns Word,'" pp. 33–37.

60. These two biblical morals also appear together in a religious tract by one of Chaucer's contemporaries; see John Clanvowe, *The Two Ways*, in *The Works of Sir John Clanvowe*, ed. V. J. Scattergood (Cambridge: D. S. Brewer, 1975), pp. 65–66 (ll. 246–50 and 283–85), advising man on how to "withstoonden" the devil.

61. See London, Lambeth Palace Library MS 209, fol. 53, the Lambeth Apocalypse, English, circa 1260–67, for a devil shooting an arrow at a woman who defends herself with a Shield of Faith; it is reproduced by Nigel Morgan, *Early Gothic Manuscripts [2], 1250–1285* (London: Harvey Miller, 1988), fig. 141, cat. no. 126. A similar shield can be seen in Morgan's *Early Gothic Manuscripts [1], 1190–1250* (London: Harvey Miller, 1982), figs. 269–70, where an allegorically "armed" knight confronts the Seven Deadly Sins. The boss of both shields is inscribed "Deus," and their three corners with the names of the Trinity.

62. Paul N. Zietlow, "In Defense of the Summoner," *ChauR* 1 (1966): 4–9, is wrong to describe the Friar so: "He brags fatuously of his ability to describe the pains of Hell," thereby displaying "overblown pretensions to knowledge of moral geography" (p. 6). Friars, like other churchmen—in a tradition going back at least as far as the apocalypses attributed to St. Peter (second century) and to St. Paul (fourth century)—did claim such knowledge: those texts, widely disseminated and widely credited, were quite specifically meant to "agryse" men's hearts, to frighten them away from a life of sin. For these earliest texts describing hell's pains, see Montague Rhodes James, ed., *The Apocryphal New Testament* (Oxford: Clarendon, corr. ed., 1953), pp. 504–55; and for a recent far-ranging study, Martha Himmelfarb, *Tours of Hell: An Apocalyptic Form in Jewish and Christian Literature* (Philadelphia: University of Pennsylvania Press, 1983). For a Middle English versification of St. Paul's vision of hell, see that appended to a translation of St. Edmund's *Speculum ecclesiae*, "Hou a man schal lyue parfytly," *The Minor Poems of the Vernon MS [I]*, ed. Horstmann, pp. 221–51 and 251–60; see also p. 405. Book III of Guillaume de Deguileville's *Pèlerinage de l'âme* offers an extensive treatment; see Merrel Dare Clubb, Jr., "The Middle English Pilgrimage of the Soul: An Edition of MS Egerton 615" (Ph.D. diss., University of Michigan, 1954), pp. 156–83. On the moral use of thinking on hell's pains, see, e.g., Arthur Brandeis, ed., *Jacob's Well [I]*, EETS, o.s. 115 (London: Kegan Paul, Trench, Trübner, 1900), 1: 231–32.

63. On this manuscript, see Morgan, *Early Gothic Manuscripts [I]*, cat. no. 51, pp. 98–99. It copies a similar page in Munich, Bayerische Staatsbibliothek MS Clm. 835, fol. 30v, probably made in Oxford, ca. 1200–1210 (ibid., cat. no. 23, pp. 68–72); the latter is reproduced by Jurgis Baltrušaitis, *Réveils et prodiges: Le gothique fantastique* (Paris: Armand Colin, 1960), p. 129.

64. London, Brit. Lib. MS Yates Thompson 13, fols. 137v–150, containing the Fifteen Gradual Psalms (Psalms 120–34); fol. 138v shows the blessed entering heaven. Lilian M. C. Randall, *Images in the Margins of Gothic Manuscripts* (Berkeley: University of California Press, 1966), describes this remarkable sequence fully in her

index entry "Last Judgment: Pains of Hell," pp. 132–33. On this manuscript, linked to the Neville family, see John Harthan, *The Book of Hours* (New York: Crowell, 1977), pp. 48–49, with color reproductions on pp. 46–47; the last of these shows fol. 139, where devils use ropes to drag off the damned, who cry out (in the legend), "alas alas tristes dolenz alas alas." Gibson, *Hieronymus Bosch* (1973), p. 77 (fig. 62), also publishes two scenes from the sequence. For a French version of Hell's pains, ca. 1400, see Kolve, *Chaucer and the Imagery of Narrative*, fig. 123; cf. that in Meiss, *French Painting . . . The Boucicaut Master*, fig. 338 (in color). Plummer, *Hours of Catherine of Cleves*, includes three remarkable images of Hell, pls. 42, 47, 99.

65. Much of Book III of Lotario dei Segni (Pope Innocent III), *De miseria condicionis humane*, ed. Robert E. Lewis, Chaucer Library (Athens: University of Georgia Press, 1978), concerns the pains of the damned, ending in this summary catalogue: " 'There shall be weeping' and moaning, wailing and shrieking, grief and torment, gnashing and shouting, fear and trembling, labor and pain, fire and stench, darkness and anxiety, anguish and harshness, calamity and want, distress and sorrow, oblivion and confusion, tortures and pains, bitternesses and terrors, hunger and thirst, cold and heat, brimstone and fire burning forever and ever" (p. 232). Chaucer himself translated this work—he names it in his Prologue to *The Legend of Good Women* (G 414–15)—though his translation is lost; see pp. 17–30 for Lewis's discussion of problems in the way Chaucer Englished the book's title.

66. For a vast range of illuminations showing Dante and Virgil viewing the pains of the damned in hell, see Peter Brieger, Millard Meiss, and Charles S. Singleton, *Illuminated Manuscripts of the Divine Comedy*, 2 vols. (Princeton, NJ: Princeton University Press, 1969), 1: 39–326. Karla Taylor, *Chaucer Reads "The Divine Comedy"* (Stanford, CA: Stanford University Press, 1989), reached me just as this lecture was to go to press. Judging from the index, *The Friar's Tale* receives no mention in her book.

67. A point made regarding *The Wife of Bath's Tale* by Carole K. Brown and Marion F. Egge in response to an article by Penn Szittya, in *PMLA* 91 (1976): 291.

CHAPTER IV

1. Eric Jager, *The Tempter's Voice: Language and the Fall in Medieval Literature* (Ithaca, NY: Cornell University Press, 1993), was the first to publish this woodcut in relation to *The Merchant's Tale* (p. 281), entitling it "The climax of the pear tree story"—a pun hard to resist. I first came upon it in Marilyn Stokstad and Jerry Stannard, *Gardens of the Middle Ages* (Lawrence, Kansas: Spencer Museum of Art, 1983), no. 67, p. 217, who publish the equivalent page from a volume in the Library of Congress. Caxton's woodcuts are in fact "freehand copies of the woodcuts in the French *Esope*, which are traced copies of those in the editions of Steinhöwel's collection." Because the German original is aesthetically superior, I have printed that version here. See *Caxton's Aesop*, ed. R. T. Lenaghan (Cambridge, MA: Harvard University Press, 1967), pp. 23–24, for an extensive scholarly introduction to the woodcuts. To allow comparison, he publishes five woodcuts from Caxton's edition as appendix 2.

2. For the text of the fable, see N. S. Thompson, "*The Merchant's Tale*," in *Sources and Analogues of the Canterbury Tales*, 2 vols., ed. Robert M. Correale and Mary Hamel (Woodbridge, Suffolk, Eng.: D. S. Brewer, 2002, 2005), 2: 534. Steinhöwel's Latin text is printed by W. F. Bryan and Germaine Dempster, eds., *Sources and Analogues of Chaucer's Canterbury Tales* (London: Routledge and Kegan Paul, 1941, repr.

1958), pp. 354–55, along with Macho's French *Esope* based upon it, pp. 355–56. These volumes, together with *The Literary Context of Chaucer's Fabliaux: Texts and Translations*, ed. Larry D. Benson and Theodore M. Andersson (Indianapolis: Bobbs-Merrill, 1971), pp. 203–73, give access to all the important analogues. For convenience, I shall refer to Chaucer's unknown source as fabliau in nature though I do not mean to restrict it to the French tradition; Italian novelle share a common vision of the human comedy.

3. Helen Cooper, *Oxford Guide to Chaucer: "The Canterbury Tales,"* 2nd ed. (Oxford: Oxford University Press, 1996), p. 206.

4. Derek Pearsall, *The Canterbury Tales*, Unwin Critical Library (London: George Allen and Unwin, 1985), pp. 193–209, covers this better than any other essay I know.

5. Kenneth A. Bleeth, "The Image of Paradise in the *Merchant's Tale*," in *The Learned and the Lewed: Studies in Chaucer and Medieval Literature*, ed. Larry D. Benson, Harvard English Studies 5 (Cambridge, MA: Harvard University Press, 1974), pp. 45–60. Jager, *Tempter's Voice*, chap. 6; D. W. Robertson, Jr., "The Doctrine of Charity in Medieval Literary Gardens," *Speculum* 26 (1951): 24–49. Many other studies might be cited, including Lorraine K. Stock's interesting semiotic reading, "'Making it' in the *Merchant's Tale*: Chaucer's Signs of January's Fall," *Semiotica* 63 (1987): 171–83.

6. For the full text see "An ABC," in *Riverside Chaucer*, pp. 637–40; it is headed, "Incipit carmen secundum ordinem litterarum alphabeti" (Here begins a song following the order of the letters of the alphabet). It is translated from Guilllaume de Deguilleville's allegorical *La Pelerinaige de vie humaine*.

7. Two books by Roger S. Wieck, *Painted Prayers: The Book of Hours in Medieval and Renaissance Art* (New York: George Braziller and Pierpont Morgan Library, 1997), and *Time Sanctified: The Book of Hours in Medieval Art and Life* (New York: George Braziller and Walters Art Gallery, Baltimore, 1988), with essays by Lawrence R. Poos, Virginia Reinburg, and John Plummer, offer expert and inviting guides to the subject. I briefly quote from *Painted Prayers*, p. 19.

8. Christopher De Hamel, *A History of Illuminated Manuscripts*, 2nd ed. (London: Phaidon, 1994), table of contents (p. 7), and pp. 168–99. On the major centers that produced Books of Hours, see pp. 184–85. John Harthan, *The Book of Hours with a Historical Survey and Commentary* (New York: Thomas Y. Crowell, 1977), is useful, as is Robert G. Calkins, *Illuminated Books of the Middle Ages* (Ithaca, NY: Cornell University Press, 1983), chaps. 6–8. All these books are richly illustrated.

9. James Carson Webster, *The Labors of the Months in Antique and Mediaeval Art: To the End of the Twelfth Century*, Northwestern University Studies in the Humanities 4 (1938; repr., New York: AMS Press, 1970), pp. 93–94.

10. On this manuscript, and others closely related to it, see Lucy Freeman Sandler, *The Peterborough Psalter and Other Fenland Manuscripts* (London: Harvey Miller, 1974); Sandler publishes all the calendar pages on pp. 16–19. January stands first in the year in the Julian calendar, introduced by Julius Caesar (B.C. 45), and retained that place in the Gregorian calendar reformed in 1582; most stone zodiacs and liturgical calendars reflect this order. But see Emile Mâle, *Religious Art in France: The Thirteenth Century*, ed. Harry Bober, trans. Marthiel Mathews, Bollingen Series 40: 2 (Princeton, NJ: Princeton University Press, 1984), pp. 69–71, for an explanation why the "calendars in stone" at Chartres, Paris, Amiens, and Reims, for example, do not all begin with January and Aquarius; and Michelle P. Brown, *Understanding Medieval*

Manuscripts: A Guide to Technical Terms (Malibu: J. Paul Getty Museum, 1994), p. 31, for a concise historical overview. Because it began a new historical era, the day of Christ's birth (December 25) proved an attractive candidate, or (as often in England) the day of the Annunciation (March 25), or (less common) the moveable feast of Easter. But in the liturgy, the Julian calendar prevailed, even though January 1 (also known as the day of the Circumcision) comes in the midst of winter, in northern climes a time especially ill-suited to that role. Hence in some popular reckonings, the year was said to begin in the spring. For instance the late fourteenth-century *On the Properties of Things: John Trevisa's translation of "Bartholomaeus Anglicus De Proprietatibus Rerum:" A Critical Text*, ed. M. C. Seymour, 2 vols. (Oxford: Clarendon Press, 1975), declares "spryngynge tyme" the "bygynnynge of the yere. . . ." bk. IX, chap. 5 (1: 523). A mid-fifteenth-century allegorical poem, *The Court of Sapience*, ed. E. Ruth Harvey, Toronto Medieval Texts and Translations 2 (Toronto: University of Toronto Press, 1984), p. 73 (2157–59) does the same: "they clepe the Ramme the fyrst sygne,/ For that in Mars, begynnyng of the yere,/The sonne in hym maketh his cours digne." Chaucer's Canterbury pilgrimage begins under the sign of the Ram (Aries), on the 17th or 18th of April, possibly for this same reason. The latter date is described as "messager to May" in the Introduction to *The Man of Law's Tale* (II 5–6]. In liturgy and calendar art, however, the year always begins with January, and that is what concerns us here.

11. Though I came upon it only after my own researches were well underway, John F. Adams, "The Janus Symbolism in *The Merchant's Tale*," *Studies in Medieval Culture* 4 (1974), 446–51, is learned and useful, though it makes no reference to the visual arts. I first tested some of these ideas in a brief paper delivered at the MLA meeting in Houston, 1980, which M. Teresa Tavormina kindly noticed in her annotations to this tale in *The Riverside Chaucer*, p. 889 (note to l. 2222). Chapter 5 of Peter Brown's *Chaucer at Work: The Making of the Canterbury Tales* (London: Longman, 1994), a pedagogically innovative workbook designed for beginning students, asks salient questions about the iconography of January, and provides some well-chosen materials toward an answer. I have benefited too from research on January-Janus conducted by David Burchmore when he was my student in Virginia, and afterward at Cal Tech. *Time in the Medieval World: Occupations of the Months and Signs of the Zodiac in the Index of Christian Art*, ed. Colum Hourihane, recently published for the Index of Christian Art by Princeton University and Penn State University Press (2007), has scant commentary, but its many pictures are useful. On January, see pp. lvi, 55–66; on May, pp. lvii, 113–25; and on the Gemini, pp. lxi, 257–65.

12. For a comparably stark example, cf. the Ingebord Psalter, made in northern France or Belgium, ca. 1200; it is reproduced by Florens Deuchler, *Der Ingeborgpsalter* (Berlin: Walter de Gruyter, 1967), pl. 1, and discussed on p. 18.

13. His name gives us (or is derived from) the common Latin name for a domestic door or gate (*janua*), as well as the name for a covered passage, an arcade, or a civic arch (*janus*) erected over a major thoroughfare. (A *janitor* in ancient Rome was a "doorkeeper.")

14. Isidore of Seville, in his *Etymologies*, a great encyclopedia not yet finished at his death in 636, wrote of him so: "They call Janus (*Ianus*) the door (*ianua*), as it were, of the world or the sky or the months. They imagine two faces for Janus, standing for the east and the west. And when they make him with four faces and call him the double Janus, they refer to the four corners of the world or to the four elements or to the seasons. But when they imagine this, they make him a monster,

not a god." See *The "Etymologies" of Isidore of Seville*, trans. Stephen A. Barney, W. J. Lewis, J. A. Beach, Oliver Berghof, and Muriel Hall (Cambridge: Cambridge University Press, 2006), p. 185 (bk.VIII.xi.37).

15. Macrobius, *The Saturnalia*, trans. Percival Vaughan Davies (New York: Columbia University Press, 1969), bk. I.9.9, p. 67 (a work difficult to date precisely, but probably before 433).

16. Ibid., bk. I.9.18, pp. 68–69. On this, and on the mythological tradition in general, see the monumental study by Jane Chance, *Medieval Mythography: From Roman North Africa to the School of Chartres, A.D. 433–1177* (Gainesville: University Press of Florida, 1994), p. 76 and *passim*, and its continuation, *Medieval Mythography: From the School of Chartres to the Court at Avignon, 1177–1350* (Gainesville: University Press of Florida, 2000). In *The Mythographic Chaucer: The Fabulation of Sexual Politics* (Minneapolis: University of Minnesota Press, 1995), chap. 8, she reads *The Merchant's Tale* in the light of Martianus Capella's allegorical poem on the marriage of Philology and Mercury (*De nuptiis Philologiae et Mercurii*), written before 439, and of medieval commentaries on it.

17. Stewart Perowne, *Roman Mythology*, Library of the World's Myths and Legends (New York: Peter Bedrick, rev. ed., 1984), p. 18. Macrobius accounts for the tradition in a different way: "Janus is believed to have had two faces and so could see before him and behind his back—a reference, no doubt, to the foresight and shrewdness of the king, as one who not only knew the past but would also foresee the future" (*The Saturnalia* I.7.20, p. 58).

18. Macrobius, *The Saturnalia*, I.9, p. 67. The entire chapter is of interest.

19. Based on the "moralized Ovid" of Pierre Bersuire, composed in the fourteenth century, this little treatise added a number of divinities (Janus among them) to that important work, and eliminated its allegorical interpretations. The Latin text reads: "Janus vero intra deorum numerum acceptus est, cui omnis rei inicium ac finem tribuebant. Hic autem taliter figurabatur. Erat rex, homo sedens in trono fulgenti radiis circumquaque. Qui duas facies habebat, quarum una ante se, altera post se respiciebat. Juxta illum quoque erat templum, et in manu eius dextera habebat clavem, qua templum ipsum aperire monstrabat. In sinistra vero habebat baculum, quo saxum percutere et ex illo aquam producere videbatur." It is edited by Hans Liebeschütz, *Fulgentius Metaphoralis: Ein Beitrag zur Geschichte der antiken Mythologie im Mittelalter*, Studien der Bibliothek Warburg 4 (Leipzig: Teubner, 1926), p. 122, from a manuscript that includes a portrait of Janus that illustrates this passage (pl. 22): Vatican Library MS Reg. lat. 1290, fol. 4, from northern Italy, ca. 1420. Janus is shown enthroned, looking both ways, holding a key to the door of a churchlike temple and (in his other hand) a rod with which he causes water to issue from a rocky cliff. E. H. Wilkins argued that Chaucer used the *Libellus* for certain details in his *Hous of Fame* and *Knight's Tale*—see his "Descriptions of Pagan Divinities from Petrarch to Chaucer," *Speculum* 32 (1957): 511–22—but this claim has been refuted by John M. Steadman in "Venus' *citole* in Chaucer's *Knight's Tale* and Berchorius," *Speculum* 34 (1959): 620–24. Liebeschütz dates the work ca. 1400.

20. *The "Etymologies,"* p. 128 (bk. V.xxxiii.3). As the translators of this volume say, "It would be hard to overestimate the influence of the *Etymologies* on medieval European culture, and impossible to describe it fully. Nearly a thousand manuscript copies survive, a truly huge number" (p. 24).

21. The colored-pavement design is probably of Italian origin (*opus Alexandrinum*). See Elizabeth Eames, "Notes on the Decorated Stone Roundels in the

Corona and Trinity Chapel in Canterbury Cathedral," in *Medieval Art and Architecture at Canterbury before 1220*, British Archaeological Association Conference Transactions for the year 1979 (London and Kent: British Archaeological Association, 1982), 5: 67–70. January may be seen in the upper left corner of fig. 15a.

22. For January with two heads in "stone calendars," see Perrine Mane, *Calendriers et techniques agricoles (France-Italie, XIIe–XIIIe siècles)* (Paris: Editions le Sycomore, 1983), figs. 27, 33, 143, 176, 221 (here also between two doors), and for an especially full and useful introduction to the whole tradition, Jill Meredith, "The *Bifrons* Relief of Janus: The Implications of the Antique in the Court Art of Emperor Frederick II," in *The Brummer Collection of Medieval Art*, ed. Caroline Bruzelius with Jill Meredith (Durham, NC: Duke University Press and the Duke University Museum of Art, 1991), pp. 97–123, with close attention to Ovid's *Fasti*, passed over in my text above. And see the densely learned entry on "Janus" by J. Toutain in *Dictionnaire des antiquités grecques et romaines d'après les texts et les monuments*, ed. Charles Daremberg and Edmond Saglio, 10 vols. in 9, 3rd ed. (Paris: Hachette, 1881–1929), pp. 609–15, old but still very useful.

23. See Francis Wormald, *The Winchester Psalter* (London: Harvey Miller and Medcalf, 1973), figs. 106 (whole page) and 107 (detail), and p. 99 for a description. For a more recent discussion of provenance and date, see Kristine Edmondson Haney, *The Winchester Psalter: An Iconographic Study* (Leicester: Leicester University Press, 1986), pp. 8 and 70. She does not discuss the calendar paintings.

24. A politically important devotional book, it was made in 1423 to commemorate the marriage of Anne of Burgundy to John Duke of Bedford. The duke, a brother to Henry V of England, dead the year before, was at the time Regent of France in the name of Henry's son, the infant Henry VI. On this manuscript and for reproductions of many of its pages (though not that of January), see Janet Backhouse, *The Bedford Hours*, Medieval Manuscripts in the British Library (London: British Library, 1990). The verses in the bottom margin tell us the little roundel shows how January carries the key of the new year and opens its door to the four seasons.

25. On this manuscript, see Lucy Freeman Sandler, *Gothic Manuscripts, 1285–1385*, Survey of Manuscripts Illuminated in the British Isles (Oxford: Harvey Miller, 1986), 2 vols., vol. II, no. 107 (pp. 118–21).

26. For a remarkable study of the history, iconography and ideology of this manuscript, see Michael Camille, *Mirror in Parchment: The Luttrell Psalter and the Making of Medieval England* (Chicago: University of Chicago Press, 1998). I echo his analysis on pp. 174–77, and quote from p. 177.

27. Derek Pearsall and Elisabeth Salter, *Landscapes and Seasons of the Medieval World* (Toronto: University of Toronto Press, 1973), reproduce three hog-killing scenes for December (pls. 52a, 52b, 52c).

28. Bridget Ann Henisch, *The Medieval Calendar Year* (University Park: Pennsylvania State University Press, 1999), chap. 2 ("Winter: By the Fireside"), offers a guide to all this, with many illustrations. A man before the fire drying his boots and warming his feet sometimes decorates February pages instead. The slippage is not really surprising: as in the case of December and January, January and February have much in common.

29. See Lotario dei Segni (Pope Innocent III), *De miseria condicionis humane*, ed. Robert E. Lewis, Chaucer Library (Athens: Georgia University Press, 1978), bk. I. 9, "Of the Discomforts of Old Age," p. 106.

30. A psalter probably from Bruges, mid-thirteenth century, now in Los Angeles, the J. Paul Getty Museum MS Ludwig 14 (85.MK.239), fol. 1, illustrating its January page with a similar scene, includes a servant or small boy drawing wine from a cask. It is from the same manuscript as my Figure IV.13.

31. A much-reproduced image from a Book of Hours illuminated in France for the English market—this one by the Fastolf Master, ca. 1440–50—dresses its two-headed Janus in a double hood emerging from a single scarlet cape over his shoulders; a high, double-wide black hat sits atop his joined heads. One of his heads, as is often the case, is bearded, the other unbearded—signifying age and youth, the old year and the new. He eats standing up (with a long bone in one hand, a wine goblet in the other), like a powerful lord eager to be about his business; two servants are at hand to attend to his needs (Oxford: Bodleian Library MS Auct. D. inf. 2.11, fol. 1).

32. For another example of feasting between two doors, see London, Brit. Lib. MS Royal 2 B. ii, fol. 1, a psalter from northwestern France, mid-thirteenth century, though its Janus has three faces rather than one.

33. For the picture in color, see Jean Longnon and Raymond Cazelles, *The "Très Riches Heures" of Jean, Duke of Berry* (New York: George Braziller, 1969), fig. 2, with commentary; or Raymond Cazelles and Johannes Rathofer, *Illuminations of Heaven and Earth: The Glories of the "Très Riches Heures du Duc de Berry"* (New York: Harry N. Abrams, 1988), pp. 12–17, valuable also for its appendixes concerning the making of this book, the duke's life, and his other manuscripts and treasures.

34. Related versions from the workshop of the Brussels Initials Master, made within the same decade or so, are reproduced by Millard Meiss, *French Painting in the Time of Jean de Berry: The Late Fourteenth Century and the Patronage of the Duke*, 2 vols. (London: Phaidon, 1967), vol. 2, figs. 718, 719; on them see vol. 1, 230–32, and on the workshop as Parisian, p. 229. Both show January warming himself at his fireplace, with a table behind him set with food and drink. This version of the month's occupation may have originated with February, which might account for the contemporary lord or well-off burgher who replaces at table the two-headed or three-faced Janus-god.

35. A famous image by Simon Bening from the Da Costa Hours, Bruges, ca. 1515, takes this even further (New York, Pierpont Morgan Library MS M. 399, fol. 2v). It is reproduced by Henisch, *Medieval Calendar Year*, as color plate 6-6.

36. *Riverside Chaucer*, p. 1128 (*Merchant's Tale* textual notes, IV 1417).

37. Gower too, treating "Love-Delicacy" as a subcategory of Gluttony, uses food imagery for sexual desire throughout (*Confessio Amantis*, bk. VI, 600 ff.) In ll. 899–950 he explores the way sexual fantasy "feeds" desire; see *The English Works of John Gower*, ed. G. C. Macaulay, 2 vols., EETS, e.s. 81, 82 (London: Oxford University Press, 1900, 1901), 2: 183–93.

38. See Karl Wentersdorf, "Imagery, Structure, and Theme in Chaucer's Merchant's Tale," in *Chaucer and the Craft of Fiction*, ed. Leigh Arrathoon (Rochester, MI: Solaris, 1986), pp. 35–62 (here pp. 50–54). (*Pirum* can also mean staff, or cudgel.) An early fifteenth-century English lyric, "I have a newe gardyn," charmingly agrees in using such imagery for the sexual act. The speaker, a young man presumably named John, boasts of having in his garden (the finest garden under the sun) a pear tree that bears only "per Jenet" (i.e., Johnny-pears, that ripen early on St. John's Day). When the fairest maid in town asks him for a graft of his "pery tre," he "grafts" her, and twenty weeks later her belly swells with new life. But when he encounters her

again, twelve months after their first meeting, she disclaims his paternity: it was, she says, a "pear Robert" and not a "pear Jonet." For the text, see *Secular Lyrics of the XIVth and XVth Centuries*, ed. Rossell Hope Robbins (Oxford: Clarendon Press, 1952), no. 21. Female desire was not always treated with such wit and delicacy.

39. Figure IV.13: for related images in this manuscript, see fol. 106, where (at the left) a nun leads the monk by a string tied to his genitals, and (at the right) he climbs a tower where she awaits him; or fol. 111, where the monk kneels before the nun, and they undress; or fol. 111v, where they copulate on the ground, alongside a pack mule carrying a load of phalluses. On fol. 132v, the nun and the monk are at it again, as he offers her his purse and erect penis simultaneously. On fol. 160, two nuns pluck penises from a tree, this time tucking them into their habits, while (at right) the monk offers a huge disembodied penis to the nun, who graciously reaches out to receive it. For a perceptive study of this manuscript and its borders, see Sylvia Huot, *The "Romance of the Rose" and Its Medieval Readers: Interpretation, Reception, Manuscript Transmission* (Cambridge: Cambridge University Press, 1993), chap. 8, esp. pp. 292–301. She interprets the phallus tree as an "audacious parody of the increasingly erotic rosebush sought by the Lover" in that poem (p. 292). Ruth Mellinkoff, *Averting Demons: The Protective Power of Medieval Visual Motifs and Themes*, 2 vols. (Los Angeles: Ruth Mellinkoff Publications, 2004), argues that the purpose of this sexual display was apotropaic, meant to ward off the devil (1: 134). Though I am not convinced by this interpretation, she reproduces the full series very handsomely (vol. 2, figs. VI.49–58). For a comparable lady of the court plucking penis-fruit from a tree, see the carved wooden casket-panel (probably from Basel, early fifteenth century) reproduced by Michael Camille, *The Medieval Art of Love: Objects and Subjects of Desire* (New York: Harry N. Abrams, 1998), p. 109 (fig. 95). The lady's lover, carved in relief on the casket's other end, stands next to a tree with leaves shaped like vaginas. For a lecherous woman wearing a fool's cap over her disheveled hair while cradling two disembodied phalluses to her chest and holding a third to her mouth, see Claude Gaignebet and Jean-Dominque Lajoux, *Art profane et religion populaire au Moyen Age* (Paris: Presses Universitaires de France, 1985), p. 190 (fig. 2). This drawing, from an early sixteenth-century manuscript, illustrates a "rebus" of Picardie, conflating *follement je vis* ("foolishly I live") with *folle mange vits* ("a foolish woman [lecherous woman] eats pricks").

40. *On the Properties of Things*, bk. IX, chap. 13 (1: 531).

41. See Wormald, *Winchester Psalter*, fig. 111; and Millard Meiss and Elizabeth H. Beatson, *The Belles Heures of Jean, Duke of Berry* (New York: George Braziller, 1974), color pl. fol. 6.

42. Figure IV.14: from a psalter possibly made in Bruges, it dates from the mid-thirteenth century.

43. The page is included in a partial facsimile, *The Hours of Jeanne d'Evreux Queen of France*, published by the Metropolitan Museum of Art (1957). The trees or branches carried by the servant are larger even than the tree in the ground between them. A late fourteenth-century colored drawing from an English almanac is also in this tradition (Oxford, Bodley MS Rawl. D. 939, section 2, fol. 5); see *English Rural Life in the Middle Ages*, Bodleian Picture Book 14 (Oxford: Bodleian Library, 1965), fig. 16a. Though crudely executed, its noble rider ceremonially displays both bird and branch. We will look at several other examples; Wilhelm Hansen's extensive monograph *Kalenderminiaturen der Stundenbücher: Mittelalterliches Leben im Jahreslauf* (Munich: Callwey, 1984), reproduces a good number more.

44. See Hansen, *Kalenderminiaturen der Stundenbücher*, figs. 35–52, for variations on this theme.

45. Webster, *Labors of the Months*, remains valuable on examples to the end of the twelfth century, with a comprehensive catalog, many illustrations, and comparative tables arranged by country.

46. It is so, for instance, in the Bedford Book of Hours, London, Brit. Lib. MS Add 18850, fol. 4, where a man carries back a green branch (or small tree) as the "occupation" for April (French, 1423); and in a magnificent French Book of Hours, early fifteenth century, Cambridge: Trinity Coll. MS B. 11.31, 32, fol. 4.

47. Quoted by Robert B. Schwartz in a well-researched essay, "The Social Character of May Games: A Popular Background for Chaucer's *Merchant's Tale*," *Zeitschrift für Anglistik und Amerikanistik* 27 (1979): 43–51 (here p. 43).

48. *Peter Idley's Instructions to His Son*, ed. Charlotte d'Evelyn (Boston: D.C. Heath, for the Modern Language Association of America, 1935), bk. II-A, 1032–33. See the "May Day" entry in *Funk and Wagnalls Standard Dictionary of Folklore, Mythology, and Legend*, 2 vols. (New York: Funk and Wagnalls, 1949–50), 2: 695–96, for a fuller account of the custom.

49. In this case May 3, a date that had some special meaning for Chaucer, still not wholly understood. The action of Book II in *Troilus and Criseyde*, for instance, begins on this same day, rapturously described (II, 50–55): it is then that Pandarus begins his vicarious seduction of Criseyde.

50. Lorraine Kochanske Stock, "The Two Mayings in Chaucer's *Knight's Tale*: Convention and Invention," *Journal of English and Germanic Philology* 85 (1986): 206–21, is thoughtful and well informed. She explores the ambiguities of this passage on pp. 215–17.

51. The Wharncliffe Hours, painted in Paris by an artist known as Maître François, ca. 1475–80, offers a supremely elegant example, he with his falcon, she with the green branch, seated together on a horse. Margaret Manion, *The Wharncliffe Hours* (London: Thames and Hudson, 1981), reproduces it in color as pl. 5. On falconry as a metaphor for love and courtship, see Camille, *Medieval Art of Love*, pp. 96–106, with many pictures. For two pictures employing a falcon as a sign of love between men, see Diane Wolfthal, "Picturing Same-Sex Desire: The Falconer and His Lover in Images by Petrus Christus and the Housebook Master," pp. 17–46, in *Troubled Vision: Gender, Sexuality, and Sight in Medieval Text and Image*, ed. Emma Campbell and Robert Mills (New York: Palgrave Macmillan, 2004).

52. *On the Properties of Things*, bk. IX, chap. 13 (1: 531). Trevisa also wrote, just before: "And May is a tyme of merthe, of love, of gladness and of likynge, for most in May briddis singith and maketh joye." And see his rhapsodic praise of the season of spring, IX.5 (1: 524). Cf. Gower's *Confessio Amantis*, bk. VII, 1045–50 (Gower, *English Works*, 2: 261).

53. IV 1693, 1742, 1888, 2157, as Emerson Brown, Jr., noted in a brief but important article, "The *Merchant's Tale*: Why Is May Called 'Mayus'?" in *ChauR* 2 (1968): 273–77.

54. See chapter 4 in my *Chaucer and the Imagery of Narrative: The First Five Canterbury Tales* (Stanford, CA: Stanford University Press, 1984) ("*The Miller's Tale*: Nature, Youth, and Nowell's Flood"), for another way in which an ill-matched marriage (age against youth) could be turned into something imaginatively finer than standard fabliau fare.

55. The May page from a fifteenth-century calendar made for Charles

d'Angoulême can sum up visually, with a little adjustment, the progress of my argument so far. It shows May as a beautiful young woman, chalk white of complexion and richly gowned, holding a green-leafed branch, being gazed at by an attentive dog at the window, alongside a husband ruddy-faced and gray of hair, surrounded by buzzing bees, who holds a glass of wine in one hand and a basket of yellow fruit in the other. He seems earnest and preoccupied, she distant and inscrutable. Indeed, she recoils from him ever so slightly. I do not equate him with January—the fruit he offers suggests a harvest month—but she unequivocally represents the May. In terms of calendar realism, their union too is unsuitable, creating a conflict between them likely to be relieved in one way or another. Derek Brewer reproduces the picture in color in *Chaucer and His World* (London: Eyre Methuen, 1978), opposite p. 121.

CHAPTER V

1. I make a point of specifying the "calendar page," because, astrologically speaking, the twelve months and their signs do not neatly correspond: the zodiac sign typically changes near the middle of the month. For instance: the sun enters Gemini around May 21 and leaves around June 21, having been in Taurus before that, from April 21 to May 21. Since virtually all illuminated calendars assign just one sign to each month, the Gemini Twins serve as the universal sign for May. There are rare exceptions: the calendar to the *Très riches heures of Jean, Duc de Berry*, for example—perhaps the most beautiful Book of Hours ever made—presents each month's "occupation" topped by a demicircular tympanum, in which a figure holding a blazing sun drives his chariot across a monochrome blue sky. The outer band of that sky is divided between the two constellations the sun will pass through, with the appropriate sign painted in each. (In April, the sky is divided between Aries the Ram and Taurus the Bull.) See the facsimile edition by Jean Longnon and Raymond Cazelles (New York: George Braziller, 1969), plates 6 and 7, for the Gemini as a naked heterosexual couple depicted twice, first in the May sky and then in that of June.

2. The last two lines specify the location of the sun *within* the sign-span of Gemini: "But litel fro his declynacion of Cancer" means it was just a few days before the summer solstice, when Jupiter's influence (his "exaltation") becomes paramount. No one, so far as I know, has perceived any further significance in this detail, and the manuscript tradition for IV 2133, meant to corroborate this dating, is corrupt: all the manuscripts read "Juyl" (July), presumably a scribal confusion, uniformly emended in modern editions to "Juyn." A similar confusion, but there quite probably intended, besets the astrological dating of *The Parson's Tale*, where the "exaltation" of the moon is incorrectly said to be "in Libra." Chauncey Wood has argued persuasively that Chaucer put Libra (the Scales) in that place for symbolic reasons. See his *Chaucer and the Country of the Stars: Poetic Uses of Astrological Imagery* (Princeton, NJ: Princeton University Press, 1970), pp. 275–97. For my purposes, focused on calendar art in relation to Chaucer's tale, the salient facts are these: the sun is in Gemini, and Gemini in calendar art is the zodiacal sign assigned to May, the month for whom January's bride is named, and to whose fresh beauty she is often compared. J. D. North, *Chaucer's Universe* (Oxford: Clarendon Press, 1988), makes a heroic attempt to decipher and interpret the precise details of Chaucer's many astrological datings, but it is an abstruse argument almost impossible to follow, full of debatable assumptions and doubtful adjustments. His chapter on *The Merchant's Tale* (chap. 14, pp. 443–55) is hugely complex and detailed—he would date the

pear-tree cuckoldry June 8—but he admits, from the beginning, that Chaucer in this tale "has left us with one or two traces of an astronomical framework the form of which it is extremely difficult, perhaps even impossible, to discern" (p. 443). I am not competent to take issue with North on his precise arguments—Chaucer himself (in North's reading) seems rather often to get astrology wrong. But I doubt that this kind of investigation, for all its challenge and potential interest, helps the ordinary reader much, medieval or modern. Calendar art, in contrast, can move us toward a more general understanding, more fully in the public domain.

3. *Confessio Amantis*, bk. VII, 1031–34, in *The English Works of John Gower*, ed. G. C. Macaulay, 2 vols., EETS, e.s. 81, 82 (London: Oxford University Press, 1900, 1901), 2: 261.

4. The exact terms of this arrangement vary: some versions send the Dioscuri to each of the two realms for six months at a time, since the constellation Gemini is visible only six months a year. Bernardus Silvestris, in the twelfth century, interpreted them as the day star and the evening star: "when Pollux descends to the lower hemisphere, Castor holds the higher, and thus Pollux descends to the underworld so that Castor may rise." See his *Commentary on the First Six Books of Virgil's "Aeneid,"* trans. Earl G. Schreiber and Thomas E. Maresca (Lincoln: University of Nebraska Press, 1979), p. 55. This may explain their otherwise odd representation in the Rohan Book of Hours (ca. 1419–27), which shows them seated side by side in the sky, one looking up, the other with his head on his arms looking down; see Millard Meiss and Marcel Thomas, eds., *The Rohan Master: A Book of Hours* (New York: George Braziller, 1973), color pl. 9. Having described them as stars, Bernardus Silvestris goes on to say "in a better way, we interpret these brothers to be the soul and the body, of which the soul is rational and immortal and thus a god, but the body is mortal. The soul endures the death of the body for a time, so that the body may then share the immortality of the spirit. . . . The body dwells in the region of life by companionship with the soul."

5. I have drawn upon accounts in *Brill's New Pauly: Encyclopaedia of the Ancient World*, ed. Hubert Cancik and Helmut Schneider, English ed., 15 vols. (Leiden: Brill, 2004), 4: 518–19; the *Larousse Encyclopedia of Mythology*, intro. by Robert Graves (London: Paul Hamlyn, 1959), pp. 204–5, 228; Pierre Grimal, *The Dictionary of Classical Mythology*, trans. A. R. Maxwell-Hyslop (Oxford: Blackwell, 1985), pp. 140–41; John Pinsent, *Greek Mythology*, Library of the World's Myths and Legends, rev. ed. (New York: Peter Bedrick, 1983), pp. 114–16; and William Smith, *A Dictionary of Greek and Roman Biography and Mythology*, 3 vols. (London: John Murray, 1876), 3: 1052–54, which remains valuable for the richness of its citation, despite its age. Of interest too is J. Rendel Harris, *The Cult of the Heavenly Twins* (Cambridge: Cambridge University Press, 1906), a sweeping, not always trustworthy book, written by a learned archaeologist-anthropologist in a speculative mode. He traces the Gemini back to prehistoric man's attempt to explain the mysterious fact of twins by postulating two fathers, one from the spirit world, deemed variously benevolent or malign, and the other from the world we share. In a number of primitive societies, Harris shows, twins have been considered patrons of fertility.

6. Figure V.1 derives from a prototype made in the previous century. See Michelle P. Brown, *Understanding Illuminated Manuscripts: A Guide to Technical Terms* (Malibu, CA: J. Paul Getty Museum, and London: British Library, 1994), pp. 14–15, for a concise introduction to such manuscripts.

7. *On the Properties of Things: John Trevisa's Translation of "Bartholomaeus Anglicus De*

Proprietatibus Rerum"; A Critical Text, 2 vols. (Oxford: Clarendon Press, 1975), bk. VIII, chap. 10 (1: 467); bk. IX, chap. 13 (1: 531). The former passage continues, "And thanne somtyme beth many werres and st[r]iffe bitwene kynnesmen and cosines."

8. The carving referred to can be seen in François Vogate, *Vézelay*, with photos by Auguste Allemand (Vézelay: Vogade, n.d.), pls. 9, 16. It has often been published elsewhere.

9. On this manuscript see Nigel Morgan, *Early Gothic Manuscripts [II], 1250–1285*, A Survey of Manuscripts Illuminated in the British Isles, vol. 4 (in 2 parts) (London: Harvey Miller, 1982, 1988), cat. no. 151a, pp. 136–39.

10. This important Book of Hours contains miniatures by the Bedford and Boucicaut Masters, and silverpoint drawings possibly by one of the Limbourg brothers.

11. That is not so, however, on the Gemini page (MS Voss Lat. Q. 79, fol. 16v) from the Leiden manuscript of Aratus's *Phaenomena*, made in the second quarter of the ninth century. It shows the twins frontally naked, one holding a club, the other a lyre (attributes borrowed from another set of twins, Amphion and Zethus, sons of Zeus by Antiope). See Ranee Katzenstein and Emile Savage-Smith, *The Leiden Aratea: Ancient Constellations in a Medieval Manuscript* (Malibu, CA: J. Paul Getty Museum, 1988), pp. 18–19 and 22–23. Roger S. Wieck, *Painted Prayers: The Book of Hours in Medieval and Renaissance Art* (New York: George Braziller, 1997), p. 34 (fig. 19), reproduces a much later example, Italian, ca. 1470, exquisite, but also slightly decadent. The further one gets from the classical period the more keenly this anxiety is felt. Michael Camille, *The Gothic Idol: Ideology and Image-Making in Medieval Art* (Cambridge: Cambridge University Press, 1989), offers a wide-ranging study. Female nudity, at least in some contexts, was a degree more acceptable. Eve offered one respectable occasion, though after the Fall she must be shown with a fig leaf, or clothed in animal skins. David lusting after Bathsheba in her bath offered another: see Thomas Kren's interesting and beautifully illustrated essay, "Looking at Louis XII's Bathsheba," in *A Masterpiece Reconstructed: The Hours of Louis XII*, ed. Thomas Kren with Mark Evans (Los Angeles: Getty Publications, 2005), pp. 43–61. The legendary martyrdom of certain female saints also "sanctified" the representation of nudity. In the present volume, my chapter on the iconography of St. Cecilia (Chapter VII) reproduces a number of such images.

12. But see Leo Steinberg, *The Sexuality of Christ in Renaissance Art and in Modern Oblivion*, 2nd ed., revised and expanded (Chicago: Chicago University Press, 1996), on the way Renaissance art ostentatiously displayed the genitals of Christ as an infant, and (less convincingly) as a dead man before burial. This second edition addresses the storm of controversy created by its initial publication. See also Richard C. Trexler, "Gendering Jesus Crucified," pp. 107–20, in *Iconography at the Crossroads*, ed. Brendan Cassidy, Index of Christian Art Occasional Papers 2 (Princeton, NJ: Department of Art and Archaeology, Princeton University, 1993). Trexler cites one Crucifixion (1407) in which a penis is apparently visible through a transparent perizonium; but it is the only medieval example he knows. (He does not reproduce it.) See p. 110n23.

13. The pages of this magnificent manuscript have been published in color facsimile as *Old Testament Miniatures: A Medieval Picture Book with 283 Paintings From the Creation to the Story of David*, ed. Sydney C. Cockerell and John Plummer (New York: George Braziller, n.d. [1969]). See p. 151 for our picture; p. 149 shows Jonathan and David pledging their love with tender gestures and joined hands.

14. I otherwise, in these chapters, quote the Douai-Rheims translation of the Latin Vulgate (1582/1609); note that some versions of the Bible title these books differently, with 1 and 2 Kings (as above) named 1 and 2 Samuel instead. The Vulgate reads, "decore nimis et amabilis super amorem mulierum."

15. Cf. their full-shouldered embrace in a manuscript of *La somme le roy*, a treatise on the Virtues and Vices, London, Brit. Lib. MS Add. 54180, fol. 107, in which they represent the highest ideal of friendship (labeled *Amistie*). They kiss, but Jonathan is shown as a much older, gray-haired man (!) presumably to avoid scandal. Dating from about 1295, it is reproduced by Eric G. Millar, *The Parisian Miniaturist, Honoré*, Library of Illuminated Manuscripts (London: Faber and Faber, 1959), color pl. 7 (p. 29).

16. I am at a loss to describe what they are up to in the Canon Table. It is reproduced by Carl Nordenfalk, "A Tenth-Century Gospel Book in the Walters Art Gallery," *Gatherings in Honor of Dorothy E. Miner*, ed. Ursula E. McCracken et al. (Baltimore: Walters Art Gallery, 1974), pp. 139–70 (here p. 147, fig. 3). The stone arch at Sacra di San Michele, Val Di Susa, can be seen in Frederick Goodman, *Zodiac Signs* (London: Brian Todd, 1990), p. 57.

17. See Florens Deuchler, *Der Ingeborgpsalter* (Berlin: Walter de Gruyter, 1967), p. 19 and pls. 2 (5) and 5 (13c), for a reproduction.

18. Venice: Biblioteca Marciana MS it. IX, 276, fol. 69; it may be seen in Peter Brieger, Millard Meiss, and Charles S. Singleton, *Illuminated Manuscripts of the Divine Comedy*, Bollingen Series 81, 2 vols. (Princeton, NJ: Princeton University Press, 1969), 2: 490. Other late fourteenth-century illustrations of this passage are reproduced on p. 489 (fig. a, from a Morgan manuscript, shows them embracing *as stars*, a design at once spiritual and erotic). The month of May is related mythographically to Mercury, patron god of eloquence (and trickery); see Jane Chance, *The Mythographic Chaucer: The Fabulation of Sexual Politics* (Minneapolis: University of Minnesota Press, 1995), chap. 8, for a mythographic reading of *The Merchant's Tale* that pays learned critical attention to this relationship. Trevisa, *On the Properties of Things*, 1: 531, offers "Maya the modir of Mercurius" as one possible derivation of the month's name.

19. Roger Wieck et al., *Time Sanctified: The Book of Hours in Medieval Art and Life* (New York: George Braziller, 1988), p. 46 (fig. e), reproduces a fine example.

20. I cite this tradition chiefly as yet another sign of heterosexual anxiety in confronting the same-sex Gemini tradition.

21. Thomae Walsingham, *De archana deorum*, ed. Robert A. van Kluyve (Durham, NC: Duke University Press, 1968), p. 50: "Pinguntur enim Gemini porrectis brachiis esse amplectentes et quasi primo pubescentes. Sic et illo, inquiunt, tempore queque iam semina radicibus inferius extensis et implicitis amplectuntur terram, superius vero pubescunt in herbam." Written in the early fifteenth century.

22. Cambridge, Trinity College MS B. 11. 4, fol. iii, provides an elegant example, made in London, ca. 1230. See also *Time in the Medieval World: Occupations of the Months and Signs of the Zodiac in the Index of Christian Art*, ed. Colum Hourihane, published for the Index of Christian Art (Princeton, NJ: Princeton University Press, and University Park: Penn State University Press, 2007), figs. 497, 498 (pp. 263–64), for other thirteenth-century examples.

23. See, for example, Anna De Floriani, *Miniature parigine del Duecento: Il salterio di Albenga e altri manoscritti* (Genoa: Costa and Nolan, 1990), fig. 5, from a Paris psalter made circa 1225. Derek Pearsall and Elisabeth Salter, *Landscapes and Seasons of the Medieval World* (Toronto: University of Toronto Press, 1973), fig. 41c, include an English example from a Peterborough Psalter now in Cambridge: Corpus Christi

College MS 53, fol. 3, ca. 1320. Sometimes the Twins appear fully dressed with shields, as in the eleventh-century Bible of Saint-Vaast now in Arras, reproduced by Walter Cahn, *Romanesque Bible Illumination* (Ithaca, NY: Cornell University Press, 1982), fig. 68 (described p. 112, and pp. 266–67). And sometimes they appear dressed, or partially dressed, behind a single shield, as at Chartres Cathedral, at the west door. See, e.g., Wormald, *The Winchester Psalter*, figs. 123, 129 (English, ca. 1140–60), for another early example. But the Twins naked behind a shield was the most common. As we shall see, the heterosexual Gemini will often be shown that way as well.

24. For instance, the Grosbois Psalter, Liège, 1261 (New York, Pierpont Morgan Library MS M.440, fol. 3). In the same library's MS M. 92, a Book of Hours from Paris, made between 1230 and 1239, the Twins lean with their elbows on a heraldic shield which *does not* cover them modestly (fol. 17); but their genitals have been scraped (erased) by a later censor.

25. A similar "gaze" from behind a shield, but here with a woman looking down at the man's genitals, can be seen in Morgan MS M. 1042, fol. 3 (a Breviary fragment from Paris, 1285–97). Whereas he looks shy and concerned, she raises a hand in astonishment or pleasurable surprise. Such images seem meant, at least in part, to divert and amuse. It can be seen in *Time in the Medieval World*, ed. Hourihane, fig. 496, p. 263.

26. See Ruth Mellinkoff, *Averting Demons: The Protective Power of Medieval Visual Motifs and Themes*, 2 vols. (Los Angeles: Ruth Mellinkoff Publications, 2004), 2: 183–87, reproduces several medieval wrestling images, all very different from the elegant Gemini version. Jurgis Baltrusaitis, *Réveils et prodiges: Le gothique fantastique* (Paris: Armand Colin, 1960), p. 152, figs. 38 a and c, offers two other striking examples. A relevant example from Ely Cathedral is reproduced by Richard Hayman, *Church Misericords and Bench Ends*, Shire Album 230 (Aylesbury: Shire Publications, 1989), p. 28.

27. Michael Camille, "'For Our Devotion and Pleasure': The Sexual Objects of Jean, Duc de Berry," *Art History* 24 (2001): 169–94, a groundbreaking essay whose subtlety and interest are only hinted at above. Thomas Kren, referencing this same essay, writes about the duke's playful relationship with the brothers Limbourg, the greatest painters in his employ, and concludes that "the roles of nudity and eroticism in the duke's books probably reflected larger appetites of their celebrated patron. They show the intimate ways in which a private devotional book might be personalized." See *Masterpiece Reconstructed*, ed. Kren and Evans, pp. 52–53.

28. I quote from the edition by Nikolaus M. Härig, in *Studi medievali* (Turin), 3rd series, vol. 19, no. 2 (1978): 797–879 (here p. 811). Alain makes clear his invention is rooted in a pictorial tradition, saying that it confirmed what "the faithful representation in the picture showed" ("In quo, sicut picturae veritas praedicabat"). Alan of Lille, *The Plaint of Nature*, trans. James J. Sheridan, Mediaeval Sources in Translation 26 (Toronto: Pontifical Institute of Mediaeval Studies, 1980), II, pr. 1, p. 79. For Alan's condemnation of homosexuality, see esp. I, mtr. 1, and VIII, pr. 4, pp. 67–72, 133–48.

29. Alan of Lille, *Anticlaudianus; or, The Good and Perfect Man*, trans. James J. Sheridan (Toronto: Pontifical Institute of Mediaeval Studies, 1973), V.8, pp. 136–37. A few lines later he describes them so: "the Spartan Twins have a special radiance as they bear the standards of Spring" (V.16–17, p. 138).

30. Cf. the exquisite miniature attributed to Venturino Mercati, from a Book of Hours, probably made in Milan, ca. 1470, reproduced by Wieck, *Painted Prayers*,

fig. 19 (p. 34); Wieck tactfully imagines as patron to this book "someone who had very individual iconographic preferences." (It comes from New York, Pierpont Morgan Library, MS G.14, fol. 7v.) In star-chart pictures of the Twins, Castor is often shown holding a sickle (an emblem of mortality) and Pollux a lyre (linking him to the higher realms and the music of the heavenly spheres).

31. Reproduced in *Regensburger Buchmalerei: von frühkarolingischer Zeit bis zum Ausgang des Mittelalters*, catalog eds. Florentine Mütherich and Karl Dachs (Munich: Prestel-Verlag, 1987), fig. 35. D.W. Robertson, Jr., *A Preface to Chaucer: Studies in Medieval Perspectives* (Princeton, NJ: Princeton University Press, 1963), calls attention to heterosexual couples thus engaged, on carved-ivory mirror backs from the mid-fourteenth century (figs. 59, 61, 62). See also Michael Camille, *The Medieval Art of Love: Objects and Subjects of Desire* (New York: Harry N. Abrams, 1998), figs. 85–86. Steinberg, *Sexuality of Christ*, pp. 3–7, 110–18, treats chin chucking with historical sweep and an extensive presentation of visual evidence. Though chiefly interested in the Virgin chucking the chin of the Christ child, a theme not relevant here, Steinberg gives its role in courtship full due.

32. Cambridge, Fitzwilliam Museum MS 36–1950, fol. 6. The Twins stand in a shoulder embrace, their hair equally long, their heads resting together, between two trees.

33. On this manuscript, see C. M. Kauffmann, *Romanesque Manuscripts, 1066–1190*, Survey of Manuscripts Illuminated in the British Isles, vol. 3 (London: Harvey Miller, 1975), cat. no. 48.

34. This illumination covers all the bases: a naked, mature heterosexual couple is shown seated side by side, in midnight-blue *grisaille*, in the cloud-filled top margin of the page; mature men carrying May branches emerge from the woods in the background at far right. On this deluxe manuscript, see John Harthan, *The Book of Hours* (New York: Thomas Y. Crowell, 1977), pp. 128–33.

35. *The Works of Michael Drayton*, ed. J. William Hebel, 6 vols. (Oxford: Shakespeare Head Press, Blackwell, 1961), 1: 163, 164–65, 182. There are other Gemini allusions in the poem as well, including reference to the way "the twofold-twynned Geminy" embrace "in their star-gilded girdle strongly tyed" (p. 198).

36. Chaucer had versified this story in some form before he began *The Canterbury Tales*, referring to it as "The Love of Palamon and Arcite" in the list of his works he incorporated into the Prologue to *The Legend of Good Women* (F 420). The title of his source, Boccaccio's *Il Teseida delle nozze d'Emilia* (The Theseid, or Story of Theseus, Concerning the Nuptials of Emilia), be it noted, focuses instead on her.

37. I owe this idea to Professor Gerhard Joseph, who proposed it in a personal letter after a lecture on *The Merchant's Tale* I gave to the Medieval Club of New York City many years ago. Representations of the male Gemini behind a single heraldic shield show them "bothe in oon armes" (having the same coat of arms) quite literally.

38. The Gemini couple in the Hours of Jeanne d'Evreux, illuminated by Jean Pucelle some ten years earlier, is likewise heterosexual, graceful, and naked. It is in New York, Metropolitan Museum of Art, the Cloisters Collection, 1954 (54. 1. 2), fol. 6.

39. Ibid.

40. See *The Wharncliffe Hours: A Fifteenth-Century Illuminated Prayerbook in the Collection of the National Gallery of Victoria Australia*, ed. Margaret Manion (London: Thames and Hudson, 1981), color pl. 5 (p. 33).

41. One of the earliest depictions of the "labor" of May in an English manuscript focuses solely on ideas of fecundity, showing shepherds working with sheep, goats, and lambs: London, Brit. Lib. MS Cotton Tib. B.V (vol. 1), fol. 5, a miscellany from the eleventh century. It is reproduced by Elzbieta Temple, *Anglo-Saxon Manuscripts, 900–1066*, Survey of Manuscripts Illuminated in the British Isles, vol. 2 (London: Harvey Miller, 1976), cat. no. 87, fig. 273. Cf. the same library's MS Cotton Julius A.VI, fol. 5 (cat. no. 62, fig. 198).

42. On this manuscript, see *The Cambridge Illuminations: Ten Centuries of Book Production in the Medieval West*, ed. Paul Binski and Stella Panayotova (London: Harvey Miller, 2005), cat. no. 88, pp. 202–4.

43. New York, Pierpont Morgan Library MS M. 280, fol. 5v. Other examples could be readily adduced.

44. It is widely published, for example, by Claude Caroly and Jacques Bussy, *Amiens et sa cathédrale* (Paris: P. Horay, 1971), fig. 72, and in *Time in the Medieval World*, ed. Hourihane, fig. 502 (p. 265). The design is thirteenth century, but the stone may not have been cut until the fourteenth century, when the west front was completed.

45. Though made in France, the psalter was owned by Robert Heryerd and his wife Johanna, who donated it to the prioress and nuns of Goring Priory, an Augustinian convent founded in the time of Henry II. See Montague Rhodes James, *The Western Manuscripts in the Library of Trinity College, Cambridge: A Descriptive Catalogue*, 4 vols. (Cambridge: Cambridge University Press, 1900–1904), vol. 1 (no. 244), p. 338.

46. Figure V.17: for the manuscript as a whole, see *Queen Mary's Psalter*, facsimile ed. Sir George Warner (London: British Museum, 1912); and for the Gemini page, pl. 132 (described p. 24). Pl. 131 shows the occupation of the month: three young men hunting with birds, one of them on a horse.

47. Compare Rome, Bibl. Vaticana MS Cod. Urb. Lat. 603, fol. 9 (a Franciscan Breviary, ca. 1320 or after, also from the workshop of Jean Pucelle), almost identical, but more elegant in execution; again a thick zone of green leaves, supported by a single trunk, encircles the loins and genitals of the Twin. I know of no reproduction. On the manuscript itself, see Kathleen Morand, *Jean Pucelle* (Oxford: Clarendon Press, 1962), pp. 47–48.

48. Richard N. Snyder has suggested to me the "king" in Figure V.20 may be an embedded portrait of Maximillian I of Hapsburg, Holy Roman Emperor from 1493 until his death in 1519.

49. Some other examples of the erotic twins in trees: Cambridge, Fitzwilliam Museum MS 118, fol. 5 (a Book of Hours, use of Paris, 1500–1510); Oxford, Bodleian Library MS Buchanan e. 3, fol. 4 (from a Book of Hours, use of Rouen, ca. 1500); and the same library's MS Rawl. liturg. e. 36, fol. 3 (a French Book of Hours, use of Rome, first quarter of the sixteenth century); and Los Angeles, J. Paul Getty Museum MS Ludwig IX. 25, fol. 5v, a Book of Hours from Rouen, ca. 1500.

50. The same library's MS M. 1000, fol. 5, a Book of Hours made in Paris, ca. 1415–25, by the Boucicaut Master and his workshop, is nearly identical, and of comparable beauty. Los Angeles, J. Paul Getty Museum MS Ludwig IX. 6 (83. ML. 102), fol. 5 is closely related (the Bedford Master workshop, ca. 1440–50), as is the May page in a Book of Hours, from Paris or Tours, ca. 1470–90, now in the Lenin Library, Moscow, published as fig. 34 in Ekaterina Zolotova, *Livres d'heures: Manuscrits enluminés français du XVe siècle dans les collections de Moscou* (Leningrad: Editions

d'art Aurora, 1991), its miniatures ascribed to the circle of Jean Bourdichon. For other examples, see the Hours of Jean Dunois, French, ca. 1450, *Illustrations from One Hundred Manuscripts in the Library of Henry Yates Thompson*, 7 vols. (London: Chiswick Press, 1907–18), vol. 5, pl. 48 (fol. 5); and Milan, Bibl. Trivulziana, Castello Sforzesco MS 2164, fol. 5 (also French, fifteenth century). John Harthan, *An Introduction to Illuminated Manuscripts from the Victoria and Albert Museum* (London: Victoria and Albert Museum, 1983), p. 31, fig. 16, reproduces such a page in color (Reid MS 17, fol. 3), possibly from Rouen, ca. 1480. He duly notes "The Gemini sign was one of the few places in Books of Hours where artists could portray nudity." New York, Pierpont Morgan Library MS M. 27, fol. 7, from a Book of Hours, probably Rouen, ca. 1420–30, recalls the same-sex (wrestling) version of this embrace, now staged naked behind a shield.

51. Cf. Los Angeles, J. Paul Getty Museum MS Ludwig IX 16 (83. ML. 112), fol. 5, from a Book of Hours, use of the order of St. John of Jerusalem.

52. The glossary to *The Riverside Chaucer* is inadequate here, glossing it simply as "struggle" (p. 1295). The monumental *Middle English Dictionary*, in contrast, under *strogelen*, (pt. S.16, pp. 961–62) provides ample evidence that it often meant "wrestle," including Chaucer's use of it in *The Pardoner's Tale* to describe the plan of two drunken young men to murder their mate: "And I shal ryve hym thurgh the sydes tweye / Whil that thou strogelest with hym as in game" (VI 828). The Trevisa, Lydgate *Pilgrimage*, and Hoccleve citations that follow in the *MED* use *struggle* and *wrestle* together as synonyms. Chaucer might have used the latter word to describe the copulation in a tree (metrically there is no difference), but *struggle* describes more ambiguously what the act of love can look like, seen from the outside, whereas *wrestle* would limit it to wrestling alone.

53. This cure by "struggling / wrestling" is Chaucer's own. Herewith a brief account of how the cuckoldry is described in the analogues or possible sources.

In the earliest Western version of the story, the *Novellino*, composed at the turn of the thirteenth century, the account of the sexual act is colorful but bland: "Now the lady was in the pear tree with the friend who was waiting for her and they enjoyed great pleasure together [*e istavano in grande solazzo*], so that the pear tree was bending this way and that with the pears falling to earth all over the husband." Her excuse, once the husband has seen what they are doing, is even more blandly expressed: "If I had not done this with him [*S'io non avessi fatto chosíe con chostui*], you would never have seen the light."

Boccaccio's *Decameron* (written in the years immediately following the Black Death of 1348–49) tells an analogous story brilliantly, but the trick that forwards the adultery (too elaborate to summarize here) is worked almost in reverse: the husband, jealous but not blind, is tricked into climbing the tree, so that the young ones can openly make love on the ground below; he is then persuaded that the tree has magical powers of distortion, showing things "that are not so" to those who look down from its branches. Even if Chaucer knew this version (*Decameron* VII.9), unprovable but not impossible, his account of lovemaking *up in a tree* cannot be derived from it. In any case, Boccaccio's account of the deed itself is oddly flat and lacking in wit—"As soon as [the husband] was up [in the tree], the lady began to take her pleasure with Pyrrhus [*la donna insieme con Pirro s'incominciarono a sollazzare*]." Pyrrhus's subsequent claim that what the husband saw was merely an "illusion" ("trasvedere") of "carnal" activity ("carnalmente giaciuto"), caused by the deceiving tree, is not much better. The tale ends on a similar note: "later, in a more leisurely fashion, Pyrrhus and Lydia took pleasure and delight [*piacere et diletto*] in each other many times. And may God grant the same to us."

Only a brief Latin fable by one Adolphus (1315) even hints at Chaucer's invention. Though a mere thirty-six lines long, much of it devoted to misogynist complaint, it phrases the wife's excuse in an interesting way. A mysterious voice, she says, told her to "sport with a youth high in a tree / And your husband will quickly be given his former sight, believe me" (*Ludere cum juvene studeas in roboris alto, / Prisca viro dabitur lux cito, crede mihi*). The verb *ludere* means "play" in a generalized way: to play at a game, to gamble, to sport or frolic, and, in the right context, can even mean "to play amorously," as it probably does here. But absent any further specification, it does not mean "to wrestle." The last line of the fable shifts the sexual metaphor completely: "Her husband honors and loves her, but another plows her."

54. On the elaborate page shown in Figure V.25, SS. Philip and the Lesser James decorate the left margin in a single roundel: because they share the same feast day (May 1), they are sometimes used to supplement the Gemini twins themselves. But not here: the Gemini, in the bottom left margin, are naked, genderless, and conjoined like Siamese twins, with two bodies and one head (a variant not entirely uncommon, perhaps another way of avoiding even implicit sexuality). Below the calendar, the occupation of the month furnishes the grandest scene on the page: an elegant boating party, its craft decked out with fresh green branches, with an oarsman drinking, musicians playing, and a court fool sitting at the back. For two other calendar pages from this manuscript, with comparable upper borders, see Bridget Ann Henisch, *The Medieval Calendar Year* (University Park: Pennsylvania State University Press, 1999), chap. 6, color pl. 15; chap. 7, color pl. 6.

55. Anthony Annunziata, in a valuable study, "Tree Paradigms in the *Merchant's Tale*," in *The Fourteenth Century*, ed. Paul E. Szarmach and Bernard S. Levy, Center for Medieval and Early Renaissance Studies Acta 4 (Binghamton: State University of New York Press, 1977), pp. 125–35, has suggested the relevance of the Jesse tree before me (pp. 128–29). For a powerful early example, see the Tree of Jesse page, frontispiece to the Prophets in the Lambeth Bible, possibly from Canterbury, ca. 1150, reproduced p. 114 (fig. 53) in *English Romanesque Art, 1066–1200*, Arts Council of Great Britain exhibition catalog, ed. George Zarnecki, Janet Holt, and Tristram Holland (London: Weidenfeld and Nicolson, 1984).

56. Emile Mâle, *Religious Art in France: The Twelfth Century; A Study of the Origins of Medieval Iconography*, ed. Harry Bober, trans. Marthiel Mathews, Bollingen Series 40: 1 (Princeton, NJ: Princeton University Press, 1978), pp. 171–77, gives a useful introduction to the tradition; see figs. 149, 151. It has been superseded by Gertrud Schiller, *Iconography of Christian Art*, 2 vols., trans. Janet Seligman (Greenwich, CT: New York Graphic Society, 1971-72), 1: 15–22, a work of remarkable sweep and concision (with several further volumes not yet published in English). See her figs. 23, 30, 31, 32 (exceptionally powerful) and possibly 35, for Jesse trees emerging from Jesse's loins. She agrees with Mâle in thinking her third group ("that of the complex image") "probably goes back to Abbot Suger of Saint-Denis" (p. 18) Arthur Watson, *The Early Iconography of the Tree of Jesse* (London: Oxford University Press, 1934), remains a fundamental study. In chapter 7, "Suger and the First Tree of Jesse," he challenges (and complicates) Mâle's account.

57. It is published, and commented upon by Kristine Edmondson Haney, *The Winchester Psalter: An Iconographic Study* (Leicester: Leicester University Press, 1986), fig. 8 and pp. 93–94. On the date and provenance of the manuscript, see pp. 7–8.

See also her fig. 81, reproducing the British Library's MS Lansdowne 383, fol. 15, for a striking early example.

58. In the lower margin, but unrelated to the scene above, Samson kills a lion with his bare hands. The picture is much easier to read in color, as reproduced in *Age of Chivalry: Art in Plantagenet England, 1200–1400*, an exhibition catalog edited by Jonathan Alexander and Paul Binski (London: Royal Academy of Arts, and Weidenfield and Nicholson, 1987), p. 451 (fig. 568). Donald Drew Egbert, *The Tickhill Psalter and Related Manuscripts* (New York: New York Public Library, 1940), offers an extensive study. On this manuscript see also Lucy Freeman Sandler, *Gothic Manuscripts, 1285–1385*, Survey of Manuscripts Illuminated in the British Isles, vol. 5 (in 2 parts) (London: Harvey Miller and Oxford University Press, 1986), vol. 2, no. 26 for the catalog entry, and vol. 1, figs. 25 (formerly the Dyson Perrin York Hours), and 96 (the Ormesby Psalter) for other relevant examples. For English pages from the period just before, see Nigel Morgan, *Early Gothic Manuscripts [I], 1190–1250*, Survey of Manuscripts Illuminated in the British Isles, vol. 4 (in 2 parts), (London and New York: Harvey Miller and Oxford University Press, 1982), figs. 104 and 239, and *Early Gothic Manuscripts [II], 1250–1285*, figs. 188 (exceptionally suggestive), 254, 286.

59. The so-called Capucins' Bible, its spectacular Jesse page reproduced in color by Cahn, *Romanesque Bible Illumination*, p. 215 (fig. 179); on it, see p. 220. On the manuscript in general, see pp. 278–79 (cat. no. 97).

60. See Schiller, *Iconography of Christian Art*, p. 15.

61. Emile Mâle, *Religious Art in France: The Thirteenth Century; A Study of Medieval Iconography and Its Sources*, ed. Harry Bober, trans. Marthiel Mathews, Bollingen Series 40: 2 (Princeton, NJ: Princeton University Press, 1984), p. 171. He reproduces the Chartres window as fig. 121. In Mâle's own descriptions of the "tree," he spoke of it as growing out of Jesse's stomach (*ventre*), though he clearly understood the tradition better than that.

62. It contributed to the Prophets' Play, in its several forms, and to a full-scale "Tree of Jesse" pageant (kings and prophets) in *The N-Town Play: Cotton MS Vespasian D. 8*, ed. Stephen Spector, 2 vols., EETS, s.s. 11, 12 (Oxford: Oxford University Press, 1991), a fifteenth-century drama cycle from East Anglia; for its text see 1: 65–70.

63. The Chicele Breviary, ca. 1408–14, now in London's Lambeth Palace, provides an example: see Kathleen Scott, *Later Gothic Manuscripts, 1390–1490*, Survey of Manuscripts Illuminated in the British Isles, vol. 6 (in 2 parts) (London: Harvey Miller, 1996), vol. 1, fig. 132, and vol. 2, cat. no. 30. The Astor Psalter-Hours, fol. 53, in the collection of Viscount Astor, provides another (from the fourteenth century): it can be seen in *England in the Fourteenth Century: Proceedings of the 1985 Harlaxton Symposium*, ed. W. M. Ormrod (Woodbridge, Suffolk, Eng.: Boydell Press, 1986), fig. 15. Mâle, *Religious Art in France: The Twelfth Century*, figs. 150 and 151, sets two contrasting examples side by side. One, from the Ingebord Psalter, ca. 1200, locates the tree behind the couch Jesse rests upon; the other, from the Psalter of Blanche of Castile, roughly contemporary, has it grow from between his covered legs. See Emile Mâle, *Religious Art in France: The Late Middle Ages; A Study of Medieval Iconography and its Sources*, ed. Harry Bober, trans. Marthiel Mathews, Bollingen Series 40: 3 (Princeton, NJ: Princeton University Press, 1986), pp. 77–78 and 205, on the late fifteenth century's preference for a seated rather than a recumbent Jesse, with the tree arising above or behind him. Fig. 42 (p. 79) offers an example. At least fifteen Jesse windows from the fourteenth century survived the English Reformation, though many of them survive only in fragments. See Christopher Woodforde, "A

Group of Fourteenth-Century Windows Showing the Tree of Jesse," *Journal of the British Society of Master Glass-Painters* 6 (1937): 184–90.

64. It can be seen in color in *The Hours of Catherine of Cleves*, ed. John Plummer (New York: George Braziller, 1966), fig. 90 (New York, Pierpont Morgan Library MS M. 917, p. 148).

65. On the status of squires, see Jill Mann, *Chaucer and Medieval Estates Satire: The Literature of Social Classes and the "General Prologue" to the "Canterbury Tales,"* (Cambridge: Cambridge University Press, 1973), pp. 115–20.

66. First, in a brief note by William W. Main, then in another by Philip Griffith, summed up and reinforced by Emerson Brown, "The *Merchant's Tale*: Why Is May Called 'Mayus'?" *ChauR* 2 (1968): 274–77.

67. A corrupt friar, "Sire *Penetrans-domos*," come to "heal" Contrition, is sharply rebuked by Peace, who compares him to a friar in favor at a court where Peace once stayed: "And was my lordes leche—and my ladies bothe. / And at the laste this lymytour, tho my lord was oute, / He salved so oure wommen til some were with childe." William Langland, *The Vision of Piers Plowman: A Critical Edition of the B-Text*, ed. A. V. C. Schmidt (London: J. M. Dent, 1978), B-text, bk. XX, 341–48, p. 262. (For the C-text version, see bk. XXII, 340–47.)

68. From a brief note by Philip Mahone Griffith in *The Explicator* 16 (1957), no. 13: "Chaucer's *Merchant's Tale*."

69. Jacobus de Voragine, *The Golden Legend: Readings on the Saints*, trans. William Granger Ryan, 2 vols. (Princeton, NJ: Princeton University Press, 1993), 2: 196–98.

70. New York, Pierpont Morgan Library MS M. 622, fol. 177, an Armenian Menologium dated 1348, from Sis, Cilicia, shows the saints holding mortar and pestle, as does that library's MS M. 12, 69v (perhaps from Tours, ca. 1500), in which they hold medicine bottles.

71. E. G. Withycombe, *The Oxford Dictionary of English Christian Names*, 3rd ed. (Oxford: Clarendon Press, 1977), p. 78.

72. Leslie G. Matthews, "SS. Cosmas and Damian—Patron Saints of Medicine and Pharmacy: Their Cult in England," *Medical History* 12 (1968): 281–88.

73. The page is reproduced in color by Page, *Astrology in Medieval Manuscripts*, fig. 45 (p. 55). Matthews (above) did not know of this evidence from York.

74. Derek Pearsall, *The Life of Geoffrey Chaucer: A Critical Biography* (Oxford: Blackwell, 1992), p. 225; Chaucer's residence in Kent may have begun as early as 1385. He probably moved back to London in 1398.

75. Blean, though not on the pilgrim's route, is no further from Canterbury than is Harbledown (two miles away) where the pilgrims hear *The Manciple's Tale*: "Woot ye nat where ther stant a litel toun / Which that ycleped is Bobbe-up-and-doun, / Under the Blee, in Caunterbury Weye?" (Prologue, IX 1–3). On these churches, and the three others, see Matthews, "SS. Cosmas and Damian."

76. See *The Minor Poems of the Vernon MS*, pt. 1, ed. Carl Horstmann, EETS, o.s. 98 (London: Kegan Paul, 1892), p. 194 (551–52). This too I owe to Emerson Brown in a brief note published in the *Chaucer Newsletter* 13, no. 1 (1991): 5. Further evidence includes a "life" of Cosmas and Damian, ca. 1400, in *Legends of the Saints in the Scottish Dialect of the Fourteenth Century*, ed. W. M. Metcalfe, 3 vols., Scottish Text Society 18 (Edinburgh: William Blackwood, 1896), 2: 293–303; it closely translates the *Legenda aurea*.

77. Brown, ". . . Why Is May Called 'Mayus'?", p. 276 and n12. The Latin verses continue, in translation: "The rich field is tilled; the vine and the tree are bedecked.

Then bees reproduce, calves are castrated, and sheep are shorn. Cheese is pressed. Bricks are to be made." Brown establishes May as a good month for medicinal healing, quoting a treatise long attributed to Bede and a poem by a ninth-century monk, Wandelbert of Prüm.

78. See Heinz Skrobucha, *The Patrons of the Doctors*, trans. Hans Hermann Rosenwald, Pictorial Library of Eastern Church Art 7 (Recklinghausen: Aurel Bongers, 1967), p. 11, citing the *Synaxarium ecclesiae* of Constantinople. Marie-Louise David-Danel, *Iconographie des saints médecins Come et Damien* (Lille: Morel and Corduant, 1958), offers a full study with many pictures, most of them late, but including two *predellae* by Fra Angelico, with multiple scenes (figs. 21–36).

79. Jacobus de Voragine, *The Golden Legend*, 2: 196–97.

80. Skrobucha, *Patrons of the Doctors*, p. 12.

81. *The Oxford Dictionary of the Christian Church*, ed. F. L. Cross, 3rd ed., ed. E. A. Livingstone (London: Oxford University Press, 1997), s.v. "Cosmas and Damian," p. 421.

82. Skrobucha, *Patrons of the Doctors*, pp. 12–15, forwarding a claim first made by Ludwig Dübner, *De incubatione* (Leipzig: Teubner, 1900), who on p. 77 prints the Greek original of the "we are not Castor and Pollux" story reported above. It is reprinted by Harris, *Cult of the Heavenly Twins*, p. 157 (note to p. 54), whose chapter 10 ("Cosmas and Damian"), pp. 96–104, accepts and builds upon Dübner's thesis. Harris's book, highly erudite but also wildly venturesome in its reasoning, must be used with caution. But chapter 6 ("Twins Are Healers"), pp. 50–54, suggests the first mission of the Dioscuri was to restore sight to the blind; and chapters 4 ("Twins: Patrons of Fertility"), 7 ("Twins Guard Truth"), 9 ("Twins in the Calendar"), 10 ("Italian Saints"), and 20 ("Concluding Remarks"), especially its final sentences echoing Theodoret, Bishop of Cyprus, p. 154, are all of interest.

83. See *Oxford Dictionary of the Christian Church*, s.v. *incubation*, p. 826, for a brief notice and useful bibliography.

84. I know of only one May page that makes any clear-cut reference to Eden, but it is very interesting. In an architectural structure filling the right margin it shows two scenes, God creating Eve from Adam's side and blessing her (below), and the Gemini in an erotic embrace, their nakedness masked by a shield (above). The Gemini here seem to be Adam and Eve depicted a second time, with lavish gold-colored wings sprouting from their shoulders, presumably to indicate their innocence. The parallel being drawn, one notes, is with the Creation, not the Fall. This image too is late, ca. 1490–1510, and can be seen in color in Page, *Astrology in Medieval Manuscripts*, fig. 36, though it is wrongly described (p. 46) as a "calendar page for June." *Time in the Medieval World*, ed. Hourihane, includes a Gemini couple naked amid trees, with the man offering the woman a piece of fruit. It evokes Eden, and if they are meant to be Adam and Eve, it must be postlapsarian—*he* offers the fruit to her. But they are better read, I think, as a traditional Gemini couple, with the fruit a tender courtship offering; it does not seem a sign of sin. It too is late: from a French early sixteenth-century Book of Hours.

85. Kenneth A. Bleeth, "The Image of Paradise in the *Merchant's Tale*," in *The Learned and the Lewed: Studies in Chaucer and Medieval Literature*, ed. Larry D. Benson, Harvard English Studies 5 (Cambridge, MA: Harvard University Press, 1974), pp. 45–60. He argues that Chaucer did highlight certain aspects of the Fall, but acknowledges that the poem's "most significant" Christian context is in its "series of references to paradise in the first part of the tale" (p. 46).

86. Damian, it is true, is compared to an "adder"—but much earlier, at the wedding feast rather than in the tree, and in a very specific sense: for having fallen in love with May, he is compared to a treacherous snake in the bosom of his master ("Lyk to the naddre in bosom sly untrewe / God shilde us alle from youre aqueyntaunce!") (IV 1786). Eric Jager, *The Tempter's Voice: Language and the Fall in Medieval Literature* (Ithaca, NY: Cornell University Press, 1993), p. 258, nevertheless makes a reasonable case for associating him with the devil.

87. For text and translation, see David Bevington, ed., *Medieval Drama* (Boston: Houghton Mifflin, 1975), p. 91 (231–32). The devil tells Eve: (1) that her husband is a fool (she agrees he's "a little hard" [*un poi est durs*]); (2) that though she thinks him lordly (*mult francs*) he is in fact servile (*mult serf*); and (3) that she, so delicate and beautiful, is the wiser of the two (*tu es plus sage*) (ll. 221–33).

88. See Henry Ansgar Kelly, "The Metamorphoses of the Eden Serpent During the Middle Ages and Renaissance," *Viator* 2 (1971): 301–27. The medieval drama, however, in order to connect the serpent with Lucifer, seems usually to have costumed the serpent as a man (referring to him in dialogue as "he"), a tradition only rarely or ambiguously represented in medieval visual art (see pp. 324–26). Kelly cites a few examples; to them might be added the August calendar page from the Rohan Hours (Paris: Bibl. Natl. MS Lat. 9471, fol. 11v), in which the serpent, coiled round the tree, shows two heads, one (looking to Adam) that of a dragon, the other (facing Eve) a man's face with a long beard. The manuscript was made ca. 1419–27. See Meiss and Thomas, eds., *Rohan Master*, color pl. 14.

89. Jager, *Tempter's Voice*; I quote from the book jacket's authorized summary.

90. There are three classic studies: Mortimer J. Donovan, "The Image of Pluto and Proserpine in the *Merchant's Tale, Philological Quarterly* 36 (1957): 499–60; Karl P. Wentersdorf, "Theme and Structure in the Merchant's Tale: The Function of the Pluto Episode," *PMLA* 80 (1965): 522–27; and Mortimer J. Donovan again, "Chaucer's January and May: Counterparts in Claudian," in *Chaucerian Problems and Perspectives: Essays Presented to Paul E. Beichner, C.S.C.*, ed. Edward Vasta and Zacharias P. Thundy (Notre Dame, IN: University of Notre Dame Press, 1979), pp. 59–69. In Chaucer's tale, the two appear as the King and Queen of Fayerye, but Pluto is nevertheless identified as having "ravysshed" Persephone out of Etna in his "grisely carte," when she was gathering flowers in a meadow (IV 2225–33). Chaucer cites Claudian as his source, though that poem is incomplete, but he would have known the seasonal interpretation of this myth from Ovid's *Metamorphoses*. As players in "the pear-tree story" Pluto and Proserpina are Chaucer's alone: the sources and analogues have the wronged husband appeal to God, or Jupiter, or introduce Christ and St. Peter as passive onlookers, bemused by the woman's ability to excuse herself, no matter what she has done. Wentersdorf, "Theme and Structure," pp. 523–24nn9–11, surveys the various interventions, and prints a translation of the Claudian original on p. 525. His conclusion is in harmony with my own: "The effect which Pluto's deed had on nature throws light on the unnaturalness of his marriage; and this unnaturalness is acknowledged in Jove's decision that Proserpina be permitted to leave her husband for a few months every year" (p. 527).

91. For the Latin text, see John Gower, *English Works*, ed. Macaulay, 2: 450 (*Confessio Amantis*, bk. VIII, preceding 2377). I quote a translation signed A.G. (Alfred Geier], included in John Gower, *Confessio Amantis*, ed. Russell A. Peck (New York: Holt, Rinehart, and Winston, 1968), p. 521. For the encounter with Venus

described above, see Book VIII 2301 ff.; I quote (or reference) ll. 2321, 2403–4, 2416, 2907.

92. I quote from the Macaulay edition: bk. VIII, 2321; 2403–4; 2424–28; 2416; 2907.

93. This renunciation marks the end of Gower's poem, though he lived out his own life quite differently. In 1398, nearing the age of sixty-eight, he married for the first time, choosing one Agnes Groundolf, otherwise unknown, but presumably a lower-class woman significantly younger than he. Historians have generally assumed that his health was failing and he needed a nurse to look after him. But Isabella Yeager suggests a richer possibility, in a well-researched essay, "Did Gower Love His Wife? And What Has It to Do with His Poetry?" Her tactful, revisionist account stresses the following facts: Gower lived another ten years, apparently in good health, during which he wrote a good deal; if help was needed, he could as easily have hired a man servant (the more common practice); one of his brief Latin poems ("Est amor"), conceivably written on the eve of his marriage, speaks of his expectation of being married "in the flesh" ("nuptorum carnis"); he provided for his wife generously in his will, and wrote a loving epitaph for her tomb, which stood near or alongside his own, though it does not survive. Yeager does not comment on *The Merchant's Tale* in her essay, but the parallels with Chaucer's January, his condition and his needs, seem to me striking. In short, though Gower too chose to marry late, he did so without January's self-delusion, and left no evidence of regretting that decision.

94. Ballade no. 880, in Eustache Deschamps, *Oeuvres complètes, societé des anciens textes français*, ed. Le Marquis de Queux de Saint-Hilaire and Gaston Raynaud, 11 vols. (Paris: Firmin Didot, 1878–1903), 5: 63–64. On it, see William Matthews, "Eustache Deschamps and Chaucer's 'Merchant's Tale,'" *Modern Language Review* 51 (1956): 217–20. Though we have no way of dating the ballade, and despite Deschamps' stated admiration for Chaucer, in Matthew's opinion "there is little reason to believe that he was influenced by Chaucer or any other poet from England, that land of giants and men with tails which he so much disliked" (p. 218). Chaucer's debt to Deschamps, on the other hand, is demonstrable and extensive.

95. Hourihane, ed., *Time in the Medieval World*, p. lv, thinks such variance may reflect the differing climates of northern and southern Europe, though it may simply register the overlap of real-life occupations within the same cycle. The months of January–February and April–May, in particular, share not only a certain kind of weather but also invite the same kinds of pleasure. As Hourihane notes, "There is never more than a month's difference in the use of these labors."

96. I am thinking, for instance, of the Wife of Bath, who attributes her character and marital history to the influence of both Venus and Mars; of the mostly ill-fated, star-crossed journeys made by Constance in *The Man of Law's Tale*; and of the character traits of the young people in *The Knight's Tale*, as expressed in the prayers they make to (and in the temples of) Mars, Venus, and Diana. Wood, *Chaucer and the Country of the Stars*, engages with each of these and more.

97. C. S. Lewis, *The Discarded Image: An Introduction to Medieval and Renaissance Literature* (Cambridge: Cambridge University Press, 1964), pp. 103–4. For a religious critique of "judicial astrology" and its claim to predict the course of individual human lives—an offense against the First Commandment—see *Dives and Pauper*, ed. Priscilla Heath Barnum, 1 vol., in 2 pts., EETS, o.s. 275, 280 (London: Oxford University Press, 1976, 1980), [I.1], 117–51. (It was written ca. 1405–10.) See Wood,

Chaucer and the Country of the Stars, pp. 12–21 and 44–50, on Chaucer's unequivocal rejection of astrological determinism in his *Treatise on the Astrolabe* (pt. I. 21, ll. 49–62, and esp. pt. II. 4, ll. 57–69), where he decisively abjures these "observaunces of judicial matere and rytes of payens, in whiche my spirit hath no faith." But he entertains (I choose the word carefully) some related ideas elsewhere. Woods briefly notices *The Merchant's Tale* "sun in Gemini" on p. 94. North, *Chaucer's Universe*, seeks to date certain events in the poem (the marriage and the onset of January's blindness) by means of highly technical calculations, centered on shifts in "lunar velocity." The Gemini passage did not deeply engage him, but for his remarks on it, see pp. 446–47, 454.

98. Gower, *Confessio Amantis*, bk. VII (1044–50); in *English Works*, 2: 261.

99. Henisch, *Medieval Calendar Year*, p. 16. Exceptions to this rule might be cited, but they are rare and late, and (as Henisch says) do not color or interact with the labor/occupation or zodiac cycle. For instance, the May page in the Hours of Henry VIII, Tours, ca. 1500, shows (in the large miniature above) a well-dressed young couple walking through the woods with flowering branches over their shoulders, and (in a small roundel below) a naked Gemini couple in sexual embrace, with a number of saints proper to that month filling the remaining space around the liturgical calendar. But the saints make no discernible comment on the other (traditional and sustained) visual programs; they are there because their feast days are in the calendar alongside. Roger S. Wieck, William M. Voelkle, and K. Michelle Hearne, *The Hours of Henry VIII: A Renaissance Masterpiece by Jean Poyet* (New York: George Braziller, and the Pierpont Morgan Library, 2000), reproduce this page in color on p. 61 (Morgan MS H. 8, fol. 3).

100. In the Steinhöwel analogue, and in Macho's *Esope*, the husband is blind, but these compositions are much later in date: 1476/77 and 1480.

101. Deschamps' *Miroir de mariage*, which Chaucer raided extensively for the first part of this tale, has much to say about a rich man's need to sire an heir. See *Sources and Analogues*, ed. Correale and Hamel, 2: 490 (290–94, 369–74) and 492 (746–73), and also the Sarum collect published on p. 500.

102. Chaucer does the same in *The Nun's Priest's Tale*, a few tales later, explicitly evoking the Fall in a beast fable nominally about chickens. (See VII 3157–71, 3230–66, 3320–21). In that tale, a proud rooster, badly advised by his favorite hen, relaxes his guard and is carried off in the jaws of a tempter-fox determined to have him for supper—a mock-tragic "fall" that almost costs him his life. At the end of this tale, in order not to disappoint those who insist on "doctrine" (lessons) in literature, Chaucer offers two brief morals: "Keep your mouth shut!"/"Keep your eyes open!" But, as anyone who has read the tale knows, his investment as a poet lies in everything that has gone before—some six hundred lines of sophisticated comic verse, inflating a brief animal fable into something so grandly human and so grandly absurd (these are chickens after all) that only a dull Jack could wish for lessons as simple as these. Chaucer uses the tale to pass in review our most cherished ways of assuring ourselves we matter in the universe—that is, the images we project, the stories we tell (including the story of the Fall), the philosophic questions we raise, the lofty position we claim as our own—relying on the beast-fable genre to divorce all these from their usual human context. Even the sovereign dignity we derive from our belief in "free will" gets put into play, since the rooster's enigmatic dream of a "fall" into a fox's mouth seems destined to come true.

CHAPTER VI

1. Jill Mann, "Chaucerian Themes and Style in the *Franklin's Tale*," in *Medieval Literature: Chaucer and the Alliterative Tradition*, pt. 1 of New Pelican Guide to English Literature, ed. Boris Ford, 9 vols. (Harmondsworth: Penguin Books, 1982), 1: 133–53; Helen Cooper, *Oxford Guides to Chaucer: The Canterbury Tales* (Oxford: Oxford University Press, 1989), pp. 230–45. The "goodman of Paris" (Le Ménagier de Paris), writing (ca. 1392) to instruct his young wife in the nature of marriage, describes the love that should unite a married couple so: "And all their special pleasure, their chief desire and their perfect joy is to do pleasure and obedience one to the other, if they love one another." The fact that mutual obedience in marriage seems to him neither fantastical, wicked, nor darkly humorous, is enough to dismiss those readings of the tale that declare *any* sympathy for its premises romantic and "nonmedieval." I quote Eileen Power's translation in her *Medieval People*, 10th ed. (New York: Barnes and Noble, 1963), p. 105; she offers an informed and sympathetic introduction to the French book.

2. Erwin Panofsky, *Studies in Iconology: Humanistic Themes in the Art of the Renaissance* (Oxford, 1939; repr., New York: Harper and Row, 1972). Panofsky alludes to these later kinds of painting (independent landscape and *nature morte*) in setting out a three-part analysis of how we come to understand the sense of a work of art: (1) a *pre-iconographic* recognition of primary or natural subject matter (recognizing an apple as an apple, a hill as a hill); (2) an *iconographic* recognition of secondary or conventional subject matter—images, stories, allegories, generally text-based, which must be learned and correctly identified; and (3) an analysis of "intrinsic meaning or content," which he elsewhere calls *iconological*, and which finds in the artifact "those underlying principles which reveal the basic attitude of a nation, a period, a class, a religious or philosophical persuasion—unconsciously qualified by one personality and condensed into one work" (pp. 3–17; I quote from p. 7). Panofsky believed that in European landscape painting, still-life and genre, "the whole sphere of secondary or conventional subject matter is eliminated" (p. 8). For problems with this leap to the third kind of analysis, see Jean Arrouye, "Archéologie de l'iconologie," in *Pour un temps: Erwin Panofsky*, ed. Jacques Bonnet (Paris: Centre Georges Pompidou, 1983), pp. 71–83, esp. 73–74.

3. Paris, Bibl. Natl. MS fr. 1586, a sumptuous manuscript containing the complete literary works of Guillaume de Machaut, made ca. 1350, may offer (on fol. 103) an early precursor. It illustrates the enchanted garden of *Le dit du lion* as a kind of forest alive with animals and birds, thus providing (in the judgment of François Avril) "one of the oldest independent landscapes in European painting." But this picture too is linked to literature, and would not have been painted without that (pre)text. Avril publishes it in color in his *Manuscript Painting at the Court of France: The Fourteenth Century, 1310–1380* (New York: George Braziller, 1978), pl. 26; see pp. 36, 84, 90 for details. See Reindert L. Falkenburg, *Joachim Patinir: Landscape as an Image of the Pilgrimage of Life*, trans. Michael Hoyle, Oculi 2 (Amsterdam and Philadelphia: J. Benjamins, 1988), for the claim that Patinir (ca. 1485–1524) created the first "autonomous landscapes."

4. In Arthurian literature above all: e.g., the fierce penitential landscape Gawain travels through in his Advent quest for the Green Castle, in Fitt II of *Sir Gawain and the Green Knight*.

5. See "The Ideal Landscape," chap. 10 in Ernst Robert Curtius, *European Litera-*

ture and the Latin Middle Ages, trans. Willard R. Trask (New York: Bollingen Foundation and Pantheon Books, 1953).

6. "The Crucial Passages in Five of the *Canterbury Tales:* A Study in Irony and Symbol," *Journal of English and Germanic Philology* 52 (1953): 294–311; little more than two pages (295–97) are devoted to *The Franklin's Tale*, but they are remarkable in their insight.

7. I am grateful to Professor Ellin Kelly not only for this photo, but for sharing with me her firsthand knowledge of the site. *The Riverside Chaucer*, p. 897 (n801), contains relevant bibliography, and notes that "the nearest high shore is at Concarneau, 35 km. away." Chaucer may have simply taken the name Pedmark from a source—written or oral—and invented the rest, or he may have conflated some personal knowledge of that site with other parts of the Finistère coast, where cliffs and rocks meet the sea much as they do in his description of the place: see, e.g., Michel Renouard and Hervé Champollion, *Bretagne* (Rennes: Ouest France, 1984), pp. 64–65 (which shows a modern ship wrecked against rocks), 68–69 (with its solitary figure standing high, overlooking the sea), and 70, 72–73, 77, 78 (all in handsome color). Bernard Henry and Marianne Henry, *Villages de Bretagne* (Paris: Rivages, 1985), includes a view, in color, pp. 84–85, looking down upon the Penmarc'h and Saint-Guénolé; it is taken from the lantern of the present lighthouse (p. 87), there being no "bank on heigh" available (then or now). Michel Renouard, *Nouveau guide de Bretagne* (Rennes: Ouest France, 1982), pp. 226–27, offers a useful description of the town; his color plate, pp. 40–41, (not of Penmarc'h) again offers something much closer to the landscape of Chaucer's poem.

8. The rocks may draw something of their symbolism from a tradition that declared this world a tempestuous "sea of fortune," with Fortune's House set on a rocky island in its midst; Chaucer knew versions of that tradition from (*inter alia*) Boethius's *Consolation of Philosophy*, Alain de Lille's *Anticlaudianus*, Jean de Meun's continuation of the *Roman de la Rose*, and Guillaume de Deguileville's *Pelerinage de la vie humaine*. I have written on the tradition at some length, with pictorial evidence, in my *Chaucer and the Imagery of Narrative: The First Five Canterbury Tales* (Stanford, CA: Stanford University Press, 1984), pp. 325–33. See Guillaume de Lorris and Jean de Meun, *The Romance of the Rose*, trans. Charles Dahlberg (Princeton, NJ: Princeton University Press, 1971), pp. 118–22 (ll. 5921–6174), for the relevant passage, and fig. 30 for an illustration; John V. Fleming, *The "Roman de la Rose": A Study in Allegory and Iconography* (Princeton, NJ: Princeton University Press, 1969), fig. 31, publishes another. But I do not think this especially relevant: in *The Franklin's Tale* the rocks must be seen as no more than rocks, if we are to assess the changing meanings Dorigen attributes to them.

9. See Derek Pearsall and Elizabeth Salter, *Landscapes and Seasons of the Medieval World* (Toronto: University of Toronto Press, 1973), esp. chap. 4 ("The Enclosed Garden"). Their citations of Chrétien de Troyes' *Cligès* and Boccaccio's *Decameron* pp. 76 and 82, are particularly apposite here.

10. See Teresa McLean, *Medieval English Gardens* (New York: Viking Press, 1980), pp. 120–27, on this double heritage of the medieval love garden. In her judgment, the *hortus conclusus* of the Song of Songs ultimately "overshadowed its archetypal partner, the Garden of Eden, and became the dominant image of Paradise and Love. . . . It was an earthly garden as well as a heavenly one and, like Eden, was interpreted both representatively and allegorically, as an image of human and of divine love" (p. 121). Paul F. Watson, *The Garden of Love in Tuscan Art of the Early*

Renaissance (Philadelphia: Art Alliance Press, 1979), is useful, esp. chapter 6, on the characteristic architecture and activities of the garden. Marilyn Stokstad and Jerry Stannard, *Gardens of the Middle Ages* (Lawrence, KS: Spencer Museum of Art, 1983), offer many images. John Harvey, *Mediaeval Gardens* (Beaverton, OR: Timber Press, 1981), surveys changing ideas of the garden from classical times through the high Middle Ages. But especially recommended is *Medieval Gardens*, intro. Elisabeth Blair MacDougall (Washington, DC: Dumbarton Oaks, 1986), a collection rich in learning and intellectual surmise: the essays by Paul Meyvaert, Anne Hagopian van Buren, Marilyn Stokstad, John V. Fleming, Derek Pearsall, and Brian E. Daley are of particular relevance here. For illuminations showing Eden as a walled garden with a turfed bench and/or with a fountain, see, e.g., Millard Meiss, *French Painting in the Time of Jean de Berry: The Boucicaut Master* (New York: Phaidon, 1968), fig. 380 and figs. 379, 381 respectively. For a French translation of the Song of Songs with the bride and bridegroom shown as medieval lovers strolling in an elegant walled garden, see London, Brit. Lib. MS Royal 15.D.III, fol. 297v.

11. I quote from *The Travels of Marco Polo* (New York: Orion Press, n.d.), pp. 48–50, with illustrations from a fourteenth-century manuscript For the equivalent material in *Mandeville's Travels*, ed. M. C. Seymour (Oxford: Clarendon Press, 1967), see pp. 200–202.

12. As is often the case in fourteenth-century manuscripts of the *Roman*, once the walled garden has been depicted, it may or may not reappear in illustrations of the action that takes place within it; for a picture from this same manuscript that shows the garden walls, see Otto Pächt and J. J. G. Alexander, *Illuminated Manuscripts in the Bodleian Library Oxford* , 3 vols. (Oxford: Clarendon Press, 1966–73), vol. 1, pl. 47, fig. 619a; cf. fig. 612. Bryan Holme, *Medieval Pageant* (London: Thames and Hudson, 1987), pp. 64–65, publishes (in color) two late fifteenth-century Flemish illustrations to the poem that show dancing and music making within the garden walls proper; John V. Fleming, "The Garden of the *Roman de la Rose*: Vision of Landscape or Landscape of Vision?" in *Medieval Gardens*, intro. MacDougall, reproduces one of these (Paris, Bibl. Natl. MS fr. 19153, fol. 7) in black-and-white, and includes a valuable discussion of the geometry (square vs. round) of the poem's garden; see also his fig. 2. Figure 12 of the present chapter is also relevant.

13. Emphatically established in *The Franklin's Tale* by ll. 849, 897, 900, 905, 988, 1015.

14. From the *Collationes* of Cassian of Marseilles, "Of Mortification," spoken by the abbot Abraham in response to Cassian's confession that he was homesick for all the pleasures of life that he had left behind; trans. by Helen Waddell, *The Desert Fathers* (1936; repr., Ann Arbor: University of Michigan Press, 1957), p. 160.

15. In Chaucer's *Knight's Tale*, Emily's walled garden *adjoins* the knights' prison tower, creating a comparable iconographic setting. There too an apparently binary opposition (life's possibilities, imagined at two extremes) first reverses its values, and then reveals at its core a profound unity. See my analysis of this setting in *Chaucer and the Imagery of Narrative*, chap. 3.

16. The full painting, of which Figure VI.4 is only a tiny detail, is reproduced in color, p. 14 (fig. 2), in Walter Prevenier and Wim Blockmans, *The Burgundian Netherlands*, trans. Peter King and Yvette Mead (Cambridge: Cambridge University Press, 1986).

17. J. Burke Severs, "Chaucer's Clerks," in *Chaucer and Middle English Studies in Honour of Rossell Hope Robbins*, ed. Beryl Rowland (London: Allen and Unwin, 1974),

pp. 146–47, notes "two well-known facts concerning the University of Orléans" in Chaucer's time: that its curriculum was entirely devoted to law, both canon and civil; and that it was "a hotbed of astrological and magical studies, not formally, but informally." He quotes a 1396 French text that refers to this double reputation, honourable for law, scandalous for "nigromancie" (the devil finds his disciples there).

18. Figure VI.5: from an encyclopedia, *Omne Bonum*. A related miniature, with two devils, is reproduced in color by Francis King, *Magic: The Western Tradition*, Art and Cosmos Series (New York: Avon, 1975), fig. 16.

19. See Laura Hibbard Loomis, "Secular Dramatics in the Royal Palace, Paris, 1378, 1389, and Chaucer's 'Tregetoures,'" *Speculum* 33 (1958): 242–55; she prints the prose description of the feast on p. 246 (and on pp. 249–50 Froissart's account of a 1389 *entrémes,* intended to stage the siege (or fall) of Troy, that was abruptly canceled by royal command due to dangerous overcrowding of the hall). Avril, *Manuscript Painting at the Court of France*, pl. 34, publishes the picture in color (commentary, p. 107); as does Charles Sterling, *La peinture médièvale à Paris, 1300–1500*, 2 vols. (Paris: Bibliothèque des Arts, 1987–90), 1: 247 (commentary and other illuminations from the manuscript, pp. 245–49).

20. The 1378 account tells us that the pageant structures were moved about by men concealed within them, and the 1389 account specifies the use of hidden wheels. See Loomis, pp. 244, 250.

21. Loomis, "Secular Dramatics in the Royal Palace," p. 244, describes some possible ways in which Chaucer might have heard of the 1378 feast, and on p. 247 does the same for that of 1389.

22. Ibid., p. 244.

23. William Tydeman, *The Theatre in the Middle Ages* (Cambridge: Cambridge University Press, 1978), p. 71 ff., discusses other medieval and early-Renaissance occasions graced with spectacular effects, including, for example, the coronation banquet of Martin I of Aragon in Saragosa in 1399.

24. See Merriam Sherwood, "Magic and Mechanics in Medieval Fiction," *Studies in Philology* 44 (1947): 567–92. The gifts brought to King Cambyuskan in *The Squire's Tale*—a brass horse, a glass mirror, a golden ring, and a naked sword, each of which has "magic" properties—deserve mention here. (They serve, moreover, as a prelude to the Franklin's treatment of magic, for his tale both succeeds and in a sense completes the Squire's). The gifts excite much speculation, including the following comment concerning the horse of brass: "it is rather lyk / An apparence ymaad by som magyk, / As jogelours pleyen at thise feestes grete" (217–19). But there too Chaucer refuses to settle for so easy an explanation, dismissing it in lines 220–24 (together with other rumors and guesses) as typical of "lewed peple" attempting to understand matters beyond them. Helen Cooper, "Magic That Does Not Work," *Medievalia et Humanistica*, n.s., 7 (1976): 131–46, writes interestingly about magic in medieval romances, including *The Franklin's Tale* (on p. 141).

25. For a convenient facsimile and translation of the whole book, see *The Sketchbook of Villard de Honnecourt*, ed. Theodore Bowie (Bloomington: Indiana University Press, 1959); the page before us appears there as pl. 59. It shows in addition (top row, not reproduced here), "How to make a saw operate itself; How to make a crossbow which never misses," and (to the right, in our detail), "How to make the most powerful engine for lifting weights."

26. See Naomi Miller, "Paradise Regained: Medieval Garden Fountains," pp. 143–44n23, in *Medieval Gardens*, intro. MacDougall, for a basic bibliography.

27. Anthony Luengo, "Magic and Illusion in *The Franklin's Tale*," *Journal of English and Germanic Philology* 77 (1978): 1–16; I quote from pp. 1, 4, 7, 9, 16.

28. As will soon be clear, I think that this blurring of several kinds of "magic" into a single category is essential to the tale and its issues, urgent and interesting in its own right. I don't think it's meant to characterize the Franklin as ignorant, provincial, or confused. A good deal of modern criticism to the contrary, I suspect the poet would have acknowledged a deep kinship with the Franklin—the pilgrim whose social class and aspirations, temperament, courtesy, and savoir faire seem most to resemble what the life records (and other poems) suggest were Chaucer's own. Chaucer does not offer his Franklin as a pattern of Christian perfection—the portrait is full of light satiric touches—but neither does he present him as his (or our) moral and intellectual inferior. The Franklin is a great "housholdere"—a man of property, with responsibilities in the world—and he fills that role in ways that bring to Chaucer's mind St. Julian, patron saint of hospitality, as well as Epicurus, the Roman philosopher who taught that pleasure is the highest human good. I think Chaucer would have been amused at how austerely certain modern critics judge the Franklin, all the while living (as Chaucer did, and as most of us do) as amply as we can. Chaucer found the more innocent forms of hypocrisy endlessly diverting, but he did not write from out of them.

29. Mary Flowers Braswell, "The Magic of Machinery: A Context for Chaucer's *Franklin's Tale*," *Mosaic* 18 (1985): 101–10.

30. Ibid., p. 101.

31. Ibid., p. 105.

32. Ibid., pp. 102–3.

33. Ibid., p. 108.

34. The lost original is thought to have been by Jan van Eyck. The present painting is reproduced in color as fig. 256 (p. 292) in Prevenier and Blockmans, *Burgundian Netherlands*, and as fig. 78 in Elisabeth Dhanens, *Hubert and Jan van Eyck* (New York: Alpine Fine Arts Collection, 1980). On it, see Anne Hagopian van Buren, "Un jardin d'amour au parc d'Hesdin, et le role de Jan van Eyck dans une commande ducale," *Revue du Louvre* (1985). Van Buren's exhaustive study of the Hesdin records (which extend from 1288 to 1536), soon to issue in a book, will significantly extend and secure our knowledge of the park's history.

35. Braswell, "Magic of Machinery," p. 103; for a fuller account, translated from a 1433 record of refurbishings, see Richard Vaughan, *Philip the Good: The Apogee of Burgundy* (Harlow: Longmans, 1970), pp. 138–39.

36. Anne Hagopian van Buren, "The Model Roll of the Golden Fleece," *Art Bulletin* 61 (1979): 359–76; I quote from p. 372.

37. Quoted by Van Buren, "Model Roll," p. 370. For the whole preface (and a more recent text, quoted here) see *The Prologues and Epilogues of William Caxton*, ed. W. J. B. Crotch, EETS, o.s. 176 (London: Oxford University Press, 1928), pp. 33–34. Van Buren reconstructs what these paintings might have been like.

38. The catalog of delights reads so in Machaut's French: "Et les merveilles, les deduis, / Les ars, les engins, les conduis, / Les esbas, les estranges choses." For both text and translation (here from pp. 210–13), and an authoritative study of the poem's tradition—"[it] is probably the most important French love poem of the fourteenth century, and it may also be the best" (p. 32)—see Guillaume de Machaut, *"Le jugement du roy de Behaigne" and "Remede de Fortune,"* ed. James I. Wimsatt and William W. Kibler, Chaucer Library (Athens: University of Georgia Press, 1988). Their color

frontispiece reproduces an illumination showing the poet within the walled park of Hesdin, writing a complaint against Fortune and her wheel.

39. Valerie I. J. Flint, *The Rise of Magic in Early Medieval Europe* (Princeton, NJ: Princeton University Press, 1991), studies the Church's accommodation of practices originally condemned as magical.

40. Richard Kieckhefer, *Magic in the Middle Ages* (Cambridge: Cambridge University Press, 1989), pp. 16–17. There is a most interesting discussion of the several kinds of magic in *The Chess of Love*, trans. Joan Morton Jones (Ph.D. diss., University of Nebraska, 1968), a late fourteenth-century or early fifteenth-century commentary on *Les echecs amoureuse*, pp. 288–304; it deserves to be better known, and richly confirms the view that magic must be taken seriously in the study of medieval culture. (The poem and its commentary still await publication in the original French.)

41. Kieckhefer, *Magic in the Middle Ages*, pp. 101–2 and passim ("the allure of machines combined with the mystery of the unexplained," p. 107). On the blurring of categories see also van Buren, "Reality and Literary Romance," in *Medieval Gardens*, intro. MacDougall, pp. 128–29, 132–33. Compare this contemporary account of a great Passion play staged in Valenciennes in 1547: "The machines (*secrets*) of the Paradise and of Hell were absolutely prodigious and could be taken by the populace for magic" (there follows a long list of machines and wonderful actions), in A. M. Nagler, *A Source Book in Theatrical History* (New York: Dover Publications, 1952), pp. 47–48.

42. Loomis, "Secular Dramatics," p. 243.

43. Figure VI.9 is reproduced in color by Avril, *Manuscript Painting*, pl. 24.

44. Braswell, "Magic of Machinery," p. 106.

45. The *Filocolo* version imagines *real* magic—magic we accept within terms of the story as genuine and successful. Theban, the magician, travels all over the world, by magical means and with magical speed, to gather what is necessary to make a garden bloom in January. It is not undercut with reference to easier, less mysterious arts (banquet entertainments, stage devices, automata), nor is its setting limited to a study full of books.

46. For a late but powerful expression of this same phenomenon, see the engraving Gustave Doré made as frontispiece to his edition of *Don Quixote*. The Don sits in a chair with books stacked or thrown all about him, waving a sword in one hand and reading from a favorite romance in the other; the air is full of his literary imaginings—knights, horses, goblins, damsels in distress—figures from books who are as real to him (that is his problem) as life itself. It can be seen, e.g., in *Gustave Doré: Das graphische Werk*, 2 vols., ed. Gabriele Forberg (Munich: Rogner und Bernhard, 1975), 1: 454.

47. Two critics have touched briefly on such a reading before me: Samuel Schuman, "Man, Magician, Poet, God: An Image in Medieval, Renaissance, and Modern Literature," *Cithara* 19 (1980): 40–54, who writes about Chaucer (pp. 40–43), Shakespeare, and Nabokov; and Derek Pearsall, *The Canterbury Tales* (London: Allen and Unwin, 1985), p. 154, who describes (in passing) the magic show at Orléans as "an almost gratuitous exhibition of Chaucer's delight in his own poetic powers."

48. See, e.g., Morton W. Bloomfield and Charles W. Dunn, *The Role of the Poet in Early Societies* (Cambridge: D. S. Brewer, 1989); Marc Drogin, *Biblioclasm: The Mythical Origins, Magic Powers, and Perishability of the Written Word* (Totowa, NJ: Rowan and Littlefield, 1989); and, with reference to the visual arts, Ernst Kris and Otto Kurz,

Legend, Myth, and Magic in the Image of the Artist (New Haven, CT: Yale University Press, 1979), esp. chap. 3 ("The Artist as Magician").

49. Ernest Gallo, *The "Poetria Nova" and Its Sources in Early Rhetorical Doctrine* (The Hague: Mouton, 1971), pp. 20–21 (ll. 120–25). Geoffrey's *praestigiatrix*, rendered by Gallo as "magician," is translated as "conjurer" by Margaret F. Nims, *"Poetria Nova" of Geoffrey of Vinsauf* (Toronto: Pontifical Institute of Mediaeval Studies, 1967), p. 20. *An Early Commentary on the "Poetria Nova" of Geoffrey of Vinsauf*, ed. Marjorie Curry Woods (New York: Garland Publishing, 1985), pp. 28–29, specifies both ("He praises the subtlety of art and says that this ART PLAYS LIKE A MAGICIAN that is, a sorcerer" ["PRESTIGIATRIX, *id est uenefica*"]), continuing, "A *prestigium* is a kind of subtle magic trick [*quedam subtilitas magice artis*] that makes something seem other than what it is, as is said about this art." A related phrase, *praestigiae verborum*, specifically signified the deceptive use of words. That Chaucer knew at least the early part of Geoffrey's treatise can be reasonably presumed: ll. 43–47 furnished him an important stanza near the end of Book I of the *Troilus*, beginning: "For everi wight that hath an hous to founde" (1065 ff.).

50. See my *Chaucer and the Imagery of Narrative*, chapter 1, for an extensive discussion of the role of mental imagery in medieval accounts of how we experience literature; figs. 5–7 are diagrams of brain function. In the picture reproduced above, the three cells have each been assigned two functions, clearly labeled: the first holds "common sense" (receiving impressions from all the senses) and imagination; the second, phantasy and estimation; the third, memory and motion (*motiva*). Also see *Roger Bacon's Letter Concerning the Marvelous Power of Art and of Nature and Concerning the Nullity of Magic*, trans. Tenney L. Davis (Easton, PA: Chemical Publishing, 1923), p. 27.

51. In expression of her nature, *Tristesse* not only tears at her hair and gown, but (in the text) scratches savagely at her face.

52. Figure VI.12 can be seen in color in Harvey, *Mediaeval Gardens*, pl. 3b. For the verbal portrait of "Sorowe" quoted in my text, see *The Romaunt of the Rose*, ll. 301–48 (*Riverside Chaucer*, p. 690).

53. The rocks seem to be Chaucer's own invention, without parallel in either of the Boccaccio versions of the story. See Geoffrey Chaucer, *The Canterbury Tales: Nine Tales and the General Prologue*, ed. V. A. Kolve and Glending Olson (New York: W. W. Norton, 1989), pp. 393–406, for translations of both the *Filocolo* and *Decameron* texts. The longer (*Il Filocolo*) version is the more likely source.

54. On the image in Figure VI.13 (and for a color reproduction) see the Germanisches Nationalmuseum (Nurnberg) guidebook, *Führer durch die Sammlungen*, ed. Peter Strieder (Munich: Prestel-Verlag, 1980), item 134 (described as an allegory of life and death).

55. John Southworth, *The English Medieval Minstrel* (Woodbridge, Suffolk, Eng.: Boydell Press, 1989), esp. chaps. 1 and 2. I quote from pp. 3, 10–11. A. A. Prins, "Notes on the Canterbury Tales (3)," *English Studies* 35 (1954): 158–62, on the meaning of *tregetour*, remains valuable.

CHAPTER VII

1. V. A. Kolve, *Chaucer and the Imagery of Narrative: The First Five Canterbury Tales* (Stanford, CA: Stanford University Press, 1984), chaps. 1 and 2.

2. A view expressed by our presider, Henry Ansgar Kelly, at the Second International Congress of the New Chaucer Society, New Orleans, April 10–13, 1980.

3. The most interesting studies include (in the journals) Donald R. Howard, "The Conclusion of the Marriage Group: Chaucer and the Human Condition," *Modern Philology* 57 (1960): 223–32; Russell A. Peck, "The Ideas of 'Entente' and Translation in Chaucer's *Second Nun's Tale*," *Annuale Mediaevale* 8 (1967): 17–37; Paul M. Clogan, "The Figural Style and Meaning of the *Second Nun's Tale*," *Medievalia et Humanistica*, n.s., 3 (1972): 213–40; Paul E. Beichner, "Confrontation, Contempt of Court, and Chaucer's Cecilia," *ChauR* 8 (1974): 198–204; Carolyn P. Collette, "A Closer Look at Seinte Cecile's Special Vision," *ChauR* 10 (1976): 337–49; John C. Hirsch, "The Politics of Spirituality: The Second Nun and the Manciple," *ChauR* 12 (1977): 129–46; Marc D. Glasser, "Marriage and the *Second Nun's Tale*," *Tennessee Studies in Literature* 23 (1978): 1–14; and see the articles listed in notes 5 and 6 below. Substantial discussion of the tale is much rarer in critical books on Chaucer, but important exceptions include Mary Giffin, *Studies on Chaucer and His Audience* (Hull, Quebec: Editions L'Eclair, 1956), pp. 29–48; Trevor Whittock, *A Reading of the Canterbury Tales* (Cambridge: Cambridge University Press, 1968), pp. 251–61; Alfred David, *The Strumpet Muse: Art and Morals in Chaucer's Poetry* (Bloomington: Indiana University Press, 1976), pp. 232–34, 236; Donald R. Howard, *The Idea of the Canterbury Tales* (Berkeley: University of California Press, 1976), pp. 288–92, 304.

4. It can most easily be read in Jacobus de Voragine, *The Golden Legend: Readings on the Saints*, trans. William Granger Ryan, 2 vols. (Princeton, NJ: Princeton University Press, 1993), 2: 318–23, or in *Sources and Analogues of the Canterbury Tales*, 2 vols., ed. Robert M. Correale and Mary Hamel (Cambridge: D. S. Brewer, 2002, 2005), 1: 491–527.

5. See G. H. Gerould, "The Second Nun's Prologue and Tale," in W. F. Bryan and Germaine Dempster, eds., *Sources and Analogues of Chaucer's Canterbury Tales* (London: Routledge and Kegan Paul, 1941; repr., 1958), pp. 664–84. The most recent such study is by Sherry L. Reames, "The Sources of Chaucer's *Second Nun's Tale*," *Modern Philology* 76 (1978–79): 111–35. She offers a critical interpretation of the tradition as a whole in "The Cecilia Legend as Chaucer Inherited It and Retold It: The Disappearance of an Augustinian Ideal," *Speculum* 55 (1980): 38–57. Bryan and Dempster have now been superceded by Reames' chapter on the tale in *Sources and Analogues*, ed. Correale and Hamel, 1: 491–527, which includes texts of the Latin sources and full translations.

6. Joseph E. Grennen's "St. Cecilia's Chemical Wedding: The Unity of the *Canterbury Tales*, Fragment VIII," *Journal of English and Germanic Philology* 65 (1966): 466–81; and Bruce A. Rosenberg's "Contrary Tales of the Second Nun and the Canon's Yeoman," *ChauR* 2 (1968): 278–91.

7. Ibid., p. 481, and pp. 278–79, respectively.

8. Brit. Lib. MS Royal 2 B. vii, fol. 278, likewise shows St. Cecilia kneeling upon the ground; it may be seen in facsimile in *Queen Mary's Psalter*, ed. Sir George Warner (London: British Museum, 1912), pl. 272.

9. On this tradition see Albert P. de Mirimonde, *Sainte-Cécile: Metamorphoses d'un thème musical* (Geneva: Minkoff, 1974), and his bibliography, p. 11.

10. On this manuscript, a Breviary painted between 1413 and 1419 for Jean sans Peur of Burgundy or for his wife, Margaret of Bavaria, see Millard Meiss, *French Painting in the Time of Jean de Berry: The Limbourgs and Their Contemporaries*, 2 vols. (London: Thames and Hudson, 1974), 1: 325–28. The posture of St. Cecilia praying before an open book is formally related to that of the Virgin Mary in many versions of the Annunciation.

11. John H. Fisher, ed., *The Complete Poetry and Prose of Geoffrey Chaucer* (New York: Holt, Rinehart, and Winston, 1977), p. 319.

12. See the plan of the church as published, for instance, by Mary Sharp, *A Guide to the Churches of Rome* (Philadelphia: Chilton Books, 1966), p. 64 (room 4: the Calidarium); or by Guglielmo Matthiae, *S. Cecilia*, in *Le Chiese de Roma Illustrate*, vol. 113 (Rome: Marietti, 1970), figs. 2, 3, and end plan (room 9).

13. Figures VII.7 and 8: a painting by an unknown Tuscan master, now in the Uffizi Gallery, originally in the Church of St. Cecilia in Florence. "The church was razed in 1367 to permit enlargement of the Piazza dei Priori and was soon rebuilt near the Piazza Signoria. If the construction was completed before Chaucer came to Florence in 1373, it was a very new edifice in a central location and might have attracted such a visitor. It was demolished in the late eighteenth century." See Geoffrey Chaucer, *The Tales of Canterbury, Complete*, ed. Robert A. Pratt (Boston: Houghton Mifflin, 1974), p. 442, with a reproduction of the painting opposite.

14. Millard Meiss and Elisabeth H. Beatson, eds., *The Belles Heures of Jean, Duke of Berry* (New York: George Braziller, 1974), reproduce in facsimile the major illuminated pages.

15. James Cleugh, *Love Locked Out: A Survey of Love License and Restriction in the Middle Ages* (London: Blond, 1963; repr., Spring Books, 1970). Chap. 8 ("Bathers") offers a wealth of information, learned in its resources but devoid of annotation. See also Vern Bullough and Bonnie Bullough, *Prostitution: An Illustrated Social History* (New York: Crown, 1978), pp. 122–23, 314 (n68), and the illustrations on pp. 113, 130. Urban Tigner Holmes, Jr., *Daily Living in the Twelfth Century* (Madison: University of Wisconsin Press, 1952; repr., 1962), pp. 166, 301 (n34) discusses domestic bathing arrangements. Lynn Thorndike, "Sanitation, Baths, and Street-Cleaning in the Middle Ages and Renaissance," *Speculum* 3 (1928): 197–98, publishes statistics demonstrating "the widespread existence of public baths in mediaeval towns."

16. Compare the fine illumination in Holmes, *Daily Living in the Twelfth Century*, facing p. 115. On baths in early literature see C. A. Kauffmann, *The Baths of Pozzuoli: A Study of the Medieval Illuminations of Peter of Eboli's Poem* (Oxford: Cassirer, 1959), pp. 1–2, for many references. Propertius, *Elegies*, I.xi.27–30, is especially interesting: the poet worries about his beloved Cynthia, vacationing at Baiae amid its famous baths: "Baiae, / where many a love affair will founder / and many a respectable girl / has come to grief, / that den of vice / that casts a slur on love itself / I HATE the place," from *The Poems of Propertius*, trans. John Warden, Library of the Liberal Arts (Indianapolis: Bobbs-Merrill, 1972), p. 24. The bath offered a common metaphor for the experience of love's passion: in Chrétien de Troyes' *Cligès*, for instance, the damsel Soredamors, once scornful of love, becomes its victim in these terms: "Amors li a chaufé un baing / Qui molt l'eschaufe et molt li nuist" (Love has heated for her a bath which heats her and troubles her greatly), ed. Alexandre Micha, CFMA (Paris: Champion, 1965), p. 15 (ll. 464–65). So too in the *Roman de la Rose*, ll. 12710ff., where La Vielle instructs Bel Acueill in what is to come ("et vos baignerez en l'estuve / ou Venus les dames estuve," etc.), ed. Félix Lecoy, CFMA, 3 vols. (Paris: Champion, 1965–70), ll. 12721–22. Robbins translates the full passage so:

> Well I know
> That late or soon, whenever it may be,
> You'll pass amidst the flame that scorches all—
> You'll plunge into the bath where Venus makes
> All women bathe. I know you'll feel her brand.

Now I advise that you prepare yourself
By listening to the teaching that I'll give
Before you take that bath; it's perilous
For youths to bathe there who have not been taught.

See Guillaume de Lorris and Jean de Meun, *The Romance of the Rose*, trans. Harry W. Robbins (New York: Dutton, 1962), p. 264.

17. For a study of the manuscript, with reproductions of its drawings and etchings, see Johannes Graf Waldburg-Wolfegg, *Das mittelalterliche Hausbuch* (Munich: Prestel-Verlag, 1957). Fols. 18v–19 show another erotic bathhouse scene, this time with several bathers (figs. 20–21). Jane C. Hutchison, *The Master of the Housebook* (New York: Collectors Editions, 1972), provides a catalog of drypoint attributions.

18. On this manuscript (and for a color reproduction of this picture) see Sydney C. Cockerell and John Plummer, *Old Testament Miniatures* (New York: George Braziller, n.d.). It illustrates 2 Kings 11:2–4. In a French Book of Hours, Cambridge, Fitzwilliam Museum MS 74, fol. 97, made ca. 1480, David and Bathsheba are shown in a bath together; two attendants draw curtains around them for privacy. Cf. François Villon's *Grand Testament*, lines 645–48.

19. The scene with Susanna illustrates Daniel 13:15–21. A German tapestry (Marburg, Elizabethkirche) from the first third of the fifteenth century represents the riotous life of the Prodigal Son with a bath scene (he in a tub with a courtesan, a table set with food and drink alongside); see Betty Kurth, *Die deutschen Bildteppiche des Mittelalters*, 3 vols. (Vienna: Schroll, 1926), vol. 3, pl. 233.

20. Although the text concerns the customs and morals of ancient Rome, the illustration is contemporary in its reference; so too is the version in Leipzig, Bibl. de la Ville MS 72, fol. 270, reproduced by Morris Bishop, *The Horizon Book of the Middle Ages* (New York: American Heritage, 1968), p. 201 (see also the illumination on p. 200). Alexandre de Laborde, *Les MSS. à peintures de la Cité de Dieu*, Société des Bibliophiles Français (Paris: Rabir, 1909), pl. 84d, reproduces a page from The Hague, Meermanno-Westreenianum Museum MS 11, fol. 69v, illustrating Augustine, *The City of God*, II.20. Three couples are shown in tubs, others are drinking and eating, and there is a prostitute in bed with a customer, in formal juxtaposition to a scene of courtly Christian ladies spinning at their distaffs.

21. John Gower, *Confessio Amantis*, bk. VIII, 484, for instance, writes of "the bathes and the Stwes" as apparently synonymous: both are closed down by the citizens of Tyre in penitential mourning for their absent prince. *The English Works of John Gower*, ed. G. C. Macaulay, 2 vols., EETS, e.s. 81, 82 (London: Oxford University Press, 1900, 1901), 2: 399.

22. *The Filostrato of Giovanni Boccaccio*, ed. and trans. Nathaniel Edward Griffin and Arthur Beckwith Myrick (Philadelphia, 1929; repr., New York: Octagon, 1978), pp. 248–51: "in certo luogo rimoto ed oscuro"; "in parte segreta" (III, vv. 25, 27).

23. From the *Legenda aurea* of Jacobus de Voragine, in Bryan and Dempster, eds., *Sources and Analogues*, p. 676. The full line reads, "Que quasi in loco frigido mansit, nec modicum saltem sudoris persensit." Compare the text of the *Passio*, ed. Mombritius, ibid., p. 684: "Quasi in loco frigido illibata perstitit sanitate: ita ut nec una pars membrorum eius saltem sudoris signo labasset." Jehan de Vignay's French translation of the *Golden Legend* follows Jacobus closely: "Et elle estoit la tout ainsi come en vng froit lieu, & ne sentit oncques vng peu de sueur." In F. J. Furnivall, ed., *Originals and Analogues of Some of Chaucer's Canterbury Tales*, Chaucer Society, 2nd. ser., nos. 7, 10, 15, 20, 22 (London, 1872–88), p. 205. Caxton's translation of the

Golden Legend reads, "a brennyng bayne which hir semed was a place colde & wel attemperyd"; ibid., pp. 217–19. In Bokenham's version Cecilia is "as myry / As she had ben in an herbere cold & grene, / For of swete no drope on hyr was sene." Osbern Bokenham, *Legendys of Hooly Wummen*, ed. Mary S. Serjeantson, EETS, o.s. 206 (London, Oxford University Press, 1938), p. 223. C. Horstmann, *Altenglische Legenden: Neue Folge* (Heilbronn: Gebr. Henninger, 1881), p. 164, records an aberrant version of the legend in which Cecilia's whole house is burned, with her inside it: "Bot all that here to her was sene / Als scho in ane erber had bene / Clene and faire with flores bright." For an Old English account of Cecilia's death, see *Ælfric's Lives of the Saints*, ed. W. W. Skeat, EETS, o.s. 94, 114 (London, 1890, 1901, repr. 1966), p. 376. One early version (thirteenth century) varies from all these in making no mention of Cecilia's cool comfort in the bath; in a weird addition of its own it describes her as playing with the waves in her bath as she preaches and converts more than four hundred: "Me caste hire In the sethende water ther-Inne al nyght heo beth / the lengore ther-Inne heo was the verrere heo was hire deth. / With the walmes heo sat & pleide & prechede of godes grace. / Mothan four hondred men bicome ther cristen In the place." Furnivall, ed., *Originals and Analogues*, p. 218.

24. Figure VII.16 is reproduced in color by Sergio Samek-Ludovici and Nino Ravenna, *Dante's Divine Comedy*, trans. Peter J. Tallon (New York: Crescent Books, 1979), p. 80. On this manuscript see Peter Brieger, Millard Meiss, and Charles S. Singleton, *Illuminated Manuscripts of the Divine Comedy*, 2 vols. (Princeton, NJ: Princeton University Press, 1969), 1: 332–39, and for pictures from other manuscripts illustrating these cantos, 2: 399–402. This version of the purgatorial punishment of lechery is consonant with, and no doubt develops from, its traditional punishment in hell. Chaucer quotes St. John on the matter in *The Parson's Tale*: "Seint John seith that avowtiers shullen been in helle, in a stank brennynge of fyr and of brymston—in fyr, for hire lecherye, in brymston, for the stynk of hire ordure" (X 840). Marital sex indulged in for the sake of "amorous love" alone is referred to as "thilke brennynge delit" later in the same discussion (X 942); see also line 209. Paris, Bibl. Natl. MS fr. 19 (a magnificent illuminated *Cité de Dieu*, ca. 1473), fol. 211, shows the torments of hell, including a pair of lechers bound together in coital position on a roasting spit, being turned by devils over a bed of red-hot coals. It introduces bk. XXII of Augustine's work. Sodom and Gomorrah had been destroyed for unnatural forms of the vice, a punishment Innocent III explained in his *De miseria*, II.25: "Therefore the Lord rained out of Himself not rain and dew, but brimstone and fire: brimstone for the stench of lust, fire for the heat of passion—a penalty fit for the crime." Lothario dei Segni (Pope Innocent III), *On the Misery of the Human Condition*, ed. Donald R. Howard, trans. Margaret Mary Dietz, Library of Liberal Arts (Indianapolis: Bobbs-Merrill, 1969), p. 51. For a fourteenth-century image of the burning cities (in Vienna, Austrian National Library MS 1191) see Eva Irblich and Gabriel Bise, *The Illuminated Naples Bible*, trans. G. Ivins and D. MacRae (New York: Crescent Books, 1979), pp. 26–27. In the *Apocalypse of Paul* adulterers and fornicators of several sorts are seen in a river of fire; see *The Apocryphal New Testament*, trans. Montague Rhodes James (Oxford: Clarendon Press, 1924, rev. ed., 1953), p. 545. In a realm of punishment less eschatological, a lecherous couple die in a hot bath in Marie de France's *Equitan*; see her *Lais*, ed. Alfred Ewert (Oxford: Blackwell, 1947), pp. 26–34; and for an English version, *Bawdy Tales from the Courts of Medieval France*, trans. Paul Brians (New York: Harper and Row, 1972), pp. 50–56.

25. The Parson at one point apparently praises the possibility of a celibate marriage: "And certes, if that a wyf koude kepen hire al chaast by licence of hir housbonde, so that she yeve nevere noon occasion that he agilte, it were to hire a greet merite" (X 945). But this occurs in his discussion of the chastity possible to widows, for whom the "if" clause is not so difficult and conditional. The "chastity" possible in marriage, his larger subject, always assumes procreation, e.g., "Trewe effect of mariage clenseth fornicacioun and replenysseth hooly chirche of good lynage, for that is the ende of mariage" (line 919, see also line 882). Howard, *The Idea of the Canterbury Tales*, p. 288, sees *The Second Nun's Tale* as "a final tale on the subject of love and marriage," arguing that "it is not about a state of life higher than marriage but about a higher form of marriage itself." His full discussion, pp. 288–92, 304, is relevant; see also p. 247n36, where he partly revises his argument in "The Conclusion of the Marriage Group," cited above. Glasser, "Marriage and the *Second Nun's Tale*," pp. 7–8, offers learned evidence for thinking "the chaste marriage . . . a problematic concern for the Church since the third century"; it was, for instance, officially condemned in the year 600. In Glasser's view, "The [tale's] marriage relationship, which lasts only briefly, is quickly converted into an alliance of the elect." I think Glasser's evidence relevant to our reading of the tale, but would argue (in company with Howard) that this marriage, however odd, remains one of its central terms. I would supplement both with an emphasis upon spiritual procreation as the mode in which Cecilia's marriage at once honors and transcends the ordinary purposes of that institution. Whittock, *Reading of the Canterbury Tales*, in a fine chapter on the legend, briefly discusses Cecilia's fruitfulness in terms of her conversions (pp. 255, 259).

26. The husband-son paradox is paralleled in *The Second Nun's Prologue*'s praise of the Virgin Mary: "Thow Mayde and Mooder, doghter of thy Sone" (l. 36). Robert P. Miller, "Chaucer's Pardoner, the Scriptural Eunuch, and the Pardoner's Tale," *Speculum* 30 (1955): 180–99, gathers together a good deal of patristic commentary on ideas of spiritual multiplication and increase. For an especially important treatment see *"De sancta virginitate,"* trans. John McQuade, S.M., in Augustine, *Treatises on Marriage and Other Subjects*, ed. Roy J. Deferrari, Fathers of the Church: a new translation (New York: Fathers of the Church, Inc., 1955), vol. 27.

27. Glasser, "Marriage and the *Second Nun's Tale*," pp. 10–11, carefully notes these rhetorical shifts in tone.

28. Dante, *Purgatorio*, trans. Charles S. Singleton, Bollingen Series 80 (Princeton, NJ: Princeton University Press, 1973), pp. 238–39.

29. See, e.g., Meiss and Beatson, *Belles Heures of Jean, Duke of Berry*, p. 262 (reproducing fols. 178, 179) for St. Agnes and St. Agatha, and *Queen Mary's Psalter*, ed. Warner, pl. 313b, for St. Margaret naked in a tub with fire blazing below (London, Brit. Lib. MS Royal 2 B vii, fol. 311).

30. The crime of the three children, like that of SS. Valerian, Tiburce, and Cecilia, lay in their refusal to worship an idol; but in, for instance, W. Nelson Francis, ed., *The Book of Vices and Virtues*, EETS, o.s. 217 (London: Oxford University Press, 1942), pp. 226–27, their example is used to prove that

> who-so wole kepe hym from brennynge, schal do awey al thing that quekeneth the fier of lecherie bi abstinences and scharpenesse of penaunces y-do to the body. Wher-of holi writ seithe that the children that weren norisched with grete boistreous metes and ne wolde not vse delicious metes were saued in the ouene brennyng of Babiloyne, wher-bi is vnderstonde the synne of lecherie, that is y-queynt bi abstinence and scharpenesse of penaunce.

Honorius of Autun, in a sermon for the feast of the Annunciation, *Speculum ecclesiae* (*P.L.* 172, col. 904 ff.) includes the children in the furnace as a type of the Virgin birth: "By the will of God the flames escaping from the furnace burnt those without and touched not a single hair of those who were within. Moreover they were heard singing in the midst of the fire, and with them the king saw one like to the Son of God. Even so the Holy Spirit impregnated the Holy Virgin with His inner fire, while without He protected her against all concupiscence." On this tradition see Emile Mâle, *The Gothic Image: Religious Art in France of the Thirteenth Century*, trans. Dora Nussey (London, 1913; repr., London: Collins, 1961), p. 149. A ninth-century French sequence, "Buona pulcella fut Eulalia," offers a particularly close parallel to the life of St. Cecilia; St. Eulalia too remains virginal for the love of God, and is thrown into a fire, where she does not burn; see R. M. Ruggieri, *Testi antichi romanzi*, 2 vols. (Modena: Società Tipografica Modenese, 1949), 2: 58–59. On this poem see Peter Dronke, *The Medieval Lyric* (London: Hutchinson, 1968), pp. 39–41.

31. This figural interpretation became a commonplace of medieval devotion, which Chaucer himself rhymes in the Prologue to *The Prioress's Tale:* "O mooder Mayde, O mayde Mooder free! / O bussh unbrent, brennynge in Moyses sighte" (VII 467). The Annunciation sermon by Honorius cited above includes it too: "Herein is a figure of the Holy Virgin; for never burning with the fire of concupiscence she yet received within her the flame of the Holy Spirit" (Mâle, *The Gothic Image*, p. 148). In the later Middle Ages it becomes part of the *Speculum humanae salvationis* and *Biblia pauperum* traditions, which use text and picture in tandem to establish the relationship. For such a picture from a *Speculum* manuscript see Roger Sherman Loomis, *A Mirror of Chaucer's World* (Princeton, NJ: Princeton University Press, 1965), fig. 131. *Illuminated Naples Bible*, p. 41, shows the Old Testament event on its own.

32. Manchester, John Rylands Library MS Lat. 19, picture no. 6 (n.p.), an Apocalypse from the first third of the fourteenth century, offers a powerful image of this torment. Cf. the version in Oxford, Bodley MS Auct. D.4.17, fol. 2 (an English Apocalypse, ca. 1250–60), or that in Cambridge, Fitzwilliam Museum MS 101, fol. 13 (ca. 1490–1500). Jacobus de Voragine, *Golden Legend*, 1: 51, recounts it so: "The Emperor Domitian, hearing of [John's] fame, summoned him to Rome and had him plunged into a caldron of boiling oil outside the gate called the Porta Latina; but the blessed John came out untouched, just as he had avoided corruption of the flesh." In a fifteenth-century collection of sermons known as the *Speculum sacerdotale*, ed. Edward H. Weatherly, EETS, o.s. 200 (1936), p. 153, St. John is put into a brass "tonne full of brennynge oyle," where he preaches the one true God, and "then bi the grace of God that hym defendid he passid oute of the vessel as vnhurtyd with the fyre as he was vnfouled with flescheliche synne." That torment, though he did not die of it, earned him the title of martyr: "And therefore is this feste of hym as though he had suffrid marterdom lyke to other."

33. On the liturgical book from which Figure VII.17 is taken, see Margaret Rickert, *The Reconstructed Carmelite Missal* (London: Faber and Faber, 1952), pl. 23b, and p. 110.

34. Robert P. Miller, *Chaucer: Sources and Backgrounds* (New York: Oxford University Press, 1977), fig. 4 (p. 114), reproduces Huntington Library MS H.M. 3027, fol. 161, which shows the saint fully clothed, kneeling within a fire built upon the ground, as the executioner strikes at her head with a sword. Unlike our Figure VII.17, this clearly offers a variant version of her martyrdom.

35. Rosenberg, "Contrary Tales," p. 281, has adduced this text before me.

36. Grennen, "St. Cecilia's Chemical Wedding," pp. 469–71, provides the essential details. Stanislas Klossowski de Rola, *The Secret Art of Alchemy* (New York: Avon Books, 1973), pp. 10–12, outlines the Great Work with unusual clarity; his book offers as well a vast collection of alchemical illustrations, many of them in color. On the nature and obscurity of alchemical illustrations see E. J. Holmyard, *Alchemy* (Harmondsworth, Eng.: Penguin Books, 1957), pp. 162–64. C. G. Jung, *Psychology and Alchemy*, trans. R. F. C. Hull, 2nd. ed., Bollingen Series 20 (Princeton, NJ: Princeton University Press, 1968), also has many illustrations, among which figs. 134, 167, 226, 227, and 268 will be of particular interest to my reader; pp. 230–32, 412–15 of his text are especially helpful regarding the chemical marriage.

37. Figures VII.18 and 19 are reproduced by Klossowski de Rola, *Secret Art of Alchemy*, figs. 27–28; Figure VII.20 is reproduced in color in the same, fig. 42; see also figs. 37, 38, 41. Chaucer declares *Rosarium philosophorum* to be his source, but as F. N. Robinson's note to line 1428 explains, the passage Chaucer versifies seems to be drawn instead from another treatise by Arnold, *De lapide philosophorum*; the relevant passage can be read in Bryan and Dempster, *Sources and Analogues*, p. 698, in the chapter on the tale prepared by John Webster Spargo.

38. Grennen, "St. Cecilia's Chemical Wedding," pp. 466–67. Jung, *Psychology and Alchemy*, pp. 35, 306–16, explores the contrasting systems at greater length. Grennen notes (pp. 469–70) that "the wedding, also represented as the marriage of Sol and Luna, is especially frequent in pictorial symbolism," though some of the examples he adduces from Jung, in his n6, seem to be in typographical error, while many important ones go unnoted (see my note 36 above).

39. Grennen, "St. Cecilia's Chemical Wedding," p. 471: "The fire under the crucible which makes all possible" is one of the "odd resemblances" and "analogies" between the saint's legend and the science of alchemy that he believes Chaucer would have noted, constituting for both a "basic narrative line, which comes down finally to a 'fixing' of a substance so that it can endure the fire's heat." As I suggest above, the narrative sequence works against such an analogy.

CHAPTER VIII

1. This chapter is an expanded version of my presidential address to the New Chaucer Society, meeting in Los Angeles, July 26–29, 1996, at UCLA, delivered at the J. Paul Getty Museum. I quote from Jill Mann's "Chaucer and Atheism," published in *Studies in the Age of Chaucer* 17 (1995): 11, 14. Seen in the global context, she writes, "feminism looks like a parochial concern. It is not gender but religion that is at the center of the present-day conflicts in Ireland, Yugoslavia, Lebanon, Palestine, Egypt, Algeria. Religion, that is, *matters*, and it matters because it has a political function. And it is because it matters that we should be prepared to evaluate and debate it, rather than treating it as something too personal or too sacred to be discussed" (p. 14).

2. Charles Muscatine, "Chaucer's Religion and the Chaucer Religion," in *Chaucer Traditions: Studies in Honour of Derek Brewer*, ed. Ruth Morse and Barry Windeatt (Cambridge: Cambridge University Press, 1990), p. 250. What Muscatine would deny is not Chaucer's orthodoxy, but "the nature, range, depth, and intensity of his religious feeling itself. It is the latter, his enveloping religiosity, that seems to me to be a late twentieth-century discovery or preoccupation" (ibid.). He rightly

deems Ralph Baldwin's monograph, *The Unity of the Canterbury Tales*, *Anglistica* 5 (1955), the ur-text of readings that allow for such feeling, at least on occasion, on Chaucer's part. And he is right to judge that monograph "remarkable."

3. Psalms 13 and 52, Vulgate numbering; in Hebrew and post-Reformation Bibles, 14 and 53. Since 13 includes most of 52, they are thought to have originated in a single psalm, entering the collection via independent textual traditions.

4. "Quis enim mundum contuens, Deum esse non sentiat?" Hilary of Poitiers, *Tractatus in Psalmos*, *P.L.* 9: 325d.

5. Augustine, *Enarrationes in Psalmos*, XIII 2, *Corpus Christianorum: Series Latina* (Turnholt, Belgium: Brepols, 1956), vol. 38, p. 38: "Nec ipsi enim sacrilegi et detestandi quidam philosophi, qui peruersa et falsa de Deo sentiunt, ausi sunt dicere: Non es Deus. Ideo ergo dixit in corde suo, quia hoc nemo audet dicere, etiam si ausus fuerit cogitare." I quote the translation by Dame Scholastica Hebgin and Dame Felicitas Corrigan, *St. Augustine on the Psalms*, in *Ancient Christian Writers: The Works of the Fathers in Translation*, ed. Johannes Quasten and Walter J. Burghardt, S.J., no. 29 (New York: Newman Press, 1960), 1: 154; only two volumes have been published so far, extending through Psalm 37. In this commentary, Augustine was no doubt thinking of Epicurus and his followers, who taught that the soul dies with the body, that the physical world can be explained by natural causes, and that the gods do not interfere in what happens here on earth. To do so would detract from the perfect bliss they enjoy in intercosmic space, where they live only for themselves. Even philosophers as benighted as this, Augustine reminds us, did not deny the existence of God(s). For a brief explication of Epicurean beliefs, see *The Oxford Classical Dictionary*, ed. N. G. L. Hammond and H. H. Scullard, 2nd ed. (Oxford: Clarendon Press, 1970), pp. 390–92, or *The Encyclopedia of Philosophy*, ed. Paul Edwards, 8 vols. in 4 (New York: Macmillan, 1967; repr. 1972), 3: 2–5. Augustine had written commentaries on the first thirty-two psalms by 392; on the rest by 420 (see Peter Brown, *Augustine of Hippo: A Biography* (Berkeley: University of California Press, 1967), p. 74.

6. Eusebius, *Commentaries on Psalms*, in *Patrologiae cursus completus*, Series Graeca, ed. Jacques-Paul Migne, 162 vols. (Paris: 1857–66), 23: 144, on Psalm 13; col. 143 offers a Latin translation: "Etsi vero, quia omnibus a natura insita est Dei notitia." Eusebius allows for a variety of atheists, including some who say God is only an empty name and does not exist at all, some who reject the true God to fabricate others who do not exist, and some who claim merely that he does not concern himself with earthly matters. Eusebius's emphasis is on hypocrisy and inauthenticity: they confess many Gods with their mouths, but hold no sound belief about God in their heart. The Greek *átheos* can mean "without God" as well as "denying God." Augustine, too, affirmed that the soul by its very nature participates in eternal Truth, reflecting the Trinity in its faculties of memory, understanding, and will. Variations on this idea will become commonplace throughout the medieval centuries.

7. Even in that century, *atheist* served chiefly as a term of abuse, without theological precision. The extensive article on atheism in *Encyclopaedia of Religion and Ethics*, ed. James Hastings et al. (Edinburgh: T. and T. Clark, 1908–26), s.v. *atheism*, 2: 173–90, remains helpful, esp. pp. 176ff. on atheism in England and France: "what was simply neutral materialism in London became often positive atheism in Paris," though markedly so only in the eighteenth century. The *OED* first records *atheist* in 1571, in Golding's dedicatory epistle to Calvin on the Psalms: "The Atheistes which say . . . there is no God." *Atheism* as a noun first occurs in 1587, in a passage defining it instead as

"utter Godlessness." *Theist*, interestingly enough, is not recorded until 1662, and *theism* not until 1678. These constitute a secondary formation, invented to oppose "atheism," not vice versa. Atheism, as Derrida might say, is always already there.

8. See Augustine, *On Free Choice of the Will*, trans. Anna S. Benjamin and L. H. Hackstaff, Library of Liberal Arts (Indianapolis: Bobbs-Merrill, 1964), p. 38; *St. Anselm's "Proslogion" with "A Reply on Behalf of the Fool" by Gaunilo and "The Author's Reply to Gaunilo,"* trans. M. J. Charlesworth (1965; repr., Notre Dame, IN: University of Notre Dame Press, 1979), pp. 116–17; and Thomas Aquinas, *Summa theologiae* Ia.2.1, ed. Thomas Gilby, O.P., Blackfriars trans. (London: Eyre and Spottiswoode, 1964), pp. 63–64.

9. Siger of Brabant, *Die Impossibilia des Siger von Brabant: Eine Philosophische Streitschrift aus dem XIII. Jahrhundert*, ed. Clemens Baeumker, *Beiträge zur Geschichte der Philosophie des Mittelalters*, 2.6 (Münster: Aschendorf, 1898), p. 1.

10. For the other examples, and a brief introduction to the genre—a subspecies of the genus *sophismata*—see Roy J. Pearcy, "Chaucer's 'An Impossible' (*Summoner's Tale* III, 2231)," *Notes and Queries* 14, no. 9 (1967): 322–25.

11. Lucien Febvre, *The Problem of Unbelief in the Sixteenth Century: The Religion of Rabelais*, trans. Beatrice Gottlieb (Cambridge, MA: Harvard University Press, 1982), pp. 336, 353. The pages between, as well as his concluding chapter, "A Century That Wanted to Believe," are of particular relevance.

12. The page is reproduced in color by Millard Meiss, *French Painting in the Time of Jean de Berry: The Late Fourteenth Century and the Patronage of the Duke*, 2 vols. (London: Phaidon, 1967), vol. 2, fig. 78, and discussed in vol. 1: 153–54 and 331–32; on Jacquemart see also pp. 151–52, 169–76, and passim. For the Pucellian model, as evidenced in the *Bréviaire de Jeanne d'Evreux*, see vol. 2, fig. 605; its fool is wilder in mood, more full of mischief.

13. The titles of those lectures will give some idea of their content: (I) "The Fool and His Hunger"; (II) "Typologies of the Psalter Fool"; (III) "The Fool as Killer of Christ"; and (IV) "The Feast of Fools Revisited." I gave them first as the Alexander Lectures at Toronto University in late 1993, and then (with the permission of both sponsors) in revised form as the Clark Lectures at Trinity College, Cambridge, in early 1994. They have been expanded into a book, now nearly complete. The present chapter begins by summarizing some of the material from the first and second of these lectures, though I reserve for the book the full range of idea, evidence and pictorial representation they require. Erotic love as a form of God-denying folly, is however new to the series, and is here addressed for the first time.

14. "Et difficile est ut incurramus in hominem qui dicat in corde suo: Non est Deus." Augustine makes the point over and over: "non multos . . . perpauci sunt . . . sic pauci sunt. . . . uix inuenitur; rarum hominum genus est qui dicant in corde suo." *Enarrationes in Psalmos,* on *Psalm* 52:2, ed. cit., p. 638. The old six-volume Oxford translation of Augustine's commentary on the Psalms was reprinted (in slightly revised and abridged form) in *The Nicene and Post-Nicene Fathers*, 1st series, vol. 8, first published in 1888, reprinted 1974 by Wm. B. Eerdmans (Grand Rapids, MI). Though its prose style is mannered and archaic, it will remain useful until the new translation (see note 5 above) is completed. (It translates Psalm 13, pp. 46–47, and Psalm 52, pp. 202–5, numbering them 14 and 53; see p. 202 for the passage under discussion.) Michael P. Kuczynski, *Prophetic Song: The Psalms as Moral Discourse in Late Medieval England* (Philadelphia: University of Pennsylvania Press, 1995), offers a useful study of the psalter's importance to medieval culture at large, and to late medieval English

writing in particular; Part I includes a brief history of psalm interpretation, with p. 21 demonstrating Augustine's prominence within this tradition, an importance Kuczynski deems "impossible to overstate."

15. [Augustine:] "qui putat Deo placere facta mala, non eum putat Deum. Si enim Deus est, iustus est; si iustus est displicet ei iniustitia, displicet iniquitas. Tu autem cum putas ei placere iniquitatem, negas Deum" (ed. cit., p. 639).

16. Günther Haseloff, *Die Psalterillustration im 13. Jahrhundert: Studien zur Geschichte der Buchmalerei in England, Frankreich and den Niederlanden* (Kiel: n.p., 1938), remains a standard study, linking the development of an eight-picture cycle to the introduction of the Paris University Bible, and tracing its influence across northern Europe. The novelty of this tradition consisted in taking its subject (in most cases) from just the first verse of the psalm. Haseloff notes that Psalm 52 was unusual in showing further development and variation after 1230 (p. 29)—testifying, I would say, to the cultural volatility of *non est deus* as a text. An earlier tradition, popular in England and Germany, had divided the 150 psalms into 3 equal groups (at Psalms 1, 51, 101), each with its own picture. This was sometimes joined to the Paris cycle to create a ten-picture cycle (Psalm 1 being common to both). This permitted an even richer decoration of deluxe Bibles and psalters and became fashionable throughout Europe.

17. Images of jesters and court fools "swerve" from the atheistic meaning of the text in a different way, proposing professional foolery and indecorum as another kind of "carelessness" about God. It is hard to imagine court fools uttering "there is no God" as part of the entertainment they offered.

18. In some cultures, the idiot was thought to bring good luck and to enjoy God's special protection; his incoherent utterances were sometimes treated as divinely inspired. The English word *silly* (ME *sely*, akin to German *selig*) originally meant innocent, blessed, and happy. On this see Edwin Radford, *Encyclopaedia of Superstitions*, ed. and rev. by Christina Hole (London: Hutchinson, 1961), "Afflicted Persons," p. 14; Muriel Laharie, *La folie au Moyen Age, XIe–XIIIe siècles* (Paris: Le Léopard d'Or, 1991), pp. 81–83, 87–107; and for a magisterial study, Michael W. Dols, *"Majnūn": The Madman in Medieval Islamic Society*, ed. Diana E. Immisch (Oxford: Clarendon Press, 1992), esp. chap. 13 on "The Holy Fool."

19. See, e.g., "Robert of Sicily," in *Middle English Metrical Romances*, ed. Walter Hoyt French and Charles Brockway Hale (New York: Prentice-Hall, 1930), p. 937 (121–28), in which the fool-king strikes the gate porter so fiercely that his nose and mouth bleed. In *La Folie de Tristan*, Tristan's entry into Mark's castle, discussed below, offers another example.

20. Figure VIII.10: the "proper" man might instead be seen as rebuking the fool, but his gaze and wagging finger seem to be pointed upward toward God.

21. Such pictures might be said to confirm a proverb well attested in both classical and medieval texts: "Timor invenit deos" (Fear first created the gods; We invent the gods out of our fear). Chaucer translated it so: "Drede fond first goddes, I suppose" (*TC*, IV 1408). See notes to *The Riverside Chaucer*, p. 1049, for other examples. In fuller form the proverb reads "Primus in orbe deos fecit timor" (Fear first made gods in the world). John V. Fleming, *Classical Imitation and Interpretation in Chaucer's "Troilus"* (Lincoln: University of Nebraska Press, 1990), pp. 83 ff., traces it to Statius, not Petronius.

22. Penelope B. R. Doob, *Nebuchadnezzar's Children: Conventions of Madness in Middle English Literature* (New Haven, CT: Yale University Press, 1974), chap. 1, offers an elegant survey of medieval attitudes toward madness, including medical

theory concerning its natural causes. Laharie, *La folie*, significantly extends that investigation and adds a careful study of the treatment of the mad and the simple within a feudal society. Angelika Gross, *"La Folie": Wahnsinn und Narrheit im spätmittelalterlichen Text und Bild* (Heidelberg: Carl Winter Universitätsverlag, 1990), likewise devotes considerable space to the medical explanation.

23. This ambivalence can be found within the Old Testament itself, most clearly in the Book of Jonah (4:11) when God changes his mind about destroying Nineveh: "And shall not I spare Ninive, that great city, in which there are more than a hundred and twenty thousand persons that know not how to distinguish between their right hand and their left, and many beasts?" The English poem called *Patience*, from the late fourteenth century, amplifies that pardon to include "sottez formadde" who cannot distinguish between the upright of a ladder and its rung, babes in arms who have never done harm, women "unwitty" who can't tell one hand from another, as well as dumb beasts who cannot sin yet cause themselves grief. God's last-minute decision to extend mercy to all these offends only Jonah, the most irritable of prophets. See Malcolm Andrew and Ronald Waldron, eds., *The Poems of the Pearl Manuscript: Pearl, Cleanness, Patience, Sir Gawain and the Green Knight* (Berkeley: University of California Press, 1979), p. 205, ll. 509–23.

24. See R. Colin Pickett, *Mental Affliction and Church Law* (Ottawa: University of Ottawa Press, 1952), passim.

25. In play 16 of the Chester cycle, Herod says:

> Methinkes this man is wonders throo,
> dombe and deafe as a doted doo,
> or frenticke, in good faye.
>
> . . .
>
> Cloth him in white, for in this case
> to Pilate hit may be solace,
> for Jewes custome before was
> to cloth men that were wood
> or madd, as nowe hee him mase,
> as well seemes by his face;
> for him that hase lost his grace
> this garment is full good.

R. M. Lumiansky and David Mills, eds., *The Chester Mystery Cycle*, EETS, s.s. 3 (London: Oxford University Press, 1974, 1986), 1: 293, ll. 187–202. The editors trace the history of the white robe from Luke 23:11 ("indutum veste alba"), via Peter Comestor's *Historia scholastica* and the *Legenda aurea*, where it is a sign of ridicule or mockery, to other late medieval English texts that unequivocally declare it a fool's garment (ibid., 2: 233n), well supported by the iconographic tradition of Psalm 52.

26. Cf. St. Bernard's commentary on "play the mountebank I will" (2 Kings 6:22), quoted by Caroline Walker Bynum, *Jesus as Mother: Studies in the Spirituality of the High Middle Ages* (Berkeley: University of California Press, 1982), pp. 127–28. For the larger topic, see John Saward, *Perfect Fools: Folly for Christ's Sake in Catholic and Orthodox Spirituality* (Oxford: Oxford University Press, 1980), and on early examples in the Eastern Orthodox Church, Alexander Y. Syrkin, "On the Behavior of the 'Fool for Christ's Sake,'" *History of Religions* 22 (1982): 150–71. Such an inversion of wisdom/foolishness underlies the account of "What the Lord Jesus Did from His Twelfth to the Beginning of His Thirtieth Year" in the immensely influential *Meditations on the Life of Christ*, once widely ascribed to St. Bonaventure. It tells us that during these eighteen years, silently passed over in the Gospels, Christ stayed at home,

apparently idle, avoiding all conversation and showing no prowess or valor, causing the people to scoff at him, saying, "He is a useless man, an idiot, a good-for-nothing, foolish, bad." At the age of twelve he had proved himself "in advance of his years in wisdom" before the Doctors in the Temple, but afterward he chose to be mistaken for a simpleton, "abject and foolish in the eyes of men so that He would be thought of as devout"—i.e., innocent and unworldly—without making any claim to special understanding. *Meditations on the Life of Christ*, trans. Isa Ragusa and Rosalie B. Green (Princeton, NJ: Princeton University Press, 1961), chap. 25, pp. 94–96.

27. For an example that Millard Meiss (*French Painting: The Late XIVth Century*, 1: 169–71) would attribute to Jacquemart himself, see the Annunciation page with its Man of Sorrows overhead from the *Petites Heures du duc de Berry*, ca. 1375, reproduced in color in Meiss, vol. 2, fig. 94. See also Charles Sterling, *La peinture médiévale à Paris, 1300–1500* 2 vols. (Paris: Bibliothèque des Arts, 1987-90), 1: 124, discussing fig. 63. For my purpose it is enough that these manuscripts are nearly contemporary, employ some of the same models, and were made for essentially the same courtly milieu.

28. "Serpentis sapientia decepti sumus, dei stultitia liberamur." Augustine, *De Doctrina Christiana*, I.xiv, *Corpus Christianorum Series Latina* 32 (Turnholt, Belgium: Brepols, 1962), p. 14; *On Christian Doctrine*, trans. D.W. Robertson, Jr. (Indianapolis: Bobbs-Merrill, 1958), p. 15.

29. Figure VIII. 16 is reproduced in color by François Avril, *Manuscript Painting at the Court of France: The Fourteenth Century, 1310–1380* (New York: George Braziller, 1978), pl. 18a, who comments "an anti-Semitic inspiration is evident in the image showing a figure beating and pulling at the hood of a Jew who seems to be drinking from something resembling a chalice" (p. 74). In my forthcoming book I discuss this illustration in a chapter called "The Fool as Killer of Christ."

30. Figure VIII.17: from a Bible made at the beginning of the thirteenth century, and possibly the earliest type of "fool" in the Paris tradition. Haseloff, *Die Psalterillustration*, pls. 5 and 6, reproduces the full cycle of psalter images from this manuscript, and notes, pp. 24–25, that this type of fool—thoughtful but somewhat sad—was soon replaced by the idiot-madman, a choice that seemed to Haseloff easier to understand.

31. This other interpretation was made current in the West by Augustine, from whence it infects the commentary tradition as a whole. It depends upon reconstruing *non est deus* to mean "he is not God," and making knowledge of Christ's Passion part of David's prophetic wisdom. "The Fool as Killer of Christ" was the subject of my presidential address to the Medieval Academy of America in 1993, as well as the third of my Alexander-Clark lectures. Because of the number of pictures its argument requires, I have reserved its publication for my forthcoming book.

32. Figure VIII.18: reproduced by Roger Sherman Loomis and Laura Hibbard Loomis, *Arthurian Legends in Medieval Art* (New York: Modern Language Association, 1938), fig. 91, discussed on p. 56. Loomis recognized that the second panel might be indebted to *Dixit insipiens* iconography: "The figure of Tristan with his club in hand and the attitude of the king on his throne were probably inspired by some such miniature in a Psalter" (p. 56). But he thinks no further on it. Tristan's haircut, a kind of cruciform tonsure in which two hairlines intersect each other, is commonplace in many Psalm 52 illustrations and may be the sort of shearing "en croiz" Tristan gives himself in the Oxford *Folie*. But see Ruth Mellinkoff, *Outcasts: Signs of Otherness in the Northern European Art of the Late Middle Ages*, California

Studies in the History of Art 32 (Berkeley: University of California Press, 1993), 1: 186–88, for another possible gloss on that text, i.e., the rough checkerboard haircut sometimes featured in late medieval representations of the fool. Julia Walworth, "Tristan in Medieval Art," in *Tristan and Isolde: A Casebook*, ed. Joan Tasker Grimbert (New York: Garland Publishing, 1995), pp. 255–99; Stephanie Cain Van D'Elden, "Reading Illustrations of Tristan," in *Literary Aspects of Courtly Culture*, ed. Donald Maddox and Sara Sturm-Maddox (Cambridge: D. S. Brewer, 1994), pp. 343–51; and Michael Curschmann, "Images of Tristan," in *Gottfried von Strassburg and the Medieval Tristan Legend*, ed. Adrian Stevens and Roy Wisbey (Cambridge: D. S. Brewer, 1990), pp. 1–17, are valuable guides to the larger tradition, but none of them comment on Tristan as fool. Merritt R. Blakeslee, *Love's Masks: Identity, Intertextuality, and Meaning in the Old French Tristan Poems* (Cambridge: D. S. Brewer, 1989), a learned and sensitive study of the Old French Tristan poems, includes a long section on "Tristan's Disguises" (pp. 59–95), including "Tristan *Fou*": "the most frequently retold of the disguise episodes in the medieval Tristan corpus" (p. 72, with sources listed in n19). Blakeslee studies the fool disguise as a punishment for sin, as a consequence of grief and guilt in love, and as a version of ungoverned passion; he derives it from the witty fool (both *ménestral* and *jongleur*); and sets it alongside the medieval wild man (a kinship developed with particular care in the Oxford *Folie*). Though a richly comprehensive account, it does not touch on Tristan's relation to the psalter fool. Jacqueline Schaefer has looked at madness in these poems in several essays: "Tristan's Folly: Feigned or Real?" *Tristania* 3 (1977): 4–16; "Specularity in the Mediaeval *Folie Tristan* Poems or Madness as Metadiscourse," *Neophilologus* 77 (1993): esp. p. 365 and 367n6; and, in collaboration with Angelika Gross, "Tristan, Robert le Diable und die Ikonographie des *Insipiens*: der Hund als Neues Motiv in Einem Alten Kontext," in *Schelme und Narren in den Literaturen des Mittelalters*, Wodan 31, no. 3: Tagungsbände und Sammelschriften (Greifswald: Reineke-Verlag, 1994), where Schaefer relates Tristan's disguise to the type of the psalter *insipiens*, interpreting the features they have in common as negative with regard to the psalm, but positive with regard to the love affair (p. 64), and presenting them as an example of inversion, the world upside-down, in which folly in one sphere becomes truth in another (p. 66). Laharie, *La folie*, had earlier (in 1991) noted that the symptoms of certain mad lovers (Yvain, Lancelot, Tristan, and Amadas) correlated with the madmen of psalter illustration; see pp. 145–52, and for their cure, pp. 224–32. So far as I know, these studies from the 1990s were the first to connect the *Folie* poems with the *insipiens* tradition.

33. See M. Domenica Legge, *Anglo-Norman Literature and Its Background* (Oxford: Clarendon Press, 1963), pp. 121–28, on the two versions. She thinks the *Folie Tristan d'Oxford* written in Anglo-Norman probably the later, with both deriving from a lost common source. Blakeslee, *Love's Masks*, pp. 133–37, offers a bibliographic guide to the many versions of the episode, including the standard editions by Ernest Hoepffner of the two *Folie* poems. They are conveniently published together, along with other Tristan poems, and translations into modern French, by Jean Charles Payen in *Les Tristan en vers* (Paris: Garniers, 1974), pp. 247–97, which I follow here. All translations I cite of the *Folie Tristan* are by Alan S. Fedrick, from *The Romance of Tristan by Beroul and the Tale of Tristan's Madness* (Harmondsworth, Eng.: Penguin Books, 1970), pp. 151–64. I wish to thank Penguin Books for permission to quote from this translation. I have changed its "Yseut" to "Yseult" for uniformity with my other texts.

34. "Las! que ferai, quant ne la voi?/Que por li sui en grant efroi/Et nuit et jor et tot lo terme:/Quant ne la voi, a po ne deve./Las! que ferai? Ne sai que faire. . . . /Tenir me porroit por mauvais,/Se por nule menace lais/Que je n'i aille en tanpinaje/O en abit de fol onbraje./Por li me ferai rere et tondre,/S'autremant ne me puis repondre" (11. 90–94, 104–9).

35. "Ses dras deront, sa chere grate;/Ne voit home cui il ne bate;/Tondrë a fait sa bloie crine./N'i a un sol en la marine/Qu'il ne croie que ce soit rage,/Mais ne sevent pas son corage" (11. 130–36).

36. "Et se fera por fol sanbler,/Quë a Ysiaut viaut il parler./Droit a la cort en est venuz,/Oncques huis ne li fu tenuz" (11. 148–51).

37. "Fox, com a non?—G'é non Picous./—Qui t'angendra?—Uns valerox./—De que t'ot il?—D'une balaine./Une suer ai que vos amoine:/La meschine a non Bruneheut:/Vos l'avroiz, jë avrai Ysiaut" (11. 158–63). The exchange of females, here wittily proposed, links Brangain's name to Yseult in a further onomastic derangement—Bruneheut—recalling the wedding night in which Brangain replaced the no-longer virginal Yseult in the bed of her husband the king.

38. "Et dit Tristanz: 'O bee tu?/Entre les nues et lo ciel,/De flors et de roses, sans giel,/Iluec ferai une maison/O moi et li nos deduison'" (11. 165–69).

39. "Moi et Ysiaut, que je voi ci,/En beümes: demandez li . . ." (11. 176–77).

40. "Jë ai sailli et lanciez jons,/Et sostenu dolez bastons,/Et en bois vescu de racine,/Entre mes braz tenu raïne./Plus diré, se m'an entremet" (11. 184–88).

41. "Or te repose, Picolet./Ce poise moi que tant fait as:/Lai or huimais ester tes gas" (11. 189–91).

42. "Fol, mal aient li marinel/Qui ça outre vos amenerent,/Qant en la mer ne vos giterent" (11. 213–15).

43. "Dame, cil cox ait mal dahé!" (1. 217). In translating this as, "My Lady, a curse on your fool" (p. 156), Fedrick misses Tristan's attack on Mark.

44. "Entre Tristanz soz la cortine:/Entre ses braz tient la raïne" (11. 573–74).

45. *Folie d' Oxford*, 11. 299–308, as translated by Lynette R. Muir, *Literature and Society in Medieval France: The Mirror and the Image, 1100–1500* (New York: St. Martin's Press, 1985), p. 104, in her discussion of the theme of "the world upside-down." Jean-Charles Payen, "The Glass Palace in the *Folie d'Oxford*: From Metaphorical to Literal Madness, or the Dream of the Desert Island at the Moment of Exile; Notes on the Erotic Dimension of the Tristans," in *Tristan and Isolde: A Casebook*, ed. Joan Tasker Grimbert (New York: Garland Publishing, 1995), writes suggestively about the poetic implications of this version of a lover's paradise: "Up there, they will be able to love in the light, no longer in the shadows. . . . As fear is forever abolished, so also will be guilt, hence the transparency"—and on its compensatory nature—"But Tristan is too lucid not to know that the luminous home beyond the clouds is simply a projection of a desperate desire" (p. 121). Payen emphasizes the profound opposition of this fantasy to feudal ideology: in the twelfth century "there is no salvation to be found outside of society, no matter how intense one's ardor" (p. 118). But he does not touch on its destructive relation to Christian ideas of salvation. Blakeslee, *Love's Masks*, pp. 53–54, 82, 92, thinks it a disguised reference to the wood of the Morois in which the two lovers for a time escape civilization and its moral codes, and to Yseult's bed chamber, where they find their greatest happiness together. That reads it well in terms of Tristan's intention; but the specific terms of his invention turn it into a (false) celestial paradise, in ways Blakeslee acknowledges only in passing, p. 53n62.

46. Figure VIII.19: On this manuscript see Loomis and Loomis, *Arthurian Legends in Medieval Art*, p. 94 and fig. 222 (folio number incorrectly cited). Mary Frances Wack, *Lovesickness in the Middle Ages: The "Viaticum" and Its Commentaries* (Philadelphia: University of Pennsylvania Press, 1990), offers a learned guide to the medical tradition. Judith Silverman Neaman, *The Distracted Knight: A Study of Insanity in the Arthurian Romances* (Ph.D. diss, University of Michigan, Ann Arbor, 1968), studies the literary tradition.

47. Eilhart von Oberge's *Tristant*, written between 1170 and 1190, includes the story several decades before the Parisian cycle of psalter illustration took form—which means the kind of madman Tristan pretends to be is originally drawn from the ordinary world of wandering fools, madmen, and idiots, just as the psalter fool in turn would be. See the translation by J. W. Thomas (Lincoln: University of Nebraska Press, 1978), pp. 145–50. But the *Folie* poems sound a deeper note by juxtaposing Tristan's fool disguise with a fool's vision of eternity—unknown in earlier versions—thus invoking the reading of Psalm 52 that interpreted idolatry—the worship of false gods—as a denial of God's existence. When Parisian psalter illustration installed a madman-moron in the Psalm 52 initial, it conferred iconographic authority upon an understanding of Tristan's folly already implicit in those texts. The Hermitage Casket (ca. 1325) reproduced above (Figure VIII.18) makes clear how readily that new iconography was assimilated, for its Tristan, with his heavy club and cross-tonsured haircut, is unmistakably derived from a Parisian typology of the psalter fool. As I shall demonstrate in my book, madness and idiocy had been converging upon the text of the psalm ever since Jerome first rendered the Hebrew word *nabal* as *insipiens* rather than as *imprudens* or *stultus*. But so far as I know, the Tristan legend is the first to overlay the figure of lover and fool in a way that carries serious religious implications.

48. For this reason I would not link Tristan together with Yvain, Lancelot, and Amadas, as though their love-madness were of a single kind (pace Laharie, *La Folie*, pp. 145–51). Concerning the other three, Neaman puts it well (*Distracted Knight*, p. 173): "The love madness in fiction comes not from love but from the hopelessness of love. It is not incurable, and the cure is always related to the cause; furthermore, the cures are never purely medical. They come either from some sign of mercy from the lady—i.e., her care of him, her forgiveness—or her repetition of some magic incantation like the linking of their two names."

49. This act of renarration has been much discussed; see Matilda Tomaryn Bruckner, *Shaping Romance: Interpretation, Truth, and Closure in Twelfth-Century French Fictions* (Philadelphia: University of Pennsylvania Press, 1993), chap. 1, for a particularly thoughtful account focused on the *Folie d'Oxford*.

50. In the Berne *Folie*, Brangain advises her lady, "Go and find clothes for him. He is Tristan and you are Yseult . . . do all you can to please him until Mark comes back from the river." In response Yseult becomes a witty jester too: "May he find so many fish that he does not come back for a week!" (Fedrick trans., p. 163). In the anonymous thirteenth-century prose version (Paris, Bibl. Natl. MS fr. 103) the queen gives Tristan costly robes and linen to wear on secret visits in her chamber. But he must revert daily to his disguise as a fool, sleeping under the stairs, in order to remain in Tintagel. When he is discovered two months later he has to flee. See *The Romance of Tristan and Isolt*, trans. Norman B. Spector (Evanston, IL: Northwestern University Press, 1973), p. 71.

51. For an elegant essay on Gottfried von Strassburg's presentation of this love as "beyond human judgment," see Esther C. Quinn, "Beyond Courtly Love: Religious Elements in *Tristan* and *La Queste del Saint Graal*," in *In Pursuit of Perfection: Courtly Love in Medieval Literature*, ed. Joan M. Ferrante and George D. Economou (Port Washington, NY: Kennikat Press, 1975), pp. 179–219. Quinn writes of the ordeal by fire: "Gottfried presents the exoneration of Isot before the highest tribunal by the direct intervention of the Deity. This is, of course, a fictitious Deity, indifferent to His own laws, but it is a daring stroke on Gottfried's part—to involve the Lord Himself in the web of deceptions which the subtle Queen weaves—to present Him as deceived or as willing to aid her in deceiving" (p. 187).

52. See Fleming, *Classical Imitation*, particularly chapter 3, "Idols of the Prince," and before him, D. W. Robertson, Jr., *A Preface to Chaucer: Studies in Medieval Perspectives* (Princeton, NJ: Princeton University Press, 1962), pp. 99, 112–13, 401 and *passim*. Michael Camille, *The Gothic Idol: Ideology and Image-Making in Medieval Art* (Cambridge: Cambridge University Press, 1989), offers a brilliant study of the theme of idol worship in medieval art. His final chapter, "Idols in the Mind," focuses on the topos of woman on a pedestal, both as an object of courtly-love desire and an idol of perverse devotion.

53. See Barry Windeatt, *Oxford Guides to Chaucer: Troilus and Criseyde* (Oxford: Clarendon Press, 1992), pp. 231–40, on "Love and Religion," for a thorough presentation of the textual evidence behind such a reading.

54. On this manuscript see Walter Cahn, *Romanesque Bible Illumination* (Ithaca, NY: Cornell University Press, 1982), pp. 221–22, and his more recent *Romanesque Manuscripts: The Twelfth Century*, 2 vols., vol. 2 in *A Survey of Manuscripts Illuminated in France*, ed. François Avril and J. J. G. Alexander (London: Harvey Miller, 1996), no. 81. Though an Englishman, Manerius is thought to have been working in France when he made this Bible.

55. In medieval iconography, the devil often has goatlike features (hairy skin, a beard, caprine horns, cloven hooves, a tail, etc.) which scholars trace back to antique representations of the nature god Pan. But his face is generally human; I know of no instance where he is shown simply as a goat. Confessions of devil worship exacted by the Inquisition describe him appearing in the form of a toad, a giant black cat, a great disembodied head, or an unusually pale ice-cold man. Beryl Rowland cites two instances in which heretics were accused of worshiping or fornicating with the devil in the form of a goat, but *in vilissimi hirci forma* may simply mean a devil with goatlike features. See her *Animals with Human Faces: A Guide to Animal Symbolism* (Knoxville: University of Tennessee Press, 1973), p. 83.

56. For instance, a late thirteenth-century relief, carved on a porch of the Cathedral of Freiburg im Bresgau shows Sensuality (Voluptas) as a beautiful naked woman draped in the flayed skin of a goat, its head covering her sexual parts—reproduced as fig. 7 in *Woman Defamed and Woman Defended: An Anthology of Medieval Texts*, ed. Alcuin Blamires (Oxford: Clarendon Press, 1992). In a sequence of Deadly Sins and Virtues illustrating Chaucer's *Parson's Tale*, ca. 1450–60 (Cambridge, Univ. Lib. MS Gg.4.27) Lechery is personified as an elegantly gowned woman riding upon a goat (fol. 233). See Roger Sherman Loomis, *A Mirror of Chaucer's World* (Princeton, NJ: Princeton University Press, 1965), fig. 179. There is nothing arcane about this tradition. Medieval bestiary lore describes the male goat (*hircus*) as "a lascivious and butting animal who is always burning for coition. His eyes are transverse slits because he is so randy. . . . The nature of goats is so extremely hot

that a stone of adamant, which neither fire nor iron implement can alter, is dissolved merely by the blood of one of these creatures." See *The Book of Beasts: Being a Translation from a Latin Bestiary of the Twelfth Century*, trans. T. H. White (London: Jonathan Cape, 1954), pp. 74–75. For a full account see Rowland, *Animals with Human Faces*, pp. 80–86. Chaucer's discussion of Lechery in *The Parson's Tale* links the sin explicitly with idolatry: "Certes, be it wyf, be it child, or any worldly thyng that [a man] loveth biforn God, it is his mawmet, and he is an ydolastre" (X 859).

57. For a closely related illustration see Paris, Bibl. Natl. MS lat. 11535, fol. 30v, where the *insipiens* (standing before an altar with a goat idol) wears a kind of pointed beret, indicating that he is a learned man. Reproduced in Haseloff, *Die Psalterillustration*, pl. 3. On this manuscript, a partial copy of the Manerius Bible (or a hypothetical sister MS), see Cahn, *Romanesque Manuscripts*, 2: no. 92.

58. Figure VIII.22: Kathleen L. Scott generously allowed me to see in advance her descriptions of this manuscript (and its sister manuscript now in Turin, discussed below) from her *Later Gothic Manuscripts, 1390–1490*, 2 vols., *A Survey of Manuscripts Illuminated in the British Isles*, ed. J. J. G. Alexander (London: Harvey Miller, 1996), where they are numbered 26 and 27 respectively. She dates the Big Bible ca. 1405–15, thinks it probably a London production, and identifies its dominant illustrator (Hand A, setting the style for several other hands) as the Carmelite–Lapworth Master, the "learner hand" of the Carmelite Missal. Scott raises serious doubts about Margaret Rickert's attribution of some of the work to Herman Scheerre.

59. See *MED*, s.v. *fol* (adj. 3), p. 675, and *folie* (noun 2b), p. 682; Chaucer frequently uses these words in this sense in his *Parson's Tale* discussion of Lechery (X.852–55, 884). For *fole femme* meaning "whore" in medieval French, see Adolf Toblers and Erhard Lommatzsch, eds., *Altfranzösisches Wörterbuch* (Wiesbaden: Steiner, 1954), cols. 1999–2000. In both languages more is meant than "foolish woman," "stupid woman," or "mad woman." *Fol'amors*, properly an antonym to *fin'amors*, could be thought synonymous with it.

60. It would narrow the meaning of the picture too much to see the lascivious couple as representing fornication merely. All sin, of course, was understood to deny God one way or another—to deny His supremacy, His authority, His commandments—and "sinners" (unspecified) occasionally appear in the inventories of commentators attempting to identify a plausible *insipiens*. But here the connection is stronger than that. The psalm text illustrated has more to do with the First Commandment ("Thou shalt have no other Gods before me") than with the Sixth (against adultery); it tells us these are God-denying fools. Cf. the Rohan Book of Hours (Paris, Bibl. Natl. MS lat. 9471, made ca. 1419–27), which shows on fol. 235 a crowd of Israelites reverencing a naked male idol while a courtly couple embraces voluptuously in their midst. Reproduced in facsimile by Millard Meiss and Marcel Thomas, *The Rohan Master: A Book of Hours*, trans. Katharine W. Carson (New York: George Braziller, 1973), pl. 123, with helpful commentary.

61. The manuscript of Figure VIII.23, too, is enormous, one of the seven largest psalters that survive from the fifteenth century. For a full description see Scott, *Later Gothic Manuscripts*, 2: 27.

62. This manuscript (MS fr. 166), splendidly begun by the brothers Limbourg, ca. 1402–4, was completed much later by a lesser painter, whose work includes the illustration of the Psalms. See Millard Meiss, *French Painting in the Time of Jean de Berry: The Limbourgs and Their Contemporaries*, 2 vols. (London: Thames and Hudson, 1974), 1: 67–68, 81–84. The mid fourteenth-century manuscript used as a model

survives as Paris, Bibl. Natl. MS fr. 167; its equivalent illustration shows a madman above, with four men playing dice below—a pastime in which (I surmise) chance or Fortune is reverenced in place of the deity.

63. See Jenny Stratford, "The Royal Library in England Before the Reign of Edward IV," in *England in the Fifteenth Century: Proceedings of the 1992 Harlaxton Symposium*, ed. Nicholas Rogers, Harlaxton Medieval Studies 4 (Stamford, England: Paul Watkins, 1994), 193–94, with a full bibliography on the question.

64. See A. I. Doyle, "English Books In and Out of Court from Edward III to Henry VII," in *English Court Culture in the Later Middle Ages*, ed. V. J. Scattergood and J. W. Sherborne (New York: St. Martin's Press, 1983), p. 172. Doyle suggests Henry V may also have commissioned Corpus Christi College, Cambridge, MS 61 of the *Troilus*, with its famous frontispiece of Chaucer reciting to courtiers; Henry's unexpected death could account for its program of illustrations being left unfinished (p. 175).

65. Lee Patterson's profound study of this poem, "Ambiguity and Interpretation: A Fifteenth-Century Reading of *Troilus and Criseyde*," in his *Negotiating the Past: The Historical Understanding of Medieval Literature* (Madison: University of Wisconsin Press, 1987), pp. 115–53, focuses on the uses made of it for the nuns of Syon Abbey. In a treatise belonging to the abbey, concerned to show how "flesshly love hideth and coloureth him undre love spirituel" (p. 121), the author quotes Troilus's song (p. 124) and ends by offering this advice regarding carnal love's "sweet poison": "Of which poison if ye lust more to rede, / Seeth the storie of Troilus, Creseide and Dyomede" (p. 127), clearly suggesting a copy of that poem may have been available to them in the abbey library. Part 3 of Patterson's chapter, called "*Troilus and Criseyde* in the Nunnery," is of great interest here, not only in its allowance for textual ambiguity, but in its demonstration that all interpretation is partial and partitive, as in this case of a monastic author writing for nuns: "Disambiguating is always, and properly, a process of deciding not what a text means but what we want it to mean. . . . One of the great achievements of Augustinian hermeneutics is to make the preemptive nature of interpretation explicit" (pp. 150–51). If the Psalm 52 illustration studied above was for a time available to at least some of those nuns, the Syon Abbey connection is rich indeed.

66. Cf. the lament in which Troilus asks his eyes why they don't "wepen out youre sighte; / Syn she is queynt, that wont was yow to lighte?" (IV 312–13). (See also IV 1429–31, where "the grete furie of his penaunce / Was queynt with hope, and therwith hem bitwene / Bigan for joie th'amorouse daunce.") Fleming's chapter "Quaint Light in Troy," in *Classical Imitation*, offers a witty history of modern criticism's occasional squeamishness concerning these puns—an anachronistic decorum that invades even *The Riverside Chaucer*, p. 1051n543, which is content to say: "Frost rightly argues against reading a pun in *queynt*, Yale Rev. 66, 1977, 551–61." But Frost's essay is belle-lettristic at best. It testifies to interpretive discomfort without producing scholarly evidence of any substantial kind.

67. In Figure VIII.25, Tristan is second from the left; Troilus last on the right. Such trays, commissioned to present sweetmeats or other offerings to a bride or mother, often depict subjects from secular poems. See John Pope-Hennessy and Keith Christiansen, *Secular Painting in 15th-Century Tuscany: Birth Trays, Cassone Panels, and Portraits* (New York: Metropolitan Museum of Art, Metropolitan Museum of Art Bulletin, Summer 1980), pp. 4–11. One of their examples, showing a mother receiving presents in her bedroom as the baby is tended by women below, has an

inscribed prayer: "May God grant health to every woman who gives birth and to their father . . . may [the child] be born without fatigue or peril," and so on (figs. 4 and 5). On the tray reproduced here, see Loomis, *Arthurian Legends in Medieval Art*, fig. 135 and p. 70; and esp. Paul F. Watson, *The Garden of Love in Tuscan Art of the Early Renaissance* (Philadelphia: Art Alliance Press, 1979), pl. 67 and pp. 80–84. He derives its iconographic formula from that first developed for the Assumption of the Virgin, notices that Venus extends her arms in the fashion of the Man of Sorrows displaying his wounds (an *Ostentatio Veneris*), and names its theme unequivocally as "the power of sex," "the power of Venus," and its subject "Our Lady of Pleasures." Granted the tray's dynastic occasion, it seems unlikely this Venus was thought of as being opposed to respectable, married love. As Watson notes, the apple trees and lush garden symbolize fecundity, creating a paradise "sacred to a deity but open to virtuous mortals"; "Venus [here] ideally replaces these worthies' consorts." Michael Foss, *Chivalry* (London: Michael Joseph, 1975), p. 96, reproduces the tray in color.

68. In an interpretive move more tactful than D. W. Robertson's, Fleming, in *Classical Imitation*, measures Troilus against the highest ideals of paganism rather than of Christianity—as though he were a pagan philosopher or statesman, whose proper study is wisdom. But Troilus is a young warrior, experiencing romantic love for the first time, and he aims at something quite different—whatever can be known of bliss within his lady's arms. I think we are meant to allow him a young man's folly, even as he seeks to make spiritual sense of it. Philosophy is certainly not his calling. Whenever he tries to think a Boethian question through, he gets the answer wrong.

69. I paraphrase here the powerful analysis by Anders Nygren, *Agape and Eros*, trans. Philip S. Watson (Philadelphia: Westminster Press, 1953), pp. 478–80.

70. Augustine, *Enarrationes in Psalmos*, Ps. 13:2: "Nemo intellegatur fecisse bonitatem usque ad Christum; quia non potest quisquam hominum facere bonitatem, nisi ipse monstrauerit" (ed. cit., 38:86); *St. Augustine on the Psalms*, trans. Hebgin and Corrigan, 1.154.

71. "Ergo Deum esse non est per se notum." Aquinas, *Summa theologiae*, la.2, I (ed. cit., pp. 6–7).

Illustration Sources and Credits

CHAPTER I

I.1. The lover offers his lady his heart; they go off together. Ivory writing tablet, French, fourteenth century. The Detroit Institute of Arts (42.136), Founders Society Purchase with funds from Robert H. Tannahill. Photo © 1994 The Detroit Institute of Arts.

I.2. Troilo's dream of a boar lying with Criseida. From a manuscript of Boccaccio's *Il Filostrato*, Naples, 1414. New York, Pierpont Morgan Library MS M. 371, fol. 48v.

I.3. A boar hunt. From an English Bestiary, second quarter of the thirteenth century. Oxford, Bodley MS 764, fol. 38v.

I.4. The eagle tests its young against the sun. From an English Bestiary, ca. 1230. London, Brit. Lib. MS Royal 12. F. xiii, fol. 49. © The British Library. All Rights Reserved.

I.5. The eagle purges its sight and descends into rejuvenating waters. From an English Bestiary, second quarter of the thirteenth century. Oxford, Bodley MS 764, fol. 57v.

I.6. Diomede's battle coat, with broach, being displayed in Troy. From a French prose translation of *Il Filostrato*, ca. 1455–56. Paris, Bibl. Natl. MS fr. 25528, fol. 89v.

I.7. Scipio's dream, looking down on earth. From a manuscript of Macrobius's *Commentary on the Dream of Scipio*, Italian, dated 1383. Oxford, Bodley MS Canon. Class. Lat. 257, fol. 1v.

I.8. Dante and Beatrice move toward the heaven of the sun (*Paradiso* XXII). Painted by Giovanni di Paolo, Italian ca. 1445. London, Brit. Lib. MS Yates Thompson 36, fol. 146. © The British Library. All Rights Reserved.

CHAPTER II

II.1. The death of Cleopatra. Engraving by Barthel Beham, ca. 1524. Photo: The Warburg Institute, London.

II.2. The death of Cleopatra. Engraving by Augustin Hirschvogel, 1547. Photo: The Warburg Institute, London.

II.3. The death of Cleopatra. Engraving by Hans Sebald Beham, ca. 1529. Photo: The Warburg Institute, London.

II.4. The death of Cleopatra, with Cupid weeping. Engraving by Agostino Veneziano, 1528. Photo: The Warburg Institute, London.

II.5. The deaths of Anthony and Cleopatra. An illustration from Boccaccio, *Des cas des nobles hommes et femmes*, trans. Laurent de Premierfait, ca. 1470–83. London, Brit. Lib. MS Royal 14 E. v, fol. 339. © The British Library. All Rights Reserved.

II.6. The deaths of Anthony and Cleopatra. *Hystoire tripartite*, Flanders, dated 1473. London, Brit. Lib. MS Royal 18. E. v, fol. 363v. © The British Library. All Rights Reserved.

II.7. The deaths of Anthony and Cleopatra. From Boccaccio, *Des cleres et nobles femmes*, manuscript dated 1410. Paris, Bibl. Natl. MS fr. 12420, fol. 129v.

II.8. The deaths of Anthony and Cleopatra. Same text as Fig. II.7, manuscript dated 1404. Paris, Bibl. Natl. MS fr. 598, fol. 128v.

II.9. The deaths of Anthony and Cleopatra. From Boccaccio, *Des cas des nobles hommes et femmes*, ca. 1410. Paris, Bibl. de l'Arsenal MS 5193, fol. 272v.

II.10. The tomb of Anthony and Cleopatra. Same text as Fig. II.9, ca. 1415. New York, formerly Coll. Francis Kettaneh, no pagination.

II.11. Anthony and Cleopatra dead. Same text as Fig. II.9, ca. 1415–20. Paris, Bibl. Natl. MS fr. 226, fol. 183v.

II.12. The temptation of Adam and Eve. Hans Sebald Beham, engraving on paper (1543), 8.2 × 5.7 cm. Gift of Mr. and Mrs. Potter Palmer, Jr., 1921.316. Art Institute of Chicago. Photography © The Art Institute of Chicago.

II.13. The Meeting of the Three Living and the Three Dead, English, ca. 1330–45. London, Brit. Lib. MS Arundel 83, fol. 127. © The British Library. All Rights Reserved.

II.14. The narrator of "A Disputacioun Betwyx the Body and Wormes" at prayer in a church. English, ca. 1435–40. London, Brit. Lib. MS 37049, fol. 33. © The British Library. All Rights Reserved.

II.15. Tomb image illustrating the same poem. London, Brit. Lib. MS 37049, fol. 32v. © The British Library. All Rights Reserved.

II.16. A woman's body debates with worms. London, Brit. Lib. MS 37049, fol. 35. © The British Library. All Rights Reserved.

II.17. A warning from the grave; the tomb of the Emperor Antiochenus visited by his steward and his son. London, Brit. Lib. MS 37049, fol. 87. © The British Library. All Rights Reserved.

II.18. The tomb of Cardinal Jean de Lagrange, 1402. Avignon, Musée du Petit Palais. Photo: © Archives Photographiques, Paris. S.P.A.D.E.M.

II.19. The tomb of Archbishop Henry Chichele, 1424. Canterbury Cathedral. Photo: National Monuments Record, London. Reproduced by permission of English Heritage, NMR.

II.20. The tomb of Bishop Richard Fleming, before 1431. Lincoln Cathedral. Photo: National Monuments Record, London. Reproduced by permission of English Heritage, NMR.

II.21. The tomb of François de la Sarra, ca. 1370–1400. Vaud, Switzerland. Lausanne, Musée d'Elysée. Photo: Archives de Jongh, Lausanne.

II.22. The tomb of François de la Sarra (detail of Figure II.21).

II.23. The tomb of Alice de la Pole, Duchess of Suffolk, granddaughter of Geoffrey Chaucer, 1475. Ewelme. Photo: National Monuments Record, London. Reproduced by permission of English Heritage, NMR.

II.24. The tomb of Alice de la Pole (detail). Conway Library, Courtauld Insitute of Art. Photograph by the late F. H. Crossley.

II.25. The death of Dido. An illustration from Boccaccio, *Des cas des nobles hommes et femmes*, fifteenth century. London, Brit. Lib. MS Add. 35321, fol. 43. © The British Library. All Rights Reserved.

II.26. The death of Dido. Ca. 1470–83. London, Brit. Lib. MS Royal 14 E. v, fol. 77v. © The British Library. All Rights Reserved. It illustrates the same text as Figure II.25.

II.27. The death of Lucrece. Same text and manuscript as Figure II.26, fol. 121v. © The British Library. All Rights Reserved.

II.28. Hercules, with Cerberus on a leash, restores Alcestis to her husband, Admetus. Catacomb painting, fourth century. Rome, Via Latina. Photo: Pontifical Institute of Christian Archaeology, Vatican City.

II.29. Hercules rescues Alcestis from Hell. An illustration from the *Libellus de imaginibus deorum*, northern Italian, ca. 1420. Vatican City, Bibl. Apostolica Vaticana MS Reg. Lat. 1290, fol. 5a v. Photo © Biblioteca Apostolica Vaticana.

II.30. Hercules rescues Alcestis from Hell-Mouth; Alcestis and Admetus (?) enthroned. An illustration from Ridevall, *Fulgentius metaforalis*, 1420. Vatican City, Bibl. Apostolica Vaticana MS Palat. 1066, fol. 228. Photo © Biblioteca Apostolica Vaticana.

II.31. Geoffrey Chaucer: portrait with a daisy. Sixteenth century. London, Brit. Lib. MS Add. 5141, fol. 1. © The British Library. All Rights Reserved.

CHAPTER III

III.1. Angry parents curse their child. Woodcut from Geoffrey de la Tour Landry's *Ritter vom Turn*, Basel, Michael Furter, 1493. Reproduced with permission from Ernest and Johanna Lehner, *Picture Book of Devils, Demons, and Witchcraft* (New York: Dover Books, 1971), fig. 23.

III.2. A carter and three horses try to move a cart of hay as three other peasants push and shove. From Luttrell Psalter, English, ca. 1340. London, Brit. Lib., MS Add. 42130, fol. 173v. © The British Library. All Rights Reserved.

III.3. *The Hay Wain*, by Hieronymus Bosch. Madrid, Prado Museum. Triptych open: paradise on the left wing, hell on the right. Dutch, ca. 1485–90. Photo: Erich Lessing / Art Resource, NY.

III.4. *The Hay Wain*, by Hieronymus Bosch. Madrid, Prado Museum. Central panel: the world as a cart of hay, from which everyone takes what he can. Photo: Erich Lessing / Art Resource, NY.

III.5. *The Hay Wain*, by Hieronymus Bosch. Detail of central panel: lovers and music makers between angel and devil, with Christ above. Photo: Erich Lessing / Art Resource, NY.

III.6. *The Wayfarer*, by Hieronymus Bosch. Madrid, Prado Museum. *The Hay Wain* triptych, outer wings closed. Dutch, ca. 1485–90. Photo: Scala / Art Resource, NY.

III.7. Staging diagram for *The Castle of Perseverance*. Ca. 1425–40. Washington, DC, Folger Shakespeare Library MS V. a. 354, fol. 191v. By permission of the Library.

III.8. An illustrated poem of the Seven Ages of Man's Life, with good angel and bad angel in attendance. English, ca. 1435–40. London, Brit. Lib. MS Add. 37049, fol. 28v. © The British Library. All Rights Reserved.

III.9. The Seven Ages of Man's Life (continued). English, ca. 1435–40. London, Brit. Lib. MS Add. 37049, fol. 29. © The British Library. All Rights Reserved.

III.10. The pilgrim's soul between devil and angel. An illustration from *Le pèlerinage de l'âme*, by Guillaume de Deguileville, early fifteenth century. Paris, Bibl. Natl. MS fr. 376, fol. 89.

III.11. St. Michael and the devil argue over a dead man's book of reckoning. From the Book of Hours of Catherine of Cleves, Dutch, ca. 1440. New York, Pierpont Morgan Library MS M. 917, p. 206.

III.12. A carter and his horse. From a French translation of Boethius's *De consolatione*, ca. 1406, illustrating Book V, prose 4. Cambridge, Trinity Hall MS 12, fol. 81 b. By kind permission of the Master and Fellows.

III.13. The pains of hell. From a London psalter, ca. 1220–30. Cambridge, Trinity College MS B. 11. 4, fol. 11v. By kind permission of the Master and Fellows.

CHAPTER IV

IV.1. The climax of the pear-tree story, illustrating Aesop, *Vita et fabulae*, printed by Heinrich Knoblochtzer, Strasbourg, ca. 1481, and copied by William Caxton for his own Aesop (*Esope*; 1484). New York, Pierpont Morgan Library MS PML 50, fol. qiij.

IV.2. January calendar page: Janus feasting, and Aquarius. Peterborough Psalter. English, before 1318. Brussels, Bibl. Royale MS 9961–62, fol. 1. Photo © Royal Library of Belgium.

IV.3. January calendar page: Janus between two doors. French, ca. 1230. Paris, Bibl. de l'Arsenal MS 1186, fol. 2.

IV.4. January calendar page: Janus between two doors. English, ca. 1150–61. London, Brit. Lib. MS Cotton Nero C. iv, fol. 40. © The British Library. All Rights Reserved.

IV.5. January calendar page: Janus feasting; Aquarius; the Old Year and the New. Bedford Book of Hours. French, ca. 1423. London, Brit. Lib. MS Add. 18850, fol. 1. © The British Library. All Rights Reserved.

IV.5a. January calendar page: Janus as porter, with pensive monk (detail from Figure IV.5).

IV.6. A sinner looking into Hell-Mouth and thinking on his death. English, between 1325 and 1335. London, British Library MS Add. 42130, fol. 157v. © The British Library. All Rights Reserved.

IV. 7. January calendar page: winter provisions, feasting before the fire. Liège, ca. 1280. Oxford, Bodley MS Add. A. 46, fol. 1.

IV.8. January feasting. From the Peterborough Psalter, English, before 1318, Brussels, Bibl. Royale MS 9961–62 (detail of Figure IV.2). Photo © Royal Library of Belgium.

IV.9. January calendar page (detail): feasting between a closed and an open door. Paris, between 1230 and 1239. New York, Pierpont Morgan Library MS M. 92, fol. 15.

IV.10. January calendar page: the Duc de Berry receives New Year's gifts. French, ca. 1411–16. Limbourg Brothers, *Très riches heures du Duc de Berry*. Chantilly, Musée Condé MS 65, fol. 1v. Photo: Réunion des Musées Nationaux / Art Resource, NY.

IV.11. January calendar page (detail): after a meal, warming himself at the fireplace. Paris, ca. 1400. Oxford, Bodley MS Douce 62, fol. 1v.

IV.12. January calendar page: feasting, attended by servants. Bourges? ca. 1500. Oxford, Bodley MS Canon. Liturg. 99, fol. 5.

IV.13. *Roman de la Rose*: a nun gathers fruit from a penis-tree, and embraces a monk (border detail). French, ca. 1330. Paris, Bibl. Natl. MS fr. 25526, fol. 106v.

IV.14. May calendar page: a man riding out with hawk, between budding trees. From a psalter, Bruges? mid-thirteenth century. Los Angeles, J. Paul Getty Museum MS 14, fol. 5.

IV.15. May calendar page (detail): a falconer with servant, bringing home the green. Jean Pucelle, the Hours of Jeanne d'Evreux. Paris, ca. 1325. New York, The Metropolitan Museum of Art, Cloisters Collection, 1954 (54.1.2, fol. 5v). Image © The Metropolitan Museum of Art.

CHAPTER V

V.1. A star chart of the constellation Gemini (the Twins). English, mid-twelfth century. Oxford, Bodley MS 614, fol. 19.

V.2. May calendar page: the Gemini as wrestlers; a falconer with flowering branch. English, ca. 1265–70. London, Brit. Lib. MS 50,000, fol. 3. © The British Library. All Rights Reserved.

V.3. May calendar page (detail): a falconer on horse; the Gemini as wrestlers. Paris, 1407. Oxford, Bodley MS Douce 144, fol. 10.

V.4. May calendar page (detail): a falconer on horse; the Gemini as wrestlers. French, ca. 1440–50. Illuminated by the Fastolf Master. Oxford, Bodley MS Auct. D. inf 2. 11, fol. 5.

V.5. Old Testament illustration (detail): David takes leave of Jonathan. Paris, ca. 1250. New York, Pierpont Morgan Library MS M. 638, fol. 32.

V.6. May page (detail): a falconer rests his horse; the Gemini as infants (putti), playing in the sun. Paris, ca. 1400. Oxford, Bodley MS Douce 62, fol. 7.

V.7. May page (detail): falconer on horse; the Gemini embrace behind a shield. French, perhaps from Beauvais, ca. 1260–70. New York, Pierpont Morgan Library MS 101, fol. 6.

V.8. May page (detail): falconer; the Gemini embrace between trees, covered by a leaf. French, ca. 1400. New York, Pierpont Morgan Library MS M. 264, fol. 5.

V.9. The Gemini (star chart, detail). Bayeux, ca. 1268–74. Oxford, Bodley MS Laud. Misc. 644, fol. 8v.

V.10. The Gemini embrace in a boat (detail). From the Shaftesbury Psalter, English, ca. 1130–40. London, Brit. Lib. MS Lansdowne 383, fol. 5. © The British Library. All Rights Reserved.

V.11. Gemini Twins "bring in the May." From the *Grandes heures* of Anne of Brittany, illuminated by Jean Bourdichon. Paris or Tours, ca. 1500–1508. Paris, Bibl. Natl. MS lat. 9474, fol. 8.

V.12. The Gemini as lovers, man and woman, between flowering trees, behind a shield. The Psalter and Hours of Bonne of Luxembourg, Paris, before 1349. New York, The Metropolitan Museum of Art, Cloisters Collection, 1969 (69.86), fol. 6.

V.13. May page (detail): the Twins as lovers behind a shield. Liège, ca. 1280. Oxford, Bodley MS Add. 46, fol. 3.

V.14. May page: bringing home the green; the Twins as wrestlers. Hours of Isabella Stuart, from the studio of the Rohan Masters, Angers? ca. 1431. Cambridge, Fitzwilliam Museum MS 62, fol. 5a.

V.15. May page (detail): the Twins as lovers between trees. German, ca. 1225–50. New York, Pierpont Morgan Library MS M. 711, fol. 4.

V.16. May page (detail): the Twins as lovers between trees. French, ca. 1260. Cambridge, Trinity College MS B. 11.5, fol. 8. By kind permission of the Master and Fellows.

V.17. May page (detail): the Gemini behind a shield, with trees and courting birds and courting lions. English, *Queen Mary's Psalter*, early fourteenth century. London, Brit. Lib. MS Royal 2 B. vii, fol. 76. © The British Library. All Rights Reserved.

V.18. May page (detail): a falconer; male Gemini, naked behind a tree. Paris, from a Breviary illuminated in the style of Jean Pucelle, ca. 1350. New York, Pierpont Morgan Library MS M. 75, fol. 3.

V.19. May page (detail): a couple ride out; the Gemini naked in trees. Normandy, early sixteenth century. Oxford, Bodley MS Douce 72, fol. 3.

V.20. May page: a King of the May (?); the Gemini in trees. French, early sixteenth century. Cambridge, Fitzwilliam Museum MS. 128, fol. 3.

V.21. May page (detail): a falconer; the Gemini in trees. French, ca. 1500–1510. Cambridge, Fitzwilliam Museum MS 132, p. 5.

V.22. May page (detail): the Gemini as erotic wrestlers. Paris, illuminated by the Bedford Master and his workshop, between 1430 and 1435. New York, Pierpont Morgan Library MS M. 359, fol. 5v.

V.23. May page: the Gemini as erotic wrestlers. Paris (use of Rome), ca. 1510. Cambridge, Fitzwilliam Museum MS 123, fol. 3.

V.24. May page: a couple ride out; erotic wrestling; music and courtship in the green wood. French (use of Rome), second quarter of the sixteenth century. Oxford, Bodley MS Douce 135, fol. 4.

V.25. May page: a May Day procession, bringing in the green. Spinola Book of Hours, Flanders, ca. 1510–20. Los Angeles, J. Paul Getty Museum MS Ludwig IX 18, fol. 3v.

V.26. The tree of Jesse. English, from the Winchester Psalter, before 1161. London, Brit. Lib. MS Cotton Nero C. iv, fol. 9. © The British Library. All Rights Reserved.

V.27. The tree of Jesse. The Tickill Psalter, English, ca. 1303–14. New York, New York Public Library, Spencer Collection MS 26, fol. 5v.

V.28. SS. Cosmas and Damian receive a physician's case. Greek, from the Menology of Basileios II, beginning of the eleventh century. Vatican City, Bibl. Apostolica Vaticana MS gr. 1613, fol. 152. Photo © Biblioteca Apostolica Vaticana.

CHAPTER VI

VI.1. The rocky coast of Pedmark (Penmarc'h) in Brittany. Photo: Ellin M. Kelly.

VI.2. The garden paradise of the Old Man of the Mountain. From an English manuscript of Marco Polo's *Li livres du Graunt Caam*, English, ca. 1400. Oxford, Bodley MS 264, fol. 226.

VI.3. The God of Love's carol dance in the *Roman de la Rose*. French, late fourteenth century. Oxford, Bodley MS Douce 332, fol. 8v.

VI.4. A harbor with rocky cliffs. Detail from a panel painting, "Madonna and child with an anonymous benefactress and St. Mary Magdalen." Netherlandish, ca. 1470. Liège, Musée Diocésain.

VI.5. Black magic: a clerk studies the heavens with demonic assistance. English, from an encyclopedia, *Omne bonum*, mid-fourteenth century. London, Brit. Lib. MS Royal 6 E. vi, fol. 396v. © The British Library. All Rights Reserved.

VI.6. Entertainment at a royal feast, Paris, 1378. From Charles V's *Grandes chroniques de France*. Paris, Bibl. Natl. MS fr. 2813, fol. 473v.

VI.7. Automata from the sketchbook of Villard de Honnecourt. French, ca. 1225–50. Paris, Bibl. Natl. MS fr. 19093, fol. 22v (detail).

VI.8. The pavilion at Hesdin, with festive courtiers (possibly a 1431 wedding) in the foreground. Sixteenth-century copy of a lost original. Versailles, Musée des Beaux-Arts du Château. Photo: Réunions des Musées Nationaux / Art Resource, NY.

VI.9. A courtly dance in the park at Hesdin. An illustration from Machaut's *Remède de Fortune*, French, ca. 1350. Paris, Bibl. Natl. MS fr. 1586, fol. 51.

VI.10. A three-cell diagram of the brain (*phantasia* in the middle cell), from Triumphus Augustinus de Anchona, *Opusculum perutile de cognitione animae*, rev. Achillini, Bologna, 1503, sig. f. (viii). London: Brit. Lib. © The British Library. All Rights Reserved.

VI.11. A portrait of Sorrow (Tristesse) tearing her hair. From a *Roman de la Rose*, French, ca. 1330. London, Brit. Lib. MS Add. 31840, fol. 5. © The British Library. All Rights Reserved.

VI.12. The Lover admitted into the Garden of the Rose by Lady Idleness, porteress of the gate. From a *Roman de la Rose*, French, beginning of the fifteenth century. On the wall, from far left, we see three other sins that exclude one from the garden: Covetousness, Avarice, and Envy. London, Brit. Lib. MS Egerton 1069, fol. 1. © The British Library. All Rights Reserved.

VI.13. An allegory of human life. Panel painting from the upper Rhine, ca. 1480. Germanisches Nationalmuseum, Nurnberg.

CHAPTER VII

VII.1. The deaths of Valerian and Tiburce, Cecilia's husband and brother-in-law. French, mid-fourteenth century. Oxford, Bodley MS Douce 313, fol. 268.

VII.2. Christ blessing the sacrifice of St. Cecilia. Oxford, Bodley MS Douce 313, fol. 332v.

VII.3. Cecilia as the patron saint of church music. Historiated initial from an Italian manuscript, late fourteenth or early fifteenth-century. Cambridge, Fitzwilliam Museum MS McLean 201, fol. 26v.

VII.4. Angel presenting crowns of lilies and of roses to the married couple. From a French Breviary, ca. 1413–19. London, Brit. Lib. MS Harley 2897, fol. 440v. © The British Library. All Rights Reserved.

VII.5. Scenes from the life of St. Cecilia. From a late fifteenth-century *Légende dorée*. The flowers in Valerian's crown are red; those in Cecilia's crown are white. Paris, Bibl. Natl. MS fr. 245, fol. 179v.

VII.6. St. Cecilia's martyrdom. From a French Book of Hours, early fifteenth century. Cambridge, Trinity College MS B. 11. 31/32, fol. 216. By kind permission of the Master and Fellows.

VII.7. The saint in majesty. From an early fourteenth-century Tuscan altar piece, originally in the Church of St. Cecilia in Florence, now in the Uffizi Gallery. Courtesy of the Ministero per i Beni e le Attività Culturali, Firenze. Photo: © Gabinetto Fotografico, S.S.P.M.F., Firenze.

VII.8. St. Cecilia in a bath, heated by flames (detail of Figure VII.7).

VII.9. Portrait of St. Cecilia. From the *Belles heures* of Jean, Duc de Berry, French, ca. 1408–09. New York, The Metropolitan Museum of Art, Cloisters Collection, 1954 (54.1.1.), fol. 180. Image © The Metropolitan Museum of Art.

VII.10. St. Cecilia in a boiling bath. Ca. 1500–1510. Cambridge, Fitzwilliam Museum MS 118, fol. 198v.

VII.11. Invitation to a bath. From the margins of *The Romance of Alexander*. Flemish, between 1339 and 1344. Oxford, Bodley MS 264, fol. 75.

VII.12. Pleasures of the bath (from the same margin as Figure VII.11).

VII.13. David looking upon Bathsheba in her bath. Paris, ca. 1250. New York, Pierpont Morgan MS M. 638, fol. 41v.

VII.14. Susanna spied upon by the elders as she bathes. From a German book of prayers to the saints, fifteenth century. London, Brit. Lib. MS Egerton 859, fol. 31. © The British Library. All Rights Reserved.

VII.15. Late fifteenth-century bathhouse. An illustration from Valerius Maximus, *Des faits et des paroles memorables*. Paris, Bibl. de l'Arsenal MS 5196, fol. 372.

VII.16. Dante, Virgil, and Statius in purgatory. From a late fourteenth-century manuscript of the *Divine Comedy*. Venice, Bibl. Marciana MS it. 9. 276, fol. 45v.

VII.17. St. Cecilia amid flames. In a Carmelite missal illuminated near the end of the fourteenth century. London, Brit. Lib. MS Add. 29704–5, fol. 160v (fragment 4/79). © The British Library. All Rights Reserved.

VII.18. The Red King (sulfur) and the White Queen (mercury), freed from impurity. From a fifteenth-century alchemical treatise by Johannes Andreae. London, British Library MS Sloane 2560, fol. 6. © The British Library. All Rights Reserved.

VII.19. The chemical union of the Red King and the White Queen. London, Brit. Lib. MS Sloane 2560, fol. 7. © The British Library. All Rights Reserved.

VII.20. The Red King and the White Queen with wings, illustrating Arnold of Villanova's earlier *Rosarium philosophorum*, in a sixteenth-century alchemical manuscript. St. Gall, Kantonsbibliothek St. Gallen, Vad. Sig., MS 394a, fol. 64.

CHAPTER VIII

VIII.1. Psalm 52: Dixit insipiens: "The Fool hath said in his heart: 'There is no God.'" Duc de Berry Psalter, Paris, painted by Jacquemart de Hesdin, ca. 1386, after a model by Jean Pucelle. Paris, Bibl. Natl. MS fr. 13901, fol. 106.

VIII.2. Psalm 52 (detail from Figure VIII.1). Madness, hunger and alienation.

VIII.3. Psalm 52: David prays to the Lord; the God-denying fool runs mad. Isabella Psalter, Paris, ca. 1255–65. Cambridge, Fitzwilliam Museum MS 300, fol. 57.

VIII.4. Psalm 52: the God-denying fool, tonsured and anguished, with fool's food and jester's "marotte." *Bible historiale*, Paris, 1357. London, Brit. Lib. MS Royal 17 E. vii, fol. 241. © The British Library. All Rights Reserved.

VIII.5. Psalm 52: the God-denying fool encounters Christ, with fool's food and club. Guines Psalter, Paris, after 1228 (ca. 1240?). London, Brit. Lib. MS Add. 30045, fol. 28. © The British Library. All Rights Reserved.

VIII.6. Psalm 52: the God-denying fool cavorts before David, naked and mad. Breviary, East Anglia, 1322–25. London, Brit. Lib. MS Stowe 12, fol. 180. © The British Library. All Rights Reserved.

VIII.7. Psalm 52: the God-denying fool in contention with some person (or persons) unseen, his body turned against itself. Psalter, Milan, beginning of the fifteenth century. Oxford, Bodley MS. Canon. Liturg. 378, fol. 59v.

VIII.8. Psalm 52: the God-denying fool eating at fool's food and threatening with his club; Christ looks down from above. *Bible historiale*, by Jean de Papeleu, presented to Charles V. Paris, 1317. Paris, MS Arsenal 5059, fol. 237v.

VIII.9. Psalm 52: the God-denying fool, with "marotte," makes music by biting the tail of a dog; Christ looks down at him in sorrow. *Bible historiale*, by Jean de Vaudetar, presented to Charles V. Paris, 1372. The Hague, Museum Meermanno-Westreenianum MS 10B23, fol. 293.

VIII.10. Psalm 52: two God-denying fools, one simple-minded, the other ostensibly sane, but wagging his finger in contention with Christ above. Huth Psalter, Lincoln, ca. 1280. London, British Library MS Add. 38116, fol. 60v. © The British Library. All Rights Reserved.

VIII.11. Psalm 52: the God-denying fool rebuked by David, eating at fool's food and carrying a soft bladder on a stick. Psalter, East Anglia, ca. 1310–20. Oxford, All Souls MS lat. 7, fol. 49v. By kind permission of the Warden and Fellows.

VIII.12. Psalm 52: a "natural" fool, hairless and naked beneath his mantle, prepares to eat fool's food while brandishing his club against Christ. Psalter, Artois, end of the thirteenth century. Oxford, Bodley MS Douce 118, fol. 60v.

VIII.13. Psalm 52: the God-denying fool, with no God in the sky, but with fool's food and "marotte." Breviary, near Ghent, early fourteenth century. London, Brit. Lib. MS Add. 29253, fol. 41v. © The British Library. All Rights Reserved.

VIII.14. Psalm 52: the God-denying fool eating at fool's food (compare the orb held by Christ), beset by dogs. Prayer book of Queen Joanna, Naples, third quarter of the fourteenth century. Vienna, Österreichische Nationalbibliothek MS 1921, fol. 65.

VIII.15. Psalm 52: the God-denying fool before King David, naked and mad. Aurifaber Bible, Paris, end of the thirteenth century. Paris, Bibliothèque Sainte-Geneviève MS 1181, fol. 184v. Photo © Bibliothèque Sainte-Geneviève, Paris.

VIII.16. Psalm 52: the God-denying fool as Jew, drinking from a chalice and tormented by a Christian. The Psalter and Hours of Bonne of Luxembourg, Paris, before 1349. New York, The Metropolitan Museum of Art, Cloisters Collection, 1969 (69.86, fol. 83v). Image © The Metropolitan Museum of Art.

VIII.17, Psalm 52: the God-denying fool as a troubled but thoughtful man. Bible, probably Paris, beginning of the thirteenth century. Florence, Bibl. Medicea Laurenziana MS Plut.15.11, fol. 286v. Courtesy of the Ministero per i Beni e le Attività Culturali, Firenze. Photo ©: Biblioteca Medicea Laurenziana. All rights reserved.

VIII.18. Tristan plays the fool (panels 2, 3, 4). The Hermitage Tristan Casket II, Paris, ca. 1325. St. Petersburg, State Hermitage Museum.

VIII.19. Lancelot plays the fool. Prose Lancelot, Amiens, 1286. Bonn, Universitätsbibliothek MS 526, fol. 404v.

VIII.20. Psalm 52: the fool as court jester. Psalter, England, illuminated, third quarter of the fifteenth century. Oxford, Bodley MS. Laud. Lat. 114, fol. 71.

VIII.21. Psalm 52: the fool as idolator, here worshiping a goat. Manerius of Canterbury Bible, illuminated by Manerius of Canterbury, possibly in Troyes, late twelfth century. Paris, Bibliothèque Sainte-Geneviève MS 9, fol. 209.

VIII.22. Psalm 52: the fool as jester in the company of courtiers and courtly lovers, God the Father looking down from above. Bible, England, ca. 1405–15. London, Brit. Lib. MS Royal I E. ix, fol. 148. Photo © The British Museum. All Rights Reserved.

VIII.23. Psalm 52: two God-denying fools (a "natural" and a jester) mock God in the company of courtiers and courtly lovers, the latter in an erotic embrace. Psalter, England, ca. 1405–15. Turin, Bibl. Naz., Universitaria di Torino MS I. 1. 9, fol. 16. Courtesy of the Ministero per i Beni e le Attività Culturali, Torino. Photo © Biblioteca Nazionale, Torino. All Rights Reserved.

VIII.24. Psalm 52: the fool at a woman's spindle, above; two fools make love to women below. *Bible moralisé*, commissioned by Philippe le Hardi of Burgundy, Paris, ca. 1470–80. Paris, Bibl. Natl. MS fr. 166, fol. 120.

VIII.25. Venus, radiant, is worshiped by famous lovers, including Tristan and Troilus (Tristan second from the left, Troilus last on the right): "queynt is the light." Birth tray or salver, Tuscany, ca. 1400. Paris, Musée du Louvre (RF 2089).

Index